Finally and In Conclusion

A POLITICAL MEMOIR

Author's Acknowledgements

I wish to thank Independent Group Newspapers, the *Irish Press* Group, *The Irish Times*, *The Sunday Business Post*, *The Sunday Tribune*, the *Irish Examiner*, the *Irish Catholic*, the *Independent*, Radio Telefis Éireann, the *Irish Medical News*, *Business and Finance*, *Hibernia*, and *Magill* for the various quotations I have availed of in completing the text. I also wish to thank Ruairí Quinn, Eddie McEvoy, Martyn Turner, the *Irish Examiner*, *The Irish Times*, the Department of Health and the Irish Council of the European Movement, for permission to reprint a number of photographs and cartoons.

Finally and In Conclusion

A POLITICAL MEMOIR

BARRY DESMOND

**NEW
ISLAND**

FINALLY AND IN CONCLUSION
First published October 2000 by
New Island
2 Brookside
Dundrum Road
Dublin 14
Ireland

ISBN 1 902602 41 2

British Library Cataloguing in Publication Data
A catalogue record for this book is available from the British Library

*The publishers have made every reasonable effort to contact the copyright holders of
photographs produced herein. If any involuntary infringement of copyright has
occurred, sincere apologies are offered and the owners of such copyright are
requested to contact the publishers.*

Cover design: Slick Fish Design, Dublin
Cover photograph: Institue of European Affairs
Typesetting: New Island Books
Printed in Ireland by Colour Books Ltd.

Contents

For Stella,
Ciaran, Marcus, Eoin and Aidan

Foreword

When I was 21 in 1957, I did what all sensible Corkmen do. I bought a one-way ticket to Dublin. I had been offered a trainee union official's job at £8 per week. I was in heaven.

My new world was sparse digs in Upper Pembroke Street, writing reports of union meetings, a liberated social life in Neary's and O'Neill's pubs, teas in the Civil Service Dining Club, Labour Party meetings, Croke Park on Sundays, and then meeting Stella. Our marriage was heaven number two.

But there was another side. Ireland was in deep economic recession. The political landscape was still the choice of Dev or Collins. Whole areas of social policy — health, education, social welfare, housing — were in profound neglect. Issues of social morality were dominated by the Catholic Hierarchy. I smelled the poverty in the mass dole queues.

This was the climate in which I worked in the trade union and labour movement. The obstacles to radical social and economic change were formidable. Public debate about equal access to higher education, child care, family law reform, adoption, contraception, divorce and abortion was grindingly reluctant to approve reforms. These issues were to the fore throughout my 20 years in the Dáil. At times it was all very depressing.

When I was first elected in 1969, the unionists began to lose their hegemony in Northern Ireland. Sinn Féin–IRA then reinvented themselves and launched almost three decades of sectarian carnage. To write about the anger I felt when walking behind the coffins of men from the Army and Gardaí is impossible.

Stella and I sought to protect our four young sons from the often sheer viciousness of those times. It was not easy. Advocating change as a full-time deputy in a minority party was a precarious occupation indeed.

When I was asked this year by Tom Garvin and Brigid Laffan of the Department of Politics in UCD to accept an Honorary Fellowship in the Department, I thought that I should record my experiences with warts, prejudices and all. I have also set out my opinions about some controversial events and personalities. I can never keep my mouth shut!

I retired this year after 43 years' work in the trade union and labour movement, in local and national politics and in the European institutions. These memoirs are an attempt to illustrate my involvement in the period. I also wanted to put the record straight about Labour's substantial contribution towards economic and social progress during these decades.

In those years our country has been transformed with phenomenal growth, virtual full employment, and a unique extent of home ownership. And we have taken our full place in Europe. I felt I should recall how our country was really put on the path of fiscal responsibility.

But the good fight is very far from over. Some prominent members of the Oireachtas with whom I often debated have disgraced themselves, their parties and our noble profession. Some powerful citizens have attempted to subvert the political process. Some have succeeded because we did not at times have public representatives strong enough to stand up to them.

My father did not take part in the War of Independence so that sleaze should infect the body politic. He and his comrades would be very angry men today. And he would want me to so record.

And he would fight again to oppose those who still owe allegiance to their private army and who would subvert the fragile institutions of our state.

I specially want to thank Margaret Carter, Stephen Collins, Joe Joyce, and Edwin Higel and Ciara Considine of New Island Books for their invaluable skills in helping me to draw these recollections together. I also wish to thank Michael O'Higgins, BL, for his considerable advice. Any omissions or lapses are entirely at my door.

When Michael D. Higgins was chairman of the Labour Party, I teased him at conferences by saying 'finally' and then speaking for another five minutes. When in exasperation he asked me to stop, I would respond with 'in conclusion' and continue to the bitter end. Hence the title of this book in tribute to the only real Minister for Arts and Culture the country has had to date.

And this is not necessarily my very last word!

Barry Desmond
Dublin
September 2000

One

A Child of Neutrality

'Here on the northern slopes of Musheramore
Mountain, Millstreet, County Cork, you are indeed
special but, nevertheless, just one more traveller
coming here in a 4,000 year continuum of travellers
visiting this place back to neolithic times.'

Michael O Muircheartaigh

Politics and rebelliousness are in my blood. My father, Con,
fought in the War of Independence and was a founder member
of Fianna Fáil before joining the Labour Party in the 1940s. He
was elected as a Labour senator and later Lord Mayor of Cork,
the proudest achievement of his political career. The Desmonds
have always been a rebellious Munster people, coming to
Ireland more than 800 years ago as the soldiers, horsemen and
camp followers of the FitzGeralds and later involved in the
various Desmond rebellions of the Tudor era. Garret Mór
FitzGerald was the chief governor of Ireland in 1478 and
probably our first real Taoiseach. Appropriately enough, at the
height of my political career I served under another Garret
FitzGerald, Taoiseach in the coalition government of 1982-87.

My father and mother were living in 13 FitzGerald Place on
the Old Blackrock Road, Cork with their first child, Noreen,
when my twin brother John and I were born in 1935. My
mother never knew that she was carrying twins until we
arrived in Harveys Nursing Home in the South Terrace. In 1935
the infant mortality rate in Ireland was 69 per thousand births
and probably much higher for twins, so survival was by no

means assured. I was christened Bartholomew after my grandfather. But my mother hated the short names 'Battie' or 'Bertie' and decided early on to call me Finbarr or Barry. And I have been dubbed many other names since then.

My father, Con, was born at Kilmeedy, Millstreet, Co Cork, in 1896. His father Bartholomew died in agony with a perforated appendix before he could reach Millstreet Hospital in 1910. His wife Hanora Casey, born 1865 at Knocknalomon, was left alone to rear nine children. She was an extraordinary, powerful woman and a native Irish speaker. As a child I was captivated by her stories, handed down from earlier generations, of the diseases and starvation of the famine, the evictions of her family and the sheer poverty of those decades.

Along with my brother and sister, we enjoyed our summer holidays as children on the tiny farm where she lived with her bachelor son, Paddy. She smoked a white clay pipe and shag tobacco in the evenings and wore an elaborate black cloak and bonnet to mass. She was 87 when she fell and broke her hip; she died of pneumonia in Millstreet Hospital. Her funeral remains clear as a bell to me today because it was the first time that my twin brother John and I shouldered a coffin to the graveside in the old St Patrick's Church Cemetery in Millstreet. We were only 17 years old.

One of my proudest boasts is that I can claim to be related to members of a Cork team who won the All-Ireland Hurling Championship but never got the cup or the medals! Andrew Desmond and P. Desmond played for Clondrohid, a small town midway between Macroom and Millstreet, in the All-Ireland Final on 28 February 1891 at Clonturk Park, Dublin. Clondrohid scored a second decisive goal and were declared the winners at the final whistle. Three hours after the game, the infamous referee changed his mind and disallowed the second goal. Their opponents that day, Young Irelands, were declared the winners. Clondrohid appealed and the game was refixed for Thurles but the Dubs refused to travel. The game was still being debated by the Central Council as late as September 1893. By then, presumably out of disgust, the Clondrohid team had disbanded. Thus were the Desmonds, not for the first time in Irish history, denied their hour of glory.[1]

As children we were fascinated by Kilmeedy Castle, originally built in 1436, and by the local river on the side of the castle. Thus we had a real sense of family roots and history which many families in urban Ireland do not experience today. I was told step by step, on my father's side, of our relationships with the Caseys, the Desmonds, the Dennehies and the Moynihans in the surrounding parishes. Stella and I returned recently to the old Carnegie Public Library in Millstreet to trace my roots back to 1810.[2] It was a fascinating exercise.

Those childhood summers with my grandmother were magical. There was no radio or television. We had the *Examiner* at midday when my uncle Paddy came home from the creamery. There was no horse on the small farm. A jennet, ferocious in nature but with a heart of iron, climbed the mountain, pulled turf from the bog and cut the hay. We had bastible bread and treacle cake made by our grandmother, potatoes and a dip of milk and onions in the evening and bacon on Sundays, all from the turf fire which never went out. And we recited the rosary every evening, with the station mass every few years. I recall being terrified going to confession to the local curate down the side bedroom before mass. We whitewashed the old house and cleaned out the yard for days before the station mass. Preparations for Sunday mass were meticulous. My father, with the open razor, would give his brother Paddy a real close shave. We were awe-struck when he held up Paddy's nose and scraped his upper lip without the slightest scar! At Millstreet church the well-off families sat up front in their donated seats, the coated women occupied the aisles and those with shawls were at the rear. Contributions from each family, name after name and the precise cash amounts, were read out by the parish priest for the Christmas and Easter dues. Great social attention was paid to each amount. And we prayed for the conversion of Russia.

In all there were three daughters and six sons in my father's family. Four emigrated to New York, three married locally. My uncles and aunts, Batty, Jeremiah, Nora and Mary, emigrated from Cobh to the Bronx in the early 1930s and returned the odd summer after the war and brought ex-US Army and Air Force coats and boots to my uncle Paddy and that which we coveted most — US dollars. Paddy remained to look after the mother and my father 'emigrated' to Cork city. My father had the bare primary education but he knew about farming. He was employed by the agricultural company, Lucy and O'Connell, in Cork as a seed sorter on the docks and in their store. In 1923 he joined the Irish Transport and General Workers' Union, a turning point in all our lives.

My mother, Margaret O'Connor, was born in 1900 at Liskelea, Waterfall, above the old railway viaduct outside Cork city. My grandmother on my mother's side, as they say, was a Dineen from the old Gaeltacht area of Kaelkill, Bantry and came to live there in a roadside cottage in the mid-1860s. My grandfather was a land steward for a local Protestant farmer. My mother went into domestic service at a young age with the Crosbie family of *Cork Examiner* fame. It was there that she learned to cook and, well into her eighties, she could produce an outstanding meal from half nothing. With Howards One Way flour, overnight porridge, spuds from our local allotment, tripe and drisheen, Evergreen bacon and Lunham sausages, nobody went hungry in our house.

The trouble with my mother was that she regularly added sienna pods, cod's liver oil, milk of magnesia and mulled Murphy's stout to our diet with dire after-effects. My mother also believed the 'phisóg' that one of twins is physically a weakling. She could never make up her mind which of us was in need of a tonic! Accordingly, we were given chicken soup and strange concoctions that certainly kept us moving in all directions. She was quite strict during the Lenten fast. We were allowed one full meal and two collations a day. The faithful had consulted Bishop Cornelius Lucey about the composition of a collation and he ruled that it was a cup of tea and a bun. The bakers of Cork duly produced substantial buns which we knew as 'Connie Dodgers'! After doing her service years with the Crosbies, my mother was employed as a cook in the Honan Hostel of University College, Cork. She often recalled in detail the burning of the City Hall and the shops in Cork by Black and Tan auxiliaries. She and my father married in 1932 and went to Dublin to the Eucharistic Congress on their honeymoon. My father told me it was the first time he had been to mass in a long time, having been banned from the sacraments by the bishop of Cork for being an anti-treaty republican.

Although he took the republican side in the Civil War, my father was shocked by the murder, as he emphatically called it, of Michael Collins. He and most of his friends in North Cork were anti-treaty at that time and he participated in the founding of Fianna Fáil in Cork city in 1926. His black and tan War of Independence medal is still a source of great family pride. We had correspondence in our home from Seán Lemass as Fianna Fáil Party organiser along with a letter of thanks to Con from de Valera. But my mother was pro-treaty and after my father died in 1974 the letters disappeared; she had relations in West Cork and was a Michael Collins supporter. My father strongly supported the successful candidature of Sean French for Fianna Fáil in the two 1927 general elections and those of T.P. Dowdall and Sean French in the 1932 and 1933 general elections. At the beginning of the war years after he became a full-time union official, he was deeply unhappy about the introduction of the wages standstill orders by Fianna Fáil. In 1941 he resigned from the party in protest. He then supported Labour Deputy James Hickey, a full-time branch secretary of the Irish Transport and General Workers' Union in Connolly Hall in Cork, who had been elected in 1938. As a child I recall Bill O'Brien and Billy McMullen from the One Big Union in Dublin coming to our house to offer my father a full-time Irish Transport and General Workers' Union job at Connolly Hall. As children we were fascinated by O'Brien's physical disability and his goatee beard. Even then he was to me a fearsome figure.

Because of my father's friendly association with many Fianna Fáil personalities in Cork city, he was most reluctant to stand as a Labour candidate. Eventually, in 1956 when 'Pa' McGrath, the local Fianna Fáil deputy, died suddenly while rushing for the train to Dublin, my father stood in the subsequent by-election. He wished, in effect, to keep the Labour seat 'warm' for the sitting Labour Deputy Sean Casey. It was my first experience of an election campaign. Labour's Cork director of elections, Tadg Harrington of the Post Office Workers' Union, had extraordinary ability and I learned a great deal about campaigning in that by-election. My father was subsequently elected to Cork Corporation and as a Labour Senator in 1961. He became Lord Mayor of Cork in 1965 and one of his proudest moments was the unveiling, with the Chief Justice Cearbhall Ó'Dálaigh, of a bust of Michael Collins by Seamus Murphy, at Fitzgerald's Park.

It was during this period that I became infected by the political 'bug'. Checking the electoral register; printing the election address; drafting the statements and leaflets; packing the envelopes; putting up the posters; taking them down; and that most vital training of all, what to say on the doorstep. I learned from Tadg Harrington, Pat Kerrigan, Sean Casey and my father. And I learned that sixth sense of extracting oneself from the doorstep of a die-hard supporter of the opposition who is determined to waste one's time with endless questions and ultimately abuse when one does not take the bait. It was a great apprenticeship in the organisation of politics. Above all else, when I canvassed in the working class houses and tenements of the city, I learned at first hand of the poverty, the ill health and gross overcrowding of many families. I still retain the smell of rotting houses and unsanitary conditions in the Cork of the 1950s.

*

In 1944 I started to keep a war scrapbook, cutting out battleships and tank pictures from the *Cork Examiner*. I recall looking out the back bedroom window of our home while the searchlights from Collins Barracks tracked the warplanes flying overhead, many of them obviously lost. After primary school at the Model Schools in Anglesea Street, Cork, my teenage school days were in the new 'secondary top' Presentation Brothers school in Turners Cross, Cork. There was a roller coaster of classes, football, hurling, and the discovery of that most forbidden mystery, sex. I was a young choirboy at Christ the King Church where I was confirmed and took the Pioneer pledge as was the norm. My dear mother used to leave the *Sacred Heart Messenger* on the hallstand so that we would be enlightened about purity and chastity. However well meant, it was too little knowledge for my curiosity. So I took to the Cork city library and after graduating to the senior section at about

14 years, I spent some hours consulting the textbooks reserved 'for medical students only'. I thus became an enlightened Corkonian!

Another eventful episode occurred when I developed a ferocious 'crush' on one of the beautiful twins who lived around the corner from us on the Old Blackrock Road. Being a twin I was fascinated by the Isaac sisters. But my mother put short shrift to my blushing interest by informing me that they were Jews and that they had crucified our Lord. I was not to go near them or to mix with those from 'Jewtown', an area of houses nearby. My second son is named Marcus, after Louis Marcus from Cork, an atonement, perhaps. When I told my mother in 1962 when Marcus was baptised she understood my rebellion. She too, in later times, had changed her views on Catholic 'dogma'.

Cork city in the late 1940s and early 1950s was of an intensely Catholic ethos. We had annual retreat visitations from the Redemptorists who, from the pulpit in St Finbarr's South church, delivered ringing denunciations, with all the men holding lighted candles, against 'the devil and all his works and pomps'. These invariably included communism, Stalinism, socialism, the evils of sex, the dangers of hire purchase and money lenders, drink and gambling, the power of chastity and purity, the greatness of young Catholic vocations to the priesthood and, of course, prayers for the African missions and the black non-baptised babies of darkest Africa. As a young teenager I was deeply impressed and at 14 years became a junior member and subsequently secretary of the Mother of God Junior Praesidium of the Legion of Mary in Mary Street. That was my very first experience of learning to take minutes of meetings and reading them out each week. We delivered thousands of copies of the *Irish Catholic*, the *Catholic Standard*, the *Catholic Herald*, the *Universe*, and *Marie Legionnis* every week to the homes of the South Parish. We ran a youth club in Copley Street where I spent many a Saturday afternoon dusting down the billiard tables. Very many of my classmates were in the Legion and together with hurling and football for Nemo Rangers, we had a busy social life.

The youth of the South Parish and Turners Cross in Cork owed a great deal to Mick Barrett, secretary of Nemo Rangers, Bill O'Keeffe, chairman and Dinny O'Mahony, vice chairman, for their pioneering efforts to rebuild Gaelic football and hurling in the area. The sheer personal enjoyment and confidence one gains as a teenager from such sports has a huge effect on one's adult development.

I knew Christy Ring when he was earning a living driving an oil and petrol lorry and was a loyal, paid-up Irish Transport and General Workers' Union member of Cork No.1 branch, of which my father was a full-time union official. He delivered oil to the local sawmill above our home on the Old Blackrock Road. He always had a few hurleys and sliotars in his cab. We anticipated his deliveries and while oil was being pumped, we used to dare him to give us a little exhibition. Although a very shy person, except on the field of play, Christy would always oblige. He carefully selected a hurley from the three in the cab, stood twenty-five yards from the large door knob on the outbuilding of the South Infirmary and from the opposite side of the road, with a flick of his powerful wrists, he hit the door knob repeatedly with deadly accuracy. We were all in awe. We all aspired to be like Christy Ring. No Corkman has yet succeeded.

I had the very dubious distinction of playing against Christy in the Cork county hurling championship. About 1950, Mick Barrett and a local committee had revived Nemo Rangers hurling and football club at the small former tennis club grounds in the Douglas Road. Those of us who had been nurtured in hurling and football at the Turners Cross school quickly joined Nemo. When I was 17 years of age I was the proud possessor of a Cork city division minor championship medal. Shortly afterwards the club entered the Cork county senior championship ranks. We were ominously drawn against Glen Rovers, Christy's club. I played right full back. I will never forget Christy Ring coming through the back line like a Panzer tank in World War II. My only hope was to run like hell, keep out of his way and bat away the ball. It was a real baptism of fire on the front line. We were hammered by the Glen who showed no mercy. But Nemo went on, from these humble beginnings, to become one of the most successful clubs in Cork city and county and won many championships at Cork and All-Ireland level.

Ever since, I have been a GAA member in Cork, Dublin and Luxembourg. My love of Gaelic games has never dimmed. And hurling comes first.

As soon as I went to UCC at 17 years, however, my interest in Catholic action and its lay organisations began to wane. Sunday mornings were a time to visit the second-hand bookshops on the Cork quays and to avoid the repeated sermonising of the Sunday masses. The UCC retreats for students were to me somewhat barren events with grown young men and women treated as prospective sinful adolescents. A small group of us used to remain in defiance in the students' canteen. We were dubbed 'the anti Christs'. I thus became a disturbed young Catholic and still remain in rebellious mood.

*

Many people in public life in Ireland have said that without the Christian or Presentation Brothers, they would not have received a secondary education. In my youth this was absolutely true. I was very proud in 1952 to matriculate from the Presentation Brothers' Scoil Chríost Rí, Turners Cross, after it was granted 'secondary top' status about 1950. We were a very small group of students — Finbar Ryan, Edmund Walsh, Conrad O'Riordan, James O'Brien and Stan O'Brien. The school principal, Brother Alphonsos or 'Allie' as we called him, was a dynamic and progressive school principal. Brother Norbert or 'Nobbie' was a brilliant teacher of English and Latin. He gave me my love of English as an enthralling subject. I hated maths but Brother Dermot nursed me through the examinations.

But there was also the dark side. There was a tiny minority of teachers who would explode and lash out at students who had failed to comprehend lessons. Nowadays there would be a riot in the class. They were, I would stress, not representative of the excellent teachers in the school. My school went on to become the outstanding Coláiste Chríost Rí which has contributed greatly to the economic, social and sporting prowess of my home city. And, of course, we had our retaliation, as when a piano wire was tied across the lower gate of the school at the end of the steep exit. We had the pleasure of seeing one of these brothers fly out over the handlebars of his bike with his suitcase of schoolbooks following behind on his way to the monastery in Douglas Street. And they never discovered who did the job!

Most of my matriculation class headed for the 'Inisfallen' boat from Cork to Fishguard and then on the night train to Euston in London. Many never settled into society there; they subsisted in low paid jobs and in lonely lodging houses. Some of my classmates ended their working lives in dire circumstances. They were ill prepared for the sudden transition to factory shift work and dangerous construction sites. Many finished up entirely dependent on the health and social services. They took to the Irish pubs each evening and every weekend and often became candidates for early alcoholism and poverty. I was much more fortunate.

I went to London each summer from 1952 to 1955 to earn my UCC B. Comm fees of £30, which was almost a month's wages in 1952. I had 'digs' in Tottenham Court Road, five beds to a room. I worked in a jam factory; in a paper plant cleaning the cutting machines and packing waste; in Walls Ice Cream plant; in a seaside pub in Clacton-on-Sea; and, inevitably, as a Paddy bus conductor in London Transport. I still have a vivid recollection of the nests of wasps in the barrels of mandarins in the jam factory. We steamed them all into the vats! For years afterwards I could hardly touch any jam. I recall the freezing ice cream storerooms in the Walls Ice Cream plant and working with Polish emigrants. I met for the first time the beautiful young women from the West Indies who found work in London. They laughed at my Cork accent and I hardly understood theirs. We were economic migrants. I meet my successors on the streets of Dublin today. I know how they feel.

But the most traumatic experience of all was one summer when I joined an Royal Horse Artillery Territorial Regiment in Whitehall as a young trainee barman. The officer in charge had to register me as a regular so I was given the title 'Gunner Desmond Byrne'. I set off for Salisbury Plain in an army truck at the princely salary of £6 per week. I lived in the back room of an army mess and bar. I learned how to tap a wooden barrel the hard way with cider all over my clothes. In the evenings we drove around the plain and our sutling truck issued the ration of rum to the tank crews. When the tank and artillery crews came into the bar in the late evening I learned, in the crudest terms, what they thought of Irish neutrality in the war. Being called 'Paddy' was almost a compliment. These were the battle hardened veterans from France and Germany. They were very bitter, as was British public opinion generally, about Irish military neutrality. I had to either take it all on the chin or get the train back to Fishguard and to Cork with no money. It was a very lonely and isolating experience. But I knew that I would return to Cork and home.

My brother John had gifted hands and he produced wall cabinets and electrical work of great quality. He became one of the first 'youth in training' technicians in the Department of Post and Telegraphs about 1951. He remained in Cork in the post office service until early retirement. He married Noreen Cummins and they have three adopted children. My sister Noreen was a quite brilliant student and became a library assistant in the Cork city library where she was a great guide for new books. She was also a gifted violinist with the Cork city symphony orchestra and drove the house scatty as she repeatedly practised her set pieces for the Cork School of Music. She married Sean Hennessy from Ferrybank, Waterford, who worked in AnCo. With a growing family of two sons and two daughters, she went back to complete her Junior Assistant Mistress teacher training course. She was a teacher for many years in a special school in Waterford city. She truly loved teaching and could not understand those who complained of stress. However, she did take early retirement and in 1997 she died quite suddenly of cancer. That was the greatest shock of all to our family's mortality and one of my greatest regrets is that we did not see more of one another.

I obtained the B. Comm. in University College, Cork in 1956 thanks to Professor John Busteed, dean of the commerce and economics faculty, and Dr David O'Mahony. They were two quite different characters. John Busteed was preoccupied with

Irish monetary developments up to about 1935 and had little interest in the economic trauma of the early 1950s. He was most gregarious and thoroughly enjoyed a good few Paddys down town with his students, much to the annoyance of the ultra conservative establishment of the college. Cork at that time was in the throes of mariology fever with the Marian year of celebrations and the new churches dedicated to Our Lady. Busteed did not favour the legacy of the autocratic UCC President Alfred O'Rahilly and regaled us with the story of Alfie challenging him if he believed in the dogma of the assumption. Busteed replied, 'My dear Alfie, every dogma is an assumption!' David O'Mahony was a thoughtful young economist who deeply distrusted the embryonic Anglo-Irish trade relationships.

*

Above all else, our home in Fitzgerald's Place and the Old Blackrock Road was a trade union and labour house. It was rented from Sir John and Lady Fitzgerald, of the Catholic ascendancy of Cork. Shop stewards called to our home because there was no telephone if an urgent dispute arose. Hail, rain or snow, my father would get up at 6.45 a.m. and cycle down to the docks to ensure that the correct union stevedore rota of dockers was employed. He fought against the dockers being paid 'against the slate' in the local pubs where they drank Murphys and Beamish and chalked up credit. And he won. He was a physically powerful man who would face down the most disruptive presence at any union meeting. He would sit up late into the night with my mother, drafting Labour Court submissions for CIE workers, flour and provender mill workers and his fellow dockers. At Christmas the whole family would face a thousand union membership cards. We made up the arrears, wrote the new cards for the following year and cursed the tedious chore. And my mother would remonstrate with my father when he would put in, from his own wages, the arrears on the union card of a recently deceased member to bring him back into benefit so that the local widow would get the 'Mortality Benefit' to bury her husband. The union's three-speed bike was carefully cleaned and oiled and kept in the front hall. My father was also a member of the City of Cork Co-operative Society, which had a popular bakery and provided cheap bread and confectionery for the working people of Cork. He travelled to the co-op meetings in Belfast and Manchester. The trail of co-op and British Labour Party literature which came to our home whetted my political appetite.

Shortly after I left college I was extremely fortunate in obtaining a job as a trainee trade union official in the head office of the Irish Transport and General Workers' Union in Dublin in 1957. John Conroy, the then general president of the union, had decided to recruit some trainee graduate officials. I was the first and Michael O'Leary was the second in 1958. Our respective pedigrees were first approved by the union. Michael's father was a senior psychiatric nurse in Cork and also a union member. We therefore had the inside track in a union notoriously suspicious of outsiders in the ranks of its officials. To have any association with the rival unions, the Workers' Union of Ireland and the Amalgamated Transport and General Workers' Union which was regarded as the 'British union', was the kiss of death to a career in the Irish Transport and General Workers' Union. But John Conroy, Jim Larkin Junior and Norman Kennedy were to change all that in the 1960s. In 1960 I became the first member of the Irish Transport and General Workers' Union to take up a staff appointment in the Irish Congress of Trade Unions when I was appointed education officer. I subsequently became industrial officer from 1964 to 1969.

To their great credit I found that the three full-time Congress officers, Ruaidhri Roberts, Leo Crawford and Donal Nevin, all coming from quite different backgrounds, made heroic efforts to develop and build a unified organisation for all of the affiliated unions. Leo Crawford was expert in handling the politics of the craft unions. Ruaidhri was quite bureaucratic but successful in developing the structures of Congress. Donal Nevin was head and shoulders over all others in the unions and over many in the public service with his masterly economic and statistical analysis. His monthly publication over many decades of 'Trade Union Information' was invaluable. I rarely met anyone from the Federated Union of Employers or from any government department who questioned the accuracy of his comprehensive work. Donal was twelve years older than me. He taught me how to lay out basic statistics and above all else not to 'chance my arm'. He insisted that I should check and recheck all data I used in any speech or lecture notes. It was a hard earned discipline which stood me in good stead all my life. Donal was also an inveterate hoarder of official documents and newspaper cuttings. These would spread out all over the small office of the Congress in the top floor over Morrisseys' auctioneers, at Lower Merrion Street, Dublin. To the dismay of my family I picked up his habit so much so that even today, discarding a newspaper without cutting out some particular political item of interest is akin to losing a close friend. When I was appointed to the European Court of Auditors in 1994 a three-ton container of papers followed me to Luxembourg!

I also had an intense interest in Donal Nevin's meticulous social and economic research for the RTÉ Thomas Davis lecture series. The series were to benefit my neglected social and political education. In 1967 Donal contributed to *The Years of The Great Test 1926-'39, Ireland in the War Years and After 1939-'52* in 1969, and opened up new assessments of our history. In 1964 he edited *Jim Larkin and the Dublin Lock Out* and it became a treasured possession of activists in the labour movement. In 1998 Donal Nevin edited *James Larkin: Lion of the Fold*.[3] This compendium, a labour of love, is an enormous tribute to his hero and a quite magnificent exposition of the economic and social conditions of the Larkin era. It is already a collector's item. When I came to Dublin in 1957, I did not fully appreciate the enormous impact Larkin had made on one of the major capital cities of Europe. To Cork people, Larkin was a remote figure. We knew all about James Connolly, Terence MacSwiney and Tomás MacCurtain. In Dublin I met many of those, particularly in the Workers' Union of Ireland, who had known and worked with 'Big Jim'. In many ways Jim Larkin Junior became my labour hero. He had a calm and powerful intellect and was an utterly convincing public speaker. He was a brilliant union negotiator who could put the craft union strategists to flight. In the 1950s there was no class consciousness so imperious as that of the maintenance craft unions.

*

In 1958 I was fortunate to travel on a post-graduate study course in the United States for four months from An Bord Scolaireachtai Comhairle. This was the first use of Marshall Aid residue funds for a post-graduate US scholarship scheme in Ireland. It was organised by the Office of International Labour Affairs, Washington, under the auspices of the US Department of Labour, as a multi-national trade union project for 'foreign specialists'. My fellow trade union participants were from Finland, India, Israel, Morocco, New Zealand, The Philippines, South Korea and Sweden. I was a red-raw 23-year-old trade unionist from Ireland. I was simply flabbergasted by New York, Washington, Michigan State University, St John's College, Annapolis, Chicago, Detroit, St Louis, Kansas City, Denver, Los Angeles, San Francisco, all of which I visited during my fascinating study tour.

In Kansas I met apartheid and racism for the first time when our fellow Indian union officer was barred from a restaurant. We all walked out. In these cities I had a real appreciation of the sheer size of American capitalism. In each area, I met the local AFL-CIO representatives and the hospitality from Irish emigrants in the American trade union movement was quite overwhelming. The study tour was strongly oriented by the American State Department towards a US versus communism stance. We met the retired US President Harry Truman at Independence, Missouri. When we asked him, he was quite adamant that he had taken the right decision to unleash the atomic bomb on the Japanese. I was quite shocked but in those Cold War days, nobody in our group demurred.

In late 1958 I returned to Dublin and a few months later met Stella Murphy who was working in the Labour Party head office as secretary to the acting general secretary, Senator Mary Davidson, who had been employed by the party since 1922. To the consternation of my mother, Stella and I were engaged to marry within nine weeks. We married in 1960 in Churchtown, Co Dublin.

Stella is a fourth generation Dubliner from St Brigid's Gardens on the North Strand. Her father Robert, like many from the area, joined the Royal Irish Fusiliers and fought in World War I. He was gassed but survived, and returned to Dublin to become a foreman bricklayer with Cramptons. The family then moved to the Soldiers and Sailors Land Trust houses in Milltown which today are for sale at £250,000 plus. But Robert Murphy refused to pass the union picket during the 1937 building workers' strike in Dublin. He was fired and emigrated to work in London. Nellie Cross, Stella's aunt, was treasurer of the Irish Women Workers' Union. Stella and I had a mutual trade union and Labour background, which was to play a great role in our lives. She is also the best political strategist I have ever met.

Two

A Corkonian Eyes a Dublin Seat

'While Fianna Fáil and Fine Gael were embroiled in civil war issues, Labour fought for social and economic progress. As the oldest political party Labour has also symbolised the continuity of democracy in Ireland.'

Dr John O'Connell, 1979

On St Patrick's Day in March 1965, at a general election selection convention for the Dublin South West constituency, I was selected as a Labour candidate at the top of the poll to contest that constituency. The other two candidates selected were P.J. Coughlan, a staunch Workers' Union of Ireland loyalist from Walkinstown, and Dr John O'Connell, then a 37-year-old popular general practitioner with a flourishing practice in the constituency. The convention was held at John O'Connell's home at 64 Inchicore Road, a large Victorian house with a well-furnished front drawing room which comfortably accommodated the delegates.

John had joined the party's Sean Connolly Branch in the city about eighteen months prior to the election. He had allegedly been blocked by the local Fianna Fáil hierarchy of Joe Dowling and Deputy Noel Lemass in the same constituency from getting a Fianna Fáil nomination for the local elections. P.J. Coughlan, a local Labour veteran, had been a member of the Galway No 1 and Athlone brigades of the old IRA, wounded, sentenced to death, and on three hunger strikes as a young man. He had been a Labour councillor from 1945 to 1950 and did not fear John O'Connell. I was financial secretary of the party and the newly appointed industrial officer of the Irish Congress of Trade Unions. I had the key support of local councillor Barney Colgan, general secretary of the Irish Municipal Employees Trade Union, and George O'Malley, branch secretary of the Dublin No 2 Branch of the Irish Transport and General Workers' Union.

John O'Connell was singularly displeased with my topping the poll. It was immediately obvious that he was determined to run a solo campaign with no expense spared. That St Patrick's evening I consulted Stella who knew the constituency well and she strongly advised that we should do an unofficial straw poll locally. We parked our young sons with Stella's mother in Churchtown Avenue and spent the following afternoon and evening knocking on doors in Crumlin, Drimnagh and Walkinstown. I was relatively unknown and with a cap on my young head I was almost anonymous.

We had prepared a sample ballot paper with the three Labour candidates, Richie Ryan and Jim O'Keeffe of Fine Gael, Noel Lemass, Joe Dowling and Ben Briscoe of Fianna Fáil and Jim Carroll, Independent. Working alone we took careful notes at each doorstep. Our conclusion was elementary. There was a very considerable Fianna Fáil vote from almost half of the households; there was a strong Fine Gael vote for Richie Ryan and ominously, there was real warmth, particularly from married women with families, for 'Dr John': 'Ah, janey, we never knew the doctor is running in de elections!' was the greeting. I was virtually unknown to most people.

We decided to pull out of the race but the real problem was how to do so, as a party officer, without egg all over my face. We decided to wait until the meeting of the administrative council of the party in Leinster House a few days later when our candidatures were due for ratification. At this meeting I announced my withdrawal, due to 'pressure of trade union work' and nominated Dr John O'Donovan, a former Fine Gael deputy for Dublin South East from 1954 to 1957 and a senator from 1957 to 1961. He was another 'Doctor John', a somewhat eccentric if charming lecturer in economics at UCD. After resigning from Fine Gael, he had joined the Labour Party and was seeking a Labour nomination. Brendan Corish, the party leader, had known him well when O'Donovan was a Fine Gael parliamentary secretary to the inter-party government from 1954 to 1957. After a fraught debate at the council meeting, John O'Donovan was substituted on condition that I would face the Dublin South West constituency council and explain my position and the AC decision! This I did to the utter fury of John O'Connell.

I beat a hasty retreat from Dublin South West and went to work in Dublin North East during that general election for Denis Larkin who was trying to regain the seat he had first won in 1954 and then lost in 1961. Denis was 57 years old and very much in the shadow of 'Young Jim', his brother and the general secretary of the Workers' Union of Ireland. He was not the most energetic of campaigners. However, it was perhaps the general election I enjoyed most. As well as working for Denis Larkin I, as the party's financial secretary, was on the Labour campaign committee along with James Tully TD, party chairman; Brendan Corish TD; party leader, Senator Jack Fitzgerald of Meath, who was a highly regarded GAA administrator; Donal Nevin; and Joe MacAnthony. Donal, almost single-handed, drafted Labour's election manifesto; I again learned a great deal about election organisation from him. We ran 43 candidates in 34 constituencies and polled 15.4 per cent of the national vote. We won 22 seats, the highest number since 1927.

We were all greatly pleased when Denis Larkin won back his seat from a decent local Fianna Fáil outgoing deputy, Eugene Timmons, by a mere four votes. Charlie Haughey had foolishly scooped the pool for Fianna Fáil, such was his rivalry with George Colley who were both in the same constituency. He polled 12,415 votes and George Colley 5,745, leaving Timmons adrift. Charlie Haughey was furious. He, and his band of supporters, were some of the most intimidating I have ever encountered outside a polling station or at an election count. John O'Connell went on to comfortably win the seat in Dublin South West.

*

Between the 1965 and 1977 general elections, there was acute tension between the rural and urban wings of the Labour Party. Its rural backbone had sustained the party with Deputies Dan Desmond, Dan Spring, Paddy McAuliffe, Paddy Tierney, Sean Treacy, Paddy Hogan, Michael Pat Murphy, T.J. Murphy, Brendan Corish, Jim Tully, William Norton and Sean Dunne. They had a healthy political contempt for those Labour activists who had failed miserably to win seats, particularly in Dublin. The tensions between some senior officials of the Irish Transport and General Workers' Union and the Workers' Union of Ireland in the 1940s and 1950s had debilitated the Labour organisation in Dublin. There was little agreement among party factions to put forward popular candidates of consequence for the Dublin city council and the Dáil.

When I joined the party in Dublin in 1957, Labour had only 12 seats in the Dáil and Jim Larkin Junior was its only deputy in Dublin. The Labour vote in the 1957 general election in Dublin was a mere 8.1 per cent. In 1961 it was 8.4 per cent; of the 30 Dáil seats in the eight Dublin constituencies, Labour held one in Dublin county with Sean Dunne, Independent Labour, and one in the city with Michael Mullen in Dublin North West. The party's electoral influence in Dublin in those years was dire. Jim Larkin was deeply hostile to the party leader, Bill Norton. I could smell the enmity between them when they clashed at the annual conference at the Teachers' Hall in Parnell Square in 1957. The non-selection of Jim Larkin to the 1954 cabinet by the Parliamentary Labour Party, under the influence of Norton, was a bitter pill for the Dublin organisation to swallow.

Larkin was head and shoulders above most of the 1954 Labour office holders. When he spoke in the Dáil he invariably attracted an attentive audience. It was widely believed that he would have made an outstanding minister. But Norton never forgave Larkin his past communist associations. Michael O'Leary and I booed Norton from the floor of the Teachers' Hall when he used this fact in his platform reply to Larkin. Michael O'Leary had also been critical of Norton. When Norton replied to the 120 delegates in the hall, one-third of whom were from his Kildare constituency, he referred to 'the young Corkman who has cut himself with his first shave'! The delegates roared at his discomfort when Michael indignantly pointed out that his cat had scratched him.

Charles Haughey's administration of the party leader's allowance in the 1980s had a much earlier resonance with Norton. Much to the fury of Larkin and many delegates, Norton retained this allowance of some £600 per annum for his exclusive political use. That bone of contention, together with Norton's acceptance of a company directorship in Co Kildare while leader of the party, was a repeated source of friction. It was not until Norton resigned as leader in 1960 that trustees of the parliamentary party were appointed to administer the allowance.

I did not know Norton well but he had an extraordinary span as leader of the Labour Party from 1932 to 1960. He was a formidable public speaker but being grossly overweight from his diabetic condition, he lacked the sheer presence of Jim Larkin Jnr. He retained the leadership of the party for almost three decades because, as he told me during one unguarded evening in the Dáil restaurant, the others were too engrossed in their constituencies and county councils to challenge him. Anyway, with Fianna Fáil having an overall majority from 1932 to 1948, nobody was interested in the chores of opposition. When Norton finally resigned in 1960 he did not move out of the party leader's small room on the ground floor of the 1932 annex of Leinster House. I was surprised when I went to see his successor Brendan Corish to find Brendan at a side desk in the leader's office; Norton and his private secretary, Mrs Correy, had moved the desk in for him while they continued to occupy the office.

Up to his death in 1965, Norton dominated Corish. He was streets ahead of Corish on Dáil strategy, the drafting of statements and legislative expertise. Brendan Corish had a severe sense of inferiority when it came to political discussions with Norton at party meetings. But he began to grow in confidence and stature in the mid-1960s.

The progress of Labour in the early 1960s was extremely difficult because Seán Lemass had assiduously cultivated the trade unions and particularly the Irish Transport and General Workers' Union. Lemass' firm support for the 1941 Trade

Union Act, which, unconstitutionally, proposed to give sole negotiating rights to 'Irish based unions', had not been forgotten by my union. Several of the senior union officials I worked with in the union's head office in Merrion Square had that special relationship with Fianna Fáil. A Cork relative of mine, who was a Fianna Fáil supporter until the mid-1960s, the late Charles McCarthy, recalled: 'Lemass managed to combine a warm co-operative approach to the trade union movement with a steely approach to the Labour Party on the general grounds that his party, Fianna Fáil, was more representative politically of the bulk of trade union members than was the Labour Party, which on a headcount was manifestly true.'

In the 1965 and 1969 general elections, however, an influx of perceived intellectuals began to come into the parliamentary party. There was a patronising assumption by some of the media that the men from rural Ireland were somehow uncultured, unread and uninspiring. Those with academic or professional experience were deemed politically superior. It could be said that the late Jimmy Tully from the Meath constituency epitomised the reaction to this 'Dublinisation 4' of the party. A former corporal in the army, Jimmy had pulled himself up in life by his bootstraps. He was an outstanding local deputy and councillor on Meath County Council and combined political and trade union activity as general secretary of the Federation of Rural Workers. He was chairman of the Labour Party for fourteen years, a non-drinker and non-smoker who eschewed the Dáil bar. He had little time for the new avant-garde socialists. At the 1970 party conference in Limerick, he referred to 'smart alecs, with the sweat dripping onto their school books, talking about the workers of this country'. I have no doubt that he had some of his scholarly colleagues in mind.

As a political novice on the administrative council of the party, I was intolerant of my elders. If a row could be foreseen I had no hesitation in diving in at the deep end. But my elders and betters were in no mood to be reprimanded by this self-anointed reformist. At one joint meeting between the parliamentary party and the administrative council in the mid-1960s, I fulminated against the deputies about their Dáil performances. 'What have you been doing on these issues all those years?' I chided them. 'We have been waiting for you, Barry!' Denis Larkin replied. I always learned the hard way.

Nevertheless I was elected vice chairman of the party at the 1966 annual conference, defeating Deputy Tom Kyne by 348 votes to 161. At that conference as well, Jimmy Tully was returned as chairman for the fourteenth year. There was a real sense of family history, too, in that my father was also elected to the administrative council at the top of the poll.

I was always opposed to our Dáil deputies holding elected party officerships, in effect a dual mandate within the party. The leader of the party in the Dáil and the deputy leader were automatically members of the Administrative Council, as were six other members of the parliamentary party. In 1967 I decided to challenge for the position of chairman, much to the annoyance of the Labour deputies and senators. Michael O'Leary TD was their nominee after Tully decided to stand down. Despite O'Leary's popularity, the rank and file of the party wanted one of their own as party chairman and I was comfortably elected.

In March 1968 I decided to seek a Labour nomination in the Dun Laoghaire constituency; quite a few colleagues had told me by then to put my candidature in place of my mouth. There were very strong local candidates, notably Michael E. Byrne, husband of Councillor Jane Dillon-Byrne; Councillor Flor O'Mahony, a young, active and quite charismatic Dalkeyite; Councillor Jim Byrne, a stalwart who appeared to be the logical successor to the late Councillor Jack Fitzgerald. Jack had unsuccessfully carried the Labour flag with great distinction in several previous general elections. In the event, there were eight contenders for the nominations including John Caviston of fish delicatessen fame in Glasthule. Dan Browne was in the chair at the convention and the votes were counted by Ross Connolly, the grandson of James Connolly, with each vote being converted into 100 votes for a true PR count. I was selected as the fourth candidate for the panel by a mere one-half of one vote on the seventh count.

It had been agreed that there would be a panel of four candidates because no general election had been called at that stage. In fact, Jack Lynch did not go to the country until June

1969. I was the complete 'runner in' in the ballot. At the convention I made a trenchant speech, promising to resign as Industrial Officer of ICTU, where I earned £1,500 per annum, and become the first full-time Labour deputy for the constituency if elected to Dáil Éireann. Following the convention, one of the four selected candidates, Michael E. Byrne, decided not to contest the general election. His decision left a panel of Flor O'Mahony, 'Jas' Byrne and myself.

There were three very fortunate developments for our campaign prior to the 1969 general election. Firstly, in October 1968 Fianna Fáil tried to replace the electoral system of proportional representation by the single vote, single seat system. As a Labour Party national officer and as Industrial Officer of ICTU, which was very strongly opposed to the abolition of PR, I had a very high media profile in the PR campaign. Secondly, Stella and I became life-long friends of Eric and Eileen Doyle. Eric led the PR campaign against Fianna Fáil in Dun Laoghaire. Eric and Eileen had many family and personal contacts in Dun Laoghaire and particularly in the Glenageary area where they lived and in Monkstown Farm where Eric was born and reared. Eric was a prominent union activist in the brewery laboratory in Guinness and was a respected member of the executive committee of the Workers' Union of Ireland. He was later to become a Labour councillor of Dun Laoghaire Corporation, a member of Dublin County Council, Chairman of the National Rehabilitation Board and a member of the Voluntary Health Insurance Board. Without Eric and Eileen's unstinting assistance, I would not have been elected in 1969.

We had one further lucky break. Deputy Lionel Booth, the local Fianna Fáil Deputy since 1957, decided, quite suddenly, to retire from the Dáil. Had he decided to contest the 1969 general election I would have been scuppered. The Dun Laoghaire constituency had a 17 to 20 per cent Protestant electorate and Fianna Fáil had an ideal such deputy in Lionel Booth. His retirement was a major blow to Fianna Fáil and it tried to close the gap by selecting Neville Keery, a young party activist who worked in Trinity College. A member of the Church of Ireland, he was married to Anne, Gemma Hussey's sister. Although he lived in the constituency, Neville was relatively unknown. He was also at a disadvantage because David Andrews, the sitting deputy since 1965, was not prepared, in any election, at least not until 1997, to split the constituency and share the Fianna Fáil vote.

These developments were singularly fortunate for the three Labour candidates. There was a strong residual Labour tradition in the constituency. There had been a strong Labour presence on Blackrock Urban District Council in the 1920s, notably from Councillors Timothy McKenna, Michael Quinlan and John Synott. Councillor Jack Fitzgerald in Dalkey and central Dun Laoghaire had held sway in the 1950s and 1960s. Dr John de Courcy Ireland, the maritime historian and secretary of the Dun Laoghaire Royal Lifeboat Association, and Ruaidhri Roberts, General Secretary of ICTU, were long-time residents and Labour activists in the area. They kept the flag flying in the sparse years.

However, the Dun Laoghaire constituency was dominated by south Dublin's Catholic and Protestant conservative ethos. There were some thirty Catholic religious orders in the constituency in 1969 with over 1,100 religious on the electoral register. And they most certainly all voted! The area had elected in earlier years a Unionist MP, Captain Dockrell, to Westminster and the Dockrell family continued to be represented in public life. Percy Dockrell's presence on the Fine Gael ticket posed no threat whatsoever to Liam Cosgrave. In my experience, Cosgrave had a flinty integrity but he was not a politician of social vision or economic perception. His success in becoming leader of Fine Gael arose from a combination of dogged determination and stubbornness backed by the great political legacy of his father. In 1973 he shrewdly eliminated possible rivals by sending Declan Costello to the Attorney General's office, Paddy Cooney to the legal Siberia of the Department of Justice and Garret FitzGerald to the outer spaces of the Foreign Affairs portfolio. His greatest attribute was his devotion to the democratic institutions of the State, and his intervention during the arms crisis of the Lynch government was critical.

The general election of 1969 was a torrid affair with Flor O'Mahony, 'Jas' Byrne and myself running three strong separate campaigns. Never before and never since then has there been such an intensive canvass by Labour in the constituency. In those days Dun Laoghaire politics were intensely parochial. I was, invariably, described as 'Barry Fitzgerald from Cork'. But I ran a rip-roaring campaign knowing that I was the underdog. We borrowed heavily and Eric Doyle brilliantly organised my canvass. I called on all of my trade union friends from all over Dublin and outside to rally to the cause. Union friends from the brewery laboratory in Guinness, Maurice King and Albert Murphy from the ESB, Albert Darby from Ballsbridge Motors, Tom Doolan from CIE and management consultant Michael Duggan, all came to the cause. They all knew the meeting spot — outside the 'Top Hat' ballroom. We had between 50 and 75 canvassers each evening and each weekend, all with one direct message 'No. 1 for Desmond'. I persuaded my father to come up from Cork with his car. Stella's mother and sister looked after our sons. Stella was a superb canvasser on the doorstep. I was dreadful because I loathed asking anybody for a vote, a mixture of embarrassment and pride.

The Labour first preference vote in the constituency was 2,570 for Flor O'Mahony, 1,386 for Jim Byrne and 2,870 for Barry Desmond. The quota for the seat was 7,508. When Flor O'Mahony was eliminated on the ninth count with 3,585 votes, I received a superb transfer from him of 2,757 votes and won the last seat with 1,271 votes to spare over Neville Keery. An expelled Labour member, Proinsias MacAonghusa, ran as an Independent Labour candidate and lost his deposit. We were euphoric. A few days later I returned to earth, handed in my office keys to Ruaidhri Roberts, general secretary of ICTU, and received a refund of £110 pension contributions. Suddenly, I realised that if I were to drop dead, Stella and the children had no insurance cover other than the social welfare widow's pension. Such were the pension schemes of the Irish Transport and General Workers' Union and ICTU, my employers since 1957, that I lost all pension entitlements on resignation, which was obligatory following my election. I immediately took out insurance for basic life cover.

Thus began twenty years in the Dáil. There were no secretarial assistants in the Dáil in those days. Our manual typewriter went up on the kitchen table and in between looking after the baby sons in the bouncer, Stella pounded out press statements, Dáil questions, policy documents and thousands of constituency representations. And the phone started to ring day and night, including Christmas Day.

Arising from that election I began a long personal friendship with Neville Keery who was nominated a senator by Taoiseach Jack Lynch and who is now a Head of Unit in the Communications, Information and Culture Directorate General of the European Commission in Brussels. Neville was always a strong Jack Lynch and Paddy Hillery supporter. He had no time at all for Haughey.

Having worked for twelve years in trade union offices, I was quite unprepared in 1969 for the daily contact I was about to have in the Dáil with deputies of quite different occupations and social positions. The Labour deputies included no fewer than three university academics, David Thornley, Conor Cruise O'Brien and Justin Keating, two medical doctors, John O'Connell and Noel Browne, and a clutch of union officials. Fianna Fáil and Fine Gael were dominated by farmers, lawyers, shopkeepers and publicans and, in Fianna Fáil's case particularly, auctioneers and agents. Their political interests and social pursuits were something of a culture shock and a new education for me. I was suddenly rubbing shoulders in the Dáil lobbies with the 16 Fianna Fáil farmer deputies and the 21 farmers in Fine Gael. John Bruton and I, both elected on the same day, could hardly have come from more different political backgrounds.

Three

Nine Quotas of Votes

'He carved out his Dun Laoghaire constituency with the tenacity of a water buffalo unwilling to be separated from his favourite patch of pampas grass.'

John Horgan, 1986

When I was first elected in Dun Laoghaire–Rathdown, I had no idea where half of the eighteen polling stations were. I did not know the names of most of the roads and estates in the constituency. I had no local relatives, no local school record, no membership of a residents' association, no sporting prowess and no previous candidature. I knew a few people from Cork in the constituency who wished me well and, as Cork people say only to their own, 'No chance up here, boy, of all places!' And yet in the seven general elections from 1969 to 1987, in the 1989 Euro elections and in the 1974 local elections, I was successful.

This convinced me that while every successful politician needs a continuous convergence of fortuitous events, a quota of personal humility is the prime prerequisite. It is the critical dimension. When one calls cold on the doorstep of a constituent, the chemistry with the voter is a volatile mix. It either starts to bubble there and then or it evaporates. I never ever asked anybody directly for a vote, not even, in desperation, for a scratch! One can tell intuitively, after meeting thousands of electors and from humiliating experience, the probable response of the elector. The key is initial eye contact. Lose this grip and one might as well close the door and the front gate there and then. Only if this body language is favourable should one dare to offer to shake the hand of the constituent. That right hand, usually, will also mark the ballot paper! To offer one's hand, have it refused, and possibly have the rebuff relayed to the family and neighbours, is worse than no canvass at all.

I apologised at every doorstep for 'dragging you out tonight'! I meant those words. I knew that if my regret was accepted I had gained a small advantage in this crucial encounter. And while I always carried canvass literature, I never offered it unless I was sure that it would be accepted. To be refused is to lose control on the doorstep. I always preferred to canvass alone but with Stella and a close friend two or three doors away, to 'come to the rescue'. I never canvassed without an electoral register which I kept under the canvass cards. To knock at a door and address the elector by his or her first name is a solid plus. And one also gathers some profile of the household from the register. Why have a prolonged and weary exchange of views with someone who does not appear to be on the register and who assures one that all politicians are a shower of gangsters anyway? Such vocal non-participants in the campaign are the bane of any canvass. And how does one extricate oneself from the invitation: 'Oh it's you! Come in here! I want to talk to you!'?

I received such an invitation from a well-known personality in Patrick Street, Dun Laoghaire. I was with Teesie Thomas who knew most people in the area. She came in with me. Before long the man produced a vicious carving knife and brandished it in our direction as he denounced the Labour Party and all its works and pomps. He clearly indicated what he wished to do to each precious part of my anatomy. He accused me of having neglected the live theatre in Dublin. And while his dinner companion implored him to behave, we circled the kitchen table in great disorder and eventually escaped. The said cabaret comedian lived off the story for years while I had to bring poor gentle Teesie down to Dunphy's lounge for a large brandy to restore her colour.

*

Nothing disrupts a canvass more than the disappearance of the candidate into a house in the middle of a large estate. I recall being rescued from some houses which were arch Fianna Fáil and who invited me in simply to delay the progress of our canvass. I knew that, on average, at least three out of every ten homes I visited were Fianna Fáil, three were Fine Gael, two were 'floaters', one would be Labour and one or two would not vote at all. Most Fianna Fáil voters did not declare themselves as such. They said that they were 'not interested' on the doorstep. They would ask, 'What did Labour ever do for us?' Eye contact clearly indicated polite hostility. However, one never lost hope. I always implored our canvassers to look for the second or third preferences from Fianna Fáil because they invariably mismanaged their vote in Dun Laoghaire with David Andrews going well over the quota. I did not mind being David's 'human surplus' because I never had a first preference quota of votes.

The Fine Gael voter in Dun Laoghaire, on the other hand, would be quite up front. 'You're number two after Mr Cosgrave' was music to my ears. Liam usually had a surplus and such transfers were gold dust. But every single number two was hard earned. Constituents would ring late at night and very early in the morning, when we were in bed with a young lad in the cot. They apologised for doing so and said, 'Mr Desmond, the travellers' horses are here in our front garden in Monaloe! We know Mr Cosgrave is very busy as Taoiseach so we decided to ring you. The horses are eating our roses. For God's sake, please help!' I would scramble for my upper set of dentures (having lost my front teeth at twenty years of age after a belt of a hurley) and while Stella cursed Liam Cosgrave softly into her pillow, I would assure my beloved constituent in the most unctuous of tones that I would take up the crisis at dawn. In the process, a few hard-earned number twos would come from that Fine Gael household, and perhaps from their neighbours, from Liam's surplus. By such endeavours was the survival of an Irish national legislator under PR ensured.

And one could also steal the odd vote. I recall an elderly Protestant lady from York Road ringing me in desperation. She had always voted for Percy Dockrell of Fine Gael. She was most irate. She had a serious water burst in her kitchen and she had phoned Percy. Percy did not wish to be disturbed and, not unreasonably, said 'Madam, you need a plumber, not a politician!' I swung into action, rang my emergency water engineer's number and had the crisis contained. I subsequently met the lady down town during election time. She intended to switch her number one from Percy to me and give Percy the number two. A number two from me to Percy was as useful as a jazz band in Mount Mellary! But she too was duly put on my list for a Christmas card.

Percy and Maurice Dockrell were two real wits in the Dáil bar. Percy told us that at Deansgrange cross roads in one election he was addressing the gathering from a horse dray. An irate lady emerged from the local pub with a good few jars in her. She shouted at Percy, 'Mr Dockrell, you're only an auld bastard!' Percy replied, 'Mother, it was kind of you to come!' Maurice recalled that at a meeting in the Liberties a woman challenged him: 'Maurice! who did you sleep with last night?' In a flash he quipped: 'Not with you, madam, thank God!' Hundreds of local people attended those meetings which were great occasions.

During my twenty years as a deputy I maintained a substantial Christmas card mailing list. All my Labour colleagues at national level, the secretary and chairperson of every residents' association, all old folks groups, sports clubs, county council and corporation staffs, local party members of whom there were about 150, and a wide circle of friends received a card from Stella and myself, personally signed. Many elderly, single, unemployed, unrelated and unbefriended constituents received their only card at Christmas from us. Year after year people said to me, 'Thank you for not forgetting me'. Sons and daughters would thank us for sending the card to their mother. Dun Laoghaire has an exceptionally large number of retired people living alone, often in very poor circumstances and in isolation. Personal contact is a priceless commodity. Those who keep in touch and who bother to do so are few and far between. Many such constituents would come once or twice a month to my clinic simply for a chat or a political gossip. I was someone to talk to in a lonely world. We received hundreds of cards in return.

*

The electorate always expects more from a Labour deputy than any other; more contributions to Dáil debates, more clarity of radical opinion on economic and taxation questions, more liberality on social issues, and greater willingness to be more available to constituents than any other politician. The hard core Fianna Fáil and Fine Gael voters are more prepared to put their party first. That was why I decided in the 1969 election to emphasise again and again that I intended to be a full-time public representative. This meant financial sacrifice to our family. I could have become a part-time political journalist, or a part-time trade union lobbyist for some public service unions. Like some of my fellow deputies I could have studied for the bar examinations with partial exemption. Stella and I decided to forego all such prospects because we did not want to have my full-time political commitment to Dun Laoghaire diluted. And above all I did not wish to be attacked as a double-jobber!

When David Andrews was elected in 1965 he began a weekly Saturday morning clinic in the Elphin Hotel on the Marine Road. It gave him a clear visibility to constituents. I decided in 1969 to 'up the ante'. I had clinics at Sallynoggin, with generous help from Tom and Mary Byrne, and at the Old Folks' Centre, encouraged by Eric Doyle, Joe Hoare and Rita O'Brien. I had a clinic every Saturday morning and afternoon at the Christian Institute, at the Church of Ireland Community Centre in Deansgrange. And then the Town Hall, Blackrock every Sunday morning with Niamh Bhreathnach. Stella and I did our weekly shopping very early on Saturday mornings. Our four sons saw me in between these clinics and our family social life at weekends was minimal. Apart from a social drink with close friends on Saturday nights, my clinic routine continued unrelentingly for twenty years. The only respites were the month of August and bank holiday weekends.

Sitting in cold and damp rooms in the middle of winter, jaded from a hectic week in the Dáil, carefully recording all the details of multiple constituents' problems, was an exercise in sheer endurance. Without this grind and the voluntary assistance at every clinic of dedicated party activists, I would never have been returned to the Dáil. And the clinics in themselves were only part of the work. Deputies in the 1970s had sparse secretarial assistance. I would spend Sunday evenings dictating and writing up the clinic notes. Stella would heave the manual typewriter onto the kitchen table every Monday morning and together we pounded out thousands of representations to government departments and the local authorities. Our baby son Eóin would coo a chorus as the noisy typewriter and the telephone spoke to his mother and father. There was little glamour in this political exercise. And the work did not stop with the correspondence. There were the regular weekly visits with housing applicants to the corporation and county council to seek reviews of their points on the housing list. It all added up to an eighty-hour week, thirty hours in the Dáil, thirty in the constituency and twenty at party meetings.

One of the inevitable features of clinic work was the regularity with which some constituents visited several deputies. I recall a clinic one Easter Sunday morning in Sallynoggin with Eric Doyle. A woman arrived with her children about her housing application. After a lengthy discussion she paused at the door as she departed and said, 'You really are great, Mr Andrews, for being here on Easter Sunday!' What could I say!

*

When I was first elected I learned a sharp lesson about the power and prestige of Liam Cosgrave in the constituency. Together with David Andrews and Percy Dockrell I attended the annual general meeting of the Priory Residents' Association in Stillorgan. Midway through the meeting the door opened and Liam Cosgrave entered. The top table to a man and woman stood up to welcome the leader of the Opposition. The residents followed suit. David and I remained seated. And then all the agenda items Liam wished to comment on were taken first. He was meticulous. His representation to have the pedestrian phase on the traffic lights on Stillorgan Hill increased by 25 seconds for the elderly residents was warmly received. In those years Liam Cosgrave ran the show and I was a bit player. After the meeting he had one Paddy and departed in style.

To my knowledge Liam Cosgrave never held a clinic. He relied on a large group of Fine Gael councillors and supporters to feed him with representations. He had been a Dáil deputy for the area for 26 years when I was first elected. He was a venerated local institution in almost every household. Church and State reposed in him. If I was to stay the pace with Liam Cosgrave, I had little option but to match him in constituency service. Dermot Boucher pointed out: 'It is very little exaggeration to say that no lamp post is erected, or no zebra crossing is painted in Dun Laoghaire without receiving the personal public imprimatur of the senior Fine Gael deputy'.[4]

*

The local deputy upsets at his peril the tranquillity of local values. Dun Laoghaire in the 1970s was very conservative. At our party's annual dinner it was clearly expected that a formal grace before the meal would be pronounced.

It fell to me to do so at one dinner in the Rose Park Hotel. I decided to change the usual format and repeated what I had heard at an ecumenical gathering: 'Bless us, O Lord, bless the food we are about to receive, bless those who prepared it and give bread to those who have none.'

The top table was then served our soup. The waitress slammed it down in front of me. She turned to the other waitress and exclaimed in loud tones: 'I told ye he was a communist! Did ye hear what he said about God and the food!'

*

Up to the mid-1990s a key element in every election was one's physical presence at polling stations, with banners and posters on behalf of the candidates. I am pleased that this practice has now ceased and that the electorate no longer have to run the gauntlet at the entrance to every polling station. During my elections I visited every polling station to thank the presiding officer, and his staff and to enquire how the poll was progressing. The staff and party workers expected each candidate 'to show their face'. Stella always stood at the Glasthule School's polling station for the whole day over a 15-year period. She came to know many of the electors and particularly those who supported her husband! I always stood from 6:00 p.m. to 9:00 p.m. at the very large polling station at Deansgrange cross roads. I stood without a sticker on my coat and never handed out literature. It was always highly effective as a final reminder to the electorate. But I had one huge disadvantage. In the dark winter campaigns I wore a cap but I was unknown without my bald 'elder lemon'. Nora Nowlan solved the problem with a sports umbrella and a tilly lamp on high which shone on the bald pate during the winter evenings. It gave me an electoral glow and halo. It worked!

An unwritten understanding existed between the deputies in Dun Laoghaire. We were frequently approached to contribute to sales of work, bingo, bring and buy sales and special collections for serious cases of hardship. We were in the front line wherever we went. We had very clear agreed limits to our contributions. We did not succumb to the disgraceful competition in other constituencies of jerseys and footballs for local football teams and massive personal sponsorship of all and sundry. I did make the occasional personal donation such as 'The Barry Desmond Perpetual Cup', which is still played for as a local charity competition.

During my two decades in the Dáil there was absolutely no limit on election expenditure by each candidate and by each party on their behalf. I competed against some very wealthy candidates who had full-time paid canvassers, and who had free bars and food at the end of each canvass day for their 'workers'. They paid for the hire of expensive election campaign headquarters, prohibitive mobile phones at the time, loudspeaker vans, advertising hoardings and unlimited multi-coloured literature, posters and house-to-house 'drops'. I fully support the statutory limits which were imposed on such splurging at election time by the Labour Party in government in the 1990s. They were long overdue. Deservedly, most of those well-funded candidates were never elected.

Another unwritten party rule was that canvassers and workers on election day were not paid by the party or the candidates. In Fianna Fáil and Fine Gael, many local activists who worked as polling clerks for their parties were paid and fed. It used to stick in my craw when some people outside the polling stations for Fianna Fáil and Fine Gael and wearing their stickers were the very people who had brought their problems to our clinics. Some constituents can be very cynical indeed. Our organisation occasionally paid for petrol when people volunteered their cars for polling day transport. In the 1960s and 1970s many families had no private transport. It was a boon to the elderly to have a lift to the polling station.

Our exercise became unstuck in 1973 when one relatively unknown supporter from Ballybrack offered his Morris Minor. As agreed, after the close of poll I gave him £10 for petrol for the day. Eric Doyle came back later to Paddy McCormack's lounge in Mounttown and said he had also given £10 to the said supporter who had come looking for his petrol money. Then Michael Byrne from the Glenageary polling station arrived and said that he had also been approached for the £10 and paid up. And soon afterwards Aidan McNamara, our Director of Elections, arrived. He too had been conned. Such are the hazards of organising an election campaign. At the European Court of Auditors we later called it 'risk analysis'!

A key element of every canvass was a visit to at least two pubs between 9:30 p.m. and 11:00 p.m. each election evening. One showed oneself at the doorstep and later on in the local lounge. We had one unwritten rule while in the pub — no canvass of customers. I usually bought one drink, the first, for our group and never indulged in the obscene practice of buying a round of drinks for the pub. In some constituencies, particularly in Co Dublin, this was a common enough occurrence. A deputy was reported to have paid for every fifth shopping trolley in a supermarket in his constituency for one hour. In Dun Laoghaire the electorate would have been aghast at such a crude attempt to buy votes.

But in the 1969 election all was not plain sailing. We went into a public bar in South Dublin one evening. Our group included the young Jane Dillon-Byrne and Stella. The barman pointed to the notice over the bar: 'No women or dogs allowed'. We were utterly taken aback and refused to go to the lounge area. We left the premises to the great amusement of the males in the public bar. At that time there were several pubs in the constituency where women were not served drink in the public bars.

*

In the 1973 election, Albert Darby, a trade union colleague who lived in Kilmacud, showed me the personal letter he had received from Liam Cosgrave asking for his number one vote. It was from Liam's home address, personally addressed and sent in a plain stamped envelope. He had been in correspondence with the deputy on behalf of local residents. Liam's letter was very personal, very short and very effective. I learned from the master and in each successive election, I sent a similar note to all those I had been in touch with over the preceding four years. These letters were most productive. I also sent other circulars, for example, to all fellow members of the Irish Transport and General Workers' Union of which I was a long-time member. However, accidents did happen.

In one election I posted a circular in Irish, signed Barra Deasun, to the 1,750 gaelgeoirí electors of Dun Laoghaire asking for their support. Simultaneously I posted a circular to the citizens of the UK in the constituency register welcoming them, following a referendum allowing them to vote in general elections, to exercise their new entitlement. Unfortunately, we packed the opposite envelopes. Some very irate gaelgeoirí arrived at our election headquarters in Patrick Street accusing me of a grave insult to their nationality and also offering the opinion that I was a 'pro Brit!' Our mistake was not repeated. Such mistakes could have been fatal because the core Labour vote rarely exceeded 3,600. I had to add 2,500 votes to come within two-thirds of a first preference quota. That was the stark electoral reality.

*

To this day one aspect of political participation I cannot tolerate is personal financial meanness in a public representative. I knew one public representative who developed a weak stomach. Only his favourite bottle for his recurring condition could keep him afloat. He invariably kept the bottle all to himself. He and his spouse had a perfect sense of timing for the cocktail sausages and the ham sandwiches at receptions. He travelled abroad to the most arid venue and uninteresting agenda. And yet the electorate bestowed him with many quotas over many decades.

My experience in the Dáil as Labour Whip was no different. It was easier to extract a ten-pound note from Saddam Hussein than to chase a small minority of my colleagues for the tenner for the Christmas gratuities for the usher and restaurant staffs of Leinster House. There were some seriously mean deputies in all parties who never had any money on them and who had always left their pristine chequebooks at home no matter what the occasion. Charity forbids me to name these well-known scrooges and the public at large would be taken aback if they really knew. Some of them will die as millionaires. They never seemed to appreciate that there are no pockets in a shroud.

*

One of the major internal conflicts in Dun Laoghaire during my twenty years was the pervasive presence of some 'anti-coalition' Labour activists. Their interminable demands for a second and third Labour candidate in the constituency made life as the sitting deputy quite precarious. A vocal minority of the constituency council of the party was always reluctant to acknowledge the fact that in these two decades of general elections, Labour had never received a quota of votes on the first count. In 1981 I addressed our selection convention, pointing out that there is always a dilemma facing every selection convention between the candidates who wanted to go forward to face the electorate and the need to ensure that Labour votes did not haemorrhage all over the ballot paper. I pointed out that in the Dun Laoghaire constituency in 1969, the three Labour candidates, Councillors Flor O'Mahony, Jas Byrne and myself, were 682 first preference votes short of the quota of 7,508 for one seat. In 1973, the two Labour candidates, Flor O'Mahony and myself, were 562 first preference votes short of the quota of 8,402 votes for one seat; we won again with

Cosgrave transfers this time. In 1977, the two Labour candidates, Councillor Jack Loughran and myself, were 2,072 first preference votes short of the quota of 7,612 to win one seat. We held our seat because of transfers from Cosgrave, Dockrell and Una O'Higgins-O'Malley.

It had been suggested that three Labour candidates posed no problem to the retention of one Labour seat and we would have a fight for a second. The reality was quite different as the record clearly showed. For example, because the Fine Gael candidates in 1977, Liam Cosgrave and Percy Dockrell, transferred 1,000 votes to Labour during subsequent counts, by virtue of the sheer strength of our campaign for high transfers, Fine Gael lost their traditional second seat, and we, fortunately, held ours. The price to be paid for every additional Labour candidate was an inevitable loss of some votes in transfers. I had no hesitation in saying in 1981 that should the rate of voting transfer drop below 70 per cent, then our party would have been fortunate to retain one seat let alone fight for a second.

In the event I raised no objection to the nominations of Councillors Jane Dillon-Byrne and Frank Smyth in the 1981 general election because I knew that Jane would attract votes from her own unique following in the borough and Frank Smyth was very highly regarded in the Dalkey–Ballybrack area. The quota was 8,029. Jane received 1,026 first preferences, had 1,625 on elimination on the eighth count and transferred 1,018 to me; Frank Smyth had 761 first preferences, had 834 on the fifth count and transferred 446 to me; I polled 5,935 first preferences and was elected to the third seat on the eighth count.

Contrary to popular political perception, my 20-year tenure in the constituency was not a 'one man show' in elections. In four of the seven general elections I contested, we had a second or third Labour candidate. We did so only after the most meticulous examination of the prospects of the candidates of the other parties. We had no less than seven Labour councillors elected over this period and we had some twelve active local branches and a well-organised constituency executive and council. These were the main ingredients of our political success. Any Labour deputy who runs an exclusive personal fiefdom in any constituency does so at his or her peril.

The secret is to 'walk softly' but always lead from the front and keep a very bleary eye on prospective candidates within one's own party. Going into every convention I used to turn to Stella and say, 'At least I know that if you are nominated, you will not contest!'

*

It will be gleaned from these recollections that I have some misgivings about the general efficacy of the current electoral system of PR. Its shortcomings are manifestly obvious. However, twice during my lifetime I have campaigned very vigorously against the abolition of PR. The merits of the alternatives proposed, mostly by Fianna Fáil and again by the current Minister for the Environment, Noel Dempsey, have not, on balance, merited fundamental changes. Pat Rabbitte summed up my feelings somewhat when he wrote: 'I am hugely sceptical about whether we can or should aspire to a political aristocracy of highly paid legislators cosseted from the importuning of constituents or financial worries.'[5]

In 1982 Michael D. Higgins published his perceptive tract *The Limits of Clientism. Towards An Assessment of Irish Politics.* This analysis of political patronage in a rural constituency graphically illustrated the interaction between clientism and the deputy, the minister of state, the councillor, the county manager and that object of all attention, the elector. In 1970 Professor Basil Chubb had drawn attention to the 'lack of serious ideological differences between the parties and a comprehensive localism in national politics'.[6] Michael D. concluded that the system was exploitative and distracted attention from the real social and economic issues of our society. While drawing attention to the consequences of the system of proportional representation, he did not advocate particular reforms. Would the introduction of the single seat transferable vote system diminish the prospect of candidates competing ferociously against one another for first preference votes? How does one overcome the incessant temptations facing candidates to indulge in local 'stroke politics'?

Michael D. and I faced the sobering reality that in the single seat system, Labour's representation would be drastically reduced. He too had to do his weekly round of 'clinics and confessions' to survive in the cut-throat politics of Galway. Even under the straight vote single seat system of the UK, the MP who fails to meet his constituents on a very regular basis faces defeat or de-selection. While Michael D. rightly held that clientism is exploitative in source and intent, I never ever asked a constituent who came to my clinics for a vote. I do believe that there is a democratic obligation on all deputies to make themselves available to community groups and individual constituents and to take their views on board, if possible. Michael D. and I knew of many deputies who spent 80 per cent of their lives in this mould night after night, year after year. They were re-elected. But is that the sole purpose of a democratic electoral system?

Under the system of PR, Ireland has enjoyed a stable political democratic structure. Government instability, even where there has been dependence on a small group of maverick independents, has not been a marked feature. I would never have been elected in a single seat constituency and my independent party stances would not have placed my candidature high on an elite party list. Perhaps these are two good arguments for the advocates of change! Another Fianna Fáil Minister, Charlie McCreevy, has, in his agreement with Noel Dempsey, supported the reduction of the number of deputies to 120 with enhanced remuneration. Mary Harney has advocated a Dáil of 100 deputies. Such a development does not require a constitutional amendment. All the government has to do, as Alan Dukes quite rightly pointed out,[7] is to revise the terms of reference of the Dáil Constituency Commission to provide for the top end of the population-per-seat range set out in Article 16.2.2. The outcome of such a reform would, in my opinion, result in a reduction in the number of Fianna Fáil, Fianna Gael and Independent deputies in the western constituencies. And Mary Harney might well lose her seat.

Any attempt to radically change the current electoral system will, in my opinion, provoke a savage response from the electorate. I now find that our party political system has never been held in such low esteem. The litany of sleaze, corruption and tribunals has greatly damaged our democratic institutions. Our political parties must first put their own houses in order, particularly in relation to the funding of campaigns, before they bring forward electoral reforms.

Four

The Hurlers Come Off the Ditch

'Leaders we produce easily, leadership is something else!'

Seán MacRéamoinn

The inter-party governments of 1948-1951 and 1954-1957 were particularly traumatic for the Labour Party. In the post-war poverty and minimal economic growth of the 1950s we had searing experiences in government with Fine Gael and the lesser parties. At my first party conference in 1957 the vote to stay out of coalitions was almost unanimous. It was not until the political upheaval in Northern Ireland in 1970 that most Labour deputies and senior figures in the party began to contemplate coalition again with Fine Gael. There was, however, no particular *grá* in the party for their leader, Liam Cosgrave. He was deeply distrustful at that time of 'your lot', as he described our party to me, and of Brendan Corish, our party leader. I found this strange because they were both deeply conservative Catholics. But the growing Labour detestation of Charles Haughey and his hard-nosed TACA supporters transcended any residual reservations about Fine Gael.

Jack Lynch had come to be regarded by us as a decent but captive Taoiseach in the clutches of a party which had grown arrogant and corrupt after sixteen years of continuous power. From 1969, Conor Cruise O'Brien became an almost permanent tribunal of inquiry in the Dáil into Haughey. Such were his acid criticisms of a range of Fianna Fáil ministers that at times I feared for his personal safety in the Dáil lobby.

In 1970 no political party favoured coalition with any other. Fianna Fáil's traditional view of its own identity did not allow for liaisons with other parties. The dominant personality of de Valera had profoundly influenced this policy. Identification of party and country contained a messianic view of the party's mission. The exegesis, which passed for party policy, was formulated under Dev's eagle surveillance. Jeremiah at his most blood-curdling could not better Fianna Fáil's disgust as they directed the attention of their audiences to the national political desecration which would follow another bout of inter-party government. Stability of government was the exclusive mantra of Fianna Fáil in sole power. The corollary was also held that inter-party governments were impractical and incompetent. They would lead onto national debility and a general confusion of the electorate. As a result, 'inter-party government' was one of the dirtiest phrases in Ireland's political vocabulary.

The crises in the Fianna Fáil government in 1970, particularly in relation to allegations about arms smuggling, and the intrigues between senior ministers and their associates, convinced Brendan Corish that the policy Labour had adopted twelve years previously was in urgent need of change. He summed up his feelings towards Fianna Fáil when he addressed our special delegate conference in Cork in December 1970. He said that delegates 'cannot be expected to share the feelings of disgust I have about them [Fianna Fáil] in their outrageous behaviour, particularly since May [when the Arms Crisis broke]. I see Fianna Fáil in action every day. I see the threat to our democracy as long as they remain unchallenged.'[8] The resolution of the administrative council of the party favouring a policy of coalition was adopted by 396 votes to 204. About 50 delegates led by Noel Browne walked out. A resolution proposed by Michael Mullen, general secretary of the Irish Transport and General Workers' Union, asking that the decision be deferred until after the general election, when a special conference would be held, was defeated by 470 votes to 307. Not for the first time did Michael Mullen wish to have a foot in both camps.

As Jack Lynch's leadership came under renewed pressure in 1973 over proposed constituency revisions and particularly from Bobby Molloy over the proposed Galway constituency changes, nobody doubted that we were entering a period in which no single party could preserve its hegemony alone in government.

The arrival of Garret FitzGerald in the Dáil in 1969 and the role of Declan Costello in the 'just society' policy change had impacted on the conservative character of Fine Gael. The Labour Party around Corish was qualitatively different from that which participated in the various inter-party governments of the late 1940s and 1950s under the dominance of William Norton. Deputy Tom O'Higgins of Fine Gael and Labour's general secretary, Brendan Halligan, were to bring Cosgrave and Corish together to form a national coalition government after the 1973 general election.

This was achieved despite the fact that there were many members of the Opposition parties in Leinster House who in the inner recesses of their minds felt that Fianna Fáil was the natural and permanent ruler of the Republic. Some senior Fine Gael deputies were more at home in the Bar Library than in the Dáil. There were some '*avant garde* socialists', as Jim Larkin Junior once described them to me, who were adamantly opposed to the evils of Irish capitalism but strenuously opposed anyone who dared change the scenario of a permanent Fianna Fáil government. This was particularly true in the trade union movement, which had always enjoyed an incestuous working relationship with Fianna Fáil, and particularly with Seán Lemass who, in turn, bestowed various directorships of state boards on many union leaders. Negative union memories of Fine Gael Finance Minister Gerard Sweetman lived on from the 1950s. Nevertheless, the prospect of an inter-party government had become an accepted strategy in Labour by 1972. But not before a protracted period of intense internal disputation had occurred within the party.

After the 1969 general election, the party's general secretary, Brendan Halligan, had convinced Brendan Corish that a 'go it alone' policy for Labour was no longer sustainable, particularly when faced with the perceived threat to democracy posed by Charles Haughey. The first definitive moment of change in our policy occurred at the private session of the party's annual conference at Liberty Hall in February 1970. Brendan Corish emerged from the debate to declare that he had an open mind on the issue and said that a special delegate conference should decide the coalition issue. In effect Corish repudiated his eve of the poll speech of 1961 when he stated that Labour would not join another coalition with Fine Gael. He was attacked for his retraction but he won the day at a bitter special Labour Party conference later in 1970. He was savagely assailed by Dr Noel Browne for his historic change of heart. Brown's attack, as usual, was so personal and vicious in its delivery that he increased the pro-coalition vote; his walk-out from the conference also increased the pro-coalition vote. Corish, at 54 years of age and after 27 years in Dáil Éireann, had learned the real facts of political life under our multi-seat electoral system of proportional representation. The hegemony and domination of Dev was at last laid to rest.

The Cork conference was my first experience of a very young Charlie Bird. He was a delegate and told the Chairman Roddy Connolly that he had sold down the river every principle his father (James Connolly) had stood for! Charlie was a very vocal anti-coalition young socialist. Peter Graham, a young communist activist, was murdered that same year in Dublin. He was brutally shot in the head and nobody was ever charged with his assassination. He was highly regarded by the two hundred or so young socialists, communists, Maoists, Stalinists and Trotskyites in Dublin at that time, many of whom went on to become pillars of the establishment. Charlie, Jack Loughran, Bernadette Devlin and Tariq Ali attended the funeral and gave their comrade their clenched fist salute to his Trotskyist heaven.

In January 1971, in reaction to the pro-coalition decision in Cork, a Liaison Committee of the Left was formed with Matt Merrigan as chairman and Dermot Boucher from Dun Laoghaire as secretary. They were joined by Councillor Pat Carroll, Desmond Bonass, Masie McConnell, Tony Dunne, Dave Neligan, Tom Carroll, Councillor Billy Keegan, John Byrne and Jim Kemmy. Noel Browne TD, David Thornley TD, and John Swift were also associated with the committee. Over the next four years they were a destructive influence in the party. Their meetings and numerous newsletters denounced the parliamentary party on almost every issue. Our participation in the national coalition government after 1973 was assailed. Their total hostility resulted in a spate of resignations and expulsions. The media had many a field day during these years. The party, in 1975, could take no more and the administrative council declared that membership of the committee was 'incompatible with membership of the Labour Party and that the principle of parallel organisations within the party is abhorrent to the democratic principles of the party'. Most of those who did not accept the ruling of the AC either resigned or were deemed to have terminated their membership.

Finally, in March 1977, the administrative council of the party cancelled the membership of Dermot Boucher for circulating a 'Liaison Special' in which he again attacked party colleagues. I had suffered greatly from his unwavering opposition in Dun Laoghaire for almost ten years. Brendan Halligan's work as general secretary of the party had often been made a sheer misery. It was the age-old story, not unique to Labour parties, of ideological factionalism from within being utterly debilitating in the development of the party and in our participation in democratic politics.

*

The 1973-1977 coalition seriously lacked internal cohesion. Conor Cruise O'Brien, Garret FitzGerald, Richie Ryan, Justin Keating, Michael O'Leary and Frank Cluskey were all talented individuals. They all had their own agendas. Some did not particularly like one another and were anything but team players in a collective government. In many ways I saw that government as a series of mutual jealousies in office.

For a minister who was so mercurial, Michael O'Leary was very successful in the Department of Labour. He was extremely fortunate in that the political climate in 1973, following Ireland's membership of the Common Market, strongly favoured progressive labour legislation. Equal pay was the big issue of the day. O'Leary had a dedicated fellow Corkman, Tadg O'Cearbhaill, as secretary of his department. Tadg tried to keep some control over O'Leary's sudden changes of agenda and they were barely on speaking terms by 1975. However, O'Leary was well served by a succession of excellent private secretaries and together they pushed forward the department's legislative programme. Legislation for equal pay was enacted, as was legislation against unfair dismissals; protection of workers facing redundancy; trade union amalgamations; a Joint Labour Committee for agricultural workers; and the Employment Equality Act. The arrangements for the election of worker–directors on the boards of certain state bodies were given statutory effect and the protection of young persons at work was secured. This is undoubtedly the best legislative record of any Minister for Labour in the state's history.

These measures were introduced at a time of considerable economic turmoil arising from the 1974 oil crisis. Unemployment and budget deficits rose as a consequence. Nevertheless, the achievements of that national coalition government were substantial with 100,000 local authority houses built between 1973 and 1977. As Minister for Local Government, Jimmy Tully introduced a major local authority tenant purchase scheme that enabled thousands of families to own their own homes for the first time. The pensionable age was reduced from 70 to 66 years by Brendan Corish. New ground rents were prohibited. The allowances for deserted wives, unmarried mothers, prisoners' wives and single women over 58 years of age were all introduced by Frank Cluskey, the parliamentary secretary to Corish who had delegated the Social Welfare portfolio to his trusted colleague. In the childcare area, the domicile care allowance for handicapped children was first introduced. And in the teeth of opposition from wealthy vested interests, both urban and rural, the highly progressive wealth tax was enacted by Richie Ryan, the Minister for Finance.

But eaten bread was very soon forgotten by the electorate when Fianna Fáil trumped it all with the exorbitant 1977 general election manifesto. We trudged from door to door in Dun Laoghaire to be met by: 'Why should we vote for you? Rates are being abolished! Car tax is going! We'll be on the pig's back!' This manifesto, combined with the self-inflicted debacles of the President's resignation and the Taoiseach's vote against contraception, put the seal on that government.

The most decisive factor in the 1977, 1981 and 1982 general elections was the cash handout promises of Fianna Fáil and Fine Gael in the three campaigns. The income tax relief promises of Fine Gael in the 1981 general election were wildly excessive and to the subsequent coalition government's credit were for the most part not implemented in their two budgets. The Labour Party in all three elections made no soft option promises. Such is our society that many electors favour short-term gain against long-term economic security even if in the process their own children ultimately face unemployment. Money urgently needed for social, health and education services, for employment maintenance and creation was squandered in the Fianna Fáil quests for political power from 1977 to 1982. It was utterly irresponsible that at such a critical period for our country, when all the scarce resources of our state should have been devoted to restoring full economic recovery after the worst recession in Europe since the 1930s, all Fianna Fáil set up for the electorate was a supermarket of free offers. And like all supermarkets the customers eventually paid at the checkout. There were 168,000 out of work and on short time, 13.2 per cent of our labour force at a cost of £7 million per week in unemployment payments.

By abolishing domestic rates and reducing income tax and car tax, Fianna Fáil said people would have more money to spend and thus more jobs would be created. The republican thaumaturges left no room in their simplistic logic for the obvious consequences that their proposals would decrease state revenue by about £250 million in 1978, a shortfall that would have to be made good from other sources. That is some £1,500 million in 1999 prices, not to mention the accumulated deficits in 1979 and thereafter. Nor was any attempt made in 1977 to explain who the real beneficiaries of Fianna Fáil largess would be. It was clear, however, that the handouts all had a property or income qualification. The more houses and cars one had, the more Fianna Fáil gave you in an inverse means test. About half the families in the country, mostly the better off, had a car and they benefited, in the short run anyway, from the reduction in motor taxation. However, those who had more than one car benefited twice or three times over.

The abolition of domestic rates in 1977 appealed to nearly all house owners. It was of no help to those with no homes or those in real need that had all or part of their rates waived. These people had to pay, through central taxation, for other people's rates. At the other end of the scale, the relatively well off property owner gained very handsomely. The Fianna Fáil inverse means test applied with a vengeance. The bigger one's house, and the more houses one owned, the more the government subsidised. The owner of a large home in Dublin, with a holiday home in Kerry, stood to gain about £900 a year in 1978 out of the de-rating of his properties. That is some £6,000 per annum today! On the other hand, 35,000 families had no houses at all. And the number of homeless had grown. And where did the new relatively wealthy spend their tax relief? In productive investment or savings? This Fianna Fáil bonanza paid for the growth of conspicuous personal consumption as winter continental holidays began, more booze was consumed and that new status symbol of Irish nationhood — trading up the house — emerged. On top of that, the relatively better off property owners realised capital gains because of the appreciation in the value of houses consequent on the abolition of rates. These were the good old days of 1977 to 1979!

*

The election in 1981 was fought on an independent strategy, with Labour reserving the right to call a conference afterwards to decide on participation in government if the situation allowed this. Labour returned 15 TDs on a vote of 9.9 per cent but was shocked at the defeat of Frank Cluskey, by then the party leader, in Dublin South Central. His loss, after only four years as party leader, shook morale. Fine Gael performed remarkably well gaining an extra 6 per cent and 22 new seats. Michael O'Leary was elected party leader and as the Fianna Fáil government had lost its majority, a coalition was a possibility. A special delegate Labour conference was held in the Gaiety Theatre in Dublin and O'Leary recommended participation in government. This was accepted.

The new government included Michael O'Leary as Tanaiste and Minister for Industry and Energy, James Tully as Minister for Defence, Eileen Desmond as Minister for Health and Social Welfare and Liam Kavanagh as Minister for Labour and the Public Service. Dick Spring, the new TD for Kerry North, Joe Bermingham and I were appointed Ministers of State. The tenure of this government was one of the shortest in the history of the State, being defeated on its budget proposals to impose VAT on children's shoes in January 1982. This was an entirely self-inflicted debacle. The Minister for Social Welfare, Eileen Desmond, had insisted on a 25 per cent increase in social welfare benefits; 22 per cent was on offer from the Minister for Finance, John Bruton. She persisted and VAT on children's clothes and shoes was introduced to meet the cost. Inflation fell to 21 per cent soon afterwards! Thus do governments fall.

It is best remembered from Labour's point of view for its establishment of the Youth Employment Agency in 1981 and by the public service pay agreement of December of that year. Both of these initiatives were brought about by Liam Kavanagh TD, Minister for Labour.

*

Following the general election, Billy Attley, the FWUI general secretary, proposed at our administrative council meeting in March 1982, on the eve of the election of the government of the 23rd Dáil, that we would not participate in that government. We all knew that the independent deputies and the Sinn Féin, The Worker's Party TDs were, on balance, disposed to vote for Haughey. I strongly felt that we should not let them off the hook. The Tony Gregory Dublin deal had already been signed by Haughey providing for 440 new houses in the Dublin North Inner City Area; 197 houses in the North Centre City Area; 150 additional Dublin Corporation craftsmen; an additional £20 million for Dublin Corporation services; increased taxes on derelict sites and office developments for inner city renewal; and a double weeks' social welfare payment in September and Christmas and so on. Gregory's vote was well and truly in the bag.

Billy Attley's motion was designed to ensure that the Labour deputies would, in effect, be impotent in the election of the Taoiseach and the government. I described the motion in the following terms: 'When you are in a cup final and you are three goals to nil down five minutes to go, you don't decide to walk off the pitch before the match is over!' As a distinguished FAI referee I hoped that Billy would at least get the point; my relations with him were fraught ever afterwards. Both Attley and Senator John Carroll, general president of the Irish Transport and General Workers' Union, also a member of the administrative council, refused to consider the quite reasonable amendment of the party leader, Michael O'Leary, that the decision on coalition should be deferred so as to keep up the pressure on Fianna Fáil and the independents.

As deputy leader I was trenchant in my support. Billy and John, supported by Mervyn Taylor and Michael D. Higgins, were quite cynical about Haughey but were most hostile to John Bruton as Minister for Finance. Bruton had done little to ensure the understanding and co-operation of the unions. When the question was put that the motion be decided on the night, there were 17 votes for and 17 against. Michael D. gave his casting vote as chairman of the party that the motion be decided there and then. It was carried by 18 votes to 17.

I was furious that Michael D. did not seek a compromise consensus and not split the party on the eve of the new Dáil. I accused him of playing 'a negative and destructive role'. Michael D. responded with injured vehemence. But one could never be angry with Michael D. for long. The party was split down the middle; the Labour deputies had to endure the cop-out humiliation in the Dáil and the union leaders returned to their secure offices having flexed their muscles. The 67 per cent of Labour voters who in an opinion poll the previous week favoured our participation in a coalition government were singularly unimpressed. Our party's image was severely damaged, as was the standing of Michael O'Leary as party leader. This also greatly pleased those who had ambitions to replace him with an anti-coalition leadership. But I was determined to put the record straight for the public and I did so in no uncertain terms. The only member of the administrative council who was really pleased with the outcome was Joe Higgins, the Irish Militant leader. Joe was now on the side of the Marxist angels. He has since become the Dáil's resident revolutionary.

*

As the 1982 annual national conference of the party loomed in Galway on the October bank holiday weekend, all the indications were that a U-turn on the policy to be pursued by the party in the Dáil would be voted through. Our policy for the previous thirteen years had been to maintain an open negotiating position on the question of our participation in government. This policy was to be dumped. The 1982 national conference was being asked, by a strange alliance of delegates, to opt for an exclusive 'minority government' posture. The preconditions for Dáil support for a minority government of either Fianna Fáil or Fine Gael would be negotiated by the administrative council of the party and subject, it was also proposed, to the endorsement of a special delegate conference. Each decision of the minority government would depend on the political crisis support of Labour. Thus would the party split on most major issues and further decline. The continuation of Charles Haughey as Taoiseach would, in effect, be assured.

How had this scenario come about within Labour? Many Labour Party activists had lost confidence in themselves as a political force espousing democratic socialist policies of true relevance to the grave economic and social issues of that period. The decline in industrial employment, massive accumulated exchequer deficits on current and capital accounts, and a demoralised public sector seemed insoluble. Many rank and file members and senior party activists did not trust the central direction of our party. And so a grand coalition of this distrust and frustration combined with the long-standing hard core of anti-coalitionists. We had many anti-coalition union delegates, some of whose executives were basically pro-Fianna Fáil or pro-Haughey such as Michael Mullen. And we also had an incoming party chairman, Michael D. Higgins, who used his considerable rhetorical talents to stir the political imagination of delegates on socialist issues but with great dexterity avoided the real crunch issue by supporting the escape clause of 'conditional support for a minority government'. He thus maintained a public purity of strategy. A new and strange ethos of the left, of responsibility untainted by power, emerged in Galway.

There was a unique amalgam of such unlikely bedfellows as Michael D. Higgins and Brendan Halligan. Brendan had been the scourge of the anti-coalitionists in the 1970s, the mastermind of scores of pro-coalition speeches, of by-election transfers and joint election programmes from 1970 to 1981 for the party hierarchy. After the February 1982 election, when the Labour vote dropped alarmingly to 9.1 per cent but maintained 15 Dáil seats, Brendan decided to capitalise on the return to power of Fianna Fáil and undermine the leadership of Michael O'Leary. Brendan and Michael had long parted political company. Halligan had disappointed ambitions and O'Leary was isolated. As the leading proponent of coalition with Fine Gael in the 1970s, Halligan now advocated that Labour in a hung Dáil should not enter any coalition government and should, issue by issue, support a series of minority governments.

While I had a great regard for the considerable intellectual and organisational ability of Brendan Halligan ever since we first met in 1967, Michael O'Leary and Dick Spring were deeply suspicious of his political agenda. It seemed that Halligan had decided to become the leader of the left, particularly in Dublin, in order to oust Michael O'Leary. By May 1982, in the Dublin North East *Labour News*, Brendan Halligan argued that it was reasonable to forecast that no party was going to get an overall majority in Dáil Éireann in the foreseeable future. He held that the reason was not hard to find. Under proportional representation, parties were supposed to get the number of seats in parliament to which they were entitled by their national vote. In the past, the government of the day fixed constituency boundaries and this had the deliberate effect of distorting the relationship between votes won in the country and seats won in the Dáil. The largest party, invariably Fianna Fáil, got the seats their votes strictly entitled them to. The last two elections had been fought on boundaries drawn up by an independent commission. They produced a gratifying close correspondence between votes won nationally and seats won in the Dáil. Halligan argued that:

> As no party, or combination of parties, won an overall percentage of the votes nobody won an overall majority of Dáil seats. So we had two hung Dáils. For those cogent reasons Labour should act as the leader of the left within this hung Dáil, and within all hung Dáils for the foreseeable future. Labour can make or break governments in a hung Dáil. It could be the most exciting and most rewarding period in the party's history.

This was all very plausible but far removed from the reality of electing a Taoiseach and a government. During this tempestuous period I confronted, in my usual 'over the top' style, those who advocated minority government chaos. The country was in a state of acute political instability. Our country's future was, to me, more important than internal divisions in the party. Minority government was a sterile proposition. I pointed out the lessons to be learned from the political blackmail of the Liberty Hall deal underwritten by Michael Mullen whereby Haughey had committed the government to spend £60 to £80 million to secure Tony Gregory's vote. I also had witnessed the extraordinary Sinn Féin, The Workers' Party 'conditional vote' of support for Charles Haughey as Taoiseach in March 1982. I saw them clambering over the Dáil's press gallery rails to do so and their manifest contradictions every month until they deserted the Fianna Fáil ship of state at the end of 1982.

After an emotional debate at the 1982 Galway conference, the composite resolution directing the party not to enter any coalition government with Fianna Fáil or Fine Gael was defeated by 657 votes to 522. It was a narrow squeak. The defeated resolution was proposed by the Dublin Regional Council and supported by no less than twenty-one branches throughout the country. But internal sanity prevailed in the party and after a heated and traumatic debate, the conference resolved that in the event of no party having an overall majority in Dáil Éireann after the next general election, the leader of the party, in consultation with the administrative council and the parliamentary party, was authorised to enter into negotiations with any of the political parties represented in Dáil Éireann on the basis of party policy as set down in the manifesto determined by national conference before the general election. It was clearly resolved that the purpose of this exercise would be to establish if it was possible to form a government with Labour participation which would further both the national interest and the socialist policies of the party. It was finally resolved that a special national conference be convened after these negotiations to receive a report thereon from the party leader and on the basis of this report to decide whether or not the party should enter into government, support a minority government or enter into opposition.

I drafted this resolution after consultation with Frank Cluskey. It was adopted in the teeth of opposition from Michael O'Leary. He favoured a proposal which would allow the party's administrative council and the Parliamentary Labour Party to jointly decide on the strategy to be adopted by the party in the Dáil after a general election. O'Leary was strongly supported by Dick Spring who had a substantial block of North Kerry delegates supporting him at the conference. In a rational western European social democratic party, this proposal was eminently sensible. However, in the party I knew from 1957, the prospect of this resolution being adopted by conference — whereby it was, in effect, being asked to divest itself of the right to determine post-election electoral strategy — was remote. Delegates simply did not trust most of the parliamentary party and, in particular, the leader, Michael O'Leary, on such a fundamental issue. This was the first and only major occasion that Dick Spring and I were on opposite approaches on a major policy issue.

Frank Cluskey, who had lost his Dáil seat because he disliked doing constituency work and was again drinking heavily, was in a dangerous anti-O'Leary mood. He and I decided that the best option for success was to bring forward the 'Special Conference' resolution. This was adopted by conference by 671 votes for and 498 against. It was proposed by the Merchants Quay Branch of Dublin South Central and seconded by the Stillorgan Branch, Dun Laoghaire; in effect, by Frank Cluskey and myself. Michael O'Leary's leadership was thus repudiated.

His role as leader was best summed up by Bruce Arnold on the eve of the conference:

> Michael O'Leary's leadership of the Labour Party has not been great. He has always relied on a mixture of personal magnetism and independent action, challenging to the party rather than conducive of co-operation and support. He has neglected the organisation, and, by default, this has led to a dissipation of energies and to internal divisions.[9]

O'Leary had become increasingly isolated within the party. A hard core had developed who were determined to keep him out of government in every circumstance. He was deeply distrusted as were those who supported him. He had to contend with hostility from the Militant Tendency of Joe Higgins, the disaffected former general secretary, Brendan Halligan, and the negativism of Michael D. Higgins, Emmet Stagg, Mary Robinson and Mervyn Taylor. The then anti-coalitionists ranged from those who favoured a liaison with Sinn Féin, The Worker's Party to those who advanced the concept of Labour's support for a minority government, presumably of either Fianna Fáil or Fine Gael.

Perhaps the single most important deficiency in O'Leary's leadership was his incapacity to sit down with colleagues for prolonged structured discussions, agree clear objectives and then follow through agreed policies with a rational approach. Like John Hume, he could not sit still at a meeting, was in a perpetually restless frame of mind during debates and sought to be the centre of all attention. O'Leary was a great wit and mimic, a fine platform speaker when in focus, but his lack of political organisation was chronic. Having known Michael since we were young students in UCC in 1953, I found his political agenda quite mercurial at times. While my time-keeping for meetings was anything but punctual, Michael's attendance could at times be quite speculative.

This was noticed by many observers, not least the American Ambassador Moore in 1973 when, in a biographical report to his Department of State about the new Minister for Labour, he strongly alluded to this characteristic of O'Leary. The ambassador reported that O'Leary, despite his casual manner, had a deep political concern for social issues. He also detailed his joining a picket at the embassy against the Vietnam war but wrote that this was typical of Labour activists at that time. The ambassador signed off his airgram by noting that O'Leary was often seen in the company of 'Dublin's prettiest girls' and that he was 'one of Ireland's most eligible bachelors'.

After the Galway conference, Michael O'Leary resigned as leader of the party. Joe O'Malley, Political Correspondent of the *Sunday Independent*, reported that O'Leary said he was not prepared to act as 'a scarecrow leader'! I was shocked when he applied to join Fine Gael. I was in Councillor Eric Doyle's home in Glenageary when he phoned and read to me the statement he had just issued. He told me I could collect the keys to the leader's office at the Dáil the following morning. I was very angry because we had been friends since we first met in UCC in 1953. We have not had a conversation since 1982. Now that passions have cooled I hope to invite him to dinner some evening to look back at what might have been.

Our 'special conference' strategy had worked, just about. The Labour Party had come very close to removing itself from the political landscape. Had the vote gone the other way, Stella and I would have seriously considered the wisdom of my remaining in the Dáil. The prospects of employment for a former deputy are generally very limited but one's pride and purpose in politics counts for far more.

When the Labour deputies came to the election of party leader, I had no hesitation in withdrawing from a contest with Dick Spring. I had been in the parliamentary party for thirteen years at that stage. I had accumulated a substantial number of colleagues who regarded me with a mixture of exasperation and chagrin. I was prone to telling my colleagues exactly how it was on most political issues! I knew that I had been a good party whip or deputy leader but I was far too independent and individualistic to be leader. Stella knew that too. I promptly opted in favour of Dick Spring.

In his first major test, he had to face a special delegate conference in Limerick in December 1982 after the defeat of the Fianna Fáil administration. Following a report and recommendation from him, conference decided to enter government with Fine Gael by 846 votes for and 522 against. The Kerry delegation was very substantial!

Dick Spring proved very early on that he was a shrewd leader who was determined not to be seen to take the party members for granted. In a master stroke before that special conference, he decided to write to all branch secretaries and organs of the party informing them that in his negotiations with the leaders of the other parties, his main concerns were:

> the creation of employment and the maintenance of existing jobs; the reform of our taxation system to ensure that those who can afford to do so will contribute their fair share and to ensure justice for PAYE taxpayers; the reversal of cutbacks in health and social welfare; the advancement of our party's policies in health, social welfare and education; the ending of the rezoning scandals and profiteering on land development etc.

The letter had a calming influence on the conference, which endorsed his report on his negotiations to bring Labour into government. Thus, Dick began a long and constructive career in Government and in Opposition. He was, in my opinion, the most successful and effective leader the party has had in its long history. Despite the many provocations on my part in Government and in Opposition over the next seven years, he and I had no serious personal disputes.

*

During the mid-1980s the leadership of the party was plagued by perpetual policy dissension between a group called Labour Left and the mainstream. We had to fight on two fronts. To add to the debilitating effects of the efforts to undermine the party leadership, we had the Militant Tendency with a jaded

Trotskyist agenda all of its own, a group of frenetic activists dominated by Joe Higgins, embedded in various sections of the party, notably Labour Youth. I spent many a weary hour with Dick Spring, Michael Ferris, Toddy O'Sullivan, Brendan Howlin, Ruairi Quinn, Ray Kavanagh, Marion Boushell, Pat Magner, Anne Byrne, John O'Brien, Jack Harte and Betty Dillon at lengthy meetings of the party's administrative council and organisation committee as we took them head on and successfully prevented them from taking control of the party. Emmet Stagg was quite determined to take over the party from Dick Spring and for a while it looked like he would succeed.

The members of the management committee of the 'Labour Left Collective' in 1986 were Councillor Frank Buckley, Frank Butler, Roger Cole, Tony Dermody, Peter McDermott, Terry Quinn and Michael Taft. Their submission to the party's commission on electoral strategy entitled 'Realignment of Irish Politics' was a quite exotic concoction. Its wide circulation within the party added greatly to the general confusion of our role in government. The strategy advocated by Labour Left was not a return to socialist opposition as in 1969, but the use of minority government support (MGS) as a political weapon. Labour could then use this power to offer or withdraw minority support from Fianna Fáil or Fine Gael on key issues in order to exacerbate the contradictions between 'the working class' and farmers in Fianna Fáil or between progressives and reactionaries in Fine Gael. In this way both parties would be weakened and fragmented and Labour 'would be intent on assimilating Fianna Fáil's working class support'.

The strategy would probably lead to quite a lot of elections. It was, as the submission stated, 'political life in the fast lane requiring a party and leadership with maximum in political acumen and nerve. The risks are high but, then, so are the stakes'. The Labour Party would also be re-organised with most power given to the national conference which would, however, only meet every other year, and which would elect the party leader, a party spokesperson for each major field, and the Administrative Council. In effect, and in the classical Marxist party tradition, the power structure of the party would be highly centralised with very considerable power being vested in the general secretary. There was little mention of the immediate problems facing this country in 1986 such as the crisis in the public finances. Grave issues such as growing unemployment and the survival of the welfare state only appeared in the context of developing 'programmatic initiative around popular issues laying the groundwork for Labour's realignment strategy'. This realignment strategy sought to 'destabilise and transform political competition', to 'fragment the conservative parties' and would require 'forcing continued elections' with the assumption that this process would need to continue for at least 15-20 years or possibly very much longer!

What happened meanwhile to effective government, to the necessary decision-making required to keep our county functioning was not discussed at all. The strategy proposed, if it worked, would so destabilise the country that little would be left for the socialists to inherit at the end of the day except an IMF or EEC controlled regional wasteland. Meanwhile the debilitating effect on the party was immense as the Worker's Party set about hoovering up the votes and the Dáil seats of the left.

*

It is interesting to assess over the decades the outcome of the various coalition permutations of the Labour Party in terms of parliamentary strength. In 1961 we decided that irrespective of the result of the election we would not join in government. We won 16 out of 144 seats. In 1965 we decided not to enter any coalition with any party. We had 22 Labour deputies elected. In 1969 we decided to 'go it alone'. We won 18 seats. (One of the great myths about our 17 per cent national vote in 1969 was that its size was due to the non-coalition socialist stance of the party. In fact the vote was a clear reflection of the fact that the number of Labour candidates was the highest ever nominated by the party in a general election. Forty-three candidates were nominated in thirty-four constituencies, which increased the party's first preference vote but lost seats in some constituencies such as Mid Cork and Waterford.) In 1973 we opted for a joint programme for government with Fine Gael. We had 19 deputies elected. In 1977 Labour stood on its record in government and succeeded in having 17 deputies elected out of 148. In 1981 we 'stood on our own' and 'kept our options open': 15 deputies were elected. In November 1982 the party, to an extent, kept its options open and 16 deputies were elected. In 1987 the party resigned from government for the first time and stood on its record in the coalition government: 12 deputies were returned. In 1992 the party offered an emphatic alternative to Fianna Fáil after an outstanding record in Opposition and obtained 33 seats. In 1997, after an aborted period in government with Fianna Fáil in a mould-breaking attempt in our political structures, there being no feasible alternative to Fianna Fáil available to the party, and after changing sides in 1994 to join a government with Fine Gael and the Democratic Left, the party won 17 seats. Back, so to speak, to square one.

With the exception of the 1992 general election which was unique, it is arguable that over almost thirty years, from 1969 to 1997, the public's perceptions of the party's economic and social policies; the calibre of Labour candidates in the local constituencies; their political reputations at local and national level; the quality of their constituency campaigns and organisation; and the extent to which the party's head office was effectively mobilised were of greater importance than the national electoral strategies of the party. But, at long last by the late 1980s, the coalition disputations in the Labour Party had been put to bed.

Five

A Colony Never Again

'We prefer Rome to Moscow or Peking!'

Brian Lenihan, EC Referendum, 1972

By late 1971, when the shape of the Fianna Fáil government's negotiated terms of entry into the Common Market became clear, the Labour Party had been in continual opposition in the Dáil from 1957. The party's deputies and senators were in a comfortable but ultimately arid opposition mould. The prospect of being in government was only taking hold. Hence, there was the assumption that the Fianna Fáil advocacy of Ireland's entry into the Common Market would be automatically opposed by the Labour Party.

At a meeting of the Parliamentary Labour Party to discuss our EEC campaign strategy, I advanced the view that an advantageous relationship between Ireland and the EEC, including Britain, was vital for the Irish people's future employment and standards of living. I said that emotional opposition, or opposition in principle, often linked with a convenient disregard for economic reality, was a political luxury. I stressed that Labour did not have a real political choice. An opposition platform should not stress dishonest arguments relating to agricultural incomes. The consequences for farmers, large and small, could only be favourable when compared with the alternatives. Opposition to Fianna Fáil or Fine Gael terms for the sake of opposition was neither responsible nor credible, in my opinion.

The Common Market Defence Campaign was formed by Michael O'Loinsigh, Raymond Crotty and Anthony Coughlan, Ireland's first euro-sceptics who were utterly opposed to full membership of the EEC. They attracted a wide cross-section of patrons, including Hubert Butler, Susan Casey, Austin Clarke, Maire Comerford, Maureen Cusack, Kadar Asmal, Austin Flannery, Monk Gibbon, Liam Hamilton, Michael D. Higgins, John B. Keane, Luke Kelly, Dr John de Courcy Ireland, Harry Kernoff, Con Lehane, Siobhan McKenna, Bill Meek, Peadar O'Donnell, Liam de Paor, Niall Toibin and many others. The inaugural meeting was held in the Mansion House and addressed by 'General' Tom Barry, Dan McCarthy and Margaret Tynan, Mayor of Kilkenny. Ian Mikardo, chairman of the British Labour Party, was the guest speaker.

The referendum the following year, 1972, was a fraught affair within the Labour movement. There was a great deal of tendentious campaign propaganda on both sides but one central reality emerged from this 'non-debate'. By a 5 to 1 majority in an extraordinarily high poll of 71 per cent, the electorate accepted that there was no credible alternative to full entry into the EEC with the UK. The alternatives just did not hold water on the doorstep canvass. The farmers of Ireland had an overwhelming case for full entry despite the inadequacies of the terms negotiated for the economy as a whole. I estimated that about half of the 17 per cent who had supported Labour in 1969 votes voted 'Yes' to EEC membership. Most trade union and many labour supporters accepted the view that there was no alternative, on net balance of advantage, to full entry.

It was most disturbing during the campaign that some electors associated the genuinely felt reservations of the Labour Party on employment and prices and other vital issues with the strident 'No' campaign of the IRA factions from Northern Ireland who came south. They proclaimed their so-called defence of the jobs of Irish workers by simultaneously bombing their fellow Irishmen out of their jobs in Carrickfergus and Belfast. They were firmly put in their place by the electorate in the referendum. I found it equally repulsive in the campaign that the same vocal minority in the Republic who refused to recognise the courts of our constitution were simultaneously proclaiming their defence of the right of the Irish people to determine their own sovereign institutions. On the eve of the referendum, Sean O'Bradaigh and Daithi O'Connell of Provisional Sinn Féin forecasted in *The Irish Times* that a majority would vote 'No'.

There were other extraordinary statements made during that campaign, too.

'The rights and liberties you are now asked to sell were dearly bought by the blood and tears of some of the noblest and honest men and women any country ever produced; let us not betray them today,' asserted the Common Market Defence Committee.

'Most of the voices on radio and television against entry, you'll notice, have Dublin accents. One thing though stands out very strongly … one and all are devoted disciples of Karl Marx. Do you find anyone among them who earns his living the hard way? Instead, you'll find E.S.B. Officials, Gardiner Street Sinn Féin, teachers in vocational schools, Kevin Street Sinn Féin, university lecturers, parlour pinks and, over all, a motley collection of £3,000 plus a year white collar-type Dublin trade union officials.' So recorded the *Farmers' Journal*.

'I was thinking about the monks who sat in the court of Charlemagne, which was the first international European Society. There is some Celtic quality in our people that will help us to understand and respond to the people on the Continent,' thus spoke Erskine Childers, Tanaiste.

'The origin of the EEC lies in Hitler's "new order" … There is no difference in the basic outlook, the morality, the social system, between the Germany of 1914, the Germany of 1939 and the EEC of 1970.' This was the conclusion of Justin Keating TD, Labour's EEC spokesman.

Michael Mullen, general secretary of the ITGWU, alleged to RTÉ deputy director general, J.A. Irvine, that the scripts of several programmes such as the radio serial *The Kennedys of Castleross* had contained subtle 'pro EEC advertising'.

'The same forces which have done so much to weaken Christianity on the continent would be given the same play here, with undoubtedly the same consequences,' said a

Common Market Defence campaign circular to convents and monasteries.

'Migrants of this kind [from EEC countries] are unlikely to become more Irish than the Irish themselves and they are very unlikely to be in the main practising Catholics,' concluded Dr Cornelius Lucey, Bishop of Cork.

'We'll walk round him, we'll walk through him, we'll walk over him,' came from Bernadette Devlin, picketing Jack Lynch.

'Almost certainly there would be more tourists in Ireland, not less, if we refused to become EEC members,' asserted Anthony Coughlan.

And 'General' Tom Barry did not like foreigners either: 'He did not want to say that everyone prepared to vote for entry in the referendum would be a traitor, but they were certainly misguided and there would come a day, not many years hence, when they would rue the day they had done so.'

Many commentators have been puzzled by the extremity of language used by Justin Keating in his opposition to the EEC. Justin, in my opinion, saw the 'No' campaign as an opportunity to become the leader of the old republican left, the hard-core trade union left and the new *avant garde* left of the 1969 Labour Party. As head of RTÉ's agricultural programmes from 1965 to 1967, he was well aware of Common Market developments. But he had great difficulty in shedding his old republican left dogmas and leadership ambitions. He was to lose his Dáil seat in the 1977 general election. The work load in his department was extraordinary at that period, and he found little time for constituency work in Dublin North where there was a strong traditional Labour vote. And the large farming vote in North Dublin had been singularly unimpressed by his posturing in the referendum campaign. Justin Keating was a brilliant and persuasive public speaker. Unfortunately, on the fundamental questions of Northern Ireland and EEC membership, his analysis never expanded beyond the old republican socialist certitudes of the 1950s.

Another politician suffered serious embarrassment in the referendum campaign. Brendan Halligan had been appointed general secretary of the Labour Party in 1969 having served as political director from 1967. He had little opportunity by 1972 to impose his very considerable ability on the party. The party's campaign committee had a somewhat exotic political membership and one of its decisions was to issue a memorandum to all the clergy of Ireland asking them to vote 'No'. Brendan did not draft the circular to thousands of priests and nuns but was obliged to append his name to the following extraordinary message:

> It is no dramatic scare to say that close to 50 per cent of our children could be living, within 10 years, on remittances from absent fathers and even mothers. The moral and social consequences can hardly be imagined with complacency. Apart from hardship to individual families, its group effects on the national psyche are incalculable. We believe, with Gabriel Marcel, that a de-humanised and abstractly 'objection' technology characterises the ethos of the pseudo-philosophical scientism which animates our increasingly denationalised and de-naturalised modern culture. In our view the social, cultural and demographic consequences of our country's full memberships of the EEC ... would be an irreparable damage to the fabric of our socio-cultural identity as a Christian people with a unique ethos.

The religious of Ireland were utterly bemused. Brendan Halligan subsequently made an immense contribution to Ireland's role in European affairs over the next 30 years. Niall Greene and Tony Browne, international secretaries of the party, opened up the isolated political culture and organisation of Labour to the policies of the social democratic parties of Europe. They were three of the foremost advocates within Labour of a positive contribution from Ireland in the development of European integration and enlargement. They have been largely responsible for the foundation of the Institute of European Affairs and its considerable impact on Irish society.

*

Following Ireland's momentous decision to join the EEC, many Irish politicians continued to ignore the grave prospect of the United Kingdom deciding to remain outside. The short-term consequences for Ireland would have been acute had the UK government's proposal to join been rejected. I was vice president of the Irish Council of the European Movement in 1975. I pointed out to our annual general meeting that it was vital that the electorate of the UK, and particularly of Northern Ireland, appreciate the grave economic and political difficulties they would bring upon the peoples of these islands if they voted for withdrawal from the Community. Many responsible members of the wider Labour movement, North and South, were convinced that the presence of a stronger socialist influence within the Community at all levels would create a new impetus towards the solution of many European problems. I called on all Labour supporters in the UK to remain with us in the wider Community, to surge forward towards economic and monetary union, to proceed with direct elections to the European Parliament, to dramatically expand the regional and social funds, to formulate a common front on energy and to join together to end the exploitation of the Third World. I put it clearly on the record to the electorate of the UK and particularly to our fellow Irishmen and women in Northern Ireland that were it not for the Republic's membership of the EEC, our living standards would then be lower, our unemployment problems more intractable, our farmers less well off and our export prospects less favourable.

I also asserted at our annual general meeting that some so-called socialists both in Ireland and the UK had shown themselves to be emotional, chauvinistic nationalists on this issue. 'There was therefore an historic opportunity for all socialists and trade unionists on these islands to deepen and diversify our influence and contributions in Western Europe. Let us develop a Community as one of which democratic socialists can be proud.' My statement received good publicity and I was roundly attacked by the hard left in the UK. Tony Benn was as articulate as ever in his fervent opposition. Although I had no particular regard for Harold Wilson, his courage and determination during the UK referendum campaign were emphatic. The result was a great relief to all of us. As Labour Party whip, I warmly welcomed the decisive vote of the electorate of the UK to remain within the EEC. The UK decision would, in my opinion, stimulate the prospects of greater industrial development, investment and exports in industry and agriculture in Ireland, North and South. Twenty years later, Ireland ratified the Maastricht Treaty. The treaty gave the community new powers to act together on economic and monetary union, on rights at work, on the environment and on foreign and security policy. This time the Labour Party was in favour. But some people never change. Ian Paisley, Eamon McCann, Neil Blaney, Bernadette McAliskey, Ruairi O'Bradaigh, Sinn Féin, Opus Dei, Irish Sovereignty Movement, and the parties of the extreme right in Europe, such as the Vlaams Blok in Belgium and the National Front in France, opposed the treaty.

Six

A Fellow Corkman

'The difference between Fianna Fáil and Fine Gael is "Dem dat know don't need to ask and dem dat don't know don't need to know".'

A Cork supporter of Jack Lynch

As a teenager I remember Jack Lynch coming to our house in Cork as a newly qualified barrister to collect briefs about workmens' compensation cases from my father. My mother, as most women in Cork, 'doted on him'. We held him in awe as he joked about upcoming matches. At that stage of his career Jack Lynch had little interest in politics. In fact he did not join Fianna Fáil until he was 31 years of age.

With my father, I used to walk from our home across from the South Infirmary down the 'Boggy Road' to the Athletic Grounds to see our heroes, Jack and Christy Ring from Glen Rovers and the other great Cork hurlers, play for club and county. I cheered on some heroic hurling battles with 'de Glen'. I recall Jack as a tall, strong, loose-limbed hurler with great timing on the dropping ball. I saw him and Sean Condon from St Finbarr's — 'de Barrs' — play centre field for Cork. They were the best pairing I have ever witnessed. I was just nine years of age in 1944 when Cork won the fourth-in-a-row All-Ireland. Jack was the only player to win six consecutive All-Ireland senior medals; hurling from 1941 to 1944 and 46; football 1945.

Hurling was our obsession. Our mentors were Christy Ring, Jack, Paddy O'Donovan of Glen Rovers, Alan Lotty of

Sarsfields, Gerry O'Riordan, Johnny Quirke of Blackrock and Sean Condon. Hurlers like the great Dr Jim Young from 'de Glen' were the 'enemies' we tolerated to play for Cork. There was no television and a little radio, so we went to the Athletic Grounds each Sunday. In 1947 my mother bought, for Christmas, on hire purchase, a radio which caused a family row. My father had sworn that nothing on hire purchase would ever enter our house. Hire purchase was the ruination of working people. He quickly mended his ways with the Kerry v Cavan All-Ireland Final from the Polo Grounds on radio from New York.

When the Cork team arrived back in Blarney by train, I went with my father to Blackpool bridge where the team paraded in horse-drawn carriages. We followed the team and the pipe band into the city where over twenty thousand supporters had gathered. Nine players on the Cork team had won four All-Irelands each. In 1943 and 1944 St Finbarr's held the captaincy, Sean Condon and Mick Kenefick being our parish heroes. The only other occasions I saw those horses were when Dev rode into town from Blackpool to address the Fianna Fáil faithful in Patrick Street.

*

Jack Lynch told me after a meeting of the Council of State, on which I served with him from 1973 to 1991, that the most vital speech he ever made as Taoiseach was in September 1969 during the Northern Ireland crisis. In that statement he renounced force in any circumstances as a means of resolving 'the partition question'. He also stated that any Irish union not rooted in consent would be a destructive union. Thus, he transformed the foundation policy of Fianna Fáil on partition. He showed great resolution, at a time of crisis, in facing up to the political sectarianism of Northern Ireland.

His policy statement has stood the test of time. Almost thirty years later, another Fianna Fáil Taoiseach, Bertie Ahern, copper-fastened that change in the Constitution of the Republic. Fianna Fáil in opposition would never have supported such major evolutions of national policy. Jack Lynch's approach to Northern Ireland had profound repercussions in Fianna Fáil and indeed in all the Dáil parties. In doing so he incurred the intense hostility of Ministers Neil T. Blaney, Charles Haughey and Kevin Boland and senior backbenchers such as Vivion de Valera.

The Northern Ireland crisis spilled over into the opposition in the Dáil. I vividly recall that Brendan Corish had similar confrontations in facing down the outbursts of deputies Sean Treacy, the late Steve Coughlan and David Thornley, Justin Keating, Dr John O'Connell and the late Michael Mullen, general secretary of the Irish Transport and General Workers' Union and a former member of the IRA. Brendan Corish had the support of deputies Frank Cluskey, Michael O'Leary, Conor Cruise O'Brien, Jim Tully, myself and the new general secretary of the party, Brendan Halligan.

In successive crises Jack Lynch, strongly supported by Ministers Paddy Hillery, Jim Gibbons, Padraigh Faulkner and Erskine Childers, was the calm voice of reason. He prevented a slide into security confrontations on the border, and put a full stop to *sub rosa* support being channelled to the Official IRA and the Provos. In doing so, Lynch owed a considerable debt to the late Peter Berry, secretary of the Department of Justice, who became gravely perturbed about the security of the state at that time. Likewise, Liam Cosgrave, the Fine Gael Leader, owed a similar debt to his confidential contacts, particularly in the Gardaí. Lynch effectively sidelined the ambitions of the republican ayatollahs within Fianna Fáil who saw his leadership as transitory. And he succeeded in doing so despite the boorish contempt shown by Prime Minister Ted Heath when the Taoiseach raised legitimate concerns about the minority in Northern Ireland with the UK government. Ted Heath was yet to learn the harsh lessons of Sunningdale when he bullied Brian Faulkner over the cliff and left him defenceless against the extreme unionists in his party.

*

A few months after I was elected to Dáil Éireann, the North erupted in the Derry Bogside and in Belfast, and in April 1970 the arms crisis broke. I had, during this period, personal trade union contacts in the public service on the ground in Dublin.

Stella and I had late night confidential briefings in our home about the attempted arms movements in Dublin port and at Dublin airport. From these contacts I had no doubt that the Taoiseach, Jack Lynch, had been kept in the dark by those who were effectively determined to orchestrate a government–IRA response to the crisis. They were only too well aware of the established procedures of government, the Departments of Justice and Defence and the Revenue Commissioners. They decided to do so because by then, they had persistently eroded the collective authority of the government. They assumed that Lynch would not have the bottle or party support to take them on.

In particular, Neil Blaney regarded Lynch as a weak and vacillating leader on the 'national question'. I knew Neil Blaney well having served in the Dáil and European Parliament with him from 1969 to 1994. He was a most intelligent and gregarious politician and an exceptional Minister for Local Government. But his detestation of Jack Lynch knew no bounds. His bitter solution to the Northern impasse was one of unreconstructed sectarianism, based on a 'Brits out and Prods out if you don't measure up' philosophy. This was anathema to Jack Lynch and most deputies.

It was extraordinary that during the crisis, Lynch agreed to delegate major issues of Northern policy to a number of individual ministers and subcommittees of the cabinet. A cabinet subcommittee of Charles Haughey, Neil Blaney, Paudge Brennan and Padraigh Faulkner was set up to monitor developments. Charles Haughey and Jim Gibbons were given joint authority to re-equip the army as Ministers for Finance and Defence respectively; and Charles Haughey was given authority to dispose of a fund for the relief of distress in Northern Ireland. Lynch always subsequently argued that he fully trusted these ministers to discharge their delegated functions in consultation with him on any sensitive issues. In the end he felt he could only trust Gibbons and Padraigh Faulkner on security issues, having by then lost all confidence in the Minister for Justice, Michael O'Morain, who was drinking very heavily at this critical period.

Lynch felt betrayed when Liam Cosgrave bluntly confirmed to him his worst fears. He acted with admirable resolution and courage. He then had a taste of the Haughey supporters as I had when I was director of elections for the late Denis Larkin in the Dublin North East by-election in 1963 and in the later campaigns by Fianna Fáil to abolish proportional representation. To stand one's ground for Labour in front of a polling station in North East Dublin in those campaigns was an acid test of one's political nerve. There was a palpable air of physical intimidation.

A further significant contribution by Jack Lynch to the democratic institutions of the State was his decision and that of the government to set up the Special Criminal Court in May 1972 to deal with growing IRA subversion. This court, free from any possible intimidation, had no compunction in convicting those Sinn Féin leaders who were members of the IRA. I well recall that, despite intense agitation from the Provos and pressure from several deputies, the Dáil parties refused to meet the demands of the then chief of staff of the IRA, Seán MacStiofáin, after he went on hunger strike. Like de Valera, Cosgrave and Lynch were not prepared to allow a challenge to the constitutional authority of the state to succeed.

A particular contribution of Jack Lynch was the impact of his leaderships on diminishing, in a major way, the residue of civil war animosity between Fianna Fáil and Fine Gael. There were 'hard men' on both sides in the 1970s. When 13 men were shot dead and 16 injured by British paratroopers on Derry's streets in January 1972, Lynch's emphatic response calmed the sense of fury which swept the country. The protests resulted in the fire bombing of the British embassy premises in Merrion Square. I was a witness from the safety of the Dáil to the protesters who assembled that evening, some of whom were IRA, in the hope that the Gardaí and army would intervene and that the confrontation would spread. Lynch and his security advisers, some of whom had sight of the embassy from the top of government buildings in Upper Merrion Street, wisely kept the army in reserve that evening. In the subsequent special Dáil debate he again kept the Fianna Fáil 'hawks' at bay. He succeeded in forging a cross-party consensus on this further crisis in Anglo-Irish relations.

In a then exceptional gesture of post civil war reconciliation, Jack Lynch also sent the army to Beal na Blath for the annual Michael Collins commemoration ceremony. Jerry Cronin became the first Fianna Fáil Minister for Defence to lay a wreath at the memorial to Collins. The true blue republicans in Fianna Fáil felt that Jack was far too soft on all of these inflammatory issues. Thus it fell to two Taoisigh from Cork City, W.T. Cosgrave and Jack Lynch, to confront two fundamental challenges to the democratic structures of the nation. They both met and won these challenges.

*

Despite Jack Lynch's preoccupation with Northern Ireland and his efforts to control the brooding hawks in his parliamentary party, he lost no time in reactivating Ireland's dormant application for EEC membership as soon as the French retracted their objections to British entry. He shrewdly gave the Department of Foreign Affairs and Minister Paddy Hillery authority to negotiate the Treaty of Accession. Since then, successive senior officials from that department have given outstanding service to the people of Ireland in the various extensions of the Treaty of Rome. Opinion polls in May 1972 were not as accepted as they are nowadays but the Taoiseach and Paddy Hillery, with the support of Fine Gael, succeeded in facing down the opposition of many in the Labour Party and in most trade unions and gained an extraordinary affirmative referendum vote of 83 per cent.

I strongly supported Ireland's application and was, not for the first time, in bad odour in my union and party. Paddy Hillery and I still recall our meeting in the Lakeside hotel in Killaloe, Co Clare, after the installation of the local Church of Ireland bishop. We assessed the prospect of a 'yes' vote a few weeks before the referendum. Paddy predicted a very cautious 60/40 win. I was more optimistic. We were both delighted with the 20 per cent 'No' result.

*

One of the most traumatic happenings to me, as assistant government whip in the 1973-1977 coalition, was the proposal of the Minister for Local Government, my late colleague, James Tully, to reduce the Dun Laoghaire-Rathdown constituency from four seats to three. I would have been dumped out of the Borough into South County Dublin to ensure the survival of the Fine Gael Deputy Percy Dockrell with the outgoing Taoiseach, Liam Cosgrave. I created holy hell, refused to budge and survived the rout of the 1977 general election.

Jack Lynch was well aware of similar situations which had occurred within his own party and of the cynical gerrymanders of Dáil constituencies by successive governments. More particularly, the repeated undemocratic carve-up of the country by Fianna Fáil had for decades cemented the party in power with overall majorities. Lynch acknowledged that the system was politically corrupt, and during and after the 1977 general election, he proposed the setting up of the Dáil Constituencies Commission with an independent membership and balanced terms of reference. In one fell swoop he cleaned up a pernicious political practice which had contaminated all parties. However, in the process, he ended for all time the prospect of overall Dáil majorities for Fianna Fáil. In effect, Jack Lynch created and laid out the ground for a succession of coalition governments which, over the past two decades, have, by and large, served the country well.

Shortly after the 1977 general election, John Horgan, the newly elected Labour deputy for South Dublin, met the newly elected Taoiseach Jack Lynch in the Dáil corridors. John congratulated Jack and then said: 'Do you realise, Taoiseach, that three of the five Labour deputies now in Dublin constituencies are from Cork!' Jack took a suck of his pipe and exclaimed: 'Ye should be ashamed of yerselves!'

*

Jack Lynch was surprised to see himself as a pragmatic successor to Seán Lemass, as a Taoiseach prepared to advocate a mixed economy within the Common Market. Apart from the

1977 Fianna Fáil manifesto, over which he very unwisely ceded control to Martin O'Donoghue and those former ministers who wanted to return to government at any price, his economic policy was to follow the advice of Ken Whitaker, Secretary of the Department of Finance who was appointed Governor of the Central Bank in 1969. Lynch eschewed the extremes of the ultra right or extreme left. In his first general election campaign as Fianna Fáil leader in 1969, he had the benefit of being confronted by a Labour party which had veered dramatically towards a left rhetoric and a 'go it alone' policy for government. The electorate was scared and despite its serious reservations about the Fianna Fáil Taca culture, gave victory to the decent, pipe-smoking Jack who had charmed the reverend mothers in every convent in Ireland, not to mention the GAA followers. All he had to do was mention the words 'Cuba' and 'socialism' and half the electorate blessed themselves and voted for Jack.

Later he told me the story of playing a round of golf in Cork. Ted Crosbie said to his caddy, 'Tell me booy! is that Jack Lynch playing golf over there?' 'Tis Jack all right,' replied the caddy. 'I wasn't sure, booy, because he seems to be playing from the left!' 'Ah, it's Jack all right, sure he can play from the left or the right, Mr Crosbie!' 'Ah yes,' said Ted, 'that's all right in politics, but not in golf here in Cork!'

I always had the impression that the Crosbies and the *Examiner* were never quite certain about the real political convictions of Jack Lynch. He seemed the classical Fine Gael barrister who had strayed into Fianna Fáil and deserved to be forgiven for doing so. But Jack did have more empathy with the Fianna Fáil working class of Glen Rovers and the GAA than with the cosy Fine Gael legal club of the city.

In the 1970s one of the constant undercurrents in the higher echelons of Fianna Fáil was a resentment of the influence of Maureen Lynch on Jack's political career. Jack was the first leader of Fianna Fáil to have no political heirs. He and Maureen were very close on all matters. She accompanied him to most public functions and many party meetings, unlike the spouses of many members of the government. She had no time at all for the brash male chauvinists of the party and their mohair suits. Neither did she share the view that the role of women in the party was to make sandwiches and pack the envelopes at election time. The Lynchs' lifestyle was quite modest. I know that they both took great pride in not owing or asking anybody for a single penny despite having to face major medical bills in later life when Jack suffered a very costly series of health setbacks. At that time their real friends were few and far between.

In the party and in government, they owed nobody any favours and asked for none for themselves. These traits ran counter to the naked power ambitions of the party. Down through the years successive spokespersons for Fianna Fáil have maintained that Fianna Fáil Taoisigh were never informed of the list of donations to the party. They repeatedly maintained that the identities of all such contributions were kept at arm's length while the party was in government. Yet Senator Desmond Hanafin recalled that in his time, as Fianna Fáil fundraiser under Jack Lynch, he showed Lynch the list as funds came in and 'if he did not like any name or if there was a bit of a scandal or a hint of anything that wasn't right, the subscription had to go back'.[10] This is an interesting confirmation of my opinion that the leaders of all the main political parties had a detailed knowledge of all the major contributions to their parties. Such lists were very closely guarded in all the parties.

*

Jack Lynch made three major political mistakes. Under pressure from his power-hungry cabinet colleagues he attempted to abolish the proportional representation system of election. The electorate admired him but did not trust his party. They opted to retain PR. He did not try again. Knowing how constituency boundaries could be blatantly manipulated under PR he opted to reform the system. He learned from his mistake and ensured, to his satisfaction, and particularly that of Maureen, that Fianna Fáil would never again obtain an overall majority. One wonders if Bertie Ahern and Noel Dempsey have learned the same lesson.

I have no doubt that the most serious mistake made by Jack was his decision, under intense back-bench pressure, to reinstate Charles Haughey to his front-bench in Dáil Éireann in 1975. I was very taken aback. From that moment his leadership of the party was at a discount. No sooner was he appointed to the opposition spokesmanship on social welfare than Haughey began to make a series of speeches throughout the country to the party's rank and file on issues well outside his brief. North of the Liffey he was even more determined to bury Deputy Conor Cruise O'Brien who had savaged him over six long years. Conor zealously provided him with plenty of ammunition for that exercise. During this period I frequently met Haughey, as assistant government whip, in the Dáil lobbies. He relished political gossip and could be most genial and charming. He always showed great courtesy to women and children who visited the House. However, he did not frequent the lowly and grim members' bar very much. He had more delicate and congenial watering holes in which to socialise. Neither did he frequent the Oireachtas restaurant. One could not blame him because in the 1970s the fare there was generally dire and the crude canteen decor even worse.

But in our casual political contacts he was quite open to me in his contempt of Jack Lynch's principal economic adviser, Dr Martin O'Donoghue, Professor of Economics at Trinity College, Dublin. O'Donoghue had clearly diagnosed the acute economic and fiscal problems facing the economy. His solution was to lavishly spend scarce exchequer resources to generate economic growth. It was a soft option which Charles Haughey privately scorned. Jack Lynch went along with the O'Donoghue solution, not confident that Fianna Fáil would win the election anyway. But once Charles Haughey was back on board with the Fianna Fáil government to implement the spendthrift 1977 election manifesto, Jack Lynch's days as Taoiseach were numbered.

Jack should have seen the writing on the wall in 1976-1977. Instead of calling a halt to the manifesto escapade, he allowed the budget of 1978 to confirm the abolition of the minimal capital taxation measures which Richie Ryan, the Fine Gael-Labour coalition's Minister for Finance, had introduced in the teeth of opposition from powerful financial interests. Jack had a clear opportunity at that stage to stop the rot because the economy recovered somewhat during 1978 with an increase in industrial output; inflation fell from 13 per cent in 1977 to 8 per cent in 1978. He lost his opportunity to make a real impact on the finances of the nation. It is fair to record that on fundamental economic issues, despite his experience in the Finance and Industry and Commerce portfolios, he did not possess the self-confidence to take on Martin O'Donoghue, to oppose the conservative advisers of the financial institutions and the strident farming and industrial lobby organisations. This approach was to lay the groundwork for his premature resignation.

As Colm McCarthy recalled: 'In 1977 Fianna Fáil discovered the Euro Dollar loan market and they mistook it for an oil find!' An integral part of the 1977 Fianna Fáil manifesto was their proposal to massively increase the numbers employed in the public sector. This was their main plank in reducing unemployment. It was parallel to the Fianna Fáil concept of 'self-financing subsidies'. When I was appointed Minister of State in Finance in 1981, I immediately requested a table to illustrate the effect of their manifesto policy. It showed that the numbers employed in the public sector increased by 11 per cent in the three-year period 1977 to 1980 and accounted for over 22 per cent of the increase in non-agricultural employment over that period. Together with major pay increases, the public service pay bill doubled between 1977 and 1980.

In many instances, substantial recruitment was not reflected in any real increase in the level of services being provided. The chaotic recruitment policy meant that newcomers found themselves in overcrowded offices, and work places were in confusion. When I became Minister for Health in late 1982, I read the departmental correspondence of the former Minister for Health, Charles Haughey, in which he asked the Health Boards why they had not yet taken up their allocation of new posts. The short and long term financial implications of what was being done were given little or no consideration.

The current revisionist economic mythology that our economic recovery derived exclusively from the MacSharry budget proposals of 1987 is an excessive nonsense. In fact, the vitally necessary decisions on public service pay moderation and the recruitment embargoes of the two coalition governments of 1981-1987 were the determining factors in bringing sanity into the management of our public finances in the late 1980s. But then Fianna Fáil are always adept in retrospective mythology. Jack Lynch should never have approved the 1977 manifesto and when elected he should have ditched it immediately.

*

I vividly recall the two by-elections in Lynch's heartland in Cork in October 1979 which hastened his resignation. While the Taoiseach was busy in the USA, the Fianna Fáil campaign in both constituencies was singularly lacklustre. The Haughey camp was not unhappy when Liam Burke and Moira Barry won the seats for Fine Gael. There was none of the usual Fianna Fáil national intensity ususally associated with the campaign. Lynch failed to anticipate the impending coup. He was shocked when it happened in his own back yard where Fianna Fáil had won three of the five seats in 1977. Thus began his final disillusionment with his parliamentary party.

Moira Barry was a superb young Fine Gael candidate in Cork North East and won the seat well. Had John Dennehy and John Brosnan been elected for Fianna Fáil, they would have probably supported Lynch's choice. And had the people of Cork city and county realised the peril facing their Taoiseach, they would have come out and supported him in droves. They were always distrustful of Haughey.

Jack Lynch's third most serious error of judgement was to prematurely resign in 1979 as party leader and Taoiseach. He seriously underestimated the capacity of Charles Haughey and his campaign team of Deputies Mark Killilea, Jackie Fahy, Tommy McEllistrim and Sean Doherty to palaver the new backbenchers. Jack and his cabinet colleagues overestimated the appeal of the staid George Colley who confidently expected the republican mantle to fall on him. George Colley was an honest but dull prospect. Unlike Charlie, he was quite incapable of glad-handing the rank and file. In the Members' Bar we told the Colley camp that on our head count he would lose. The political correspondents and particularly Michael Mills of *The Irish Press* also anticipated a Haughey win. Colley's election team which included Martin O'Donoghue and Desmond O'Malley were relative amateurs compared to those of the Haughey camp who exploited every ounce of dissatisfaction and disappointment among the backbenchers. And one should never underestimate the capacity of Dáil deputies to express fervent simultaneous support to each leadership candidate, particularly when they have the opportunity to do so 'in confidence'. Thus, Jack Lynch and George Colley were conned into a leadership election.

Most of my fellow opposition deputies put money, early on, on a Haughey victory. In the event, Haughey beat Colley by 44 votes to 38. George Colley, Des O'Malley, Martin O'Donoghue and others such as Eoin Ryan Senior were never to accept the Haughey takeover of the party. Therein lay the seeds of his ultimate demise. He was never to gain an overall majority in any subsequent general election. Jack and Maureen Lynch, George and Mary Colley were shocked by the outcome of Jack's resignation and even more so by the contempt shown by Charles Haughey and his supporters to them in the immediate aftermath of the contest. There then followed the infamous 'flawed pedigree' speech of the leader of Fine Gael, Garret FitzGerald, on 11 December 1979 in the Dáil when he attributed these words to the career of Haughey prior to the vote on his nomination as Taoiseach.[11]

In the synthetic furore contrived by Fianna Fáil about this valid comment, Garret's tribute and that of Frank Cluskey to Jack Lynch took second place. Garret FitzGerald said that Jack Lynch's greatest achievement was that he had led Fianna Fáil 'along the path of moderation in relation to Northern Ireland. We can only regret that he has been brought down before his time by a small group of ambitious men, having served his party and his country well'.

*

However, not all of Jack's political appointments were mistaken. In 1977 he appointed Ken Whitaker to the Seanad. It was an inspired choice because he was the most outstanding civil servant the state has employed. I still have my first edition of the White Paper Economic Development of 1958 which he wrote shortly after he was appointed Secretary to the Department of Finance in 1956. He was the first senior civil servant to have the personal self-confidence and authority to give to the government of the day a programme which was the basis of the First Programme for Economic Expansion. As a trainee union official employed in the head office of the Irish Transport and General Workers' Union in early 1957, I grew to admire his rational and detailed economic analysis of a relatively impoverished country.

Jack knew well in 1977 of Ken Whitaker's distrust of the former Minister for Finance, Charles Haughey. Whitaker had given the Taoiseach sound advice on the situation in Northern Ireland in 1970 when half his cabinet were in turmoil. His period in the Seanad was marked by searing criticisms of Fianna Fáil economic policies. For example, in January 1982, he addressed the United States Chamber of Commerce in Ireland in trenchant terms. The Whitaker broadside was clearly aimed at successive Ministers for Finance, but in particular he was perturbed about Haughey. He said: 'The policy of borrowing heavily to meet current Exchequer needs, pursued in the aftermath of the first oil price shock in 1973 but largely brought under control by 1977, was renewed recklessly in 1978 and has gained an impetus so strong that only sustained and Herculean efforts can arrest and subdue it.'

A volume of essays by Fionan O'Muircheartaigh in 1998 celebrated Ken Whitaker's honourable roll call of public service from 1934, a year before I was born, when he entered the civil service as a clerical officer. When my eldest son Ciarán joined the service as a clerical assistant in 1978, I pointed to the example of Ken Whitaker. In my opinion, his most important legacy was his uncompromising intervention in political economic debates between 1977 and 1982. And we have to be grateful to Jack Lynch and Garret FitzGerald for their successive nominations of Whitaker to the Seanad.

*

In September 1983 we were all shocked by the sudden death of George Colley. It was rumoured that he had gone to London for a cardiac procedure because he did not wish his opponents in Fianna Fáil, and particularly Charles Haughey, to learn about his condition. When I attended his funeral in Rathgar there was a palpable air of tension between his supporters and those of Haughey. His old friend Senator Eoin Ryan read the oration at the graveside at Templeogue. As Mary Harney cried at the graveside and as the Haughey camp looked stony-faced, Eoin placed particular emphasis on the one great quality of Colley:

> George Coley was a man of integrity. This has been said by many people, particularly in the last few days, but it cannot be said too often. It is a quality which is not universal among those who administer our affairs. I speak of a quality which is far wider than mere financial rectitude. A man of integrity is a man who has a set of standards, a philosophy, a conviction as to how he should order his life — and who lives in accordance with these principles.

Sixteen years later when Jack Lynch died, Charles Haughey was to face the same hostility in Cork city during the State funeral. This time Haughey had the grace not to go to Jack's graveside. And another of his enemies, Desmond O'Malley, gave the oration and spoke in the same trenchant terms as Eoin Ryan. The most pervasive ingredient of the atmosphere at the funeral was the guilt of Fianna Fáil. As fellow Corkman, Eoghan Harris rightly pointed out, there was a great deal of collective hypocrisy at Jack's funeral. Apart from sparse ritualistic references to Lynch at the *Ardfheiseanna* and in the formal histories of the party, he was airbrushed out of their republican consciences.

The last occasion on which I attended a meeting with Jack Lynch was in 1993 when he spoke to the Institute of European Affairs in Dublin. He read a paper on his lengthy involvement in Ireland's joining the European Economic Community. He was 76 when he prepared the paper and the Institute asked Dr T.K. Whitaker and myself to propose a vote of thanks. He was in great form that evening. It was a rare occasion because he had written his personal recollections of his involvement in the government negotiations from 1961 to 1972. He was Minister for Industry and Commerce from 1959-1965, Minister for Finance 1965-66 and Taoiseach from November 1966 until late-1979.

Jack Lynch recalled the most memorable of the meetings he had with the heads of government of the Six about Ireland's application for full membership of the Common Market. It was with President de Gaulle in November 1967. He recalled that the Irish team included Charles Haughey, Minister for Finance, Ken Whitaker, and Hugh McCann. He had a long meeting alone, except for his interpreter, with President de Gaulle in the Elysée Palace. De Gaulle indicated his support for Ireland's membership of the EEC but asked if associate membership would suit us because of our close economic links with Great Britain whom he thought ought not to be associate members of the Common Market. Jack assured him that he had not considered associate membership. Jack said: 'In a meeting later that day between General de Gaulle and our officials, Ken Whitaker and Hugh McCann, he repeated what he had said to me and of course got the same response. We did get the impression that there could be a long delay before negotiations with the UK would be resumed but we got an indication of French support for an interim arrangement for Ireland in this event. We did not respond enthusiastically to this.'

There is still a residual myth about de Gaulle, that he had a special affection for the green island. He may have enjoyed the solitude of our beaches but those of France were paramount. Jack Lynch said: 'This was at the end of November 1967 and at the meeting of the Council of Ministers three weeks later, notwithstanding the support of the other five member states of the Commission for ultimate membership of the UK in certain improved economic circumstances in Britain, the negative view of de Gaulle prevailed. In February of the following year, I again met the British Prime Minister Harold Wilson. He was apprehensive lest we might make some unilateral arrangement with the Six on a less than full membership basis but I assured him that our aim was full membership with the UK and the other applicant countries.'

At that Institute meeting, I pointed out that the people of Ireland had particular cause to be grateful to Jack Lynch, Paddy

Hillery and Ken Whitaker for the determination with which they pursued full membership of the Common Market for Ireland. Jack revealed to the gathering that following the resignation of de Gaulle in April 1969, Italy, Germany and the Benelux countries explored the prospects of enlargement:

> There followed a review at European Council and Commission level of the possible accession of new members and there emerged a suggestion, an ominous one as far as we were concerned, of a Community of Seven of which the UK would be the extra member. Our fears of such a development were strengthened by the setting up of a committee under Jean Monnet, who has often been described as the 'Father of Europe', to examine this question. We conveyed strenuous objections to such a development. Uncertainty continued until a summit meeting of the Six held in December 1969 agreed to the re-opening of negotiations between the Six and all the applicant member states subject to establishing a basis for negotiations.

The nation owes Jack Lynch a particular debt because not only did he lead us into the EEC but later into the European Monetary System and its exchange rate mechanism in 1979. These were the acts of a true republican. After his paper, we had a few drinks. Jack loved a glass of Paddy. He would slip away from Maureen with his driver and fellow GAA man Aidan Breslin for the pleasure. In later years he was a director of Irish Distillers Ltd. When the board, in a marketing review, considered removing the map of Ireland from the label on the bottle, Jack protested: 'You can't do that. I know when to stop when I go down the bottle and reach Athlone!'

Seven

The Master of Mendacity

Where is the noblest Roman of them all, the Mussolini of the Irish economy, the man who only had to make the well-schooled imperial gesture with the hand and everything falls into place as thousands of officials scurry off to do his bidding?

John Kelly, Dáil, 04.11.1981

I was astounded when Liam Cosgrave, Taoiseach, called the general election in June 1977. I could have told him that the feeling on the ground was decidedly anti-government. But the ministers were exhausted from more than four years of economic recession and unremitting opposition from Fianna Fáil. Moreover, there were clear indications of economic improvement. The government would have been well advised to go to the country the following October, before the resumption of the Dáil. Without the Dáil as a vehicle for opposition opportunism and pre-election skirmishes, Fianna Fáil would have been at a disadvantage. And truculent government backbenchers can threaten all they wish during a summer recess. Early October also provides a great opportunity for ministers to get out on the road in the summer and meet the people. But Cosgrave foolishly yielded to the pressure for an early summer election.

And Fianna Fáil, with Professor Martin O'Donoghue as economic adviser to Jack Lynch leading the charge, had its infamous manifesto ready. It called for a major 'once off' increase in the current budget deficit to finance major increases in public spending; cuts in personal taxation; abolition of capital taxation, i.e., the wealth tax; abolition of domestic rates and the virtual abolition of road tax.[12] At that time, Charles Haughey was only semi-attached to the Fianna Fáil front bench as the spokesperson on health. I vividly remember meeting him in the corridor of Leinster House and he assured me that he thought O'Donoghue's proposals were off the wall. Most economic commentators thought likewise. Even my Labour colleagues in the Dáil, not renowned for their budgetary discipline, were incredulous. But the electorate bought the package and the national coalition was dumped. Senior civil servants in the Department of Finance were aghast at the prospects.

*

Charlie Haughey, reincarnated as Minister for Health and Social Welfare, steered well clear of the impending budgetary crisis as he cultivated the grass roots to oust Jack Lynch. The 1979 budget was a shambles due to serious over-estimation of revenue, spending over-runs in several departments and a prolonged postal strike. Charlie was in his office in *Áras Mhic Diarmada* and showed generous sympathy to the local postal strikers who congregated in Keatings pub nearby. After he became leader of his party and Taoiseach later in 1979, he exorcised Martin O'Donoghue and all associated with him from the Fianna Fáil body politic. Haughey was regarded at that time by some economic commentators as a clever accountant and an astute businessman who had accumulated property and wealth. He was extremely well briefed and undoubtedly well read on economic affairs.

My scepticism about him at the time was based on conversations I had with the late George Colley who was conscious that his father and mine had both been founder-members of Fianna Fáil. I first met Colley as a union official in the 1960s when he was chairman of a number of Joint Labour Committees in the Labour Court. Even when I discounted the intense leadership, constituency and family rivalry between these two deputies, I still noticed the abiding distaste of George

Colley towards Haughey. Colley may have been politically dull and indecisive but his utter honesty shone true. Right up to his death he expressed great reservations to me about Haughey. My second source was the late Denis Larkin, also a fellow deputy of Haughey's in Dublin North East. Denis was a very circumspect individual but he too gave me an unflattering political assessment. Denis and the late Frank Cluskey were close on those issues. I believe that this formed the mainspring of Cluskey's dislike for Haughey.

The close relationship of Haughey with the business community goes back to the mid-1960s when he and Seán Lemass drew up the TACA organisational blueprint. Kevin Boland recalled the first dinner in the Gresham Hotel of those who paid the £100 basic subscription: 'We were all organised by Haughey and sent off to different tables around the room. I think the whole cabinet was there. I know the extraordinary thing about my table was that everybody at it was tied in somehow or other with the construction industry.' He laughingly recalled, 'Of course, I was Minister for Local Government at the time.' Kevin Boland insisted, 'I never did a thing within my department for a TACA member.'[13]

I believed him. Kevin Boland had little time for Haughey. When Boland was Minister for Social Welfare, Haughey had annoyed him about the appointment of a local social welfare officer. Boland called him 'that little bloody blueshirt'.[14] Haughey's father was a captain in the Free State Army during the civil war and he continued to serve in the army until 1928.

*

I first met Charles Haughey in March 1961 when we spoke at a meeting of the College Historical Society in Trinity College. I was a mere 26 and Haughey was ten years older and Parliamentary Secretary to the Minister for Justice, Oscar Traynor. He was an accomplished but not an inspiring public speaker. He was cultivating the gravitas of his father-in-law, Seán Lemass. I was impressed. Throughout the 1960s our paths crossed again, mostly in by-elections. I knew that he was a consummate political operator from my conversations with Frank Cluskey, Denis Larkin and Michael Mullen, who greatly admired Haughey. Haughey adroitly set out to cultivate particular niches of support in Irish society. A classic example was the income tax exemption for creative artists and authors, which was all very laudable but is still being paid for by the general body of taxpayers. Another niche was the development of his island retreat, Inishvickillaun, which so impressed the Fianna Fáil cohorts in Dingle. They behaved like the Kerry jury, which said to the judge: 'We find the defendant not guilty but recommend that he not do it again!' I often wonder how much it cost the ESB to lay on electricity to the island. Where was the cost benefit analysis? Who authorised the expenditure?

But it was some twenty years after we first met that I began to have clear political confirmation that Charles Haughey could behave in a quite ruthless manner to obtain and retain political power. He had crucially persuaded Michael O'Kennedy to vote for him as leader of Fianna Fáil in December 1979. George Colley had naively assumed that he had O'Kennedy's vote in the bag. Michael O'Kennedy had his reward when he duly became Minister for Finance and was then nominated EEC Commissioner in 1980. Meanwhile, O'Kennedy introduced an extraordinary budget in early 1980. Dermot McAleese in January 1980 pointed out that in 1979, Ireland's net official asset position had deteriorated by £800 million — £300 million by running down reserves and £500 million by increasing liabilities.

As an Opposition deputy, I became deeply suspicious about the published Book of Estimates for 1980. Later that year the supplementary estimates amounted to a staggering total of £463.5 million for the year. The only conclusion I could come to was that the 1980 budget provisions had been understated as a matter of political expediency. There was also the exceptional supplementary estimate at year end for the health vote of £126.4 million. This was also quite startling.

Most of us were very surprised in December 1980 when Haughey appointed Gene Fitzgerald as Minister for Finance to succeed O'Kennedy: Fitzgerald had voted for George Colley. It was seen as a move by Haughey to try to improve the ailing fortunes of Fianna Fáil in Cork following his political coup against Jack Lynch. When I arrived in the Department of

Finance in mid-1981, it seemed to me that there had been a 10 per cent cut across the board in the provisional estimates for 1981. More alarmingly, this seemed to have been done with no consequential policy changes! Thus, the published 1981 estimates inevitably faced serious overruns of expenditure.

I and many others had half-expected Charles Haughey to take the budgetary situation by the scruff of the neck in 1980 and remedy the situation. His television broadcast of January 1980,[15] in which he clearly spelled out his intention of cutting the level of the public sector borrowing requirement, was electrifying. But within a month it became obvious that he had no intention whatsoever of implementing his public assurance. His lack of candour again came to the fore. His February 1980 budget seriously overestimated buoyancy of revenue. Income tax receipts were supposed to increase by no less than 48 per cent! The Central Bank, the National Economic and Social Council and the Economic and Social Research Institute were clear that the 1981 budget was just about the last opportunity to escape from general international disquiet.[16] The government hoped for £200 million from 'limited privatisation' proposals to finance the public capital programme with no details provided; most financial analysts predicted a current budget deficit of some £650 million to £700 million. The PSBR could have gone as high as 20 per cent of GNP for 1980. Charlie had clearly lost his nerve.

*

When the coalition government came to office in June 1981, I was, on the nomination of Tanaiste Michael O'Leary, appointed by the Taoiseach, Garret FitzGerald, as Minister of State at the Department of Finance, ostensibly 'with responsibility for economic planning'. The Minister for Finance was John Bruton. He was a very energetic, open and frank minister if somewhat politically naive. We had one point of total agreement: namely, the confirmation beyond doubt that Charles Haughey, from the date of his election as Taoiseach in December 1979 to the date of his exit from that office in mid-1981, had almost bankrupted the country. And we knew that many public servants shared our shocked opinion. However, knowing the consummate capacity of Haughey to deflect all criticism and revise fiscal history, I sought internal verification of the impact of his venal policies.

The overall budgetary situation was exceptionally bad by any standards. Senior officials of the Department of Finance pointed out to me that the pre-July 1981 budget deficit was projected at £947 million or 9.5 per cent of GNP. As a result of our very tough July budget, the outturn in 1981 was a current budget deficit of £802 million or 7.3 per cent of GNP. Internationally in 1981 we were in the unenviable position of having by far the highest deficit in the EEC. Next came Belgium and Italy. Both were having serious economic difficulties but their deficits were only 4 per cent to 5 per cent of GNP.

An integral part of the background briefings of Charles Haughey in 1980-1981 was that borrowing for current purposes was first initiated in a major way by the national coalition government of 1973-1977. He contended that by the time he took over, it was a firmly established practice. In fact the first occasion in the history of the state in which a current budget deficit was deliberately planned was in 1972-1973, by George Colley, Minister for Finance, before the national coalition government assumed office. The coalition governments of 1973-1977 and 1981-1987 were cursed by being elected to office at times of acute recession. When the oil crisis struck in 1973-1974, that government deliberately borrowed for current purposes in order to sustain economic activity. It is very relevant to note that this action was in accordance with the advice given by international organisations to governments generally at the time.

As Minister of State in Finance in September 1981, I considered the situation to be so serious from the perspective of Labour's participation in government that I decided to brief the political correspondents. I pointed out that it was evident from the reaction to the mid-1981 Budget and other measures that the public was not fully aware of the critical state of the government finances inherited by the new administration. Many electors felt perhaps that they had had enough of bad news. I pointed out that this government did not intend to run away from the realities of economic life, and, however painful, the unvarnished facts must be made known.

Time and again over the previous two years, Fianna Fáil had attempted to conceal the real extent of the financial crisis. The stark reality was that public expenditure as a percentage of GNP had increased from 54.4 per cent in 1979 to 70 per cent arising from the 1981 Fianna Fáil January budget. Fianna Fáil had borrowed and spent in all directions to retain power. I pointed out to the correspondents that in some Eastern European countries, the outgoing prime minister and half his cabinet would be transported to the nearest salt mine for such a policy. In 1981 there was a universal public mood that such was the dire state of the economy, the country could not afford to do much about alleviating poverty and social distress. And yet each day in 1981 the country could afford £2 million pounds on alcohol. In 1981 our well-heeled citizens spent £4 million at the Galway races. And yet we could not afford any money to house our travelling people. With a life expectancy of 47 years, most of them are now dead. 1981 was a year when the first flush of rezoning of Dublin County Council farm lands enhanced each acre by £35,000. In that year alone, £300 million was spent on charter holidays while our childcare services were sparse.

*

One particularly alarming document had been in circulation confidentially in the Department of Finance. It was an internal report of a working group of the department on 'Future Budget Policy' of April 1981. It was of such a controversial nature at the time that its publication was not recommended by the group. Haughey and Gene Fitzgerald were no doubt well aware of its contents. It was then and remains today a revelation of the exchequer slide of the country during this period. The senior civil servants from the department who prepared it were: Maurice O'Connell, Assistant Secretary, Budget and Planning Division, Finance (later Governor of the Central Bank); Eamon Clarke, Assistant Secretary; Robert Curran, Second Secretary (later Second Secretary of the department); Michael Neville, Assistant Secretary; Gabriel Noonan, Assistant Secretary; Michael Somers, Principal Officer, Finance Division (later chief executive, National Treasury Management Agency); Patrick Mullarkey, Assistant Secretary (later Secretary General of the

Department of Finance); and Michael Tutty, Principal Officer (later Second Secretary of the Department), who acted as Secretariat. Declan Brennan, Department of the Public Service, participated in the group as an observer. He was subsequently to become Secretary of the Department of Education.

Their report clearly illustrated the crisis in the public finances. They stated that unless there was a significant slowdown in the growth of our foreign debt, it was likely that foreign bankers would either discontinue lending to us or, at the very least, impose much more stringent conditions on loans to us. If large deficits were sustained on a continuing basis, they would cripple the economy because of the cost of funding them and lead to the rapid exhaustion of our borrowing ability with the current deficit rising at an alarming rate to a level of about 13½ per cent of GNP in 1986. Overall Exchequer borrowing requirements were estimated at over 22 per cent for 1986. The group considered that a fall in real per capita incomes was an unavoidable part of any medium-term strategy in the circumstances. The group felt that statutory controls would probably be necessary for at least part of the period. There could be widespread and extreme industrial action.

This authoritative group of senior public servants advanced the view that substantial progress towards elimination of the current budget deficit could only be achieved through radical changes involving increased taxation and severe restrictions on public expenditure. They went on to make a series of stark proposals on public expenditure cuts which, almost 20 years later, are such as to raise the few hairs on the heads of even the baldest of former ministers. And the proposed taxation measures were equally draconian. Among measures they proposed was the freezing of capitation grants to secondary schools to save £10 million; raising the age of entry into school to six years to save £30 million; doubling exam fees to save £1.5 million; increasing health contributions from 1 to 2 per cent (yield £70 million); reducing coverage of medical cards to 25 per cent of the population to save £20 million; increasing charges to private and semi-private patients by £20 million; cutting children's allowances by £42 million; re-imposing rates and cutting housing subsidies to yield £100 million; and phasing out food subsidies to save £52 million.

I was shocked to the core when I read these proposals. When public servants of such stature had to inform Charles Haughey and Gene Fitzgerald of such major proposals, then the economy was undoubtedly in crisis. And more was to follow. They went on to propose a 10 per cent decrease in income tax bands to yield £74 million; that the PAYE allowance should be frozen to yield £60 million; that non-mortgage interest relief should be abolished to save £12 million; that short-term social welfare benefits be taxed to save £17 million; that VAT be increased from 10 to 12.5 per cent to yield £142 million; that road tax be reintroduced to yield £25 million; and that petrol and gas taxes be increased to yield £60 million.

And these public servants added further pain to their proposed litany of suffering. They put forward the view that there should be no special pay increases for five years and that new posts and the filling of public service vacancies should not exceed 1 per cent each year. Public service employment had increased by 31,000 from 1977 to 1981 arising from the Fianna Fáil manifesto of 1977.

The Department of Finance was, to say the least, a demoralised outfit. It had some very capable and dedicated senior staff. Maurice Doyle, Assistant Secretary in charge of the public expenditure division and an aspiring Secretary, was in a mood of black cynicism about the good intentions of all politicians. The outgoing Secretary, Tom Coffey, was virtually on his way to the governorship of the Central Bank. There was an air of polite despair from him that the realities of soaring budget deficits and consequential borrowing would be fudged by office holders once again. But the new Minister, John Bruton, resolved to reassert the primacy of the department. In classic Fine Gael mould he knew what was best for people even if they did not like the medicine one bit, as distinct from his Fianna Fáil predecessors whose populist policy was to give the punters whatever they wanted.

My tentative consultations in those eight months as Minister of State with the trade union and employers' organisations about the prospects of an economic and social plan for the 1980s were regarded by the cabinet as an interesting, sincere but an irrelevant exercise. In this exercise I was ably assisted on a voluntary basis by Tony Browne, Catherine McNamara and Peter Cassells. The concept of 'social partnership' did not exist and Michael O'Leary was not particularly interested at that time. Instead, I got to know all about Monsignor Horan, Charles Haughey, Padraig Flynn and their Knock Airport £12 million extravaganza!

In 1982 the monsignor sent me a postcard saying, 'Barry, I prayed for you at Knock!' At least he had a sense of humour about taxpayers' monies. An effective local airport could have been constructed closer to Castlebar for about £3 million at that time. But the monsignor had great notions about an international airport. Local fawning politicians, particularly from Fianna Fáil, were terrified about crossing him. I was not impressed. At least £6 million of exchequer monies, equivalent to £20 million today, was wasted. I was, or course, lashed by Charlie and his Mayo cohorts. These scarce monies, which could have vastly improved the road network to and from the West for all, were frittered away. Since 1986 there had been an explosion of air travel. The 1999-2000 winter schedule of Knock International Airport contained twelve return flights per week to London Stansted, and four return flights per week to Manchester!

*

So dire was the budgetary situation when the coalition government was formed in June 1981 that immediate action was imperative. John Bruton introduced his budget and he pointed out that 'in the absence of corrective action, the current budget deficit would be nearly £950 million, equivalent to 9½ per cent of GNP'. He also pointed out that excesses in capital expenditure could 'bring the overall Exchequer borrowing requirement to £1,973 million or 20 per cent of GNP'. In that budget, the government sanctioned increases in ESB and CIE charges; the continuous increase in public service employment since 1977 was cut back; the 10 per cent VAT rate was increased to 15 per cent; increases were imposed on telephone and postal charges, beer, spirits, wines, tobacco, petrol, stamp duty and excise duty on cars. The road tax on cars that had been abolished by Fianna Fáil in 1977 was reintroduced. The bank levy was introduced for the first time. The incoming government had committed itself to set up a Youth Employment Agency. To finance the agency, a one per cent levy was imposed on incomes.

As a result of these emergency measures, John Bruton ensured that the 1982 deficit was reduced by £450 million. These measures were a bitter pill for any junior Labour Minister in Finance to swallow. But I gulped and fully supported these measures in the national interest. Likewise the independent deputies Noel Browne, Jim Kemmy and Sean Dublin Bay Loftus saw no alternative to supporting the government. For the first time in my political career I found elderly constituents on the street talking to me about the national debt. The profligate policies of Fianna Fáil had come home to roost with a vengeance.

During that critical period we had been in danger of progressing into an autocracy dominated by one party leader whose resources were suspect but unknown. It is critical to appreciate that the culture of Haugheyism was all-pervasive in Fianna Fáil from 1979 onwards. We had to wait for an accident of a businessman's affidavit to bring the culture into the public gaze. Many of Haughey's associates are still in positions of power. The Taoiseach, Bertie Ahern, in 1998 was constrained to say: 'Personally, of course, I do not want to see more fall on the head of Charles Haughey. He is a good man who served the country well and I think he has taken a hell of a lot of knocks and he is getting older.' That was when it transpired that his leader had pocketed some £1.3 million in business subsidies towards his lifestyle. By the time Haughey's extracurricular income had reached an alleged £8.5 million, Bertie found the situation 'deeply shocking' in May 2000. Really! Some politicians have perfected the capacity to cry out of one eye.

*

I was assistant government whip, deputy leader of the Labour Party, and a member of the Council of State in 1982 when Brian Lenihan attempted to telephone President Patrick Hillery to persuade him to decree a change of government without dissolving the Dáil. The Fine Gael-Labour government had fallen after eight months and Charles Haughey wished to become Taoiseach without an election.

Paddy Hillery has never confirmed the sequence of these events or named those involved. I have no doubt he recorded what happened and I have no doubt there was an attempt to short-circuit the democratic process. To his great credit President Hillery refused to entertain these approaches.

Eight years later this incident became centre stage in the presidential election. I was shocked when Haughey decided to dismiss the Tanaiste — 'my old friend of thirty years' — from his government. Desmond O'Malley, Charles Haughey and the Fianna Fáil director of elections, Bertie Ahern, showed little compassion towards the seriously ill Lenihan. Brian allowed his party to use him once too often.

*

The Irish economic recovery began in 1982, not in 1987, a date so beloved by Fianna Fáil revisionists. They are still determined to airbrush the budgets of the early 1980s out of our economic history. Those who assert that Ray MacSharry as Minister for Finance and Charles Haughey as Taoiseach in 1987 were responsible for the recovery confound the realities of that decade. They vehemently opposed every single measure to control public expenditure proposed by the coalition between 1982 and 1987. The 1988 and 1989 MacSharry budgets were a belated conversion to keep public expenditure under control. It is patent nonsense to suggest that in 1987 Fianna Fáil rescued a bankrupt economy. The record shows that because of the major efforts of Fine Gael and Labour in government from 1981 to 1987, the balance of payments deficit, which we inherited in 1981 at 15 per cent of GNP, had been wiped out. Pay increases of 12 to 17 per cent per annum had been reduced to an average of 5 per cent by 1987. And we got scant support from Fianna Fáil spokespersons, including Ray MacSharry, in these earlier endeavours. In 1983 exchequer borrowing was 16.2 per cent of GNP. Ray MacSharry was handed on a plate a 6 point reduction to 10 per cent of GNP in 1987. This selective amnesia of Fianna

Fáil apologists is barefaced. I shudder to imagine what would have happened had Charles Haughey been Taoiseach from 1981 to 1987. The country was fortunate that Garret Fitzgerald and Dick Spring came on the scene at that time.

In the Dáil I found Ray MacSharry to be a chronically insecure person. He considered his Dáil seat to be precarious and at one election count, conceded defeat before being elected. After the 1987 election we compared notes about our financial insecurity. I told Ray I had an overdraft of some £10,000. He said that his was £50,000. I was not surprised when he decided in 1989 that he wanted to be appointed Ireland's EU Commissioner. Haughey was aghast and did his utmost to persuade MacSharry to continue in government. But Ray was determined to never again depend on the electorate for himself and his wife and family.

Much to MacSharry's fury, Haughey took his time before confirming his nomination to Brussels. Ray was one of the very few associates of Haughey who was not cowed by him in any way. Had MacSharry remained in national politics, I have no doubt that he would have succeeded Haughey as Taoiseach. Those who had attempted to proffer him a blandishment in 1983, on condition that he would ditch Haughey, were not forgiven by MacSharry. The trauma of these events, the most serious of which was orchestrated by a native multi-millionaire, created a deep cynicism in MacSharry about Irish politics. He was relieved to depart from active politics at the young age of 51. And he went on to become the most successful Irish EU commissioner since Paddy Hillery.

Many of Charles Haughey's supporters were so enthralled by him that, as John Kelly noted, 'if Charlie broke wind Síle de Valera would whinny'! Many senior deputies such as George Colley, Desmond O'Malley, David Andrews, Martin O'Donoghue, Jack Lynch, Frank Cluskey, Denis Larkin, Padraig Faulkner, Garret FitzGerald, Gerard Sweetman, Dick Spring, Jim Gibbons, etc., had the deepest of suspicions about the sources of his apparent wealth but like myself had no sustainable proof of his activities. It is now clear that he was touting without shame for money from the business community to sustain his ambitions and exotic lifestyle. We shall probably never know the identities of all those whom he asked for money. I have met some brazen political chancers in my time but Charlie takes the biscuit. Across the floor of the Dáil he lectured us all about the necessity to tighten our belts in the national interest while he hoovered up the thousands of Irish punts from glugger Irish businessmen who fell for his charm and the trappings of power. As one builder put it to me: 'Ye are all jealous of C.J.! Sure if he got a few bob, there might be a few shillings for us as well!'

I was in Leinster House on the October evening in 1982 when Haughey defeated the 'no-confidence' motion proposed by Charlie McCreevy. Haughey had insisted on an open roll-call vote of the parliamentary party, a classic bully-boy tactic. This procedure was decided by a show of hands of 50 to 27 against. Haughey then defeated the motion by 58 votes to 22. Haughey's intimidating supporters, who crowded the visitors' bar of the House, gave vent to their tribalism when the result was announced. I saw Jim Gibbons being assaulted and knocked down in the corridor as he left Leinster House. I was shocked by this disgraceful scene. Gibbons was a decent and honourable deputy who never recovered from this attack.

That was the culture of the time. Haughey and his banker bagman, Desmond Traynor, believed that they were above the people and above the law. Charlie was one of the greatest political charlatans who ever wore shoe leather in Dublin. That that conclusion is offensive to Dublin people is only relieved by the fact that he claimed affinity with so many other counties in Ireland. And the shock of it all is that of the scores of gullible businessmen who funded his lifestyle, only a handful have ever confirmed their contributions. Those who have done so have only confessed because they were sussed out by a tribunal of inquiry. And do the Irish people really care? One wonders, indeed. John Cushnahan MEP told me that in the Euro election campaign in Munster in 1999 he did not hear a single comment about Charles Haughey. It surely speaks volumes about our sense of morality.

However, I do know that there are many honourable deputies and business supporters of Fianna Fáil as Dr Rory O'Hanlon, TD, chairman of their parliamentary party, has so rightly pointed out. Tens of thousands of electors of great personal integrity still support Fianna Fáil. Charles Haughey brought disgrace on my own father who was a founder-member of Fianna Fáil in 1926 in Cork. He demeaned the proud and honourable offices of Taoiseach and President of Fianna Fáil. That is a real and terrible legacy which we will never erase.

Yet he had an exceptional ability to attract and manipulate a coterie of propagandists. John 'Backbencher' Healy of *The Irish Times* was a prime example. Healy exchanged brilliant and perceptive political journalism in his later years for weekly eulogies of Haughey. I rarely met a journalist who relished politics so much. The sheer cute hoorism and strokes of Haughey greatly impressed Healy. He was to die in 1991 before his icon's sleazy fall from grace. He would have been greatly pleased that his Taoiseach, Charles Haughey, led tributes to him on that occasion. However, one can become so close to the coalface and to personal relationships that journalistic objectivity goes out the windows. There were few tributes from the Opposition leaders on Healy's sudden death.

Let us not forget that at the 70th anniversary celebration of Fianna Fáil at the RDS in 1996, there were very enthusiastic speculations among the faithful that Haughey would be the party's favourite for the presidency. On that occasion he received a prolonged ovation of welcome. These were the very supporters about whom Bruce Arnold wrote: 'They sustained him, disaster after disaster. They accepted all his arrogance, they remained silent as he perjured himself, time after time, they knuckled under in a humiliating way, irresolute, cowardly, pathetic.' The video of the history of the party for the occasion did not even mention the arms crisis of 1970, which led to the sacking of Haughey and Blaney! Had Haughey run for the presidency with the support of his wealthy backers, he would probably have won. The disgrace of the nation would have been complete.

In the end, the master of venality himself in 1983 posed the one question which has yet to be answered to the electorate at large: '... are the policies and its leader in the future to be decided for it by the media, political opponents or worst, business interests pursuing their own ends?'[17]

In 1996 Martin Mansergh was invited by Fianna Fáil to write a chapter on Charles Haughey for its book *Taking the Long View*, published to mark the seventieth anniversary of the foundation of the party.[18] He titled his chapter 'Charles Haughey: A Legacy of Lasting Achievement'. Perhaps he should now re-write his eulogy, starting with his assessment as to how Haughey managed between 1979 and 1992 to milk some £8 million from the system, to sustain his political career and his lifestyle.

Eight

An Icon Revisited

'All of us in the government who are Catholics are ...
bound to give obedience to the rulings of our
Church.'

Seán MacBride, Minister for External Affairs, 1951

The Noel Browne I knew was a person somewhat different
from the stuff of popular Irish political legend. When I came to
work in Dublin in 1957 as a trainee Irish Transport and General
Workers' Union official, I attended political meetings where he
was the key speaker. He had a semi-persecuted presence as if
he expected the Special Branch or the agents of the Catholic
bishops to come in the door at any second and shoot him dead!
He had an anguished voice in which all of his declamations
began in a soft whisper. His modulated agitations mesmerised
me as an impressionable Cork émigré. I had come from Michael
O'Leary's 'Padraig O'Conaire Branch' of the Labour Party in
UCC, aptly labelled because we felt we were 'the blind leading
the blind' in the tradition of that great Irish poet. Noel Browne
was to us the ultimate voice in radical socialism.

It was not until much later that I found that he had a very
patrician approach to those who gave their support. His
economic analysis of Irish capitalism was repetitive and ill-
defined. Furthermore, he was quite dismissive of any criticism.
However, no other politician can claim to have held high office
in four political parties, been returned twice as an independent
TD and a senator, all in three Dáil and TCD constituencies over
35 years of political activism. But he was, in my experience,

quite incapable of consistent loyalty to the democratically elected executive of any of the parties he joined. He had, as the former senator and historian John A. Murphy wrote, 'a bleak, melancholy and increasingly embittered temperament'.[19] However, despite this harsh assessment, there are areas where Dr Browne does emerge with considerable credit.

Noel Browne, physician, psychiatrist, minister, senator, made a remarkable political impact on Ireland's young democracy between 1948 and 1951. His major contribution was as Minister for Health from 1948 to 1951. He provided drive and momentum to the completion of the Department of Health's programme of construction of sanatoria and the planned major hospital programme. He resigned from Clann na Poblachta in 1951 after failing to introduce the Mother and Child Scheme, which had been produced by Fianna Fáil as part of the 1947 Health Act. He had naively consulted from bishop to bishop about the scheme, from Michael Browne of Galway to John Dignan of Clonfert, to Cardinal D'Alton and Archbishop McQuaid. He then blundered into resignation and abjectly told the Dáil that 'as a Catholic I accept unequivocally and unreservedly the views of the Hierarchy on this matter'.[20] As Professor J.H. Whyte pointed out in his book *Church and State in Modern Ireland* it was Noel Browne who raised the issue in the first instance by asking the hierarchy for a ruling on his inherited Fianna Fáil proposals. After that, he finished up going nowhere politically although he remained in public life for another 30 years.

After the 1948-1951 debacles in government and in the Clann na Poblachta party, he elevated himself above it all in self-ordained political martyrdom. And yet while we down on earth were campaigning within the trade union and labour movement for fundamental reforms, Browne had no compunction in voting for the Fianna Fáil budget in 1952, one of the most savagely conservative in the history of the state. He joined Fianna Fáil in 1953 after supporting de Valera's nomination as Taoiseach in 1951; he became a member of that party's committee of twelve; he became joint treasurer of Fianna Fáil; lost his seat in 1954; was elected as an independent in 1957 and was duly expelled from Fianna Fáil in 1957;

founded the National Progressive Democrats in 1958. This party's opening statement was strange in that it proposed to make Ireland 'an example for the world of how a Christian people can create a Christian State'.[21]

Browne joined the Labour Party in 1963. As financial secretary of the party I strongly supported his application and that of Jack McQuillan. But, after a fraught relationship, he was excluded from Labour in 1977 for contesting the general election against the party, having deservedly failed to be ratified as a candidate. He was elected again as a deputy and voted for Garret FitzGerald as Taoiseach in 1981. He founded the Socialist Labour Party in 1977 and resigned from that party in 1981. And in this strange political odyssey he also managed to become vice chairman of the Labour Party in 1967 and a TCD senator in 1973. None of his many loyal workers, who followed him from party to party, rated even a footnote in his biography. His political gyrations fostered factions within progressive politics in Ireland in this period as he led young political radicals on his ego merry-go-round.

*

By the early 1950s the concept of sanatorium treatment of TB was being revised arising from the introduction of the new drug streptomycin. As Dr Ruth Barrington recorded in her outstanding *Health, Medicine and Politics in Ireland, 1900 to 1970*, 'The groundwork had been done and the system was already in action'[22] when Noel Browne arrived in the department. I reiterate these facts because Noel Browne stated on many occasions that he initiated the TB eradication programme. I swallowed this myth until I became Minister for Health in 1982 and carefully checked the limited surviving records of that period. The data was sparse because in his memoirs, Browne shamefully records that following his resignation and before he left the Custom House he ensured that 'all documents in our files likely to be used or misused against us were destroyed'! This was an outrageous act by Browne. But surviving records do show that a White Paper was published in 1946 by the Department of Local Government and Public Health entitled

'Tuberculosis', drawn up by Dr James Deeny, the department's Chief Medical Officer.

It stated that the regional sanatoria, which the department had already begun to build, would cost £2 million and would be drawn from the Hospitals Trust Fund. Three years before Noel Browne arrived in the department, the Tuberculosis (Establishment of Sanatoria) Act, 1945 had been enacted. Very significantly, treatment in the new sanatoria was to be free to everyone, irrespective of income. The 1947 Health Act also uniquely provided for the payment of maintenance allowances to TB sufferers. In the first year, 1945-1946, a half million pounds, the equivalent of a major capital programme today, had already been spent. In fact, many hospitals had been built before the war stopped the programme in the early 1940s. The truth behind Browne's elaborate claim is that Minister Dr Jim Ryan had already drafted and enacted the TB legislation and financial provisions. Dr James Deeny in fact planned the adoption by government of the sanatoria programme. Dr Browne gave it a final push, no more and no less.

The result was that the TB death rate fell dramatically from 123 per 100,000 in 1947 to 73 per 100,000 in 1951. This is not in any way to deny Noel Browne his part in combating this public health scourge. His precise contribution is particularly well assessed by Dr James Deeny in his occasional paper *Towards balancing a distorted record*.[23] Ruth Barrington in her book referred to Dr Deeny as a man 'whose ideas were to make a fundamental contribution to the future direction of health policy'.[24] J.H. Whyte in his *Church and State in Modern Ireland* acknowledged of Deeny: 'It seems to have been he more than any other individual who was responsible for the shape which legislation took in Ireland.' Those who regularly adulate Noel Browne should reflect on these calm assessments. Too many people in Ireland live in mythology rather than reality.

*

Maurice Manning wrote of Noel Browne in 1986: 'He frequently gave the impression of being unable to accept any point other than his own, of imputing base motives to those who opposed him and of having a limitless supply of moral superiority and self-righteousness.'[25] David Hanley also wrote about him in 1987: 'While Noel Browne loves humanity, he does not actually like most human beings.'[26] His life story *Against the Tide* was a vicious litany of people he supported and then scorned, from de Valera to John A. Costello, from David Thornley to Brendan Corish. It was a poisonous denigration of some 90 persons he came across in his career. For example, I did not share the Communist Party views of fellow Corkman Mick O'Riordan but he earned my admiration and that of fellow social democrats for fighting against fascism in Spain. Betty Sinclair of the Belfast and District Trades Union Council was greatly respected for fighting the cause of the exploited women workers of Belfast. Nicholas Boran, executive member of the ITGWU, and Castlecomer branch secretary, had his fellow miners x-rayed for the first detection of pneumoconiosis in Ireland. I knew and admired these outstanding socialists. I personally saw their great work in the trade union movement. Yet Browne dismissed all three as 'entirely ineffective people'.

As Brian Trench noted in 1986: 'His characterisations were marked by a streak of cruelty'.[27] Browne's reflections on David Thornley, who tragically was an alcoholic and died in 1978 aged 43, were particularly cruel to his family and friends. David and I were both elected in 1969. I knew of his outstanding campaigns for Browne in the 1951, 1954 and 1957 general elections. As David Hanley wrote in 1987: 'Almost nobody escapes the deeply contemptuous lash of this great humanitarian's tongue.'[28] Any deputy, such as myself, who dared favour a coalition strategy was automatically dubbed a coward and a self-seeker by Noel, despite the fact that in 1969 he strongly advocated coalition with Fine Gael to me and others in the party. I found his attitude disturbing, to say the least, in view of the enthusiasm with which he joined no fewer than four political parties after serving in the first inter-party government of no fewer than five parties. I fully share the view of Joe Deasy, President, Irish Labour History Society, and a respected observer of the period, that Browne's biography 'while valuable and brilliant, is marred by being very bitter, unbalanced and in parts, extremely inaccurate. Some portraits are grossly offensive, while others are ill-judged. He slandered left people like Jim Larkin, Junior and Justin Keating. He arraigned a whole gallery of political figures and parties right across the spectrum. His chapter 'The Left In Ireland', is mostly an ill-considered wish-wash'.[29]

*

The fallacy that he originated the 'Mother and Child Scheme' was acknowledged by Browne when he produced his famous brochure, *An Mhathair is a Leanbh*. He wrote: 'My authority for this service is the will of our people, unmistakably expressed through the Oireachtas in the Health Act of 1947, which the former administration passed and which the present government endorses.' An examination of this brochure shows that in these days of programme managers and advisers Noel Browne led the way in 1948. His Mother-and-Child brochure, with the Hynes, Coady, Duncan and Morath photographs, was a masterpiece of its time. He employed two outstanding journalists, Aodh de Blacam and Frank Gallagher, to great effect and rapidly created a saviour image to the consternation of the conservative medical profession. The misguided and paternal Catholic bishops were led a merry dance by some IMA consultants in the voluntary hospitals who saw Browne as a threat to their professional status. The objections of the Catholic hierarchy were threadbare and based for the most part on a paternalistic concept of Catholic sociology. However, most commentators on Browne's career have failed to stress that the scheme was based on Dr Jim Ryan's Health Act of 1947 and the Health (Financial Provisions) Act, 1947.

The glaring inexperience of Browne as a minister is also evident from his presentation of his scheme to the government. He had a clear duty to formally put the scheme by way of a memorandum to government for decision. After careful checking I have come to the conclusion that he never actually did so. Basic submission to government was and still is an elementary precondition for any hope of success. As Ruth Barrington rightly pointed out, Browne 'neglected to ensure the government's support for the details'. Astoundingly, on 27 March 1951, the Department of the Taoiseach could find no record of any submission by Browne to the government of proposals for a Mother and Child Scheme. Had he heeded the sound advice he received from Jim Larkin Junior, who told me at length in 1962 about his efforts to advise Noel Browne on the issue, and from the officers of the Irish TUC, he could have overcome the minefields laid for him by the IMA and the Catholic hierarchy. There was the prospect that the Mother and Child Scheme might not have been blown sky high.

For whatever reasons, possibly as a result of his earlier tuberculosis, there was his absence from some 80 out of 261 meetings of the cabinet during his three years as minister. This certainly did not help his cause and surely stands as the all-time record for such absences since the foundation of the state. Shortly after 1951 Fianna Fáil, wherein Ministers Seán Lemass and Jim Ryan had singularly poor relations with the hierarchy, and particularly with Archbishop McQuaid, implemented the scheme. As the late Clann stalwart, Con Lehane, rightly observed, Browne 'is constitutionally incapable of listening to criticism'. In fairness to Browne his sheer political inexperience, being appointed Minister for Health by Seán MacBride on his first day in the Dáil, aged 32, was a recipe for political turmoil. From my 20 years' experience in the Dáil, half of which was in government, I have concluded that the Taoiseach or party leader in coalition who appoints a newly elected deputy to the government, is, for the most part, storing up a great deal of unpredictable trouble.

*

In his biography Noel Browne deals in a very cursory manner with the considerable ideological influence of one of his main protagonists, Dr James MacPolin, who was the Chief Medical Officer for Limerick. He was an ultra Catholic corporate statist; a virulent anti-communist whom he defined as anybody who questioned the self-interest of the Irish Medical Association or who proposed publicly funded general practice. He was a doctor who believed that his profession had a very special place in God's scheme on earth. He wrote: 'The power of authority to do this (medical) work is from God via creation ... this power does not come from the people to persons in power, let them be ministers or minor local officials — it is from God.'[30] Dr

MacPolin went so far in his interpretation of 'The Divine Scheme of Things', as he put it, that the preservation of moral circumstances was paramount 'even if such preservation involves the person remaining in bad health'. He went on to assert that 'all current talk about abolishing "means tests" on certain services is totally immoral'. He further argued that Catholic preoccupation, in its moral teaching, with the rights of private property extended to an exclusive system of private medical practice. Public health, he ordained, was secondary.

Noel Browne never fully appreciated the extent to which MacPolin's moral strictures permeated the approach of the bishops and the medical profession to his reforms. When I read the edicts of MacPolin, I began to have some sympathy for the plight of Browne.

*

In April 1998 there emerged from a most unlikely source, namely, the voluminous archives of the late John Charles McQuaid, confirmation in a very definitive way of the real political and social ethos of the Irish governments of the 1940s and 1950s. I found McQuaid's papers a striking personal record of his almost total domination of the government of 1948-1951, including, in particular, of Seán MacBride, John A. Costello and Noel Browne. He saw Browne's scheme as creeping socialism invading the health services. When the 1947 Fianna Fáil Bill had proposed free medical care for mothers and children under 16 years of age, McQuaid had the hierarchy privately convey to de Valera that it was 'entirely contrary to Catholic social teaching... and the rights of the medical profession'. When Browne pushed forward the same scheme, Dr McQuaid did not delay in exerting his influence over 'the most obsequiously obedient government to episcopal authority in the history of the State', an assessment of Ronan Fanning.[31] In Fanning's opinion 'it is almost impossible to exaggerate the near feudal deference of Costello and his ministers to the hierarchy in general, and to the Archbishop of Dublin in particular'.

As early as 1951 the Archbishop reported to the standing committee of the hierarchy that the Taoiseach, John A. Costello, whom he had recently met three times, had given him 'the assurance that whatever the Church declares to be right in respect of Mother and Child Health Service will be unequivocally accepted by him, even if the minister had to resign or the government falls'.[32] Thus, Noel Browne was doomed from the start. Two further factors sealed his political burial. His leader, Seán MacBride, had already grovelled at the feet of the Archbishop following his election to the Dáil in 1947. He brought a letter to Dr McQuaid which stated: 'I hasten, as my first act to pay my humble respects to your Grace and to place myself at your Grace's disposal. Both as a Catholic and as a public representative I shall always welcome any advice which your Grace may be good enough to give me and shall be at your Grace's disposal should there be any matters upon which your Grace feels that I could be of any assistance.' Whereas, John A. Costello bent the knee to the Archbishop on every occasion, Seán MacBride seemed determined to go down on all fours, even to the extent of renewing his pledge of obedience after each election.

Down through the years from the late 1950s, I was never a fan of Seán MacBride despite the adulation that many chic republicans and impressionable advocates of civil liberties bestowed on this cynical political opportunist. So much for the former chief of staff of the IRA in 1936.

One of the great ironies of that time was that all members of the inter-party government, including William Norton and Noel Browne, were obsequiously deferential to the Catholic hierarchy. McQuaid recorded that at the height of the crisis over the Mother and Child Scheme, Browne called on him at his own request and 'asked me to believe that he only wanted to be a good Catholic and to accept fully the Church's teaching. I accepted that attitude'.[33] So much for the fearless solitary radical crusader. Then there was the extraordinary statement of Browne to the Dáil during the course of his resignation in 1951: 'The hierarchy has informed the government that they must regard the Mother and Child Scheme proposed by me as opposed to Catholic social teaching. That decision I, as a Catholic, immediately accepted without hesitation.'

Browne failed to appreciate that the Catholic Church had, of course, many avenues of approach for support in the cabinet.

Richard Mulcahy, Seán MacEoin, William Norton and Joe Blowick were Knights of Saint Columbanus. John A. Costello had been a member in the 1920s.[34] While I deplore Noel Browne's appalling decision to destroy his departmental and ministerial documents relating to the Mother and Child Scheme on the eve of his departure from the Custom House, I do understand his decision to release a selection of the presumably confidential correspondence. Church–State relations were never the same again.

In addition there was the unique absence of the Secretary to the Government from those government meetings Browne attended. Apparently Seán MacBride distrusted the Secretary and the cabinet agreed that he would not attend cabinet meetings. Liam Cosgrave was the then government chief whip and it seems that it fell to him to record the decisions of the government. This was an extraordinary responsibility given the great sensitivity of many of the issues which faced that government. I have never heard Liam Cosgrave elaborate on these events. In the early 1980s when I introduced, as Minister for Health, legislation relating to adoption, child care, family planning and the nursing profession etc., I took great care to maintain a clear distance from the hierarchies of all the churches on all such issues. I had learned the lessons of Browne. Despite this I had my share of reactionary opposition.

*

It is interesting to note that within the 1948-1950 government there were tensions other than those which surrounded the Mother and Child Scheme. As a member of a coalition government from 1982-1987 I was present when government decisions relating to capital murder were taken. By 1982 this was no longer a defining issue around the cabinet table. Dr Browne at a meeting at University College, Galway, in 1996 recalled:

> On the issue of capital punishment, both myself and Mr MacBride opposed on two occasions the government's decision not to advise the President to exercise clemency. We were opposed by the majority

of the cabinet. The debate in cabinet was conducted under the sympathetic chairmanship of the Taoiseach. There was no time limit to the discussion which went on until we had exhausted our arguments, yet left our cabinet colleagues unimpressed. Finally the question was put and a vote taken; we were defeated. Two men went to their death. We, no matter what we might have felt, became hangmen by proxy. This then is the essence of the minority party's dilemma in coalition in a microcosm.

It is of particular interest to note that neither he nor MacBride threatened to withdraw from government on this most fundamental of all human rights, the right of life itself. I still recall the government meeting in mid-1986 when the Minister for Justice, Alan Dukes, brought to the notice of the government the case of Noel Callan who was under sentence of death by hanging for the murder of Sergeant Patrick Morrissey. The Special Criminal Court, in December 1985, found Michael McHugh and Noel Callan guilty of the capital murder of this garda acting in the course of his duty. They were both sentenced to death. They had robbed £15,000 from Ardee Employment Office. Sergeant Morrissy had given chase. In each of the eight cases up to then where the death sentence had been imposed, the President, acting on the advice of the government, commuted the sentence to 40 years' penal servitude with a clear understanding that there would be no remission. Sergeant Morrissy was murdered by Michael McHugh in a particularly callous manner, having first wounded him in the leg during pursuit and as he tried to prop himself up, he shot him in the face. Noel Callan had a sawn-off shotgun and rifle. Following the government decision to advise the President to exercise clemency towards Noel Callan and commute the statutory sentence of death, I had a very mute explanation to offer to my garda sergeant driver that evening other than that, as a matter of principle, I was opposed to capital punishment. Tony Boyce was singularly unimpressed. We drove home in silence. Tony understood.

*

The veiled contempt of Noel Browne in his biography towards Jim Everett, the Labour deputy and Minister from Wicklow, was deplorable. Stella and my father knew James Everett quite well. He was organiser for the Co Wicklow Agricultural Workers' Union which was later to merge with the Irish Transport and General Workers' Union. He was jailed for six months in 1918, 1919 and again in 1920 for organising strikes and demonstrations against the dreadful working conditions of his members. He was appointed a judge in the Sinn Féin courts 1920-1921 and succeeded in every election from 1921 to his death in 1967. I admired the fact that he was the first deputy in any county council in Ireland to initiate a scheme of council scholarships to secondary schools for the children of working people in his county. He also won our respect for the devoted manner in which he and his wife, who had no children, educated the whole of the Kavanagh family in Wicklow town, including his nephew Liam Kavanagh, former Labour deputy whom he wished to be his successor in the constituency.

Jim Everett also had another admirable quality. He was the first Minister for Justice, to my knowledge, who refused all petitions sent to him by those who had been convicted of drunken driving. It had been the practice of his predecessors to exercise clemency in relation to those convictions. In 1956 I had just joined the party in Cork when some classmates of mine were going to the Thomas Ash Memorial Hall at Father Matthew Quay to join the IRA. Jim Everett, as Minister for Justice in the 1954-1957 inter-party government, had many of these naive young men arrested as they participated in some mad escapades against RUC barracks on the border. It took real courage to so act in government in those days. Many of these young men began to appreciate that there was more to the partition of the island than the simplicities of the propaganda of the IRA.

Jim Everett, of course, was no paragon of virtue. He tried to lever one of his supporters into a sub-postmastership in Baltinglass when he was Minister for Post and Telegraphs in the first inter-party government from 1950-1951. It backfired badly and did great damage to that government. The fact that

Fianna Fáil were adept at such practices cut no ice. The electorate always demanded better from Labour.

Perhaps one reason for Noel Browne's dismissal of Jim Everett was Browne's failure to win the by-election nomination in the Wicklow constituency, after Jim Everett's death in 1967. Noel had lost his Dáil seat in the 1965 general election and he had failed to get elected to the Seanad. He had been elected vice chairman of the party and I was chairman. I asked Noel to consider running in Wicklow. He lived in Bray and before becoming Minister for Health in 1948 had worked in Newcastle sanatorium. He agreed to contest the nomination. I personally canvassed every single branch of the party in Co Wicklow on Browne's behalf. I spent months doing so at considerable personal expense in our battered Volkswagen. I incurred the ire of the Everett and Kavanagh loyalists. On the day of the convention I went to Noel's home in Bray; his wife Phyllis was also there. The late Sean Dunne was chairman of the convention. To my consternation Noel refused to go to the convention to address the delegates. I was administered my first severe dose of his cavalier disdain for the rank and file of the party.

In the event, the delegates decided by a decisive majority to back Liam Kavanagh. After great pressure from myself, Browne eventually agreed to speak at one meeting in support of Liam in Bray. Stella and I, in turn, eating humble pie, campaigned day and night for Liam Kavanagh, against the might of the Blaney and Boland machines. Eventually, I was forgiven for my sponsorship of Browne. Liam was elected in the 1969 general election and in every general election until 1997. In the 1982-1987 coalition government he was held in great esteem by Garret FitzGerald. He was a quiet kingmaker in the parliamentary party.

*

In a highly controversial article in *The Sunday Press* in September 1970, Browne revisited the issues of contraception, abortion and homosexuality. He caused consternation in the Labour Party. I was a brand-new deputy and my colleagues were furious by Browne's decision to go solo on what were then regarded as extremely sensitive issues. He wrote:

> From my medical practice, concerned as it has been with the disturbed adolescent, I have been forced to conclude that there can be no greater human tragedy for both mother and child than the unwanted child. I believe then, logically, that contraceptive advice and techniques should be widely available. Equally, for the mother whose emotional and physical health could be preserved by its application, I am convinced that in certain cases therapeutic legal abortion also should be permitted and available. We also should adopt sensible and humane laws in regard to homosexuality, as well as extending even further the recent liberalising changes in our censorship laws, both in literature and the cinema.

In the political culture of the Dáil in 1970, these statements deeply upset most of Labour's deputies. Even those of us who shared Browne's views in the comfort of the more liberal Dublin constituencies, such as mine in Dun Laoghaire–Rathdown, came to the conclusion that he was once again working his way out of yet another political party. We also knew, as did Browne, that the prospect of the Fianna Fáil government or any other combination of deputies introducing such reforms was remote. At that time one of Browne's staunchest supporters, the newly elected David Thornley, described him as one who opted 'to stand apart from it in glorious and impotent righteousness, like Stylites on his tower'.[35]

By 1971 I sensed that Browne had become increasingly embittered, not only with our party but in particularly with the Catholic Church. He decided to launch a full frontal attack on all aspects of the Church in Irish society. In a speech at a Labour dinner in Tramore, he stated:

> The hard truth is that the Catholic Church is one of the most dedicated, resilient, obscurantist and conservative political machines in the history of man, which only now is entering into its decline the world

over. As bishops, archbishops and cardinals they are isolated from the stress of earning their living, becoming unemployed, and forced to emigrate, marry, found homes and families. Consciously or otherwise, many of them have chosen their celibate lives because they find the whole subject of sex and heterosexual relationships threatening and embarrassing. Their judgement, then, cannot be trusted on these issues.

These sweeping assertions, some 30 years ago, caused great offence among the religious and in the electorate as a whole. The party decided to issue a rebuttal. It stated:

To suggest that many of those who chose the religious life do so out of fear of sexual relations is an insult to men and women who regard their vocations as a service to God and humanity. Those who make that choice have the right to be respected for it. Dr Browne spoke for himself when he levelled that charge against the clergy. We may say the same goes for his reference to Confession which is a Sacrament of the Catholic Church and, as such, is held sacred by Catholics. It is not the function of politicians to denigrate the beliefs or practices of any religion.

A major public row was, of course, inevitable and simmered on during 1971 in public. But Browne was determined to escalate the dispute. In a statement to *The Sunday Press* in 1972, he stated:

Every proposal to improve the social fabric of our society, to reorganise our economy, to increase national wealth, provide jobs, reduce emigration and unemployment, improve our health and education services, provide proper conditions in which our aged poor could grow old in dignity, became a mortal sin and so forbidden. For those men and women who have in the past consciously or unconsciously sought the monosexual surroundings of religious orders because of their sexual immaturity or uncertainty in heterosexual relationships, there is a growingly enlightened attitude about these problems in all our communities.

The obedient Catholic had turned full circle.

Browne had us all in a political and sexual tizzy. His pointed pearl of truth about some aspects of priestly life was lost in the political turmoil. He was working himself out of the party.

*

Despite Noel Browne's outpourings during the 1970s against coalition, he expressed quite ambivalent views about the issue on occasions. From my first-hand observations of his attitude I am strongly of the view that had Brendan Corish, Michael O'Leary or Frank Cluskey offered him the prospect of again being a minister he would have trimmed his attacks. In an interview with *This Week* magazine in 1970, he was of the view that Labour should contemplate a coalition, provided 'Labour's minimal demands of ministries endowed with maximum powers must be: 1. Finance, 2. Agriculture, 3. Industry & Commerce, 4. Education. In these departments there must be certain undertakings given by our co-partners in government.' He also advocated that the party leadership 'must designate the individual members of the parliamentary party to which these ministries are to be allocated and that this information should be placed before a special party conference with whom the final decision should rest as to whether or not the party should enter the proposed alliance'.

When it became quite evident around this time that Browne had long forfeited any prospect of ministerial office because of his temperament and extreme individualism, he turned on successive party leaders at party conferences. These annual events became utterly discordant and abusive affairs. Browne's speeches, beginning in a very low voice and rising in denunciation, had capitalism in crisis within minutes. He invariably denounced the platform, particularly Brendan Corish, and culminated in the classic 'walk out', usually in time to catch the train from Cork to Dublin.

*

The Dublin Artane constituency selection conference in 1977 was, in many ways, the watershed in Labour's relationship with Browne. He had decided to shift his base from Dublin South East where Senator Ruairi Quinn had come to prominence, having lost out in the constituency in 1973 by a mere 38 votes. The Artane constituency executive invited Browne to become a candidate and I, as party whip, was appointed chairperson of the convention. I was accompanied by Dr Aidan McNamara from the Dun Laoghaire constituency executive who took a verbatim note of the meeting. We prepared an impeccable report for the Administrative Council of the party in case we all finished up in the High Court.

As soon as Noel was selected, I read out the party pledge to the convention and to Browne. It was duly witnessed by two delegates and signed and dated by Noel. The following morning on RTÉ radio, Noel began to equivocate once again about his prospective role in the parliamentary party and in the Dáil. He was quite unsure if he could support the party in government. Even Catherine McNamara, Aidan's wife and an admirer of Browne, was shocked.

But the Administrative Council was not and refused to ratify Browne as a candidate. He ran as an independent, and in effect excluded himself from the party. He was duly elected to the Dáil. But at last we had removed an albatross around the neck of the party who had kept flying in ever-decreasing circles.

By that stage he and Matt Merrigan were the bane of the life of the party leader, Frank Cluskey, who, in a more thoughtful way, was much more radical than either of them. Unfortunately, Frank's work rate over those critical years was seriously affected by his heavy drinking and chain smoking. Immediately after their expulsion from the party in 1977, in yet another article in *The Irish Times*, Dermot Boucher of the 'Liaison of the Left' group proposed that 'the Labour Left, with its allies, should proceed with the task of creating for the first time in this country a genuine Socialist Party'. At last he had his very own party when he, Merrigan, David Neligan and Desmond Bonass proposed the formation of a new party at a meeting in the Ormond Hotel, Dublin. Tom Carroll of Rathmines acted as secretary.

An interloper at the meeting from Labour Party head office reported to Flor O'Mahony of Cluskey's cabinet that 'Noel Browne followed the crowd [about 35] while implying strongly that the chances of the new party succeeding were slim'.[36] In 1978 David Thornley, who had lost his Dáil seat in June 1977, joined the new Socialist Labour Party, stating that he had done so because 'there is no man in politics I respect more than Noel Browne, despite our occasional differences. If the SLP is good enough for him, it's good enough for me'.[37] Browne never returned the compliment in his biography.

However, the SLP was soon destined to implode with Browne in his customary role as the detonator. In May 1978, Browne once again availed of the benign columns of *The Irish Times* to declare that 'Irish Republicanism in a developing crisis will become an even more intolerant, authoritarian and repressive philosophy and presents a real threat to the nominally democratic institutions of the state.'[38] He was, he wrote, referring to the Sinn Féin Republican tradition of Pearse, Griffith, Collins and de Valera which he professed to despise. Browne did not spare the Provos in his critique. He asserted:

> Whatever its objectives in the minds of Official and Provisional Sinn Féin, the Northern struggle now has all the appearances of being in the narrow Catholic sectarian tradition of peace. In its social or political morality with its secret 'army councils', it is akin to the Italian secret society, the Mafia, and the men who govern it, the Mafioso leaders of the corrupt and evil organisation. In its political philosophy, if it can be called that, Irish republicanism bears no relationship whatever to any kind of social democracy or socialism that I know of.[39]

I had many disputes with Browne but on this issue we were in total harmony. However, seven months later the first president of the Socialist Labour Party, Matt Merrigan, told the 1979 conference of the SLP that the party was not against the Provisionals' bombing campaign, as such, but was opposed to it when it meant death or destruction of workers. Merrigan was the district secretary for the Republic of Ireland of the

Amalgamated Transport and General Workers' Union whose membership was predominantly in Northern Ireland. His statement caused uproar even in the SLP. Jack McQuillan said that he had attended the conference and 'was very disturbed by expressions of sympathy and support for the Provisional IRA expressed by delegates'.[40] He said that when he heard Matt Merrigan's statement 'it was the end of the road for him as far as the SLP was concerned'. Jack McQuillan was a highly regarded radical but, as a former army officer, he was well aware of the murderous policies of the Provisionals.

Michael O'Leary, the deputy leader of the Labour Party, promptly invited Browne to rejoin Labour but there was no enthusiasm within, least of all from myself as party whip. Frank Cluskey's right shoulder went up and down yet again, he drew on a fag and said, 'That's Mattie for you, comrades!' Browne resigned from the SLP shortly afterwards. Once again he had my full support!

*

In his 1986 memoirs, Browne explained that because of the ravages of TB which decimated his family he 'had lost the belief that I could ever again form permanent friendships or lasting relationships'. It was in that framework that I knew Noel Browne from 1963 to 1977. He was, to quote his own words, 'a solitary and introverted person, I have always actively disliked public life'. However, he had particular qualities that one must record and respect. In flailing against the dragons of conservative departmental secretaries, a jealous and utterly conservative Archbishop of Dublin, himself a doctor's son, an introverted IMA and the very timid Houses of the Oireachtas, Browne did politicise the Department of Health portfolio. However, he failed to consolidate that achievement or lay the foundations of a national health service in Ireland. He was not the only Irish health minister to fail in that regard.

Secondly, he unequivocally advocated fundamental social reforms in the laws relating to divorce, homosexuality, capital and corporal punishment, adoption, illegitimacy and contraception. He did fight to keep these issues in the forefront of public opinion despite ferocious hostility. He had sparse Dáil or Seanad support on most of those issues. From 1969 to 1981 when we were both deputies, I strongly supported many of his views notwithstanding that he frequently availed of those sensitive issues to cause those whom he disliked the maximum embarrassment.

Thirdly, he did have a very clear-cut appreciation of the implications for all Irish people of the sectarian and political divisions in Northern Ireland. He never fell for MacBride's cultivated veneer of physical force and pseudo republicanism. He steadfastly refused to be sucked into the Official IRA, IRSP, INLA and Provo mindset of violence and sectarian politics. I once asked him when we travelled very early one Sunday morning down to Eileen Desmond's by-election in Cork in 1965 — to my surprise Noel produced a Sunday Missal and insisted that we attend mass together on the way at Mitchelstown — if the fact that his father was an RIC sergeant in Waterford who transferred to Derry had influenced his attitude to the IRA. He was very upset and he did not elaborate on the RIC connection but I learned then of his withering contempt for the IRA. For these saving graces he is to be greatly admired.

There was one other truly saving grace in the long career of Noel Browne. Phyllis and Noel Browne were a constant happy couple for over 60 years. They first met when she was 16 and he was a young Trinity medical student. They married in 1944 and were blessed with two daughters. As Phyllis Browne recalled in her book: 'We had a wonderful even life together and no rows, ever. The children never heard him or me raise our voices.'[41] She said in an interview with Brenda Power that Noel and she believed that 'life means nothing at all if you don't leave the world a better place than you found it'.[42]

Noel Browne most certainly made a major contribution to Irish society in that regard. However, he craved political love and acclaim throughout his career. Many of those who worked unceasingly for him were discarded. And those who in any way questioned his strategies or pronouncements were unmercifully cast aside. The consummate politician will always attempt to convince the electorate that he is not a politician. Noel Browne nearly succeeded. He died unrequited in his passion that he alone knew what was best for the Irish people. He was, perhaps, an iconoclast who liked playing God.

Nine

Some Fellow Mavericks

Ní heolas go haontís
(If you want to know me, come and live with me)

Old Irish proverb

The first real maverick I ever met was Michael Mullen. When I became a trainee Irish Transport and General Workers' Union official in 1957, I was sent to the Dublin No. 4 Hotels and Catering Branch of the union in Parnell Square. Michael Mullen was the branch secretary. He was 36 years old and had come up through the ranks of the union in Dublin as a shop steward in Ever Ready Ltd.

As the key union official in Dublin for the hotels, catering and restaurant trade, he completely dominated the industry. Most of the trade was unionised with closed shop agreements, and casual vacancies were notified by employers to the union. All casuals were vetted by the branch and sent to the employers. In time a very large number of such employees came from Dublin North West which coincidentally was to become Michael Mullen's Dublin Corporation and Dáil constituency and from around the Navan Road where he lived. No employer dared to cross him and if they attempted to do so they were quickly told of his IRA and republican past. The Dublin No 4 branch secretariat was brilliantly organised by Francis Lambert who was the powerhouse behind Michael Mullen. I learned a great deal from Francis about office and union organisation.

Among the highlights of the year for the branch were the Dublin Spring and Horse Shows at which the union supplied all the part-time labour. Michael Mullen drank heavily. I recall my first midday visit with him to the Spring Show in 1958. After multiple gins and tonics and wine with Lawlor's of Naas and salmon mayonnaise for lunch I was, to the great amusement of Michael, locked out of my mind. I was in 'digs' in Upper Pembroke Street in Dublin 2. I still do not know how I made my way from there that afternoon. But I woke up early next morning spread-eagled against the railings of St Stephen's Green in my only good suit. I had been violently ill. I was utterly inexperienced about booze. I was 23 and I learned a very sharp lesson about keeping up with hard drinking union officials. However, I learned fast and after work we adjourned almost every evening to the Granby Bar in Parnell Square where I first learned to enjoy a real pint of Guinness.

From 1961 to 1965, with the Labour Party in opposition, Michael Mullen was also a dominant figure in Labour trade union politics in Dublin. He was the sole Labour deputy in Dublin. Michael O'Leary, Frank Cluskey and Denis Larkin were elected in 1965 and his influence began to recede. He concentrated in his union career on becoming a national group secretary in 1964 and retired as a Labour TD on becoming general secretary of the union in 1969.

However, with the eruption of conflict in Northern Ireland, he was back on familiar republican territory. He strongly supported Bernadette McAliskey and Tony Gregory and the Prisoners' Rights Organisation. His statements as general secretary of the union scared the daylights out of his fellow general officers; Fintan Kennedy and John Carroll had no desire to see Liberty Hall bombed by the loyalist paramilitaries. The general officers were also concerned to ensure that the very substantial sums collected from the union's membership in the Republic for the relief of Catholics in Northern Ireland would not fall into the wrong hands.

Michael Mullen was in his element with an inside track to Charles Haughey and the Fianna Fáil government. He became the classic 'Fianna Fáil trade union man' with access to state boards and all government departments. However, that was rudely interrupted with the election of the national coalition in 1973.

Too many Labour deputies, myself included, were unduly dependent on financial support from the union's political fund, which was, in effect, dispersed by Michael Mullen. Brendan Corish, the leader of the party, was also very heavily dependent on the support of the Irish Transport and General Workers' Union membership in the Wexford constituency. Corish, as Tanaiste, gave Mullen's name to Liam Cosgrave who appointed him as one of the 'Taoiseach's eleven' to the Seanad. No sooner was he appointed than he did everything possible to undermine the government. In particular, he vehemently objected to the Criminal Law (Jurisdiction) Bill which allowed the courts in the Republic to try people for crimes committed in the North.

Eventually, Michael Mullen's health gave up on him and he died in the early 1980s. He was a gregarious, astute operator who never lost an opportunity to seek transient popularity with the electorate.

*

When I was elected to the Dáil in 1969, Deputy Oliver J. Flanagan was one of the fathers of the House, having been elected on a monetary reform ticket in the Laois-Offaly constituency in 1943. He joined the Fine Gael Party in 1950. I did not know many members of the Knights of Columbanus in the Dáil but I knew that he was one.

He told me that the secret of his huge vote was his incessant correspondence with his constituents and his personal representative in each townland. For example, a supplication for a medical card warranted a letter to the Minister for Health, the Chief Executive Officer of the Health Board and the County Manager. He then had three responses assuring him that they would look into his request, which he duly forwarded to the constituent. They in turn wrote to the CEO of the Health Board who, of course, had exclusive statutory authority to issue such cards. He replied to them in turn and they again wrote to Oliver who forwarded all correspondence to the constituent. Even if the constituent was clearly ineligible in the first instance, he and his family were most impressed by this stream of official responses all in official Oireachtas envelopes.

And in every townland his local man placed the mass card from Oliver J. on the coffins of the dead, all pre-signed in anticipation of that most certain of local events. He fixed up the cost involved with his man every month. If Oliver was in opposition in the Dáil and a problem was clearly insoluble, he had no hesitation in strongly recommending his constituent to go and see Paddy Lawlor or any other Fianna Fáil deputy since 'they now had full power to resolve the issue'. Truly a man of the people!

Oliver J. had no doubt about the insidious role of the 'intellectuals' in the introduction of contraceptives to holy Ireland. In the 1974 Dáil debate on the issue, he said:

> If the journalistic world can rake up any piece of filth or dirt that will disturb the true sincere Christian conscience they seem to flourish in it. All this being sponsored by intellectuals, intellectuals who find themselves in high places unexpectedly and who feel they can push over their false, unchristian, anti Godly and disastrous well-made theology. The whole thing is bad, immoral, evilly-designed, evilly-disposed with intent to corrupt the innocent.

It was no wonder to any of us that he was conferred with the Knighthood of St Gregory the Great by Pope John Paul I in 1978. The most any God-fearing deputy and his wife could hope for in their lifetime was a semi-public audience with the pope and the all-important photograph of the occasion in Rome. This was an extraordinary honour considering the anti-Semitic outburst of Oliver J. in the Dáil in 1943: 'There is one thing that Germany did and that was to rout the Jews out of their country ... where the bees are there is the honey and where the Jews are there is the money.'[43]

Oliver J. was the quintessential conservative in his social attitudes. He was deeply suspicious of the EEC, and stated that he never danced a step in his life, never took a drink and never backed a horse.[44] Throughout his career he was quite outspoken in his adamant views: 'There was no sex in Ireland before television.'[45] But Oliver's sense of public probity did not extend to the issue of political patronage. On the *Late Late Show* in 1968 he stated: 'I am a firm and convinced believer in jobbery... any time I hear of Fianna Fáil ministers being criticised for putting their friends into jobs, I am angered because I am not in the same position to put my friends in jobs.'[46] When Oliver resigned in 1987 he was very pleased that his son, Charles Flanagan, was elected. Charles is in a very different mould to his father. He could be a prospect for the next Fine Gael leader.

*

My last 'meeting' with Dan Spring was at his funeral in Tralee on 8 September 1988 at Hogan's Funeral Parlour, Tralee. Thousands of men and women from all walks of life, from all political affiliations, from the mountains of the Kingdom, queued in silence for many hours to give their farewells and thanks to their Labour deputy and close friend. Among those who paid tribute were fellow workers of Dan's who showed rare courage and independence as mill workers in Tralee and joined the Irish Transport and General Workers' Union. Dan was then only 24 years of age and went on to organise the local authority and bog workers and negotiate major gains in their conditions of employment. He became their Transport Union branch secretary in 1940. In those hectic years Dan's passionate love of Gaelic football blossomed. He captained the Kerry All-Ireland team in 1940 to bring the Sam Maguire Cup home for the first time to the Strand Street Club.

But there was more than the union and football to Dan Spring. He cared deeply about the welfare of the people of Kerry. The need for reformed government programmes for social welfare, local authority housing, health and education services were his campaigns. His politics were a direct and practical application of social democratic principles so often derided by the articulate aristocracy of the left. The people of North Kerry recognised Dan's untiring work at local and national level by returning him to Dáil Éireann for a record 38 successive years. While Dan was also of the strong republican Labour tradition in Kerry, he never raised a hand in violence against his fellowman. He had no time at all for the 'pub republican'. His pride and joy and that of his wife Ann, who was also an outstanding politician at local level, was to give their son Dick to his country as Tanaiste and leader of the Labour Party.

Dan was a maverick, in its most democratic sense, because he had a blunt independence of political approach in his long political career. Ann Spring did not tolerate undue intrusions from strangers in her political role. She was a delegate to the senior citizens' parliament in Luxembourg, a major media event of the European Parliament, in the mid-1980s. A BBC camera crew was harassing her to do an interview about her son the 'Eire Deputy Prime Minister'. In exasperation she consented to tell a story on camera. She spoke about the sheikh who came to London with three sons. One wanted a Boeing 747 so he bought one at the airport. The second wanted a big boat so he bought the *Cutty Sark*. The third son wanted a big white elephant so the sheikh bought him the BBC! And off went Ann in high glee!

*

When I first met him in the South Tipperary constituency during the 1961 general election, I thought Sean Treacy had the potential to be leader of the Labour Party. Other trade unionists of the time, including Jim Larkin Junior, were of the same opinion. Sean was then a prominent officer of the Irish Shoe and Leather Workers' Union, working in a shoe factory in Clonmel. He was a forceful, articulate platform speaker in an era when after-mass meetings were all-important. He had none of the cultivated pompous tone and accent and the magisterial mannerisms which enveloped him in his later years. He was Mayor of Clonmel and there was enormous pride in the town and county that the Irish Labour Party had been formed there in 1909. He was elected as a Labour deputy in each general election from 1961 to 1982.

Coming from a Fianna Fáil background — his grandfather was a Fianna Fáil Councillor — and representing a very traditional republican county, it was no surprise that he clashed with those of us in the Parliamentary Labour Party who were utterly opposed to the embryonic campaign of violence of the IRA in Northern Ireland from 1969 to 1972. Annual conference and parliamentary party confrontations between Conor Cruise O'Brien and Sean Treacy were the order of the day. Brendan Halligan, as general secretary of the party, sought to minimise extreme reaction on Northern Ireland in the parliamentary party, particularly from Sean Treacy, Justin Keating, David Thornley and Steve Coughlan. All of the political parties in the Republic were polarised on the issues of Northern Ireland at that time.

Brendan Corish, quite cleverly, took Justin Keating into the national coalition cabinet in 1973. He also proposed to elevate Sean Treacy to the position of *Ceann Comhairle* and he remained, more or less, elevated ever after. He was again very fortunate when, as an independent deputy in 1987, he was re-elected *Ceann Comhairle*. Most of us in the Labour Party were understandably cynical that Treacy accepted the post of *Ceann Comhairle* during the weekend before the formation of the 1987 government, knowing full well that, in a tied vote for Taoiseach, he would be obliged by precedent to vote for Charles Haughey. When the vote was tied at 82:82, Sean Treacy did just that and gave the country Haughey once again.

Sean Treacy had finally parted company with the Labour Party in 1985 during a Dáil vote over the Health (Family Planning) Bill which I had brought before the Dáil. He made his views known in no uncertain manner on an RTÉ *Today Tonight* interview with Una Claffey. Una knew Sean Treacy quite well from her own days in the Labour Party in the 1970s. Referring to the fact that thousands of young people were using contraceptives, she asked whether 'this indicates that there's a huge demand for contraception in this country'. Sean Treacy replied, 'Well now we're going to have the floodgates opened if this measure passes.'

He went on to assert: 'I cannot be expected to legislate for promiscuity or immorality ... I believe that contraception of the nature implied in this Bill and on such a large scale undermines the sacrament of marriage, certainly undermines family life as we know it in this country, and is by and large injurious to the whole fabric of our society. I do not condone it.'

Una Claffey then asked if he would follow his own religious views or those of people to whom contraception was acceptable on moral grounds. He again replied: 'My natural instincts, my family upbringing, the teaching of my Church, my own strong ingrained feelings in the matter, tell me it is wrong, it is intrinsically wrong, and on a matter of fundamental principle with me I'm opposed to it.'

On the same RTÉ TV programme, I made the point very strongly that: 'It is offensive, it is humiliating, and it is contrary to all concepts of moral order, that I should have to go to a doctor and get an authorisation or a prescription for a packet of condoms, and then hawk that down in a country town to a local chemist. That's what I'm trying to reform and there's nothing licentious, or nothing promiscuous, nothing floodgatery, about that at all.'[47]

But all to no avail. Sean Treacy voted against the Bill and lost the Labour whip. I regret to record that, on balance, he was no great loss.

*

In an interview with Dick Walsh of *The Irish Times* in 1976, Deputy David Thornley said: 'When I get very depressed, I drink too much. When I voted for the Criminal Law (Jurisdiction) Bill I went on a batter for a fortnight.'[48] David had voted for the measure having threatened not to do so. A three-line Labour whip was imposed by the Parliamentary Labour Party, which was in government largely because of the growing threats of the Provos, North and South, to political democracy in the Republic.

In that article, Dick Walsh brilliantly summed up the initial impact of David Thornley on Irish society in the mid-1960s. He wrote:

> David Thornley swam into public vision in the middle of the 1960s when it had seemed to some that revolution might emerge from the barrel of a cathode tube. It was the brightest period of current affairs' programmes on RTÉ, and David Thornley was one of its brilliant interviewers. He had behind him a powerful academic career, as student, lecturer and Associate Professor of History and Political Science at

> Trinity College. He was admired for his incisive style
> as he faced occasionally reluctant politicians and was
> criticised for liberalism, radicalism, socialism even, by
> those who found the thaw uncomfortable.[49]

When David Thornley joined the Labour Party in the run up
to the 1969 general election he was a popular national figure
throughout the country. Stella and I were enthralled by David
on the RTÉ Division and the twice-weekly *Seven Days*
programmes. RTÉ and David were fortunate in that Muiris
MacConghail, who had scrapped the *Hurlers On the Ditch*
programme, proved a brilliant head of these new programmes
from 1966 onwards. However, he should have stayed with RTÉ
and the academic establishment at TCD. His opposition to
Fianna Fáil and his exposé with Professor Basil Chubb on RTÉ
of the likely outcome of the abolition of proportional
representation, as proposed again by Fianna Fáil in 1968, was
decisive. It was a real tragedy that he was unable to apply the
real talents he showed on RTÉ to the real world of politics.

When David was elected to the Dáil he had considerable
difficulty with the Board of TCD agreeing the terms of his leave
of absence as a TD. The board wrote to David in October 1969
as follows: 'The board has considered your request that it
should revise its decision concerning persons on leave of
absence who stand for, and obtain, re-election to the Dáil for a
further session. The Board is not prepared, at this time, to
change its original decision that persons securing re-election
will be considered to have tendered their resignations, the three
months (or other period) being calculated from the date upon
which the individual concerned secures re-election.' I had some
sympathy for David on this issue because UCD seemed much
more supportive of their staff being elected to Irish political
office.

Following Ireland's membership of the EEC in 1972 and the
formation of the National Coalition Government in 1973, Jimmy
Tully and Brendan Halligan offered me one of the Labour seats
in the European Parliament. I turned down the lucrative dual
mandate and it was then offered, against my advice, to David
Thornley. It was the kiss of death to David. His drinking
escapades in Brussels and Strasbourg were dreadful and caused

acute anguish to the Socialist Group in the parliament. But once appointed there was virtually no way his mandate could be revoked by the party. In the debacle, David lost contact with his working class constituency of Dublin North West and his future Dáil prospects were doomed.

In December 1972 he appeared on a platform outside the Mater Hospital demanding the release of Seán MacStiofáin, the Provo leader, who was on a hunger and thirst strike. The Provos were openly contemptuous of his presence. They regarded Dáil deputies as sell-out 'Free Staters'. Meanwhile Johnny Stephens decided that his time had not yet come to die for Ireland and the Provos and David had no new martyr for ould Ireland to shoulder with the flag. Most deputies were aghast at David's behaviour; his benign support of the Provisionals baffled many people. He had inherited a fervent Irish Catholic republicanism from his mother and his aunt in Sandymount who sent him *Sean Treacy and The Third Tipperary Brigade* and Dan Breen's *My Fight for Irish Freedom* when he was nine years of age. Was it any wonder then that David became quite obsessive about the role of Pearse and that in the Dáil he was prepared to support Neil Blaney's motion for the repeal of the Offences Against the State Act?

I was particularly incensed by David Thornley during the 1972 mid-Cork by-election. Senator Eileen Desmond, who had lost her seat in 1969 because we had stupidly put up two candidates, was an outstanding candidate. She was a person of immense integrity and a political rarity in a very male oriented Labour Party. She had entered the by-election campaign with a political halter around her neck, namely, Labour's opposition to Ireland joining the EEC: that opposition had hardly impressed the small dairy farmers of mid-Cork. David proved to be an additional menace during the by-election.

If Labour had any hope of winning, it had to depend on Fine Gael transfers. In effect, there was an unofficial coalition understanding. But David was a national novelty in the election in Cork and bemused the electorate with his increasingly eccentric opinions. At Rylane Church, Co Cork, he advised the voters to decide for themselves whatever way they wished to cast their second preference votes.[50] As he travelled around the

Junior Praesidium, Legion of Mary, 1950.
John (left) and Barry Desmond (centre)

Carrying the Starry Plough at Patton's strike, Monaghan, 1959

On O'Connell Bridge with Stella, during our engagement

Leaving for our honeymoon, 1960

*Three Republicans at Fitzgerald's Park, Cork. President Cearbhall
Ó Dálaigh and my father, Con Desmond, as Lord Mayor of Cork,
unveil the memorial to Michael Collins, 1964*

First day in Dáil Éireann, 1969

*Charles Haughey with Jack and Maureen Lynch following Haughey's
reinstatement to the Fianna Fáil front bench, 1975*

*The Parliamentary Labour Party, 1977, with Frank Cluskey as leader and
Michael O'Leary, deputy leader*

Resisting the tide – victory at the 1977 General Election with (l-r) Paul Doyle, son Ciaran and Michael Duggan

Campaigning with (l-r) Fergus Ingram, Tom Doolan, Niamh Bhreathnach, Dick Spring, Barbara Murphy and Stella in the 1982 General Election

*Labour's candidates in the 1979 European Parliament Election
(clockwise from left): Michael D. Higgins, Jane Dillon-Byrne, Michael O'Leary,
Dr John O'Connell, Liam Kavanagh and Eileen Desmond*

Facing three General Elections 1981-82 (clockwise from left), · with Ciaran, Marcus, Eoin, Stella and Aidan

constituency that morning in his flamboyant green sports car, he accepted a loud speaker from the Aontacht Éireann party who had blared out 'The Men Behind the Wire' to the churchgoers.

Brendan Corish, Brendan Halligan, and councillor Con Moynihan, Eileen's director of elections, were beside themselves as to what to do with David. He had already attended a well-publicised Fianna Fáil function during the campaign at the home of Willie O'Brien, a Fianna Fáil businessman and a fervent Jack Lynch supporter. After the by-election, which Gene Fitzgerald, 40 years of age and with a strong GAA background, won comfortably for Fianna Fáil, I denounced David's behaviour as 'adolescent and irresponsible'. Despite these diversions, Eileen Desmond polled 6,700 votes and established herself as a clear Labour favourite to win back her seat in 1973.

At that time, the SDLP were in some disarray on their Northern Ireland policy. Different noises emanated each day from Gerry Fitt, John Hume, Ivan Cooper, Austin Currie and all. I made the caustic point in an *Irish Times* article that 'the SDLP put their names into a hat each morning and selected 'a leader for the day'. To my chagrin both David Thornley and I were censured at the meeting of the administrative council of the party in September 1972. All members were directed to refrain from attacking colleagues in public. At that meeting Noel Browne was also censured for attacking Brendan Corish in public. Brendan Halligan wrote to me stating that 'I am running around like a madman putting my fingers in the various holes that have appeared in the dykes.' He was referring to the various stroke pulling and publicity coups which were endemic in the party at that time. Brendan had an utterly thankless job as general secretary and performed it with heroic endeavour. And my personality trait of enjoying 'having a cut' at opponents was increasingly known.

David also had a fixation about weapons. One afternoon in 1974 he arrived in the visitors' bar in Leinster House with a large case, which we assumed was a cello, given his great interest in music. He opened it for all to gaze upon. It was a substantial elephant gun! He waved this weapon around to the consternation of deputies and visitors alike. Eventually, Frank Cluskey prevailed on him to hand it over to a former corporal of the army, namely, Jimmy Tully. On another occasion, David arrived at the social evening at the Labour Party conference in Salthill with a loaded weapon in his trousers belt. Dan Spring remarked: 'Jasus, lads, we better do something before we have another by-election on our hands!' With that Dan, who had quite an intimidating presence, marched over to Thornley, congratulated David on his 'protection' and asked if he could examine the weapon. David was flattered and surrendered the gun whereupon Dan fled the scene with it. He threw it straight into Galway Bay! He returned to the gathering and assured David that his gun was in safe hands. David had a good tenor voice and gave us a fine rendition of 'Galway Bay'. Ann Spring reluctantly bought Dan a large Paddy for his heroic deed. We knew how Dan had done the deed because midway through David's song, Dan turned around with his dead-pan half-grin and said, 'The gun goes down over Galway Bay'!

David was 40 and in poor health when he appeared on the Provisional platform in Easter 1976. He lost the Labour whip as a consequence by 22 votes to 3: I was the whip. There are many politicians who should never drink alcohol and David was undoubtedly one of those. The sheer stress of a political career is more than capable of pushing many a politician over the top. In the morning one would meet David in great good humour singing a John McCormack number, the soul of good company. By late evening he would have had a complete change of mood. David died in June 1978. To his credit, Liam Cosgrave visited him in hospital on a regular basis. David's dear wife, Petria, was a charming woman who tried her utmost to save her husband. David left a talented family. Gerry Thornley has inherited David's talents in his writings. What a waste of a brilliant colleague.

*

A classic example of the effect of political office on the man was Dick Burke. We were elected in adjoining constituencies in 1969. He was a very pompous politician. His cultivated gravitas drove me to distraction. I do not know from where he absorbed this image; he certainly did not imbibe it from his time in the Christian Brothers juniorate. Most people I knew from Co Tipperary, and there were some rare accented individuals in the racing and aviation industries, were perplexed by the arrival of this exalted accent. I saw Dick's new personality emerge after he was elected to Dublin County Council from the dignified enclave of Fine Gael Mount Merrion where he lived at that time. After his election to the Dáil he became chief whip for Liam Cosgrave.

Such was his identification with Liam's policies that he was appointed Minister for Education in 1973. In 1975 I became involved in supporting the pioneering efforts of Michael Johnston, Aine and Bill Hyland, Desmond Green, Hilary Pratt, Helen Fahy, Mike Norris, Patricial Lyle, Mary Bean, Noreen O'Brien and others to set up the Dalkey School Project. My interest arose from my time as education officer of ICTU in the 1960s. I was a member of the 1964 national steering committee of the OECD survey of investment in education in Ireland in co-operation with the Department of Education. This was my first contact with Paddy Lynch of UCD and Bill Hyland who had worked in the UN Statistics Office and the Central Statistics Office in Dublin.

Attending these discussions was an education in itself. Paddy Lynch was the inspired director of the survey. Bill Hyland rammed home to the committee the scandal that in 1964 there were no more than 13,153 students at university in the whole of Ireland. Only 14 per cent of those over 18 years of age were in full-time education. In 1974, he was among a group of parents who met in Rosse's Hotel in Dun Laoghaire and founded the Dalkey School Project. I have now been a trustee of the Dalkey School Project for 25 years. When I first spoke at a symposium organised by the project in 1975, I pointed out that under the national coalition government, integrated schools were a most unlikely prospect. I stated: 'Is it any wonder that the youth of Ireland should murder one another from different ends of the same street when they are now educated separately from one another in separate denominational schools in the same locality.'[51]

For the whole of 1975 and 1976, Dick Burke resolutely refused to meet a delegation from the project or to allow his officials to do so. Meanwhile the parents of this mixed area of Co Dublin had but one choice from the minister: denominational education. We saw the proposed national school as a pilot project, which would be child-centred, multi-denominational, co-educational and run by a democratically elected management committee. We were accused of fostering 'a school catering for atheists and humanists'.[52] But I was very pleased when Jack Lynch, as leader of the Opposition, spoke out in favour of such pilot schemes where a majority of parents wished to test such an innovation. He had been strongly advised to do so by David Andrews and Martin O'Donoghue who were very supportive of the project.

Immediately after the 1977 general election Michael Johnston, the unbowed chairman, and Desmond Green, treasurer, met the new Minister for Education, John Wilson. He gave them the go-ahead while warning that he decried triumphalism from all quarters. He proposed an opening date of July 1978. We had our first classes in a house in Vesey Place, Dun Laoghaire. Many years later Aine Hyland became a distinguished Professor of Education at University College, Cork. Thousands of children and their families have benefited from this school since 1978. The 'Council of Social Concern' of Ely House, 8 Ely Place, Dublin 2, which denounced the project, was put in its place. Liam Cosgrave and several of his fellow Fine Gael ministers had hoped that the project would fade away. He was quite wrong. A quarter of a century later, there are 18 multi-denominational schools in the Republic with an enrolment of some 3,000 pupils. I have no doubt that, together with the small number of integrated schools in Northern Ireland, they stand as a testament to the prospect of a far better system of education for the whole of this island.

Dick Burke did not endear himself to the FitzGerald liberal wing of Fine Gael in this process in the 1970s. In 1977 Liam Cosgrave duly rewarded Dick by insisting on his appointment as Ireland's European commissioner. When he returned to contest the general election in 1981 he confidently expected to be appointed Minister for Foreign Affairs. But he was never to see ministerial office again. Jim Dooge was an eminently better choice for this portfolio. As Dick said, in his self-assessment: 'If I may use that expression, it makes me more sad than mad. It was the general expectation that I was to become foreign minister.'[53]

*

In 1965 Dr John Connell cantered home to win the second seat in Dublin South West, the constituency and election I had wisely and voluntarily withdrawn from. Labour had 19.5 per cent of the vote, up from 5 per cent in 1961. Little was he to know that Fianna Fáil would redraw the constituency to take in part of Co Dublin and that he would be landed with a formidable adversary in a sitting Labour deputy, the late Sean Dunne.

The main ingredients of O'Connell's vote-getting success were his extensive medical practice in the constituency; his numerous voluntary and paid constituency clinic workers; his phenomenal personal energy; his ability to join the populist mood on many social issues; and, with his considerable editorial and printing skills, an ability to publish excellent newsletters, election addresses and leaflets. But for all of these attributes he was a political maverick. He possessed an explosive temperament when he was crossed. But this behaviour did not deter the complete loyalty of his local workers and supporters.

In 1969 John O'Connell and Sean Dunne won two seats for Labour in Dublin South West. They polled an astonishing 44.3 per cent of the first preference votes between them. It was the year I was first elected in Dun Laoghaire–Rathdown but I only sat for a few weeks in the Dáil with the two of them. Sean Dunne who was already in very poor health and the campaign proved too much for him. Sean had given up the drink in 1956 after he was declared bankrupt and lost his Dáil seat. He had misappropriated funds of the Federation of Rural Workers for political purposes. To his credit he emigrated to England, worked to pay off his debts, returned, stood for the Dáil in 1961 as an independent and was re-elected. He rejoined the Labour Party for the 1965 general election.

Sean too was quite an individualist, with a devastating turn of wit in the Dáil. In his youth he had been a member of the IRA and was interned by de Valera's government during World War II. He used to regale us with the stories of how he waved the tricolour in the distinguished visitors' gallery in Stormont and was evicted and how he adopted most unusual tactics to recruit farm labourers to the union in the farm of Maynooth College. It seems that the college authorities had the option of negotiating new pay rates or seeing the hay sheds go up in flames!

His untimely death caused mayhem in the Dublin South West constituency. Cora Ryan, Sean's widow, failed to win the Labour nomination. Another perennial maverick, Mattie Merrigan of the Amalgamated Transport and General Workers' Union, was selected. Such was his opposition to the idea of coalition that he indicated to Fine Gael voters that they could stuff their transfers. He lost the by-election.

After the 1973 general election both O'Connell and I were very disappointed that we did not become office holders. Since 1964 I had worked my head off for the party at Dáil and national level. But Liam Cosgrave as Taoiseach did not want another parliamentary secretary (as Ministers of State were then known) in Dun Laoghaire. In any event Frank Cluskey had succumbed to very heavy drinking. He had given Brendan Corish an absolute assurance that if appointed parliamentary secretary he would stop drinking. I could not demur about the plight of a close friend and the heroic support he was receiving from his wife Eileen. To his great credit Frank remained entirely off the booze for the duration of the government right through to the election in mid-1977.

Instead, I became assistant government whip to John Kelly of Fine Gael but O'Connell was left out in the cold. We had all found it extremely difficult to forgive him for his unilateral sponsorship of a meeting in March 1972 between Harold Wilson, Leader of the Opposition in the House of Commons, and the Provisional IRA leaders at his home in Inchicore. Wilson had acted in a completely cynical manner having met the government and the Parliamentary Labour Party that morning in Leinster House and never uttered a word to Corish about the proposed meeting. Corish never forgave Wilson and rarely spoke to him thereafter. O'Connell paid a high price to Brendan Corish for his solo run. It was a time of great tension as the party endeavoured to present a united front on Northern Ireland. Garret FitzGerald was later to describe the duplicity of Wilson as 'an appalling act of treachery to another democratic state'.

In one aspect of his political career John O'Connell was most unfortunate. Most sitting deputies do not have to face by-elections in their constituencies. In my twenty years in Dun Laoghaire–Rathdown I had none. O'Connell had the deaths of Sean Dunne in 1969 and Noel Lemass in 1976. Whereas 1969 was utter bedlam, in 1976 O'Connell set out to prove to the party, to Fianna Fáil and to all and sundry that he could transfer his full vote to any candidate of his choice. To the utter astonishment of all, he chose Senator Brendan Halligan, the general secretary of the party. Halligan himself was taken aback. However, he saw at last the prize of a Dáil seat at 39 years of age.

He had been political director and general secretary of the Labour Party since 1967. He was no stranger to Dublin South West having been born in Rialto, attended James Street Christian Brothers Schools and the College of Technology in Kevin Street. He first worked in CIE, Inchicore, before working as an economist with the Sugar Company. At the party selection convention he gave a solemn assurance that, if elected, he would continue to serve his constituents in Dublin South West. He was later to deeply regret this public promise when he realised that O'Connell intended to gobble up all Labour votes again in the general election in 1977.

Brendan was an outstanding candidate. He was an impressive exponent of party policy and a brilliant campaigner. Johnny O'Connell put the Labour cream on the campaign when he issued a letter to every elector in Dublin South West indicating that he had 'personally proposed his friend and colleague, Senator Brendan Halligan'. John had Brendan as his surrogate candidate and Halligan duly romped home. John O'Connell had proved himself once again. However, Brendan's promise to remain in Dublin South West was to haunt him again and again when he ditched South West and sought to run north of the Liffey, away from John O'Connell. It was described at the time by Bruce Arnold in the *Irish Independent* as 'Halligan's political suicide note'.[54] He failed to be elected in Finglas. He was an excellent deputy with real leadership potential. But he seriously underestimated O'Connell and when he jumped constituencies he earned the fatal carpetbagger tag.

John O'Connell's next major clash with a member of the party's 'elite' was in the European parliament elections in June 1979. Michael O'Leary and he both stood and ran two quite separate, hostile, brilliant and bitter campaigns. It was ironic that neither deputy had a passionate preoccupation about European affairs up to that point in their careers, although Michael O'Leary did favour Ireland's entry to the EEC. John O'Connell also had a total aversion to flying anywhere in any aircraft. But they both won two of the four Euro seats in Dublin. Within two years they had both resigned these seats.

The decline of the population in Dublin inner city constituencies and the redrawing again of Dublin South Central and Dublin South West posed new problems and new friction in the 1981 general election, this time between John O'Connell and Frank Cluskey, the party leader. We tried desperately to persuade O'Connell to move to Dublin West but he would have none of it. He ran as an independent and the leader of the party was defeated. John O'Connell was duly deemed to have 'self expelled' himself from the party. Thus, by this unique turn of events, Michael O'Leary became party leader and Tanaiste in the new government. But not before Johnny did one more twist.

Jimmy Tully, Labour's deputy leader, offered Doctor John the position of *Ceann Comhairle* for the new government in June 1981. By then, however, O'Connell was assiduously courting Charles Haughey whose home in Kinsealy he had visited on a number of occasions after the election. I suspected that he was hoping that Charlie might deliver his lifelong ambition, namely, to receive his seal of office at Aras an Uachtarain as Minister for Health. But Charlie had not lost all of his marbles; he knew that he could not deliver the doctor's ambitions. O'Connell's apologia for his intended ditching of Haughey in favour of Tully was to place an extraordinary advertisement in the evening newspapers, the *Evening Press* and the *Evening Herald*, on 23 June 1981. It was quite exceptional in the history of Western European parliamentary democracies. It read as follows:

> Since you are the people who have placed your confidence in me as your representative in Dáil Éireann, I would like your guidance as to what action I should take on that day. It would be greatly appreciated if you could indicate your wishes by completing the slip below and returning it to me at any of the thirteen addresses listed.

Dr John then asked each elector to indicate as follows:

I would like you on my behalf to: -

(1) Vote for a F.F Government   ☐
(2) Vote for a F.G. Government   ☐
(3) Vote for a F.G./Labour Coalition ☐
(4) Vote for a F.F./Labour Coalition ☐
(5) Abstain from voting   ☐

The Dáil met five days later and O'Connell, having wrestled with his conscience and his constituents over the period, informed the Haughey camp that they wanted a change of government. I do not recall the detailed result of this historic survey being announced. I do recall trying to explain to Stella why I had voted, after all these strange adventures, for John O'Connell as *Ceann Comhairle*. She noted sarcastically that we were now both members of the Council of State and that we finally deserved one another. We looked forward in trepidation to being in government with O'Connell in the chair. But O'Connell's admiration for Charles Haughey and his support for Haughey's ultra nationalism were not strong enough to dispel the honour and perks of office. As *Ceann Comhairle* he would teach us all how to respect his office.

During the period of office of the 1982-1987 coalition government the vituperative attacks by O'Connell on the Labour Party and on myself as Minister of Health were a daily occurrence. In 1979 he had written in his pamphlet *The Labour Party — 20 Questions* that Labour was the social conscience of Irish politics and that: 'Labour is the only political party in Dáil Éireann which is committed to a free comprehensive health service, and a free comprehensive family planning service should be a right to all women.'

I was shocked by O'Connell's utter cynicism in the Dáil vote on my Health (Family Planning) Bill. Dick Walsh, the brilliant political columnist with *The Irish Times*, was scathing in his criticism of Doctor John: 'Dr John O'Connell's run for the cover of the Fianna Fáil whip this week would have done justice to an Olympic sprinter. Never mind that he had derided the Act being amended. All converts — to Fianna Fáil and the anti-contraceptive lobby — were welcome.'[55] After the vote the editor of the same newspaper quoted O'Connell in 1974 on the then Contraception Bill: 'We are hypocrites if we start talking about denial of rights in Northern Ireland when we refuse to grant the right of people here to practise contraception if they wish... I do not think we should discriminate between single and married people. It is a matter for their own conscience. It is their own decision.'[56]

When O'Connell subsequently decided to join Fianna Fáil in 1985, Frank Cluskey saw an opportunity in the 1987 general election to even up old scores. In Dublin South Central, Fianna Fáil selected Ben Briscoe, Mary Mooney and John O'Connell. O'Connell was attempting an extraordinary three-card trick; being elected in virtually the same constituency under three different labels: Labour, Independent and Fianna Fáil. But he had not contested an election since 1981 having been elected *Ceann Comhairle* on two occasions and was at a considerable disadvantage. John finally met his match in Mary Mooney, an 'Alderman' from the Liberties who had a formidable personal machine. Frank Cluskey won back his seat and John O'Connell lost his by a mere 354 votes to Mary Mooney.

O'Connell was re-elected to the Dáil in 1989 but, to his intense disappointment, was not allocated any post in government. But he was Minister for Health from February 1992 to the end of that year. Within six months of obtaining his life's ambition from Albert Reynolds, who apparently was deeply impressed by O'Connell's pleadings for the health portfolio and appointed him in a reshuffle, he was in some difficulty. Padraig Yeates wrote in *The Irish Times*:

> His support for a medical ombudsman last May was headline grabbing but has yet to be acted upon, as has his proposal in March to introduce identification cards to combat under age-drinking. His energy and commitment are obviously undiminished by the years and he is still the maverick he was then. Whether he can radically change the system or be merely a bull in a china shop remains to be seen.[57]

A minister for a mere ten months, John O'Connell was in office for far too short a period to make a major impact. I am hardly in a position to provide an objective assessment. However, I do know that some senior officials in the department were profoundly relieved when the general election was called in November 1992. Both Fianna Fáil and Fine Gael experienced electoral disaster. In the aftermath, Dick Spring insisted that John O'Connell be excluded from any position in the Fianna Fáil–Labour government. Albert Reynolds did not need much convincing on that issue at that stage. As John Boland used to remark: 'The mills of God grind slowly but, by Jasus, in Dáil Éireann they grind exceedingly small!'

John O'Connell was a Dáil deputy during a period when there was no financial limit on election expenditure by any candidate or any party. For some, the sky was the limit. And there was no disclosure by any individual elector of his or her contributions to candidates or to political parties. John O'Connell was apparently quite wealthy. He set up the *Irish Medical Times* in 1965 and by all accounts it was quite profitable. He was undoubtedly a tireless and excellent editor. Nine years later he sold an interest in the paper to Haymarket, owned by Michael Heseltine, the former Conservative Minister for Defence. It seems that in turn it was sold to the Smurfit Group but O'Connell remained as editor. He also owned MIMS, a comprehensive monthly listing of drugs. All in all, John

O'Connell had the financial resources to finance a political career.

In February 1993 Dr O'Connell announced his resignation from the Dáil on medical grounds. He was, according to John Horgan, 'a highly competitive loner ... his manner has been nothing if not volatile ... he comes across as a deeply disappointed man'. He was the quintessential maverick who, in his own words in his biography *Doctor John* in 1988,[58] was someone who suffers from 'chronic ingrown political naïvety'. He was a rebuffed Fianna Fáil aspirant in the local elections in 1960; Labour party member in 1963 and deputy until 1981; Independent TD until 1985; coalition *Ceann Comhairle* in 1981 and Fianna Fáil *Ceann Comhairle* in 1982; Fianna Fáil deputy from 1985 to 1987; then one of the 'Taoiseach's Eleven' in the Seanad; and then back as a Fianna Fáil deputy and a mercurial Minister for Health. This political chameleon has been all over the place.

O'Connell should have stuck to his first profession, medicine, and should have avoided the transient populism of politics. He had an outstanding local reputation as an excellent general practitioner and he was generous and unstinting in his time with his patients. Many members of the Houses of the Oireachtas had good reason to thank him for his medical advice and consultations. Had he stuck to medicine he could have emulated that other great local doctor, Paddy Leahy (1917-1998) of Ballyfermot, who was a radical social agitator and a reformer on major issues such as contraception and abortion.

Finally, it would be entirely unbalanced to record the Dublin South West constituency politics as a mere interplay between various political chieftains. There were a hard core of dedicated Labour Party activists there whose sole concern at all times was the advancement of Labour representation at local and national level. All tribute must be paid to members such as Paddy O'Mahony, Charlie Gunning, Mrs McPartlin, May and Dan Geraghty, George Butler, Tom Lennon, Des Geraghty, Una Claffey and Myles O'Brien to mention a few. Without their dedication there would have been no Labour Party in the constituency and no disputation at all about any Dáil seats.

Ten

Limerick — You Were No Lady!

'After the government fell Brian Lenihan came to Limerick, to Michael Herbert's bar in Lisnagry, to offer me the job if I supported them, but I told him I had no interest in it. I hadn't come to the Dáil to just be Speaker!'

Jim Kemmy

The Labour Party has been described frequently, with some truth, as a convenient umbrella for local political independents. Deputy Steve Coughlan personified parochial representation to an extraordinary degree. All politics are, of course, local and without local preoccupations no deputy will be elected. But there must be a balance between local considerations and national obligations. Steve had little real interest in the latter. He moved from party to party and was a republican and IRA sympathiser in the 1930s. He was a Clann na Poblachta Mayor of Limerick in 1951. He only lost on the last count by 29 votes to the Labour Minister Mick Keyes in the 1954 general election. And then he switched to Labour and won a Dáil seat in the 1961 general election. He had worked hard to build up his publican and bookmaker businesses. These are extremely difficult to run at a profit if one is an active local politician and Steve was no exception.

My first real clash with Steve came in the run-up to the 1969 general election. The party decided to run three candidates in East Limerick and as an officer of the organisation committee, I was never forgiven by Steve. Mick Lipper and Tony Pratschke were selected as the other two candidates. Des O'Malley had been elected in a by-election in 1968 following the sudden death of his uncle Donogh O'Malley, Minister for Education. Mick Lipper had come within 900 votes of defeating O'Malley for the seat and as a consequence was much feared by Coughlan. But he retained his seat with the strong backing of the *Limerick Leader*. Tony Pratschke polled 366 votes. I met Coughlan in the Dáil bar afterwards and he greeted me with: 'Well, bollocks Desmond, are you happy now with your leap year candidate?'

My next clash with Steve came shortly afterwards with the visit of the South African rugby team to Ireland. I was a founder member, the first secretary, and then a committee member of the Irish Anti-Apartheid Movement. Louise and Kadar Asmal were the architects of the organisation. We mounted an historic march to Lansdowne Road in opposition to the Ireland–South Africa match. I went to Limerick and at a press conference urged that the Limerick city council should not give a civic reception to the racially selected team and the pro-apartheid South African Rugby Board. Steve Coughlan was irate. 'What a dammed cheek for this jumped up overnight politician to come to Limerick to tell us how to act!' he said. 'I want to warn these extremist offbeats that Limerick holds no future for them. Let them pack their bag and baggage before they are crushed without mercy!'

I was warned by many people not to put my face anywhere near Limerick again. I was assured that I would receive a Garryowen boot 'up the transom'. Brendan Corish, who was very supportive of the Anti-Apartheid Movement, implored me not to become embroiled in another Coughlan fracas. I stayed away and the demonstration was peaceful enough. The popularity of rugby in Limerick and the reporting of the *Limerick Leader* ensured a pro-Springbok occasion. A new group, 'the National Movement', organised opposition to the 'dictation of Dublin'. They marched in favour of the Springboks with banners such as 'God Bless Christian Anti-Communist South Africa'. When they clashed with anti-apartheid protestors, the *Limerick Leader* said they had been attacked by Maoists. On the day of the match, the *Limerick Leader* ran the headline: 'Why I like Limerick, by the Rev. Dawie De Villiers'. A day earlier it had banner headlines reading: 'Welcome Boks' while inside it carried an editorial saying that the anti-apartheid slogan in Dublin was 'stifle the Press'. When the rugby team left, the paper again had a banner-size heading reading: 'The Strong Silent Types Fly Out'. This story included a quote from De Villiers which read: 'I hope Limerick is more typical of Ireland than Dublin.'

But we were very successful in a campaign that is still well remembered by anti-apartheid activists. The Dublin part of the tour went ahead under great public protest. The IRFU were a spineless lot of alickadoos. The President, the Taoiseach and all ministers boycotted the Dublin match. The Belfast match was cancelled under the Public Order Act. Limerick lived up to its reputation.

Steve Coughlan's favourite political ploy was to flush the reds and the Maoists from under the bed and out of Limerick city by any and every means. To these groups he was quite willing to add Jim Kemmy and itinerants. At the city council in 1964 he described itinerants as 'a plague, far worse then the locusts of long ago'! Jim Kenny had become his arch tormentor around 1966 and faced down Steve at local level in the Labour Party. But Steve still had the red revolutionary youth in his sights!

In January 1970 the *Limerick Leader* took up the crusade: 'We say that the Irish Revolutionary Youth Movement must be crushed in Limerick and they must be run out of this city without delay. We call on everyone and particularly the clergy and the trade unions of Limerick to rise up and unite to crush the menace that is threatening the youth of this city today.' Coughlan was not slow to follow. He said a day later: 'As Mayor of Limerick I wish to alert the citizens to the dangers of the insidious propaganda being distributed by left wing agents of a foreign power. The *Limerick Leader* has already drawn attention in forceful terms to this grave situation and I add my voice to theirs and issue a solemn warning while there is still time.'

But it was the use of emotional language laced by local prejudice and a few jars which landed Steve in the local and national headlines time and time again. His bark was far worse than his bite and at times he seemed to enjoy his notoriety as when he lauded the various Irish dairy products produced in Limerick. He addressed the National Dairy Council thus: 'Some of us are inclined to take this liquid product for granted, but if we are to lay the foundation for a future generation, and avoid being decadent, we must look to the fundamentals, and give milk our first consideration. In my home which comprises my wife, two boys and a girl and myself we drink 10 pints of milk a day and we eat 3 lbs. of cheese a week. The cow is truly our second mother.'

Eventually, and not before its time, the Labour Party and the Limerick electorate tired of Steve Coughlan. In the 1977 general election he received 3,553 votes and lost his seat to Mick Lipper, a Labour Alderman, an unassuming CIE train driver and a famed Limerick and League of Ireland centre forward who was elected as an Independent. 'Dobber' Lipper was gladly accepted into the Parliamentary Labour Party. Steve Coughlan's tempestuous innings as a Labour deputy over 16 years had come to an end.

*

My political relationship with Limerick evolved in many ways around the turbulent careers of Steve Coughlan and Jim Kemmy. Jim and I were born within a year of one another in two Munster cities, had an intense trade union background, and learned our love of books in the public libraries and in our early emigration to London. We both opposed anti-Semitism, apartheid, sexism and clerical domination of social issues. Unlike Jim I was fortunate in that my father did not die of tuberculosis when I was a teenager. And I did not have to face the vicissitudes of politics in the East Limerick constituency.

Jim Kemmy joined the Labour Party in Limerick in 1963 and was elected to the administrative council of the party in 1968. He served on it for three years and was a supporter of the 'New Republic' line ('the seventies will be socialist') in the party before the 1969 election. He resigned from the Labour Party in 1972 over coalition and established his own socialist organisation in Limerick city. He founded a small newspaper, *The Limerick Socialist*, and he also became editor of *The Old Limerick Journal*. During the 1970s he supported the 'Two

Nations' theory, advocating that Protestants in Northern Ireland have the right to self-determination. He was elected to Limerick Corporation in 1974 and again in 1979 and topped the poll in his area.

He won a Dáil seat in 1981 and continued to build a solid local base. Fianna Fáil thought they had a soft touch in Kemmy and Charles Haughey tried do a Gregory-style deal with Jim or parachute him out of the way into the *Ceann Comhairle*'s chair. Neither strategy worked, as Jim recalled: 'I wasn't trying to do a Gregory-type deal. I could have done that very easily'. He comfortably retained his seat in the February 1982 election. He then formed the Democratic Socialist Party. In the November 1982 election Labour fought back and took a constituency seat. However, Kemmy was re-elected to the Dáil in 1987 and in the 1989 general election he was elected on the first count, exceeding the quota by 1,500 votes.

During the course of the controversial abortion referenda in the early 1980s, Jim Kemmy was a particular target of the pro-life cohorts in Limerick. Jim had pointed out the inherent contradictions in the proposed amendments to the Constitution and for these he was branded, as was Dick Spring in Kerry, a pro-abortionist. He recalled: 'It was difficult and disheartening and disconcerting, right enough. The *Limerick Leader* ran a campaign against me, called me an abortionist on the front page, wrote about me in an editorial called "The Stench of Death". In convents and schools they told children I was killing babies. I remember one child pointed me out to his mother and said, "Is that the man who kills babies, Mam?".' Jim was responsible for setting up the Limerick Family Planning Association and played a leading part in the success of the clinic. This clinic could not recruit a local doctor; one had to commute from Dublin.

Kemmy was intensely proud of his Limerick origins. The city was never a particular favourite of mine or Stella's but Jim held that there had been great changes, all to the good, to his beloved city. He lavished praise on it: 'The average citizen in Limerick is cosmopolitan and open towards rugby. It is a cultured city. Limerick is teeming with artists and art exhibitions. It is a music-loving city. The influence of the garrison is always there. The garrison reed band is there, and the pipe and drum band. Even the name Young Munster derives from the Munster Fusiliers.'

*

In 1974 Jim Kemmy, then a local Alderman, refused to attend the consecration ceremony of Bishop Jeremiah Newman, holding the view that the money would be far better spent on relieving local poverty. At that stage in his career Newman had made pronouncements which on social and economic issues were a strange mixture of *Rerum Novarum* sociology, the Catholic principle of subsidiarity and the evils of socialism. Jim Kemmy was unimpressed. (I found myself in a similar situation in 1984 when I did not attend the consecration of Bishop Kevin McNamara in Dublin's Pro Cathedral. McNamara had, from Saint Brendan's pulpit in Killarney, publicly admonished me about divorce and contraception while I was present, as Minister for Health, at a mass for the deceased members of the Irish Medical Organisation after their annual conference dinner. I did not walk out of the church, as I was sorely tempted to do, because Stella and the Secretary of the Department, Liam Flanagan, were with me in the church and I did not wish to embroil them in a scene. The IMO delegates were embarrassed and Liam Flanagan's views on Kevin McNamara were unprintable. I could, therefore, well understand the stance of Jim Kemmy in Limerick.) However, when Bishop Jeremiah Newman of Limerick died in April 1995, Jim Kemmy said that he had grown to have 'affection and personal regard' for him.

In many ways this tribute epitomised Kemmy's political life in Limerick. Jim fought cancer and Bishop Newman fought alcoholism. In his tribute to Bishop Newman, Jim Kemmy wrote:

> One of my most vivid memories is of Easter Saturday 1985, when he phoned me out of the blue and invited me to come and see him, right away, at his home. It was a cry from his lonely heart, immediately after the passage of Barry Desmond's Family Planning Bill, in spite of Dr Newman's loud and severe strictures. He

was badly shaken, both physically and mentally, and deeply depressed by the enactment of the bill. It was a scene worthy of Graham Greene or Franz Kafka. He was at his most vulnerable. He feared that Europe would be overrun by hordes of Turks, Russians and Algerians, as a result of family planning in the more developed European countries. I tried to convince him that people have a natural vitality and gaiety and that they would continue to procreate long after both of us were dead and forgotten.[59]

Jim was referring to Bishop Newman's interview with Olivia O'Leary in 1985 in *Magill* magazine. The bishop was in no doubt about the impact of contraception on the population of Europe. 'In a hundred years, the average number of children born to German women had fallen from 3.5 to 1.25,' he said. 'There will be nobody in Europe shortly.' The immigrant workers from Morocco and Algeria were breeding faster than Europeans, he argued. But why should that matter, she asked. He warmed to his theme. 'Charles Martel stopped the Moors from coming beyond Tours. Don John of Austria stopped the Turks,' he declared with a flourish. But why should it matter that immigrant workers had a higher birth rate than Europeans, she asked. 'If you want a Europe that is made up of Turks and Algerians, fine. But it's worse than that. We could be overrun by the Russians,' warned the bishop.[60]

Kemmy never bore any enmity towards Newman despite the bishop's successful effort in 1977 to prevent his election to Dáil Éireann. At that time Steve Coughlan was generally perceived in Limerick to be on the way out and Kemmy, the independent socialist candidate, had developed a solid basis of support in the city and particularly in Garryowen. The election in the East Limerick constituency was one of the hardest fought in the field and almost all shades of Irish political opinion were represented. Apart from the overwhelming swing to Fianna Fáil, the election in Limerick was remarkable for one other factor, the last-minute intervention of Mick Lipper on a 'Democratic Labour' ticket. Lipper's intervention was decisive in preventing Jim Kemmy from winning a seat or from going very close to it. Lipper played his trump card: the *Irish Press* announced in a lead story that Dr Newman, Bishop of Limerick, had come out in favour of the 'victimised' candidate and had signed a petition, part of which stated: 'We make this request because he is the only Labour representative we would vote for.'

Newman's support, far from being a spontaneous, hasty decision, was part of a carefully arranged plan to prevent Jim Kemmy from being elected. Lipper was able to convince the bishop that if Kemmy was given a clear field, especially in the working-class Garryowen and Southill areas, he would be elected or else would poll a large vote. Lipper told the bishop that he was the only candidate capable of beating Kemmy in Garryowen and Southill. Newman had no hesitation in bringing the political influence of the Church behind Lipper. In the week before polling day this influence came to the fore. Priests preached sermons about the duty of the people to vote for Christian candidates. The word was passed down from high places to clergy, teachers and policemen to give their votes to 'the bishop's man'. And there was a particular concentration of priests and nuns in Garryowen and Southill. Kemmy and Lipper were largely competing for the same vote.

In the event Lipper won out, and it was no surprise to learn that of his 5,224 first preference votes, 71 per cent (or 3,656 votes) of his second preferences went to Kemmy. So, it is clear that had Lipper not stood and had these second preference votes been translated to Kemmy's vote, the seat would have been won by Kemmy.

Kemmy had resigned from the Labour Party in 1972 largely on the question of coalition. His personal manifesto in that election was quite radical. He advocated the right of the Northern Protestant people to opt for the state of their own choosing, and the democratic rights of Catholics and the complete separation of Church and State; full family planning facilities as a basic human and civil right; and the democratic control and management of schools and colleges. During the crisis period of Northern Ireland politics between 1969 and 1972, Kemmy participated intensely in the internal party debates.

It was surprising to many that a Limerick party activist so steeped in the traditional politics of that city should emerge with a quite radical analysis of the conflict in Northern Ireland. Stephen Collins, in his obituary of Jim Kemmy, recorded that: 'He adopted a very hostile stance to extreme nationalism and was a strong supporter of the two-nation theory in the 1970s, the basis of which was that Northern Ireland was entitled to remain part of Britain for as long as a majority of the people living there wanted. This involved Kemmy in a campaign for the repeal of Articles 2 and 3 of the Constitution. The fact that he could carve out a political base for himself in Limerick by expressing such unorthodox views was an indication of his great courage and perseverance.'[61]

When Jim was interviewed by James Downey in 1981, he explained the development of his approach:

> About 1972 my attitude to Northern Ireland changed. It was a painful, difficult transition for me from the traditional nationalist line. I felt it was impossible to coerce the Unionists and saw the futility of using guns and bombs, which would only lead to sectarian civil war. While there had been discrimination against Catholics, I felt that the civil rights movement had been perverted and distorted into another attempt to coerce the Protestants into a united Ireland. Articles 2 and 3 of the Constitution are a barrier to genuine dialogue. We must have unity of the people in the North through friendship and good neighbourliness. It's futile to tell the Catholics that so-called liberation is around the corner. Bigotry is two-sided. We don't see the bigotry in our hearts.[62]

But perhaps the most emphatic enunciation by Jim Kemmy of the situation in Northern Ireland came at the national conference of the Labour Party in Waterford in 1993 when, as chairperson of the party, he said:

> The bombing in Warrington, which so cruelly robbed two young boys of their lives, triggered an emotional reaction from the Irish people who have one message for the terrorists; 'You have no mandate from the

Irish people; we want you to stop this carnage'. This conflict should be seen for what it is; it is a brutal, sectarian war being waged by callous, vicious men. It has nothing whatsoever to do with social justice or human liberation. The reality, whether we in the South like it or not, is that the Northern unionist population value their British citizenship. They do not wish to be liberated by anybody but especially not by the IRA who claim that they are trying to liberate them from the clutches of British imperialism while at the same time they are murdering and maiming them.

Despite his resignation from the administrative council of the Labour Party in 1970, most Labour activists always had a high admiration for the bruising battles he fought to the very end. Like many others, I was delighted when he rejoined the party in 1990. Dick Spring handled the negotiations with the Democratic Socialist Party with great sensitivity. Kemmy and Spring always favoured the political unity of the left and almost a decade before the merger of the Labour Party and Democratic Left, Jim Kemmy had this to say about his experience: 'We also learned a lesson from the DSP: that there is no room for a third political party on the left in Ireland. Also, I wanted to demonstrate to the Workers' Party that this is how it should be done. The more the Workers' Party discards the Eastern European model of democratic centralism, and the more it goes down the democratic socialist road, the more like the Labour Party it will have to become.'

When Jim Kemmy finally succumbed to cancer at 61 years, just three months after his re-election in 1997, Ray Kavanagh, general secretary of the Labour Party, paid a particularly appropriate tribute to our colleague. He wrote: 'At a time when politics is a profession under scrutiny and suspicion because of recent and current investigations about money for politicians, we are jolted in our indifference or in our cynicism when confronted with the early death of a man whose entire life was service to his people, his city and his country. Far from being on the receiving end of political contributions, this big-hearted man could never refuse an entreaty, even from the most chronic and recidivist of down and outs. "Christmas," he said to me, "is a very expensive time; there are still many poor people in Limerick".'[63]

For a person who could write and edit journals with such clarity, Jim Kemmy's speeches and radio/television interviews were often quite difficult to comprehend. In his tribute to Jim, Alan Murdoch wrote: 'Personal qualities of warmth and integrity, and pronouncements, on national radio or in the warmth of a small bar, couched in a deep rumbling Limerick dialect so thick it could sound like provincial French, attracted fierce loyalty.' Alan Murdoch also recalled the hilarious episode in the Dáil between Jim Kemmy and Deputy Willie O'Dea of Fianna Fáil: 'His principled judgements on the less virtuous national figures such as the former Taoiseach Charles Haughey carried a Moses-like gravity. Fellow Limerick TDs such as Fianna Fáil's diminutive Willie O'Dea would wince when Kemmy spotted that their local rebellions against party whips softened by the time they reached the seat of power. 'It's no use being Mighty Mouse in the constituency and then just a church mouse in the Dáil' he quipped.'

That great doyen of Irish political journalism, Dick Walsh, political editor of *The Irish Times*, aptly summed up the role of Jim Kemmy. He wrote, as a radical neighbour from Clare, following the passing of Kemmy: 'There are times when you listen to tributes to people you've known, especially those in public life, with more than a growing sense of disbelief. Was this, you wonder, the person you'd known? I listened yesterday to the tributes to Jim Kemmy, from friends like Frank McCourt and colleagues like Dick Spring, from those who'd opposed him, like Bertie Ahern, or campaigned against him like Des O'Malley and Michael Noonan; and the sense of recognition grew. Here was someone of impressive size and depth, a man who enjoyed humanity so much and was so honest in his convictions — about literature, history and culture, as well as politics — that you couldn't fail to share his pleasure.'[64]

But the last words went to Dick Spring, who also shared a common passion with Jim — rugby in Limerick. He said of Kemmy: 'A giant of a man in every way, a passionate advocate, a determined representative, a thinker and a doer, he was one of the most remarkable politicians of his generation. Above all, he was a remarkable man whose warmth, generosity of spirit and courage were never more manifest than in his final illness.'

Steve Coughlan, Ted Russell, Jim Kemmy and Donogh O'Malley, assuming that they are all together, are no doubt still slugging it out in the celestial Chamber!

Eleven

The Loss of Innocence

'I'm taking no Peugeot. I want a car with the star!'

Quote attributed to Padraig Flynn
when he first became a Minister

When I was appointed Minister for Health in 1982 I was
ensconced in a state car and I went to the Custom House.
Dermot Condon, the Secretary of the Department, jokingly
informed me, 'Minister, the bells did not precede your arrival.' I
thought he had a quirky sense of Cork humour until I realised
that he was referring to one of my predecessors, Seán
MacEntee, from 1957 to 1965. Apparently when MacEntee
arrived at the Custom House each morning the usher at the foot
of the stairs rang a loud bell. The minister then proceeded up
the stairs and down the corridor to his office. Each assistant
secretary and principal officer stood at the door of his office.
(There were no women!) Fianna Fáil in government certainly
knew how to keep the civil service in their place.

In my time I came across somewhat similar behaviour. One
minister made it known to colleagues that their fellow socialist
would prefer to be addressed as 'Minister' even in private. Such
are the temptations of government when the big job goes to the
head of the newly inflated appointee. I repeatedly saw one
minister, well known for his political self-righteousness,
ostentatiously wait at the door of his department, empty
handed, until the usher inside came to hold the door open for
his volatile presence to enter.

169

Between 1969 and 1989 I spent ten years on the government benches and ten in opposition. Opposition is a frustrating and occasionally very productive period. As a lowly minister of state in the Department of Finance and as a double portfolio holder in Health and Social Welfare I had a fascinating five years in these offices. Ministerial office changes most opposition deputies in depth. As soon as the Dáil ushers call one 'Minister' and the post office technicians arrive at one's home to install the scrambled and ex-directory telephone line, the world begins to change. One warns the teenage sons not to use that phone to call their friends. Two garda drivers from the garda depot in the Phoenix Park are appointed, chosen by the minister. I contacted two gardaí at the depot, Tony Boyce from Carrigart, Co Donegal and Aidan Breslin from Clonee, Co Meath. That was in 1981 and we have remained firm friends ever since.

I came to know Tony Boyce in rather strange circumstances. One evening, while driving on the Bray Road in my clapped out Volkswagen, the car caught fire. It had just been serviced. The metal straps on the battery under the rear seat had been crossed over in error. By pure mercy a state car was passing at the time. The garda driver stopped and dashed over with a fire extinguisher just as I was about to put my late father's crombie coat on the fire. After he lost his seat, Frank Cluskey recommended his garda driver to me and, to my surprise, it turned out to be the same person — Tony Boyce.

The daily arrival of an armed garda driver at our home transformed our household movements. The fact that they were armed fascinated our sons who had never seen a loaded weapon until then. This is but one aspect of the transformation that overcomes the opposition politician when he or she becomes an office holder: he becomes a new political personality. As such he can easily 'lose the run of himself'. Irrespective of his status he must always be available for constituents. Charlie McCreevy tells the story of a local supporter calling to his house on Christmas morning. 'I thought I would get you in! Will you ever fill in the form for me.' Charlie duly did the needful but pointed out that the form needed to be certified by a doctor. He pointed out that his constituent should go nearby to the GP's residence 'to finish the job'. 'Ah Charlie, I could never do that, it's Christmas morning!' exclaimed the beloved voter. Such is the reality of a minister's life.

The minister inherits spacious offices with direct lines to fellow ministers and the Taoiseach. He has a bevy of advisers and a private secretary, usually a higher executive officer, who often has had experience of other portfolio holders. He also has a well-staffed constituency office. His departmental secretary, assistant secretaries and principal officers ensure that the minister understands all sides of every question. They profess, of course, to be entirely non-political; however, political eunuchs are a rare species in the civil service. He discovers within weeks that delegations to his office bring one common plea: more money for their urgent needs. No matter how impressed the minister may be by their special supplications he will be sharply reminded by his secretary general that 'there is no provision, Minister, in this year's estimate'. And so another batch of letters of regret with the minister's signature wing their way to the special interest groups. The gloss quickly wears off his promises as the Department of Finance battles to control his ambitions.

Then he learns that only government decisions are circulated after cabinet meetings. Effusive protests are unrecorded. He either accepts collective decisions or resigns. Which minister ever did so in year one? Within a month or two a personality change often occurs in the minister. His voice loses some of its opposition stridency. He is no longer querulously negative and reactive. He practices, in the privacy of his office, the reading of turgid civil service scripts. He will probably attend a private media grooming on television interviews and presentations. He begins to suffer from that in-built failing of every successful politician — a growing belief in his own infallibility. He orders his first hand-tailored suit and dinner gear. His spouse persuades him to discard the cheaper shirts and invest in a dozen sober ties. He acquires a front bench manner suggesting a tolerance to contend patiently with opposition spokespersons. And he steers clear of irritating backbenchers. He sprinkles his Dáil contributions with the most recent departmental briefs. And if he is indecisive he begins to suffer from policy paralysis.

His civil servants repeatedly point to all the problems they would face if they were to implement his long-cherished pet projects. He recalls that in opposition he assailed the government of the day but must now go along with the Department of Finance pressure for a standstill in his estimate. He feels like Austin Currie who vehemently supported the rent and rates strike against internment and then had to accept, as Minister for Housing in the Northern Ireland executive, that cash deductions could be taken from the social security benefits of protesters. Once you take the Queen's shilling — in this case, the Taoiseach's telephone call and the President's seal of office — you follow the cabinet drum. The ideology of his party's policy documents are politely ignored by senior civil servants. If he is really exceptional he will shine and cast off the grinding frustrations of being a 'hurler on the ditch' opposition spokesperson. As Liam Cosgrave said in a rare interview with Ursula Halligan, being a minister in government is 'the real thing'!

When I received my seal of office in the Aras from the President, it was promptly taken from me by his secretary, and we proceeded to do as did the government of 1948. Our first meeting was held in the impressive Council of State meeting room in the Aras. Unlike that 1948 government, however, we did not send a telegram to the Vatican conveying our intention 'to repose at the feet of Your Holiness' and assure him of our filial loyalty as our first decision. Somehow or another I could never imagine Garret FitzGerald and Dick Spring doing as did John A. Costello and William Norton.

Other changes flow too from the seductive temptations of office. The minister may allow the job to go to his head as he is saluted by the Air Corps officer as he boards the government jet for a European Council meeting. He may preen himself as he uses the Aer Rianta VIP lounge at Dublin airport. He is ushered into executive class seat number 1C, the first aisle seat, in the Aer Lingus service to Brussels. His ego may inflate further on being met by the Irish ambassador at foreign airports. Parallel to this transformation is the impact on the minister's wife and family.

The ultimate ministerial arrogance is of course the manner in which the garda drivers are treated by some office holders. The vast majority of ministers behave impeccably during their tenure of office. But some behave as colonial governors, treating their drivers as coolies, leaving them waiting all hours of the day and night, winter and summer, outside pubs, restaurants, football matches, party functions and clinics. Drivers have, for some ministers, brought the children to school and the spouse to the hairdresser. Some ministers I knew stopped little short of directing those gardaí to cut the grass and do the laundry. Stella and I could never accept that any driver should have to wait in a car for hours outside a minister's house. But wait they often did or else the minister would phone the barrack master at the depot and have the driver removed forthwith. One minister I knew believed that the drivers should know as little as possible about his business, no driver lasted more than six months. He went through 11 drivers in his time. He nearly had a garda drivers' soccer team.

Garda protection was introduced in the Civil War period when the lives of members of the government were in great danger. During other more recent periods, such as the 1973-1977 government, ministers were also threatened and full security was necessary. I am strongly of the view that all ministers should have every facility in the performance of their duties. However, there should be a very clear and fully enforced code of conduct for all office holders about the use of official transport, particularly during by-elections and general election campaigns. A top-of-the-range car and two garda drivers for each office holder and the substantial subsidy from the state funds provided to each minister of state for their transport needs costs the taxpayers several million pounds per annum. In most northern European democracies, such facilities are very strictly controlled. In the earlier years of the state I knew of one rural minister who used to drop off a few calves from the boot of the Merc at the fair on the way to Dublin. The gardaí in the transport detail in the Phoenix Park soon tired of cleaning out the boot and this unique farm subsidy came to an odorous end!

The minister's disposable income also increases substantially. He and his spouse are invited to dinner at the American, British, French and other embassies. New outfits for the spouse are at last affordable. Some ministerial families begin to lose the run of themselves entirely. Unless the new minister has had a severe apprenticeship in the Dáil, the dangers of contacting this occupational disease are considerable. Nevertheless, when the new minister occupies the government front bench for the first time as the Taoiseach reads out the list in order of seniority in Dáil service, he looks to his newly bedecked spouse in the visitors' gallery and they both adapt the IRA slogan, *Tá ár lá anseo anocht*. But once the electorate gets a whiff of this arrogance, the minister's days are numbered. No political party is immune from this infection. There is no substitute for humble and comprehensive political experience well in advance of ministerial elevation.

There is one further ominous danger in such office. Ministers have no particular need to drive their private cars while in power and the departments usually maintain a well-stocked drink cabinet in the minister's office. The temptation to have a liberal stiff drink after a savage day's work or after a political crisis is immense. I have known several ministerial alcoholics and some very heavy drinkers in office. Those of us who served and survived were very fortunate indeed.

And then that remarkable confirmation of the new ministerial status arrives. The minister is due to attend an EU Council meeting and no ordinary Irish passport in the maroon Galway colours will suffice. The diplomatic passport is requested. It is carefully dated for expiry well within the life span of the government just in case the minister falls under a bus, a rather unlikely event. The Department of Foreign Affairs jealously vets the issue of such documents. The fact that they confer no exceptional status above and beyond the ordinary citizen is beside the point to a status-conscious minister. After all, the millionaires of Ireland do not have such a prized possession. As the Clare manager, Bill Loughnane, said: 'You can have all the money in the world but you cannot buy an All-

Ireland hurling medal.' Likewise the ministerial passport. But ministerial expectations tend to grow. I knew one minister who insisted, when in Paris, on staying at the Irish Embassy. Normally ministers enjoy a suite at a top-of-the-range hotel. The long-suffering ambassador who has to meet the minister at the airport has little option. And woe betide the private secretary who fails to provide full VIP treatment at airport departure and arrival for the august presence.

The new minister becomes somewhat paranoid about security when on official business abroad. Before going to Brussels I was advised not to phone Dublin on the Council's or Commission's general phones for any sensitive instructions. It was presumed that such calls were intercepted by the Belgians, the British, the French and the Germans. As far back as 1982 I was assured that the UK at Cheltenham monitored selected telecommunications between the Republic of Ireland, the UK and mainland Europe. I have no doubt that they were interceptors of immense competence. I also invariably assumed that many documents at Council level were, even at preliminary working paper and initial translation stage, in the hands of 'the enemy'. Most major governments have 'their people' well positioned at all critical levels. The British government for decades has had its 'eyes and ears' well embedded in Irish structures. In turn, the Irish government has its 'travellers' on the ground in Northern Ireland and in London. Most government ministers on either side would not be aware of the identities of such 'travellers'. Too many lives would be at stake.

The European institutions are all porous, quite apart from being hives of political gossip and personal intrigue. Those who prepare 'SECRET' and 'For Minister's Eyes Only' documents in Ireland, in Northern Ireland and in the United Kingdom know quite well that sooner or later, and generally sooner, the document will be copied in whole or in part and will be leaked. Such documents are sometimes cynically circulated to fly a variety of unofficial political kites. As the official saying goes, 'Anything told in confidence should only be repeated in confidence'. Some mandarins, anxious to convey secret information to their masters, prepare named and numbered documents, usually on one A4 page, to be circulated at a restricted meeting with no secretariat and no interpreters present. This non-document is distributed only to those present at the meeting. Following discussion and decision they are collected there and then by the secretary to the government or by the secretary general of the European Union institution. But some of us, even without the help of speed reading courses, would memorise such pages with studied nonchalance, noting the key word of each paragraph during the discussion. After the meeting it was not too difficult to reconstruct such secret documents. Kleptomaniacs are a very dangerous species in and out of government.

And when the ego is full blown, the minister concludes that his good name must be in the papers every day. I knew one minister who insisted on five press releases being issued about his good deeds each week, one for each working day. He had party leadership pretensions which were never to bear fruit. His staff was driven to distraction. His favourite party song was 'One day at a time, Dear Jesus'. When his staff saw him coming they recited the refrain under their press releases. Another junior minister had similar notions of daily public acclaim. When he received the morning papers in his office each day he would rail at his staff and throw the pages in the air in disgust when he could not find his press release. One of his party advisers, now a distinguished EU food regulatory lawyer, packed it in after a mere two weeks. He could take no more. The massage of the image can become all-consuming work for some appointees.

All politicians have their own particular contacts with the media. I was no exception. I have always been very circumspect in my contacts with journalists employed outside the Oireachtas Press Gallery and the regular European affairs correspondents. I knew of one feature writer who had free accommodation in a US hotel provided the hotel's name was favourably mentioned. Furthermore, the hotel management regularly informed this columnist of details about politicians staying in the hotel. On learning of this practice, one former minister of my acquaintance contacted fellow ministers. There was from then on a marked absence of politicians in that hotel.

Over 20 years in the Dáil I thoroughly enjoyed my daily contacts with the political correspondents. There was a great deal of sharp repartee and trust between myself as Labour whip and the old guard of Michael Mills, Arthur Noonan, Maurice Hickey and Michael McInerney. From the 1980s onwards we had many a joust with Dick Walsh, Donal Kelly, John Foley, Denis Coughlan, Sean Duignan, Joe O'Malley, Stephen Collins, Liam O'Neill and Chris Glennon. To sit in their minimal garret room at the top of Leinster House and face a formidable grilling over an embarrassing Labour fracas left sweat under my armpits. And then the first women political correspondents arrived: Geraldine Kennedy and Una Claffey took no prisoners at all. I regularly floated a juicy half story to see how the grain of truth would travel. Their subsequent queries on the flyer would drive the other side into a tizzy of briefing.

There is one matter which many ministers in the past dared not publicise. The incoming minister learns quite sharply about the incompatibility between membership of government and secret membership of any other organisation. In December 1982, the incoming Taoiseach Garret FitzGerald wrote to each one of us: 'Anyone who may be a member of such an organisation, or has in the past been a member and has not formally resigned, must do so and inform me of the fact that he has done so.' Is it any wonder that Garret was so detested by the Knights of Columbanus? Joe O'Malley reported that in the formation of the National Coalition in 1981 two ministers notified such resignations to the Taoiseach.[65] I do not have to wonder too much who they were.

During my time in cabinet, I had a somewhat tempestuous relationship with some of the trade unions affiliated to the Labour Party. For example, the Federated Workers' Union of Ireland was very aggressive in the 1980s when they demanded that we pump scarce taxpayers' money into the ailing Clondalkin Paper Mills. The affiliated unions were fiercely critical at all times of Labour in coalition while incessantly demanding the fruits of office. And these were plentiful. They were expert in playing off Fianna Fáil and the Labour Party in successive governments to secure membership of the boards of state bodies. For example, at that time the general officers of my union were directors of NET, the National Enterprise Agency, Bord Fáilte and a general secretary was a Taoiseach's nominee to the Seanad. And yet time and again some senior union spokespersons accused Labour ministers of a sell-out in government.

The unions were expert in soft-soaping Fianna Fáil ministers whereas most Labour ministers simply told them the plain unvarnished facts of many an unpalatable situation. And there were a lot of unpalatable situations around in the early 1980s from Irish Shipping Ltd to Dublin Gas. At times one detected an element of resentment that a fellow union colleague had reached the pinnacle of the political ladder. But ministerial responsibilities have their compensations. The Minister for Public Enterprise, for example, appoints the boards of directors of Aer Lingus and Aer Rianta, other than the elected worker-directors. There is usually fierce competition among the faithful for the supreme perk of an Aer Lingus directorship. For decades, members of that board had free premier travel on scheduled flights for life! In recent years this benefit has been changed. New directors now retain free travel, after they leave office, only for the period they have served. Former Taoisigh, however, have free premier class travel for life on Aer Lingus.

Each government has had different methods of appointment to these boards. When Haughey became Taoiseach, each government department was directed to forward a list of all upcoming vacancies to his office. In the coalition governments, most senior appointments proposed by the ministers were jointly agreed by the Taoiseach and the Tanaiste before being rubber stamped by the government. Almost all such lists invariably contain a quota of the parties' loyalists. Their qualifications were often a matter of some conjecture. In my Health and Social Welfare portfolios the appointments were much more mundane. I had considerable difficulty in finding suitable persons to serve on public hospital boards, on advisery health and pension committees, all on a voluntary basis. The professional social and medical staffs who participated were unstinting in their contributions.

One of the great strengths of the Fianna Fáil party is that it generally tries harder not to let its senior ministers get above their station in life. But it generally fails to do so. A classic example occurred when a delegation of ministers assembled at Baldonnel Airport's VIP lounge for government transport to the northern talks in Belfast. One ebullient minister breezed in with his usual loud bonhomie. As was his custom he interrupted those reading the morning papers with a litany of his latest achievements. Another senior minister had just returned from Rome where he had represented the Irish government at a special ceremony for Irish martyrs for the faith. He interrupted his colleague in his tracks. He said that after this momentous event in Rome, His Holiness the Pope had graciously seen him off at Rome airport. As he went up the gangway to the plane, the pope touched him on the arm and said, 'Isn't it a pity that your friend in government turned out to be such a bollocks!' Dead silence descended on Baldonnel as the civil servants dived back into their morning papers.

*

One of the most traumatic losses of innocence on the part of all new ministers is the extraordinary process of implementing a legislative reform. Grandiose election promises are one thing; a bill in its final form is quite another experience. As soon as the minister is once again reminded of his party's promise, he asks his departmental secretary to allocate a senior official to the work. This official, often burdened with other pressing tasks, must research how the issue is dealt with in other jurisdictions; he or she must discuss the issue with other staff in the department; they may contact pressure groups and outside experts for their views; they may conclude that the minister's promises were 'off the wall'. But he is not to know yet. A draft government memorandum is then prepared indicating why the legislation is urgently necessary; the cost to the exchequer or the consumer is estimated; the positives and negatives of the legislative scheme are stated; and the parties affected are listed. Meanwhile the minister is fretting as his party colleagues badger him about the delay. Eventually he is presented with the memorandum.

But he is bluntly informed by the secretary of his department that first of all it must go to all other government departments for their observations prior to submission to government. There is no way of circumventing cabinet procedures. This second process will take several further months. The minister's frustrations grow. An election promise can only be recycled so often in speeches to the party faithful. The political correspondents grow sceptical. The memorandum must go to the Department of Finance. There the neolithic mandarins come out of their caves in Upper Merrion Street and gobble up all the passing papers. Their response is usually prompt and invariably negative. The other departments usually hold their fire. Their ministers will have their own legislative priorities. Ministers may be of the same party but internal ambitions and the jealousies of colleagues may intrude. As a consequence they may delay their responses and these may be less than enthusiastic. But with dogged persistence the minister eventually forwards his memorandum including all the other departments' observations and his counter-opinions. All copies must be channelled through the government secretariat in the Department of the Taoiseach.

The legislative proposals are then discussed at length in cabinet. On the assumption that the minister is given approval, the draft heads of the bill go to the Attorney General. He then forwards it to the parliamentary draftsman. The fun then really starts. The minister descends into despair as his baby grows old. Two years have passed. The political correspondents note his legislative inactivity. His wife notes that his sleep is troubled. He takes it all out on his long-suffering private secretary who harries the draftsman. However, the latter must now familiarise himself with all of the complexities of the issue. He must ensure that the draft has no constitutional impediments and is in accordance with EU law. Meanwhile the unfortunate draftsman is harassed by other government departments to expedite their competing bills. He must draft each page, stamp it and return the bill to the department. And back goes the bill to the government again for final approval.

The novice minister has little idea of the daggers that lie around the corners of Government Buildings. The messengers from Finance lurk in the shadows. They submit a final memorandum with a 'Certificate of Urgency'. Finance proposes that, in the event of the bill being approved for circulation to the Dáil, the costs of implementing the provisions of the bill should be met from 'savings' from within the minister's own department. In effect, no new resources, no enhanced budget line for the minister. Finance's public expenditure division innocently proclaims that it has no political agenda, either with a small or big 'p'. This, of course, is utter nonsense. Every thought, work or deed of Finance is intensely political. Those who protect the holy grail of the book of estimates are, at all times, shrouded in an elegant pretence of official neutrality. The minister may have his bill but he has no money to implement his cherished reform. Game, set and match to Finance.

Other factors may now conspire against the hapless minister. The media interest in the issue may wane. The Taoiseach may no longer include a reference to the bill in his speeches. The government press office may no longer be preoccupied with the bill. The whip's office may provide a lowly inclusion of the bill in the government's legislative programme. The minister's press conference is poorly attended. The minister has to fudge his replies to planted questions about resources in his forthcoming estimate. This shining light of the government's legislative programme no longer adds lustre to the government or to the minister. And there are still five stages in the Dáil to surmount!

The innocence of the minister has been violated. He or she learns the hard way what it is really like to be a minister. And the departments size up the next office holder appearing on the horizon. It is like being measured for one's third order habit for the coffin on the way to hell, or purgatory, or a place of rest.

*

It seems quite strange today to many politicians but the advent of mobile car telephones for the very privileged few in 1974 was a novel event. Three government ministers, Conor Cruise O'Brien in Post and Telegraphs, Paddy Cooney in Justice and Paddy Donegan in Defence, had these phones installed in their state cars. These were the phones of a private company in Rathfarnham, Co Dublin and had a radius of fifteen miles around Dublin. The three ministers were the envy of their colleagues. I recall Frank Cluskey in his car coming up Westland Row to the Dáil. As we drew abreast of Paddy Donegan's car, suddenly the Minister for Defence grabbed his phone and started waving his hands. Frank turned to me and exclaimed, 'Jasus, will ye look at Donegan declaring war on Russia!' Unfortunately these phones were a short-lived affair. The mandarins in the Department of Post and Telegraphs declared that they were being operated without a licence! The embarrassed ministers had to surrender their phones. There was a long delay before they were reconnected. An example of the absence of such technology in the 1970s was when Taoiseach Jack Lynch was in Blarney, Co Cork in 1972 at a Fianna Fáil by-election rally in support of Gene Fitzgerald. Jack had to leave the platform and go to the local garda station to learn of the British Army's launch of Operation Motorman in Northern Ireland. The information technology and communications systems of 2000 have certainly transformed the political process.

*

When Dermot Nally, secretary to the government, reached for his little black-covered notebook, I knew that we were in for a long discussion around the government table about Anglo-Irish relations, usually about Northern Ireland. Such has been the government tradition since the 1920s. The notes taken were not circulated and were not read at the following government meeting. Only government decisions were circulated. When Dermot Nally retired in 1992, he had served five of the state's nine Taoisigh in ten governments over a period of twenty years. He also attended almost every European summit from 1973 to 1992. He was one of the principal drafters of the Anglo-Irish Agreement in 1984.

He was a civil servant of utter discretion. When I would go on a fishing expedition in cabinet after some whiff of scandal or conflict of public interest, usually away outside my remit, an exercise I thoroughly enjoyed, Dermot would arch one eyebrow behind the glasses, smile politely and refuse to be drawn. In the midst of the most ferocious of arguments in government, frequently on my part with the Minister for Finance about the precarious Health and Social Welfare estimates, he would remain calm and unflappable. He had a profound knowledge of the minutiae of the estimates and could be most helpful in his factual analysis of the situation. His drafting of decisions, there and then at government meetings, was cryptic in a distinctive but unambiguous longhand. Problems sometimes arose in that, by the time they were typed up and reached one's department by army messenger an hour or so after the cabinet meeting, a Finance watchdog had endeavoured to put a spin or caveat on its contents. But Dermot knew how to protect his ministers from the marauding ambushes of Finance. I always ensured that I obtained a photocopy of his pink hand-written drafts. I delivered these immediately after the meetings to my accounting officers, Dermot Condon, Jim Downey and Liam Flanagan. They too had excellent relations with Dermot Nally.

The only occasion on which Dermot Nally became agitated with me was when I harped on about the issue of exchange controls. Charles Haughey's 'shadow' spokespersons had claimed that because of government policies, money was flooding out of the country. After I had belaboured the point Dermot flashed a note across the table to me. It read, 'Can you really work exchange controls in a country where external trade accounts for 110 to 120 per cent of GNP?' For once I simply shut up: I still retain the note.

Nally's finest achievement was in relation to the protracted and intense negotiations with the Thatcher governments over the Anglo-Irish Agreement. Sir Robert Armstrong and he had an excellent relationship despite the mercurial and tempestuous reactions of Thatcher to the unfolding events. Dermot Nally, Garret FitzGerald, Peter Barry and Dick Spring were a very formidable front row in the negotiations. It must have galled their team manager, Dermot Nally, that Charles Haughey and Brian Lenihan in 1984-1986 showed such cynical disdain in opposition towards their achievements. At that time Haughey was in a destructive mode about Northern Ireland. Dermot Nally must have had considerable satisfaction when Haughey as Taoiseach in 1987 had to shed his naked opportunism and row in behind the Agreement. Such are the joys of being a senior civil servant.

But there remained one intriguing question — who would he have voted for as Taoiseach? For Jack Lynch, I surmise yes. For Charles Haughey, a definite no! For Garret FitzGerald, a possible yes. And knowing Dermot, I could be very wrong.

Dermot Nally also fulfilled another vital function. He organised the meetings of the government's security committee. The membership in my time were the Taoiseach, Tanaiste, Minister for Foreign Affairs, the Ministers for Justice and Defence and the Attorney General. No reports of the work of the committee were formally presented to the cabinet. They met the garda commissioner and the chief of staff of the army, as the agenda demanded. Other ministers did not have sight of those agendas or of any minutes. I have no knowledge of the structure of the committee in the Lynch and Haughey eras. Dermot Nally, over a long period, was privy to these secret discussions and security decisions in the national interest.

I initially had some reservations when John Boland, as Minister for the Public Service, showed great courage and imagination in proposing the introduction of the TLAC (Top Level Appointments Committee) system in the civil service. But what of the future of those most talented senior civil servants whose appointments at secretary and assistant secretary levels would terminate after seven year? The issue was not resolved when the new system was introduced. I was also upset that the Department of Foreign Affairs managed to obtain an elitist exemption from the new scheme. Garret was far too susceptible to the old boys' network of Foreign Affairs. The very thought of some 'half educated principal officer' from Social Welfare or Agriculture being promoted to an ambassador post in Iveagh House sent shivers down the Belvedere College spines. The civil service had its own very special brand of inverted snobbery. But I was reassured when Dermot Nally was appointed chairman of TLAC. The system has been invigorating. It loosened the taint of political patronage within the civil service. A new public service meritocracy began to emerge. John Boland, as Minister for the Public Service, fought his way, as a coalition condottiere, through layers of civil service empires in the process of reform.

*

In Ireland, the role of the permanent civil service in supporting and promoting policy development has always been important. In the mid-1980s there was a pervasive hostility towards the civil service in the body politic and in the media. The criticism ranged from suggestions of laziness, privilege and waste to accusations of excessive overtime working, as well as the assumption that every single person working anywhere in the public sector had high wages and pensions, both inflation proofed, and permanent employment. It was indeed a worrying feature of the grave economic crisis that, instead of inviting everyone in the country to try to find a way out of our difficulties, conflict and class divisions of one type or another were exacerbated. The deep divisions between the PAYE sector and the farming community and the self-employed were widespread.

It was always traumatic for me to agonise with the secretary and personnel officer of the Department of Social Welfare about our memorandum to government proposing the termination of office of a civil servant. No matter how serious the charge or conviction, we knew that often a whole family faced devastation. And I never passed the buck to my successors. Fortunately, these instances were very rare. Jim Downey and I still admire the level of public probity in the Department of Social Welfare, which employed some 3,400 staff and handled billions of cash every year. Other personnel issues arose in the Department of Health where I recall one civil servant who did not speak to me for two months because he had not been promoted. For all my belligerent reputation, I took it on the chin and offered it up for my ministerial sins.

Of course the preoccupations of social snobbery are not exclusive to Irish political society. While the private sector inculcates a dog-eat-dog mentality, the public sectors, in Ireland and in the European institutions, are riddled with obsessional hierarchical status. I recall in one government department when an individual was promoted from HEO to assistant principal. He was known for years to the porter on the door as 'John Joe'. On the morning after his promotion when he was so greeted once again, he reminded the hapless porter that from now on he should be addressed only by his surname. By the time he arrived up in the lift to his new office, word was all over the building. He could never understand why his standing in the department nose-dived overnight. Likewise I saw a ferocious row in the European Parliament when an A4 administrator on promotion to A3 demanded an office with two windows. These were the status symbols of that institution. On such trappings is the architecture of the new Europe built. As each new member state takes its place, a fresh outbreak of promotional fever will convulse the bureaucracies of the institutions.

A real problem facing most Labour ministers in government is negotiation on staff issues. I was a well-known trade unionist. Those on the opposite side of the table were invariably union colleagues. I was constrained to act as a transient public service employer with the Departments of Finance and the Public Service crawling up my back. There was no place to hide. My own union, the Irish Transport and General Workers' Union, and the Psychiatric Nurses Association were two of the most difficult to face. We were, in the health services, in the throes of integrating decades of male and female psychiatric nursing. The reluctance of some male nurses to co-operate was immense in some hospitals. I had to face down a serious dispute in Castlebar hospital on this issue. Eamonn Hannon, the CEO of the Western Health Board, showed great bottle on that occasion.

I berated Finance and the Office of Public Works about the dreadful conditions of employment for staff in many of our so-called 'employment exchanges'. Jim Downey, Secretary, and Mick Carroll, Personnel Officer of the Department of Social Welfare, did heroic work in this area. We received regular deputations from Billy Lynch and Paddy Woods of the Civil and Public Service Staff Association. They played a very effective 'hard man–soft man' approach. Paddy Woods was a superb negotiator. He had extraordinary contact with his rank and file. But Billy Lynch had a unique turn of phrase. He would address me thus: 'Minister, you are putting a cordon bleu around our claim!', 'Minister, you have a DIY staff embargo policy!', 'Minister, you are throwing your bread upon the waters!' 'Minister, you are holding a smoking pistol', 'Minister, you will give our side psychosomatic disorders!' and 'Minister, the CPSSA has reached the end of its redeployment tether!' But nobody dared take Billy Lynch for granted. For every long letter he wrote to our departments, he got prompt and detailed replies. And there was always Paddy Woods to point us in the right direction when Billy would say, 'Minister, our union's capacity is being zilched and you must examine your ledger balances tonight!'

*

When I experienced the interaction between ministers; between the political parties in government; between the government and the social partners; and between government and opposition, I began to appreciate the appropriateness of the observation of George F. Will in 1976 that 'Voters do not decide issues, they decide who will decide issues'. I appreciated the extent to which ministers had centralised administrative functions in their title. In the Department of Social Welfare, I was upset by the universal use of the phrase 'I am directed by the Minister for Social Welfare' in circulars and letters. A great deal of the work of the department related to the decisions of deciding officers and appeals officers and the use of the expression created the impression that I had actually made the decision. Jim Downey and Mick Carroll shared my objections and issued a direction to have it removed. It was a minor reform in departmental culture.

Another loss of innocence comes in government when one develops a thick skin towards some highly partisan media comment. In government we had two centres of regular criticism, the *Sunday World* and the *Irish Press*. In 1984, one *Irish Press* editorial declared, 'Mr Desmond has been thrashing about in the Department of Health. Among his notable victories to date ... the denying of incontinence sheets to itinerants'![66] There was no truth in this offensive assertion. I replied to the editor describing the comment as 'gutter political comment' and that 'personal political abuse only merits my contempt'. At least he published my reply.

But every minister must also be prepared for the inevitable banana skin. I was host to a ministerial delegation of senior health specialists from Iran. We welcomed them to an excellent dinner of Irish lamb, orange and apple juice. They visited a number of Dublin hospitals. Just before they went to St Vincent's Hospital my private secretary went ahead to check the arrangements. He stopped in his tracks when he saw the sign in the main hall: 'Welcome to Our Iraqi Friends'! One never knows when catastrophe is about to strike. Another delegation to Ireland, which caused some eyebrows to raise, was that led by the Chinese Minister for Health. We wanted to show him a typical Irish farm outside Tullamore. After a warm welcome of tea and cake from the farm couple, the delegation decided to inspect the premises. To our consternation they started in the bedrooms and worked down to the kitchen. And then they got down to business asking the farmer, through the interpreter, his annual income. There was silence. Surrounded by health board and departmental officials, the farmer replied 'enough!' The translation perplexed the Chinese. They asked again. This time the farmer said 'We are comfortable!' That really flummoxed the visitors.

*

Between 1973 and 1990 I attended every meeting of the Council of State. The Council advised three Presidents during this period on diverse legislative measures. President Erskine Childers was well known to most members of the national coalition government in 1973. It was clear to me from the chit-chat before the Council meetings, and during the tea, cake and Paddy afterwards, that Liam Cosgrave as Taoiseach and Erskine had a considerable mutual empathy. They both feared any prospect of political subversion. If anything, Erskine was more conservative than Cosgrave in that regard. He knew of my antipathy towards Haughey and during our conversations he did not hide his feelings about his former government colleague. He told me that he regarded him as 'a traitor to Fianna Fáil'.

My appointment to the Council of State by the President in 1973 had a rather bizarre touch. I was summoned to meet him in 1973 after his election. I had never been to the Aras before. After Dev's tenure of 14 years, the Office of Public Works had barely commenced refurbishment. It had a musty look about it, even to the book one signed on entry. Erskine asked me if I would serve as one of his seven nominees on the Council. He gave as his principal reason the fact that he had greatly appreciated my support for his 1970 Health Act. He had also admired 'your late father, Deputy Dan Desmond'. His comment put me in a rare pickle. To deny my presumed paternity could scuttle my prospect of seven years on the Council. On the other hand, I could hardly face Deputy Eileen Desmond and explain to her that her late husband, Dan, now had a 38-year-old son! As straight faced as possible I explained to the President that my father was former Senator Con Desmond adding that of course that we Desmonds were all very inter-related. I assured Erskine that I too had greatly admired Dan Desmond as did my wife Stella. Erskine recovered his dignity and he confirmed my appointment that evening, much to the chagrin of my more senior colleagues in the Dáil. On such twinges of fortune are political careers constructed.

Erskine told me that during the second inter-party government in the 1950s he had, in opposition, taken up a part-time marketing position with Pye (Ireland) Ltd. He had enjoyed his entrepreneurial sabbatical. Following the next general election he was back in government as a minister. Pye closed his account and sent on the balance of monies due to him for his endeavours. Such was the culture of rectitude within Fianna Fáil that Erskine consulted with the Chief about the cheque. Dev directed, much to the displeasure of Erskine, who was noted to count his pennies, that the cheque be returned to Pye, which he did forthwith. Those were the days!

The President's sudden heart attack and death in 1974 came as a shock to the whole body politic. I always held the view that Childers was regarded by Fianna Fáil as a traditional decent Protestant prop. He was never an integral part of the inner party core. Maureen Lynch and Rita Childers were quite conscious of the extent to which their husbands were being used by the TACA brigade. Maureen Lynch was disdainful but Rita Childers was contemptuous. After her husband's death the Fianna Fáil parliamentary party invited her in 1975 to a mass in memory of Bean de Valera, President Childers and three deceased Fianna Fáil deputies. She declined and released her reply to the media. She wrote: 'There will be no representative of the Childers family present. The late President would not benefit from the prayers of such a party. Happily for him he is now closer to God and will be able to ask His intercession that his much loved country will never again be governed by these people.'

Whereas Erskine and Jack Lynch had a considerable bond cemented by their mutual detestation of Haughey, the President who followed Childers, Cearbhall Ó Dálaigh, had a nationalist agenda all to himself. It was clear from his quotations *as gaeilge* and from his well-worn Irish copy of the Constitution at Council meetings. He told me that 'I am a Republican in the Fenian tradition'! He was not joking. One sensed that he had no time at all for the Cosgraves, the Costelloes and the O'Briens. He would have been more appreciative of Allen, Larkin and O'Brien. His feelings were reciprocated by Cosgrave and Paddy Donegan. He appointed Siobhán McKenna to the Council. James Dillon whispered to me that her legislative experience was 'somewhat theatrical' as she gave her opinion to the President on the constitutionality of the provisions of the Act against forcible entry.

Later in 1980-1982, with Paddy Hillery as President, Jack Lynch and Liam Cosgrave curtly acknowledged the existence of Charles Haughey as Taoiseach at such meetings. They were in and out of the Council meetings as fast as wild hares on the Mushera mountain meeting strangers.

The Council meetings were very formal. The secretary to the President circulated before the meeting a copy of the Bill forwarded to him for signature and copies of the relevant Dáil and Seanad debates. The Taoiseach and the Attorney General were invariably the first to respond to the President's invitation to advise him on the constitutionality of the Bill. The rest of us spoke once giving our personal opinions. The Presidents always indicated that they would give full consideration to our advice but gave no indication at the meetings of their ultimate decisions which, under the Constitution, was theirs and theirs alone.

Twelve

With Garret in Recession

'Sic transit gloria Coalitionis.'

Fergus Pyle, 1987

I was in awe of Garret FitzGerald's prodigious output of economic analysis, mostly in *The Irish Times* from 1959 onwards, when I first met him in the early 1960s. He and Professor Louden Ryan had a major influence on the economic and social development of modern Ireland through the Committee on Industrial Organisation and the National Industrial and Economic Council. The trade union movement, notably in the contributions of Jim Larkin Jnr, and Donal Nevin played a major constructive role in these bodies. At a time when there were many vociferous anti-Common Market individuals in influential positions, Garret FitzGerald together with Mary Robinson, Miriam Hederman, Denis Corboy, Eoin Ryan Snr, the late Michael Sweetman and Michael Killeen, and a few junior heretics in the Labour Party, emphatically supported Irish membership. We were determined to break the apron string of our dependence on a declining UK economy for future economic growth. FitzGerald made his mark on this period as a rising star of acknowledged ability and political ambition. In ICTU, leaders such as Ruaidhri Roberts advocated long-term economic and social plans and the forerunners to the national pay agreements. Unfortunately, Ruaidhri's blind spot was his hostility to the EEC.

Garret and I were elected to the Dáil in 1969 in the adjoining constituencies of Dublin South East and Dun Laoghaire–

Rathdown. He had been a rather late joiner of Fine Gael in 1964 at 38 years of age. Liam Cosgrave's first words to me after my election were, 'If your lot had not persisted with your anti-coalition tripe we would be in government tonight.' FitzGerald had four prevailing interests on entry to the Dáil. First, to lead Fine Gael and become Taoiseach. To do so he was determined to oust Liam Cosgrave. Liam went of his own accord in 1977. Garret had yet to learn the rule that a successful conspirator talks to as few confidants as possible. Second, he was determined to find a resolution to the Northern Ireland impasse. Third, he wished to attach Ireland more securely to the processes of European integration and, finally, he wanted to define more clearly in the Constitution the separate roles of Church and State in relation to major social questions. He succeeded in his first objective. He failed honourably in his second because, feeling that time was not on his side, he wrongly excluded the Unionists from successive agreements. He succeeded in his third objective, and made heroic, if limited, progress in the fourth.

It is evident from early in his career that with his family background in the Civil War, FitzGerald seemingly felt destined to rule and to reconcile. He was comfortable in the rarefied world of UCD economists who purported to know at all times what was best for the people. He spoke on numerous issues in the Dáil, so much so that the Fine Gael front bench was alleged to consist of twenty-one Garret FitzGeralds. He had none of the cultivated gravitas of Charles Haughey or of his adversary's ruthless management of political power. Haughey was prepared to pander to the worst elements in his party to retain control. I recall a social concern group telling me about their deputations to Garret and Charlie. Garret exuded genuine appreciation of their plight and showed frustration with the inability of the system to deliver resources to them. Months elapsed, much correspondence ensued but there was no delivery. Charlie severely questioned them, virtually accused them of being anti-Fianna Fáil hacks, and poured hostile doubts on their social commitment. But weeks later he delivered the cash on the dot. This outcome was largely because most public servants greatly feared the lash of Haughey's tongue. The merits of the supplication were secondary to Haughey. His intervention in the Talbot Company closure, which guaranteed public service jobs to redundant car assembly workers, was a classic example of his approach.

When Liam Cosgrave became Taoiseach in 1973, he clearly resolved to put FitzGerald, the 'mongrel fox' in chief, back into his den. As shadow spokesman for Fine Gael on Finance since 1971, FitzGerald was confident that he was destined for the Finance portfolio. He was so sure of his prospects that he visited the Department of Social Welfare in preparation for his first budget, much to the surprise of Frank Cluskey who was already designated as parliamentary secretary by his minister and leader, Brendan Corish. Frank promptly told Garret 'to get stuffed'. Cosgrave gave Brendan Corish the first option of going to the Department of Finance, more as a courtesy than as a serious offer. Corish wisely declined because of his lack of confidence in economic matters. Cosgrave then offered the position to Richie Ryan, Garret's arch opponent. Richie's views were much more in tune with those of Cosgrave. They both disliked 'unearned income'.

FitzGerald, who had meanwhile been in and out of Finance drawing together the draft budget, was shocked, his wife Joan more visibly so. In my opinion Cosgrave feared that FitzGerald would prove to be entirely too progressive a minister in Finance for the old guard of Fine Gael. Thus did Cosgrave also level the score against one of the prime movers in the abortive putsch which had developed against him within Fine Gael throughout 1971 and 1972. As assistant government whip to be, I viewed these intrigues with great glee. They culminated in the dramatic events of a fateful evening in December 1972 when bombs exploded in the centre of Dublin. In their wake, Fine Gael reversed its earlier opposition to passage by the Dáil of the Offences Against the State (Amendment) Bill. Had there been a Fine Gael parliamentary party vote of confidence earlier that evening before the bombing, Cosgrave might well have been ousted by a small majority. Funny old worlds were not invented only by Margaret Thatcher!

In that setting it was ironic that Cosgrave gave FitzGerald the lifeline of Foreign Affairs to subsequently parachute himself into the Fine Gael leadership in 1977. Cosgrave gave Ryan the poisoned chalice of Finance. 'Red Richie' and 'Richie Ruin' were by 1975 smeared all over the country, particularly for his courageous introduction of the wealth tax and measures on farm taxation under great pressure from Labour. This fatally undermined his ambition to succeed Cosgrave. In the event, Ryan and FitzGerald proved to be two of the best ministers in their respective portfolios since the State was founded. The crucial role of the Department of Foreign Affairs had greatly increased following Ireland's joining the EEC only ten weeks before. FitzGerald's contributions to the European Council meetings were exceptional.

The 1973-1977 period of office coincided with the disastrous oil crisis from the end of 1973. Richie Ryan had to find the tax resources to bear the brunt of massive inflation. Social welfare budget increases of 15 to 25 per cent were the order of the day. Ryan still succeeded in reducing exchequer foreign borrowing between 1976 and 1977. That government might have survived the economic crisis but it lacked vital internal discipline. Cosgrave as Taoiseach voted against his own government's contraceptive legislation in the Dáil which, on a minimal basis, authorised chemists to sell contraceptives to duly married couples. Together with John Kelly, the Taoiseach's parliamentary secretary and the government's chief whip, I had tried to muster a majority for the contraception legislation. We were flabbergasted that the Taoiseach of the day did not inform his cabinet or the whips of his intention to vote with an opportunistic opposition.

This episode undermined Cosgrave's and the government's authority from 1974 onwards. The conservative educational policies of the Minister for Education, Richard Burke, did little to enhance the liberal image of the government. The ill-discipline in the daily pronouncements of Minister Conor Cruise O'Brien on a variety of issues provided regular cannon fodder to Fianna Fáil. But it was the attack by Paddy Donegan, Minister for Defence, on President Cearbhall Ó Dálaigh in late 1976 and the Taoiseach's handling of the president's consequential resignation that ensured that the government lost public confidence. The president had, quite correctly, referred the Emergency Powers Bill to the Supreme Court. I had been re-appointed to the Council of State by President Ó Dálaigh and I was shocked that Cosgrave did not accept Paddy Donegan's offer of resignation from the government for his insult to the president. When I raised the issue at a Parliamentary Labour Party meeting, I was greeted with a show of great hostility from all Labour ministers towards Ó Dálaigh.

The tension between the government and the president was clearly evident soon after his nomination in December 1974 following the sudden death of Erskine Childers. Most ministers, with the exception of Garret FitzGerald, regarded him as a difficult Fianna Fáil sympathiser in the Aras and not to be entirely trusted to share the government's views on emergency legislation to combat subversion. Despite his distinction as Chief Justice from 1961 to 1973 and a Judge of the European Court of Justice in 1973-1974, he was still suspect in the eyes of the government.

The government during this period had very good reason to be paranoid about the security of the state. Fine Gael Senator Billy Fox was murdered by the Provos in 1974; the IRA had fomented hunger strikes in Portlaoise in 1975 and the Provos threatened to assassinate ministers if the hunger strikers were to die. Dr Tiede Herrema had been kidnapped and rescued in 1975. In 1974 the Provos bombed Birmingham and murdered 21 people. Dublin and Monaghan were bombed by Northern paramilitaries and 33 people died. I was in the Dáil when the car bombs exploded. We heard the thuds from Nassau Street. We were shocked. In 1976 the Provos assassinated the British Ambassador, Christopher Ewart Biggs, in South County Dublin. Paddy Cooney, the Minister for Justice, stood his ground and said 'the challenge confronting the state had to be resisted at all costs'. The Provos never forgave him. He was unbending in his determination to face them down. They.would have assasinated him at that time. Paddy was given Garda security for some 19 years. Provo subversion in the Republic did not flourish then.

In this setting there was a growing suspicion towards Cearbhall Ó Dálaigh. He was a person, in my experience as a member of the Council of State, of great intellect, good humour and politeness. He found it difficult to understand my detestation of the Provos. However, the behaviour of Paddy Donegan in calling him a 'thundering disgrace' was inexcusable and the failure of the Taoiseach and members of the government, including Garret FitzGerald, to repudiate his action in public did little to enhance the overall reputation of that government. Garret did convey his great concern to the president in private, before his resignation, as did I. I did not go public because I had no desire to embroil my fellow six Council of State members appointed by the president and the government in a further public debacle. But I should have gone public irrespective of the outcome. To this day I feel that I let him down very badly when I voted with the government in the subsequent vote of confidence in the Dáil. We won by 63 votes to 58 and lost the president.

After his resignation, he told me that Liam Cosgrave as Taoiseach had only called on him on four occasions during his two years in the Aras to brief him on affairs of State. He regarded this level of briefing as insulting. I agreed with him. Liam Cosgrave simply could not overcome his deep distrust of him. The president and his wife Mairín were, in my opinion, not sorry to end their exile in the Aras. In an interview after the debacle, Paddy Donegan said that he was 'a walking Zombie' due to a car accident when he made the Ó Dálaigh comment and added, to his credit, that he bitterly regretted his 'unwarranted attack'.[67] He said that when he rose to make the speech at the lunch at the Mullingar army mess, his thoughts had centred on Garda Michael Clerkin's murder in an explosion at Portarlington by the IRA two days before. Minister Donegan did in fact have a car accident the night before at Monasterboice. He also knew that the IRA had decided to set off bombs in Dublin to mark the signing of the Emergency Powers Bill into law. They were severely warned off from doing so; it was made clear to them through security sources that there would be severe repercussions if they did. They heeded the warning.

Most people today do not fully appreciate that at that time there was a very serious trial of strength between the IRA and the government of the day. Paddy Donegan also said in the interviews that 'I knew that I had a problem with alcohol and those events gave me a period of deep thought.' He went into hospital thereafter for three weeks' treatment. Paddy should never have been appointed to the Defence portfolio. Liam Cosgrave was far too loyal to his old supporters. A Taoiseach must stand apart and make hard choices.

*

After the extraordinary Fianna Fáil campaign of 1977, Garret took over the leadership of Fine Gael and its 43 deputies. Most Fine Gael ministers of the 1973-1977 cabinet supported Peter Barry for the leadership. However, Peter withdrew when he realised the way the wind was blowing and Garret 'won in a hack in a field of one', to borrow Cosgrave's parlance. As Basil Chubb aptly pointed out, 'When, in 1977, Fine Gael, the second largest political party and traditionally the most conservative, chose Dr Garret FitzGerald, an intellectual pledged to a social democratic programme, as its new leader, it was obvious that times were indeed changing.'[68] Within a few years FitzGerald had confounded his critics and transformed Fine Gael. He and the party's outstanding general secretary, Peter Prendergast, toured the country visiting every constituency. We had a European Christian Democrat in cahoots with a liberal. They created a political buzz of liberal social democracy. They cut away dead wood and planted winnable candidates who were subsequently elected.

This transformation of Fine Gael during 1977-1981 is one of FitzGerald's notable achievements. From being the closed Civil War party of the ranchers, the Law Library, UCD and the defenders of the faith, he shifted it towards a party of the just society pioneered by Declan Costello who had first invited Garret to join the party in 1964. Garret swung Fine Gael firmly in the direction of the centrist European Christian Democrats. In the general elections of 1981 and 1982, Fine Gael increased its representation to 70 deputies, giving FitzGerald two periods as Taoiseach. FitzGerald had a clear personal understanding with Frank Cluskey, the Labour leader, that they would seek to form a Fine Gael/Labour coalition following the 1981 general election. This prospect came horribly adrift when Cluskey lost his seat in that election. It was a disastrous period for Labour.

As a Labour office holder in government in both FitzGerald's periods as Taoiseach, I am not best placed to judge these governments objectively. While the short-lived 1981-1982 coalition failed to have its budget passed by the Dáil, it did above all else reverse the worst excesses of Haughey's administration and restored integrity to the State's budgetary process.

One of the saving graces of the June 1981 government was the appointment of Jim Dooge, an inspired choice from the Senate, as Minister for Foreign Affairs. Senator Jim Dooge had outstanding intellectual ability, was very constructive in inter-party negotiations, contributed greatly to the successful Fine Gael election campaigns and had a very considerable reputation at the European Council. Alan Dukes was another excellent choice as Minister for Agriculture, being appointed on his first day in the Dáil. However, Garret saddled the new government with his proposed £9.60 tax allowance per week for stay-at-home spouses. John Bruton, the Minister for Finance, announced an 18 per cent VAT rate on children's clothing and footwear in the 1982 budget and the complete failure of Garret and Michael O'Leary as Tanaiste to appreciate the negative political impact on the Independents supporting the government parachuted the coalition out of office. In a classic Fine Gael budget formulation, with the trap set by the Department of Finance mandarins, the VAT proposal was made at the government table when Eileen Desmond, as Minister for Health and Social Welfare, opted for a 26 per cent increase in social welfare rates as against a 20 per cent increase with no VAT proposal. John Bruton had yet to learn not to box himself into a corner on budget options. Despite the budget disaster, I found, as a Minister of State in Finance, that in the subsequent general election the people accepted our assessment of the state of the nation's finances. And John Bruton played a blinder on this fundamental issue in the campaign.

*

Garret was not a particularly good judge of ministerial potential within Fine Gael. This largely arose from a somewhat academic disdain for the wisdom of having a pint and a political chat with individual deputies and party organisers. These informal opportunities provide a real assessment for a party leader of the capacity of a deputy to manage a government department and act as a team colleague. Rather, he relied greatly on Peter Prendergast, the party's general secretary, and on confidants such as Frank Flannery, Derry Hussey, Bill O'Herlihy, Pat Heneghan, Edna Marren, Sean O'Leary, all key members of the Fine Gael strategy committee, and, of course, on Joan, his wife, and Gemma Hussey. Gemma handbagged John Boland out of the education portfolio in 1982 into the Department of the Public Service. He had done an excellent job despite his caustic temperament and a zero allocation of exchequer resources from Finance.

Garret appointed John Bruton after the 1981 general election as Minister for Finance. He had been a deputy since 1969, had four years experience as a parliamentary secretary and was Fine Gael spokesperson on Finance in 1981. Yet, at 34 years of age, he was relatively inexperienced for the job and despite his frenetic activity in the department was regarded at official level as Garret's voice. I was Minister of State to Bruton during that government. We could hardly believe the state of the public expenditure estimates we inherited from Haughey: 85 per cent of the projected deficit for the year had already been expended by mid year. Many departments had major overruns. The 1980-1981 Books of Estimates were so flawed that, arguably, they could have referred the demands to them from their ministers to the Comptroller and Auditor General. Had that been done, real manners would have been put on Haughey and his cabinet. My faith in our public service took a hammering at that time.

My short eight months as Minister of State in Finance, ostensibly with a brief for economic and social planning, was an invaluable insight into the inner workings of that department and of government procedures as a whole. As Labour whip and having played a major role in the general election, I had expected to be appointed to the cabinet. Michael O'Leary, within two weeks of being elected leader following Cluskey's general election defeat, brought Labour into government with Fine Gael. This was no mean achievement in his first flush of leadership. However, an unexpected issue arose. Frank Cluskey's political prospects appeared dead. I saw a way of keeping him in the parliamentary party and in the public eye by proposing to O'Leary that the party should nominate Frank to fill the MEP vacancy. This vacancy, I presumed, would immediately follow Michael's appointment as Tanaiste in July 1981. Michael had been elected to the European Parliament in June 1979 along with John O'Connell.

To my astonishment and that of the chairman of the parliamentary party, Joe Bermingham, O'Leary indicated that he had no intention of resigning until late into that autumn. No doubt by that time he would have attempted to deal with his arch rival Cluskey who had beaten him to the party leadership in 1977 by a mere one vote on the second count. O'Leary and Cluskey thereafter had mutual conspiracy theories about one another. I threatened to call a special meeting of the parliamentary party to deal with the issue. O'Leary capitulated and Frank was nominated. However, I had burned my boats for a minister's post. I had considerable doubts about Frank's survival as an MEP in the temptation-laden ambience of Brussels and Strasbourg. However, it was his lifeline and Frank was re-elected to the Dáil in 1982.

*

Garret FitzGerald in government recorded some notable legislative and political achievements. He and Dick Spring concluded the Anglo-Irish Agreement of 1985, which was another watershed in reconstructing political democracy in Northern Ireland. The Dáil agreed the second Family Planning Bill (1985). We introduced the Deposit Interest Retention Tax (DIRT) and established the national lottery. We also introduced the Child Care Protection Bill, passed the historic Single

European Act and the Extradition Act. Unfortunately Garret made an ill-prepared effort to reform and modernise legislation in the area of marital breakdown and divorce. Above all, however, he swung public opinion away from the dangerous rhetoric of Haughey on Northern Ireland. In his role as Taoiseach in presiding over these and many other progressive measures, he unfortunately succumbed to the political temptation of being involved up to his ears in every proposal. He wanted to redraft every government memorandum and every decision. His energy was prodigious and he was reluctant to delegate. The stream of notes and enquires, particularly on budgetary issues, was unceasing. No minister could ever claim that he or she was denied a fair hearing at the cabinet table. In short, Garret regarded himself as the government and secretary to the government, despite the outstanding Dermot Nally. And he nearly succeeded.

*

In the final months of the 1982-1987 government, Garret decided to send, on 18 November 1986, a memorandum to each minister on the electoral system. The Taoiseach asserted: 'There is widespread agreement that the present form of proportional representation is damaging our political system as a result of the pressures on deputies who have to service multi-seat constituencies with populations of 60,000 to 100,000 in competition not merely with political opponents but also with members of their own party.' He went on to analyse the merits of the two most often proposed alternatives and concluded: 'The substitution of single-seat constituencies, either with the 'straight vote' as proposed in 1959 and again in 1968, or with even the alternative vote, would, however, under Irish conditions create an excessive turnover of seats at elections, and would tend to give an advantage — possibly a very big advantage — to the largest party.'

His alternative involved about two-thirds to three-quarters of the Dáil (*viz.* 110-120 members) being elected by alternative vote in single-seat constituencies and the remainder being elected by a special type of system which would be based on party lists pre-selected before the election and would be filled according to the parties' first preference votes. His informal memorandum was quite comprehensive. It caused considerable bemusement among us all. However, the government was in the throes of multiple budget disputes at the time. I do not recall any further discussion on this issue.

In 1991 Gerald Barry neatly summed up the situation on electoral reform. He wrote: 'Of the major political parties Fine Gael is the only one which committed itself to changes in the electoral system. That was in 1987 when, almost entirely at the discretion of party leader and outgoing Taoiseach, Garret FitzGerald, the party programme proposed the abolition of the current form of multi-seat constituencies. They were to be replaced by single seat constituencies where the voting system would remain the single transferable vote.'[69] Gerald went on to give his cryptic assessment: 'On balance, however, it is the larger parties which stand to gain. The bigger single seat constituencies were to be, the more would they be likely to benefit.'

I have no doubt that my former constituency deputy, Liam Cosgrave, favoured a single seat constituency with transferable votes system. I sensed on several occasions that he was disappointed that Fine Gael did not go for his compromise and that of young Paddy Norton of the similar 'Norton Amendment'. During the 1959 referendum on PR, Jim Larkin Junior assured me that from his Dáil experience he favoured the single seat STV system. He conceded that initially the Labour Party would lose seats but was strongly of the opinion that thereafter the party would gain. He was very critical of the machinations of the redrawing of the multi-seat constituency boundaries at that time and of the internal party competitions for Dáil nominations under the PR system. However, because the Labour Party and most union leaders, notably Ruaidhri Roberts, were strongly opposed to the abolition of PR, he kept his counsel to himself.

But Garret was as persistent and as prolific as ever. Ten years later Garret again reiterated: 'The alternative would involve electing perhaps half the Dáil by preferential voting in single member constituencies and then compensating for the inevitable non-proportionality of the outcome of this vote by adding a similar number of members so as to ensure that each party has a proportional share of Dáil membership.'[70] We are still a long way away from a coherent and rational political debate on the democratic reform of our current electoral system. Fianna Fáil's earlier crude attempts to abolish PR have left a great affection within the electorate for the current system. I doubt very much if the body politic wishes to revisit this debate.

*

As the 1987 election loomed, there were increasing divisions in government between the Fine Gael and Labour ministers on the content of the 1987 budget. By that stage Gemma Hussey, as Minister for Social Welfare, had learned the facts of real life on low income from the secretary of the department, Jim Downey. Her Fine Gael background preoccupations about 'incentives to work' and 'over compensation ratios in social welfare' got short shrift from the bachelor Jim who virtually lived in his office. Although he resided in one of the old Mespil apartments and then in Burlington Road, Dublin 4, for most of his career, Jim Downey had little time for those who loved working people but only those who worked. He often pointed out to the cutters in Finance and to myself and Gemma that we should 'as an unemployed married couple' try to live on £49.75 per week, with a medical card and on differential rent. Bob Curran, Paddy Mullarkey and Michael Horgan, all dedicated officials from Finance, knew that they had formidable opponents in Jim Downey, Eddie McComiskey and John Hynes from Social Welfare.

Gemma learned the hard way about social deprivation and she transmuted into a fifth Labour minister. Garret was hugely protective of Gemma so Labour usually won. However, in Health I was a prime target of John Bruton for cuts. By mid-1986 Dick Spring and I had resolved that we had achieved some basic reforms and efficiencies, long overdue in the health estimates, and that we would reject any new campaign of health cuts by Bruton. Our Fine Gael colleagues were under no illusions. Having worked and suffered together for over four years, there were no recriminations when the Labour ministers decided to withdraw from government in January 1987. To Garret, I gave my reason for resignation:

> The Estimates and Budget framework for 1987 which has emerged from our government's discussions contain major reductions for health and social welfare expenditures which I cannot support. While in the lifetime of this government, which faced a daunting financial situation from the start, reaching agreement on the budget each year was inevitably difficult, the essential compassion for the underprivileged and vision for the future which was in evidence in earlier years was regrettably lacking on this occasion.

I went on to point out that I had taken numerous actions in the national interest to achieve economies, often against the tide of popular opinion, to eliminate abuse, improve efficiency and to increase cost effectiveness in the provision of services. I also pointed out that I had introduced important legislative changes including the Misuse of Drugs Act, the Health (Family Planning) Act, the Children's (Care and Protection) Bill, the Adoption Bill, the Clinical Trials Bill, the Nurses and Dentists legislation and the Tobacco Regulation and Bill. I also stated that I was pleased that we did establish the Commission on Social Welfare, the National Social Services Board, the Combat Poverty Agency and the National Pensions Board.

Garret replied: 'We have worked together for the good of our country during four years in an atmosphere of mutual loyalty and respect. I think we shall all retain warm memories of this partnership.'

On the day before we resigned from government, Jim Mitchell, Minister for Communications, circulated a memorandum proposing that Knock Airport should be designated a free port under the Free Ports Act 1986. I was shocked by the minister's statement that this status for Knock would be 'a magnanimous attempt by the government to assist the promoters in securing some return on the project'. This proposed major concession simply flabbergasted me at a time when every copper of State revenue needed to be protected. Strange how ministers go out of focus just before they leave office. Had the proposal leaked, one could only imagine the uproar in Galway, Shannon, Cork and Waterford, not to mention Dublin airport. The whole country would have had to become one big free port.

On the morning we resigned, our departures from the Council Room were emotional. I returned to the Custom House for the last time in the Merc from the Garda Depot. I had a final drink in my office with my private secretary, Alan Smith. He had been a tower of discretion when I was in my most argumentative moods. And my first private secretary, Chris Fitzgerald, also joined us, a civil service 'politician' to his fingertips. They eased my pain of exit from public office.

*

Immediately prior to our resignations, there was some speculation about the position of the Attorney General, John Rogers. He was the nominee of his close confidant, Dick Spring, when he was appointed by the Taoiseach in December 1984. On his appointment as Attorney General, his fellow barrister Brian Lenihan called him 'an innocuous junior barrister whose only achievement has been to write facetious scripts for the Tanaiste'. Brian Lenihan in politics invariably sold himself short. He was a man for the soft political option, enjoyed the good life, was lazy and unfortunately constantly played to the baser instincts of the Fianna Fáil gallery. He repeatedly failed to stand up to Haughey on crucial issues such as the Anglo-Irish Agreement in 1985. When Haughey referred to the Rogers appointment as 'John who?' Brian applauded. So much for the normal courtesies from colleagues at the Bar. Brian was cast by Fianna Fáil as their resident Tony Bennett. Handsome, gregarious and very bright, he could sing the party song at the Ard Fheis. But Tony Bennett gave up the booze. Brian was a wasted talent.

John Rogers had been very closely involved with Dick Spring in the formation of the coalition government. For two years prior to his appointment, he had given voluntary and invaluable legal advice to the Tanaiste and the Labour ministers. The Law Library had a very large body of Fine Gael supporters, some of whom were greatly peeved when John

Rogers landed the top job. It was quite clear to me in government that Peter Sutherland and Gemma Hussey had Fine Gael nominees in mind. They were furious with Garret when Dick Spring, as Labour's price for Peter Sutherland's nomination as EU Commissioner, insisted on the appointment of John Rogers. Garret knew only too well that on such issues, one did not mess around with Dick Spring.

To our great satisfaction, John proved to be an outstanding Attorney General. Unlike some of his predecessors he was a full-time occupant of the office. He did not rush away from government meetings for lucrative consultations. The issues he faced were extremely complex, for example, illegitimacy, marital breakdown, extradition and personal injury. These and many others such as the Stardust claims were handled with sensitivity and ability. The Fine Gael elite and begrudgers in the Law Library had to concede, by January 1987, that the first appointee from the ranks of Labour as Attorney General was a success. But chagrin was not confined to Fine Gael. In November 1984 the chairperson of the Labour Women's National Council, Marie Woods, had written to the Tanaiste and Labour ministers proposing that Mary Robinson should be nominated for the post. Marie was an adviser in my department but there was no way that Dick Spring or myself would have done so. Mary Robinson was a supreme individualist who, on legal and constitutional issues, was undoubtedly of great ability and energy. However, I felt that she would have attempted to unduly impose her will on the government.

Throughout Mary Robinson's eight years in the Labour party, 1976-1984, there was a distinct clash of political cultures. Frank Cluskey, Dick Spring and I were always preoccupied about the future of our party. Our family backgrounds had reared us in that milieu. Mary's was decidedly different. We found it hard to forget her advocacy of 'minority government' in 1982. Dick was quite uncomfortable with her. He felt he would be more at ease with John Rogers. Mary said: 'The way I saw it at the time was that I felt uniquely motivated, qualified and skilled.'[71] Mary Robinson did possess these qualities in abundance. But, on balance, John Rogers was the right choice.

Dick Spring was not to be forgiven by Mary. Not even when he approached her to be Labour's presidential candidate and not even when he nominated her for the contest. And after the election I was dumped from the Council of State after 17 years of nomination by three successive presidents. This occurred without even a telephone call or a mere letter of thanks. For the first time in decades there was no person from the ranks of Labour on the Council. And there has been none since.

A measure of John Roger's sense of the Constitution emerged when it became clear that the Labour ministers had decided to withdraw from government in 1987. John sent the following advice to the Taoiseach and the Tanaiste on 9 January:

> The Attorney General is the adviser to the Government in matters of law and legal opinion. Article 30.4 provides that 'the Attorney General shall not be a member of the Government'. This is a guarantee of the Attorney General's independence. His exclusion from the inner circle of Government serves to underline his independence. It is important that in the exercise of his functions the Attorney General should not be subject to the direction or control of any other person or authority. The resignation of Ministers for reasons to do with matters of economic or social policy does not give rise to a situation in which the Attorney General should resign. In fact it is important that he should not do so in such circumstances as this serves to underline the independence of his office. The Attorney though a political appointee must be in a position to put political considerations aside and to adopt an independent approach as legal adviser to the Government. JR.9.1.'87.

John Rogers served our country well.

*

Garret FitzGerald was the first Fine Gael Taoiseach to keep his political functions separate from the Catholic Church. John A. Costello said on the Mother and Child Scheme that he took his line on social and moral issues from the Catholic bishops.[72] Liam Cosgrave, in effect, adopted a similar role on these questions. Garret was truly different. However, being with Garret in government was akin to riding an energetic but unpredictable thoroughbred at full gallop, day and night, for over four years. It was all very dramatic and exhilarating even if one was liable to tumble off at any moment.

I am proud to have been associated with FitzGerald and Spring in those years in our endeavours to move our country and our people towards a more pluralist society. There was no ambiguity about our attitude or approach to dealing with IRA terrorism. This unequivocal policy contributed to the IRA–Sinn Féin leadership reassessing their policy of violent terrorism and to their contemplation a decade later of the prospect of a cease-fire. In advocating this policy we sought to have the government and administration of Northern Ireland shared jointly by all and devoted to the real interests of all its people. Above all, Garret FitzGerald sought to ensure that our democratic institutions were governed and managed with integrity for the benefit of all. When the coalition government first entered office in mid-1981 and again in 1982, the budgetary situation was dire and the estimates were in a total shambles. It took six grim years to bring public expenditure under control. As Michael McDowell rightly wrote in 1993: 'In retrospect, Garret FitzGerald obviously saw Fine Gael and Labour as natural allies. Between them he saw the basis for building social democracy in Ireland. Unfortunately for that point of view, the 1982-'87 coalition took office at a time and in circumstances where history and the state of the public finances completely pulled the carpet from under the implementation of social democratic policies.'[73]

As Minister for Health and Social Welfare, I bore the brunt of this essential exercise for over four years in the national interest. I was proud of my role even if I nearly saw my political demise in the process. For 20 years, the people of the Dun Laoghaire–Rathdown constituency elected a somewhat confrontational deputy who always preferred 'to tell it as it was' and who enjoyed every minute of the exercise in the democratic process. I shall always be in their debt.

Thirteen

With Alan and John in Finance

'We were broadly aware of the fact that people were avoiding tax. And all this had to be corrected, this was wrong. Everybody agreed it was wrong. For God's sake, whatever you do, don't rock the boat. The boat being the exchange rate. That was the culture ...'

Maurice O'Connell
Governor, Central Bank, 1999

I always thought that I was a particularly intransigent person on political issues until I experienced Alan Dukes at first hand. Once he reached a conclusion in government it had the finality of fast-drying concrete.

The interminable and debilitating cabinet disputes about public expenditure cuts that marked the 1982-1987 coalition government could largely have been avoided if we had introduced Deposit Interest Retention Tax (DIRT) and the National Lottery in 1984. These two major innovations could have contributed an initial £200 million per annum to the 1984 budget and substantially more in subsequent years. But Alan and most of his Fine Gael ministerial colleagues had been thoroughly indoctrinated by the Department of Finance and by their party's economic advisers in the belief that draconian cuts in public services, and particularly in the social services, were a prerequisite to fiscal recovery. They balked, of course, at severe cuts affecting the professional middle classes and the better-off farmers. The introduction of DIRT would have claimed back some vital revenue from these sectors for the State. The Department of Finance, the Revenue Commissioners, the commercial financial institutions and the Central Bank were aghast at the very idea of DIRT. However, the Labour ministers and Garret FitzGerald were major exceptions to this school of thought.

Shortly after the formation of the government in 1982, it was agreed to set up an inter-departmental group 'to consider the question of a withholding tax, including reference to yield, effects on liquidity, capital flows and savings'. There were no references to tax equity, evasion by non-residential accounts, all issues which had featured in the initial cabinet debate. The working group of eight was dominated by four senior officials from Finance who also held the chair and secretary positions. There was one nominee each from the Revenue Commissioners, the Department of the Taoiseach and the Central Bank.

William Scally, an economist and Labour activist who had been seconded from the Irish Sugar Company to the Department of the Environment as adviser to Dick Spring, was also a member of the group. Nine months later, in November 1983, the group reported a unanimous recommendation against the introduction of the tax. The principal conclusions put forward by the group were:

> In considering whether a withholding tax should be introduced, a critical consideration is that it would be likely to lead to a substantial outflow of funds even if non-residents were excluded from the scope of the tax. This would pose a clear threat to the official external reserves which are volatile and must be maintained at an adequate level. The effects of the tax elsewhere in the economy are more difficult to assess. Its impact on the level of financial savings and interest rates is difficult to predict but could be adverse. It could have an effect, which is also difficult to predict, on the distribution of funds between financial institutions, it could, for instance, lead to a loss of resources in the building societies. The strongest argument for a withholding tax is that it would increase the yield from tax on interest. The

tentative estimates in Chapter 7 show that, if the tax were introduced on 6ᵗʰ April 1984, the full-year potential net yield would lie in the range £65 to £95 million and for 1984, when repayments would be minimal, £100 million.

However, the group did have some tentative observations to make on the taxation system. They noted:

Changes in the existing system could, in theory at least, increase the yield from tax on interest. The changes which could be considered include: full disclosure by all institutions of all interest except that paid to non-residents; abolition of existing exemptions; increase in the composite rate in the case of building societies; bring forward the date of payment of tax under the composite rate arrangements; curbing the use of bogus non-resident bank accounts.

But the issue did not go away. After a traumatic brainstorming government session in August 1984, in the midst of dire budgetary predictions for 1985, Alan Dukes was virtually directed to submit a scheme for a withholding tax on deposit interest. He did so in October 1984. He pointed out to government that: 'The estimate of yield from a withholding tax must, therefore, be viewed with extreme caution − it should be regarded as indicating an order of magnitude... it is tentatively estimated that the potential full-year yield from tax on deposit interest, i.e. withholding tax at 35 per cent would be of the order of £215 million.' He went on to advise the government about the situation in 1983 on non-resident owned deposits in the Irish system:

A withholding tax, even though excluding non-residents, could still result in significant outflows of funds from Ireland. Fears that the new tax would be extended or a greater fear of disclosure in the case of those using accommodation addresses could give rise to significant outflows. At end-1983, non-resident owned current and deposit accounts totalled £2,269 million of which about £800 million was denominated in foreign currencies. A substantial withdrawal would be disastrous for the external reserves.

Alan then threw in the opposition of the Central Bank for good measure. Tom Coffey, former secretary of the Department of Finance was now the Governor of the bank. While the bank enjoyed a clear statutory independence, it was no surprise to see a convergence of views between it and the Department of Finance. The minister reported to the government that the Central Bank 'has grave reservations about the introduction of a withholding tax in present circumstances ... In particular, it would be essential not to exclude the building societies from the institutions to which a withholding tax would apply in view of their existing overall favourable treatment'.

Finally, Alan Dukes was in no doubt about his advice to the government. He stated: 'The Minister for Finance strongly advises against the introduction of an interest withholding tax because of the very serious effects it would have on the economy.... The tax would be likely to have a very significant impact on the level of domestic interest rates and on the financing of the Exchequer borrowing requirement. Because of the many uncertainties involved, there can be no guarantee that the withholding tax would produce a substantial additional yield for the Exchequer.'

But the Minister for Finance did not have the last word on this fundamental tax reform. DIRT was introduced after the 1986 budget after prolonged pressure from the Labour ministers. Under the Finance Act of that year, financial institutions were obliged by law to retain a portion of the interest due on all deposits other than accounts held by non-residents who were exempt from DIRT because they were intended for the use of foreigners working in the country on a temporary basis or people living abroad who wished to invest their money here. Irish residents were not eligible to hold such accounts.

One must recall that the new DIRT tax was introduced at a time of high inflation and high interest rates. By using the financial institutions to retain the tax, it provided the government with a highly effective way of tapping into the growing profits of many Irish savers who kept their money on deposit. A great irony of this situation was that Alan Dukes was reshuffled out of the Finance portfolio prior to the enactment of that Finance Bill. I suspected at the time that his obdurate opposition to DIRT was a major factor in Garret FitzGerald's decision to move him. Alan was allocated the Agriculture portfolio on his very first day in the Dáil in 1981 where he should have remained; he would have proved to be an outstanding minister in Ireland and commissioner in Europe.

After the resignation of Garret FitzGerald in 1987, Alan became party leader. Unfortunately he treated his parliamentary colleagues as a senior psychiatrist treats a group of psychotic patients. Alan knew he was the sharpest consultant in the Dáil hospital. It never dawned on him, despite several warnings, that the patients might rebel and change doctors. And they did just that.

In the light of the Dáil Public Accounts Committee's inquiry into DIRT in 1999, it is of particular interest to note that among Labour ministers and advisers in 1986 there was considerable dissatisfaction about the relationship between the government and the Revenue Commissioners. There was a perception among us that the commissioners were ordained to be responsible to nobody but themselves. There was a strong view that we, the government, could enact tax legislation but the commissioners would interpret it and implement it in their own good way. The senior officers of Finance and Revenue had, in our assessment, a rarefied inter-locked relationship apart from the government of the day.

Dick Spring was strongly of the view that an element of ministerial accountability should be inserted into this relationship. In November 1986 he wrote to John Bruton proposing that: 'A fundamental change in the system and management of Revenue collection is essential. This could require a Minister specifically in charge of Revenue Administration with cabinet status and the abolition of the Revenue Commissioners as such. The Fifth Report of the Commission on Taxation found that the administration of taxation has virtually broken down. It contained many recommendations for change and a number of these should be implemented.'

This was an unheard-of proposal. In his letter to John Bruton he was very careful to point out that: 'Legislation setting up the new Ministry would have to preclude the Minister from interfering in the affairs of individual taxpayers.' But John Bruton would not hear of it. John had become part of the system. The capacity of the senior public servants to absorb their ministers to their immutable bosoms is immense.

In December 1986 John Bruton replied to the Tanaiste:

> I do not agree with your main proposal here. There is in fact a cabinet minister at present in charge of tax administration, namely, myself. I could not countenance a second cabinet minister dealing with tax matters. I think it unlikely that our colleagues would either: they probably feel one minister dealing with that subject is more than enough! Tax administration is in any case work of an executive rather than a policy nature and seems quite inappropriate for a cabinet minister to discharge as his sole function. I would also be strongly opposed to the abolition of the Revenue Commissioners since this would be seen as removing from the tax administration its independent status. In practical terms, if a minister were to take on the executive functions of the Revenue Commissioners, it is difficult to see how he could avoid being drawn into the affairs of individual taxpayers.

The autonomy of the Revenue Commissioners was preserved. As far as John was concerned, all was well within Dublin Castle bar a bit of a shake up now and then. We now know more about the Revenue culture of those years. Had Dick Spring's proposal been considered by the government at that time, a great deal of the trauma of recent years could have been overcome. The current role of the Minister for Finance in government is one of multiple responsibilities. Dick Spring, Fergus Finlay, John Rogers, Willie Scally and myself believed that the classical Anglo-Irish governmental fiction that the Chairman of the Revenue Commissioners should be a repository of remote independence from the executive should be reformed.

I also believe that the appointment of the Revenue Appeals Commissioners should be subject to the Top Level Appointments Committee.

*

John Bruton has been a central figure in Fine Gael for more than 30 years, serving in government in five departments for 13 years and as Taoiseach from December 1994 to June 1997. And he was still only 53 years of age in 2000. We were both elected to the Dáil in 1969. I am 12 years his senior and from a totally different background. He was Clongowes, King's Inns and a wealthy farming background.

In 1981-1982 I was his minister of state in Finance. We were both shocked by the state of the public finances. In that short government he worked day and night. He was a whirlwind of political energy. He never walked to meetings: he ran, consuming takeaways on the way.

I admired his integrity. Apart from his crucial intervention in the successful divorce referendum in 1995, his political judgement was poor. In the government of 1982-1987, he misjudged Dick Spring, Frank Cluskey and myself on several occasions. Frank was the ultimate conspiracy theorist; John and he never saw eye to eye.

Labour's 1992 election campaign was the culmination of four years of an outstanding opposition performance by Dick Spring. He became the most trusted politicial leader in the Dail. A political romantic, Fergus Finlay, had a brilliant capacity to highlight injustices in Irish society. His scripts were instant and searing. With John Rogers as close confidant, and Pat Magner and Ray Kavanagh feeling the party's pulse, we won 32 seats. I had a ball as director of elections

John's most serious misjudgement was in the aftermath of the 1992 general election. He assumed that he was going to be ditched as leader of Fine Gael. His negotiating options with the other party leaders were circumscribed by his internal critics. He then wrote his suicide note. On 4 December 1992, nine days before the Dáil reconvened, he wrote to Dick Spring excluding the Democratic Left from any Fine Gael-Labour government. To add blood to the note, he proposed that the PDs should be included.

I went on a RTÉ radio programme a day later. I informed Nora Owen that when Dick would meet her leader, he would 'put manners on him'. And Dick did just that when they met alone in the Shelbourne Hotel's Constitution Room. What perturbed Dick more than anything else was the insistence by John, in a letter to him prior to their meeting, that a prime 'parameter' of such a government was 'an agreed budgetary position for each of the five years'. This had a distinct whiff of our exhausting disputations of 1982-1987. And the PD vinegar was now added to the wound. This would have been our coalition of nightmares.

I was shocked by John's naïvety. He pushed Spring into the loving Longford embrace of the astounded Albert Reynolds. Desmond O'Malley then came to browbeat Dick. They had such a slagging match that O'Malley stormed out leaving his overcoat behind. He came back for the coat: that was all he got. Both he and John Bruton lost out.

In 1992 Dick Spring was by far the most popular leader in the country. In an opinion poll during the election campaign on their preference for Taoiseach, the national sample gave Spring 38 per cent, Reynolds 20 per cent, Bruton 13 per cent and O'Malley 13 per cent. This gave rise to the strategic proposal for a 'rotating Taoiseach'. Subsequently, of course, Dick rotated Albert Reynolds and John Bruton!

One of my most memorable clashes with John Bruton was when he succeeded Alan Dukes as Minister for Finance in the closing months of the 1982-1987 coalition. Had I lost the battle, I would have walked out of government there and then.

The issue was fundamental. It related to the income eligibility guidelines for medical cards. There were three categories of eligibility for health services. The category to which a person belonged determined what services he/she should pay for, and what services he/she was entitled to free of charge. The three categories were those persons who were unable without undue hardship to arrange general practitioner services for themselves and their dependants. About 37 per cent of the population were in this category. Secondly, persons, together with their dependants, whose annual income was below a specified limit, £13,500 from 1 June 1985. About 48 per cent of the population were in this category. And thirdly, persons, together with their dependants, whose income was above the specified limit. About 15 per cent of the population were in this category.

In October 1986, the Department of Health wrote to the Secretary of Finance indicating that the current year income guidelines for medical cards were to be revised from 1 January 1987, in accordance with the increase in the consumer price index, i.e. by 3.1 per cent. This had been a long established practice for the previous 16 years. In November 1986 I was shocked to receive the following from John Bruton: 'I have no option but to refuse sanction for any increase in the guidelines for 1987. I will leave it to you to ensure that the Chief Executive Officers of health boards abide by this decision. It is not open to them to act unilaterally; the Attorney General has advised that my sanction is required to the setting of criteria for eligibility for medical cards.'

I replied immediately to the Minister for Finance:

> The proposals for increase are purely an updating of the change in money values over the past year and will not in themselves result in any increase in numbers of cards issued and consequently will not involve any additional expenditure. Your decision, therefore, will involve a withdrawal of cards from persons whose financial circumstances have not changed in real terms. A refusal to make the required adjustment will be seen to be a further attack on the less well off and most vulnerable members of our society.

The battle-lines were clearly drawn. However, John Bruton was, in my experience, an extremely stubborn minister and I was not surprised to receive a missile by return from the army dispatch rider which read:

> My decision on the medical card guidelines stands. You understand well the resource constraints that

makes this essential. I must leave it to you to ensure that employees of health boards, who are ultimately responsible to you, carry out the functions for which they are well paid from taxpayers' money. It will also be for you to decide what legal steps need to be taken to ensure that these employees do not step out of line. You may also wish to discuss the matter with your Accounting Officer, as he could also be open to criticism by the Comptroller and Auditor General and the Public Accounts Committee if he is seen to be involved in the spending of public monies without proper authorisation.

Notwithstanding this emphatic admonition by John, I knew that the weight of political argument was on my side. John Bruton was dogged by an uncanny predisposition to pick the wrong budgetary issues on which to make a stand. He had decided to elevate the issue into one of principle. Of all the cuts devised by his departmental officers, it was unquestionably the most regressive and politically untenable. I contacted John and privately pointed out to him that in 1984 there were 18,751 medical cards issued in his Co Meath constituency concerning some 37,000 persons, many of whom were married couples with a gross income of less than £95.50 gross per week or, if they had three children under 16 years, less than £127.00 gross per week. But my explanations were all to no avail.

I decided to send him a final note before raising the issue as a '12 o'clock item' (when we could raise issues of urgent public importance) at the next government meeting. I wrote to John that November:

I cannot see how you can sustain your 'decision' that there should be no increase in these guidelines for 1987. Quite apart from my total disagreement I would point out that the outcome would be to <u>lose</u> control of the eligibility situation and worse still we would be forced to climb down. This is because in exercising their discretion on the issue of eligibility for medical cards the CEO's are exercising a quasi-judicial function, comparable to Social Welfare

Deciding and Appeals Officers. In this they are not
subject to Ministerial direction.

But John was as unbending as ever. He clearly intended that
the will of Finance would prevail. He was like his fellow
Meathman, Tommy O'Dowd, going for goal in Croke Park,
head down, oblivious to injury or direction. A few days later I
handed around at the government meeting the draft newspaper
advertisement on the guidelines I proposed to publish as my
Christmas gift to the electorate. The Chief Executive Officers of
the Health Boards were unaware of the ministerial dispute;
there was no leak to the media in any way. I had forewarned
my Labour government colleagues of my clash with John
Bruton.

As soon as I placed the issue on the cabinet table, John went
'ballistic'. He again reiterated all his correspondence. I reeled
off the number of medical card dependants in Cork, 135,000,
and saw Peter Barry's eyebrows shoot up; in Westmeath,
25,000, and I saw Paddy Cooney wince; and in Waterford,
32,000. Austin Deasy did not bat an eyelid! In Dublin there
were 250,000 dependants and even the Taoiseach stopped dead
in his calculations when I emphasised that number with an
emphatic flourish. I further pointed out that thousands of
pensioners, the unemployed and welfare recipients in all other
counties would lose their medical cards as they came up for
renewal. The Taoiseach decided to do a 'tour de table' and I
won the day.

John Bruton went pale and wrote a note to the Taoiseach.
Garret did not read it out but passed it to the Tanaiste.
Meanwhile, John had gathered his papers and left the cabinet
room. We had no doubt that either he had resigned or
threatened to resign. Things looked ominous.

Garret suggested a coffee break. Dick turned to me and
muttered, 'Barry, you have fucked it up, again!' I responded
'Great issue for an election, Dick!' However, it was Dick who
went over to the Finance offices by the tunnel in government
buildings to talk to John. The government meeting resumed
about an hour later with John back in his place in more ways
than one. The Taoiseach called 'next business' and not a further
word was said. The advertisement appeared the following

Sunday. There was no animosity between John and myself. It was up-front coalition business.

However, Finance did have the last word. The government decision contained the proviso that in future the prior agreement of the Minister for Finance would be required and that this should be confirmed in a future statute. As far as I know no amendment was ever introduced.

*

I was to have one further major health estimate battle for Budget 1987 with John Bruton. In 1985-86 the General Medical Services Scheme, including drugs, cost about £112 million. Because of the growing number of persons eligible for the scheme due to increased unemployment, the increased price of drugs and our ageing population, the cost of the scheme had risen from about £92 million in 1982.

John's solution was one of long standing in the Department of Finance, namely, to introduce a £1 charge per prescription for medical card holders. This, he argued, would be a disincentive to over visitation of GPs and over-prescribing of drugs. John had a complete aversion to anything that was 'free'. He loved working people provided they worked! The £1 charge became a matter of political principle. The scene was set for another confrontation.

Meanwhile, I had sought the authority of the government to pursue negotiations with the medical profession on a new form of contract for the GMS, which would provide for payment primarily on the basis of capitation and for a superannuation scheme for such GPs. The total costs of both would not exceed the existing levels of expenditure on the GMS Scheme. I informed the government that I was satisfied that no possibility existed for agreement on a new method of payment for doctors without the provision of a pension scheme. The only effective option remaining to bring the cost of the GMS under control was to bring about a change in the method of payment, i.e. from the fee-per-service system to one based on capitation.

The response of John Bruton was quite explicit. He held that: 'Detailing of expense elements such as pensions could have repercussions for the basis of payment of other groups such as sub-postmasters or architects or barristers or veterinary surgeons who also rely to a substantial extent on the public sector for their incomes.' The Minister for the Public Service, John Boland, indicated that he had fundamental objections to the State providing a pension scheme for GMS doctors. I put on the record:

> With regard to the question of a £1 per item prescription charge the Minister for Health is totally opposed to the introduction of such a charge. It would require amending legislation which he would not be prepared to sponsor. He would regard such a proposal as inequitable in so far as it has an impact on the least well-off sectors of the community who, by definition, are unable to meet their primary health care needs without undue hardship. Furthermore, the Minister considers that a charge would be quite ineffective in producing savings because of the incentive provided for both doctors and patients to maximise the quantity of drugs supplied on each occasion when a prescription charge is levied.

I also rejected as unrealistic the proposal that capitation payments in future would be composite in nature, as proposed by the Minister for Finance. I had already indicated my belief that a formal pension scheme was necessary for the achievement of desired changes in the GMS. I strongly held the view that the virtual absence of investment in general practice was a major contributory factor of escalating demands for impatient treatment. GPs in the British NHS were also independent contractors but had a statutory pension scheme. However, despite the intensity of our positions there was no decision on the issue in government. All ministers knew that Finance had been peddling the £1 prescription charge since about 1981. But the issue did not fade away at this point.

The general secretary of the Irish Medical Organisation, Michael McCann, and the president, Dr Ken Egan were well aware of my difficulties on these issues. They were guardedly in favour of my approach, understandably so because of the extreme diversity of opinion within the IMO on all such issues.

For example, Dr Sean Baker, with whom I had severely crossed swords over services at Bantry Hospital, held the view that 'Barry Desmond's statement that he is going to bring in pensions should be treated with the contempt it deserves'.[74]

John Bruton then wrote to confirm that he was totally opposed to any pensions offer being made to GMS doctors. I replied that I had outlined at length in the memorandum before the government the reasons why I considered it entirely reasonable to provide a contributory pension scheme in the GMS, in association with capitation. At this stage I was wholly 'pissed off' by the behaviour of John Bruton. I knew he had an appalling remit in curbing public expenditure but he was like the Kerry firing squad that formed a circle for the execution. I wrote to him: 'I suggest that you concentrate on an analysis and understanding of the strategic issues in the health services rather than scouring the papers for material with which to chastise your colleagues. I regret the necessity to copy this letter to the Taoiseach and the Tanaiste.'

Thus John and I wished one another a Happy Christmas. It was to be our last festive season together. On Christmas day I realised that I had qualified for my public service ministerial pension. Stella and I would have given up our pension entitlements to win that battle!

*

One of the stranger issues to come before the government in 1986 — and one on which I found myself on the same side as John Bruton — was the future of the Queen Victoria statue by John Hughes, RHA, which was unveiled at Leinster House in 1908 by Lord Aberdeen, the Lord Lieutenant. It rested on a three-sided stone pedestal which also supported, close to ground level, three smaller bronzes, 'Fame', 'Ireland at Peace' and 'Ireland at War'.

In 1946, the Clerk of the Dáil requested the Commissioners of Public Works to provide an immediate increase in car-parking space in the courtyard at Leinster House by the removal of the monument if the government had no objection. In 1947 the government approved the removal of the monument and it was taken to the grounds of the Royal

Hospital, Kilmainham the following year. When the restoration works there were about to commence, it was further removed to Daingean, Co Offaly, where it was stored.

The Lord Mayor of Sidney, Australia, had asked if the Queen Victoria statue could be acquired as a gift or loan to be located in front of the newly restored Queen Victoria Building in Sidney. John Bruton strongly objected to the removal of the statue from Ireland and sought the approval of the government to put it on display on a secure site to be chosen by the Office of Public Works. The monument was, in his opinion, representative of one of the many traditions in Irish history. It was part of our heritage in no less a way than Norman or Viking remains.

However, the Taoiseach agreed in principle with the Australian request. I could never fathom why Garret favoured the Australian approach. Perhaps the Australians had been given particular expectations. Some years later, Garret maintained that the statue was 'particularly ugly', which was a strange justification for its export. Notwithstanding the objections of Peter Barry, Minister for Foreign Affairs, with which I fully agreed, Her Imperial Majesty was deported to Sydney. Even Éamon de Valera did not support such a policy in 1938 and more recently his granddaughter, Síle de Valera, pointed out that 'these sculptures have a story to tell. They were part of our history'.

No doubt Australia will become a Republic in time and I hope the famous statue by John Hughes will not be hidden away again.

Fourteen

Mother Church is Disobeyed

'Today's rulers are attempting to do with condoms
what their predecessors did with bread and circuses.'

Bishop Brendan Comiskey, 1991

'Deputy, do you think that if the government were to approve a
regulation whereby a married couple could buy twelve
condoms per month from a chemist that the Labour Party
might support such a measure?'

So said Erskine Childers to me, in all seriousness, one
afternoon in 1972 in the Dáil. He was Tanaiste and Minister for
Health at the time and the Magee constitutional challenge had
failed in the High Court. I assured him, tongue in cheek, that I
would consult with Brendan Corish. When I informed my party
leader, he was astonished. We decided to keep this bizarre
approach under wraps: nobody wished to embarrass poor
Erskine. In any event the subject was anathema to Brendan as a
devout Catholic. A year later Erskine was President of Ireland!

Shortly after I was elected to the Dáil in 1969, the
contraception issue came to the fore in public debate. Stella and
I had been married for nine years. We had two young sons,
Ciarán and Mark, and Eoin was expected in June 1970. We had
more than a mere political interest in the issues that arose at
that time. We rapidly developed a strong personal distaste for
the prurient pronouncements of various Catholic clergy on the
question.

In the early 1930s, it was perfectly legal to buy or sell
contraceptives in Ireland. But in the mid-1930s there came an

amendment to the criminal law which expressly forbade the sale or importation of contraceptives. The Censorship of Publications Act was amended to forbid the advocacy of the 'unnatural prevention of conception'. In 1963, the National Maternity Hospital in Holles Street opened a marriage guidance clinic that gave advice only on the rhythm method. By 1967 pharmaceutical sources were quoted as saying that sales of the pill had increased by 50 per cent over 1965. At the end of 1967 it was estimated that 12,000 Irish women were using the pill. Dr Eoin O'Dochnartaigh of University College, Cork, commented at the time that as a result of the moral and medical confusion surrounding the dispensation of the contraceptive pill, Ireland probably had the highest rate of cycle irregularity in the world! In 1968 Dr Jim Loughran, one of the most courageous general practitioners of the era, arranged a private meeting in a Dublin hotel to discuss, as he put it, 'Family Planning in Ireland'.

The first family planning clinic, known as the Fertility Guidance Company Ltd, was set up in 1969 in Merrion Square, Dublin. The clinic opened with no fanfare, and five doctors shared a rota to operate for two hours on two nights of the week. On the board were two pathologists, a consultant gynaecologist, two general practitioners, a registered nurse and a social worker. The seven were Jim Loughran, Robert Towers, Joan Wilson, D.O'B. Hourihane, Marie Mullarney, Yvonne Pim and Michael Solomons who later described how things were managed: 'Couriers of all sorts would bring supplies. Pills were easy to get as cycle regulators but caps and condoms were a difficulty. I would bring them over, my family would, friends of friends would.'

Senator Mary Robinson and two fellow independent senators made the first move to amend the 1935 Act in 1971. They introduced the Criminal Law (Amendment) Bill 1971 which proposed to permit the sale of contraceptives in stated outlets. The Senate refused a first reading and the bill was never published. Deputies Noel Browne and John O'Connell made a similar effort in the Dáil in 1972 but they too were voted down. These bills were minimalist but such was the vehemence of opposition that both Houses denied them the democratic opportunity to debate the bills. Any hope of rational public debate on Senator Robinson's bill in 1971 was dashed when John Charles McQuaid, Archbishop of Dublin and Primate of All Ireland, stated in a trenchant pastoral message:

> Given the proneness of our human nature to evil, given the enticement of bodily satisfaction, given the widespread modern incitement to unchastity, it must be evident that an access, hitherto unlawful, to contraceptive devices will prove a most certain occasion of sin, especially to immature persons. Such a measure would be an insult to our Faith; it would, without question, prove to be gravely damaging to morality, private and public; it would be, and would remain, a curse upon our country.

Stella and I were deeply offended. His statement was a direct repudiation of the statements issued by the leaders of the other Christian churches in Ireland. In effect we were both immoral and criminals. The archbishop's curse upon us was reminiscent of clerical denunciations of centuries past.

It seemed to us that the bishops were transfixed by the personal self-determination of a couple availing of contraceptives. They seemed obsessed by the sexual act. Such preoccupations, by a group of celibate priests, mostly much older than us, seemed downright unhealthy. It was all very disturbing to us in our own marriage which, like most, had its own trials and tribulations. These clerical certitudes, stated with such dogmatic intent, were a brusque intrusion in our family life. We were conscious that many priests did not share such extreme views on personal morality. However, we were left with the profoundly disturbed feeling that a clergy that lives alone, thinks alone about sexuality, pronounces alone and moralises about lonely strictures on family life, sadly, dies all alone. As Frank McCourt put it: 'The Catholic Church in Ireland left a national legacy of retarded sexuality. It is hard to forgive damage like that.'

We continued to have many a discussion about the strange preoccupation of the Catholic hierarchy with the allegedly 'permissible family planning methods'. I was aware that a book by a Catholic doctor (*Laws of Life*) advocating the use of the infertile period was banned by the Irish Censorship Board in 1941. The board considered that the indiscriminate spreading of knowledge about the 'safe period' could lead to indecent conduct and public immorality. This method was being widely promoted in Cork by Bishop Cornelius Lucey. If one wanted to adopt 'the Billings-Lucey method', one merely had to go along to any of a number of Cork churches where one would be given a full and detailed explanation of what was claimed to be 'a natural method of family limitation'. The explanatory leaflet at the time read: 'Remember the rule for early safe days when you begin to use them — dry day, safe night, skip a day ... do not forget to put white baby stamps on the 1, 2, 3, days after the last day of the peak...' Such was the Billings Method. Stella and I found it extraordinarily difficult to appreciate how this method was less 'artificial' or more 'natural' than taking a daily anovulant pill. Strange were the preoccupations of the Catholic hierarchy in their determination to keep us from 'the occasions of sin'.

Another significant intervention in this debate came from the Irish Theological Association in May 1972. The association had set up a working party to examine and make recommendations on provisions in the Constitution and legislation of the Republic which might be considered discriminatory or diverse on religious grounds. The association was primarily an organisation of people teaching theology in Ireland. The working party included Enda McDonagh, Professor of Moral Theology, T.C. Kingsmill Moore, formerly a judge of the Supreme Court, Seán MacBride, SC, G.B.G. McConnell, Presbyterian minister, Louis McRedmond and Mary Robinson. Among its many recommendations was that Section 17 of the 1935 Criminal Law Amendment Act be amended to remove the restrictions on the freedom of choice in methods of family planning. One can only imagine the ire which this report provoked in the hierarchy which saw one of its outstanding theologians, Enda McDonagh, subscribe to the reforms proposed by the working party.

Senator Mary Robinson's second private members' bill received a first reading in 1973 but still faced a formidable phalanx of adversaries. It differed from her first bill in that it proposed to transfer jurisdiction from the Minister for Justice to the Minister for Health but was defeated by 32 votes to 10 in 1974. During that debate in the Senate, the Minister for Justice, Paddy Cooney, announced that the government intended to introduce its own bill. Little did he appreciate that his own party colleagues and government members would also scuttle his bill. A measure of the die-hard attitudes of the 'old guard' of Fine Gael was the contribution of that party's leader in the Senate, Michael J. O'Higgins. *The Irish Times'* editorial was scathing: 'For the Fine Gael leader in the senate to say that "in this country, the common good happened to be for a 90 per cent or more Catholic majority" is surely strange in the era of Sunningdale and a proposed Council of Ireland. This country!'[75] Mary Robinson and her co-sponsors, Senators Trevor West and John Horgan, had displayed great courage. The defeat of the Robinson Bill was marked by the first demand by the anti-contraception lobby in the Houses of the Oireachtas for a referendum on this contentious issue of social policy. It was the forerunner of the pro-life and abortion referenda demands.

In the meantime, though, the Supreme Court had given a majority judgement on the Magee case in 1973, deciding that the ban on the importation of contraceptives was contrary to the Constitution and hence not part of our law. The judgement was to the effect that married couples were entitled not to have reasonable access to contraceptives denied to them and that the ban on importation was such a denial. It was to have a profound impact and it paved the way for the ongoing reform of the legislation over the next two decades. One of the judges, Justice J. Henchy, presented the essential facts of this historic case:

> The plaintiff, Mrs Magee, who is aged 29, lives in the restricted quarters of a mobile home with her husband, who is a fisherman earning about £20 a week, and their four children; during each pregnancy she suffered from toxaemia; during her second pregnancy she developed a serious cerebral thrombosis from which she nearly died and which

left her temporarily paralysed on one side; and during her last pregnancy she suffered from toxaemia complicated by hypertension. She has been advised by her doctor that if she becomes pregnant again there will be a very great risk that she will suffer a further cerebral thrombosis... Because of her medical history of vascular thrombosis and hypertension, her doctor advised against an oral contraceptive and recommended instead an intra-uterine device, to be used with a contraceptive jelly. But when the packet containing it was sent to her by post, it was intercepted and seized by the customs authorities.[76]

In January 1974, David McConnell who lectured in genetics in Trinity College, Dublin, and who was managing director of the non-profit making Family Planning Services Ltd wrote:

On December 19th, the Supreme Court found in favour of Mrs Magee that there was a personal and private right to space one's family. The very next day the Attorney General issued summonses against the Irish Family Planning Association and Family Planning Services, and shortly afterwards a consignment to me of literature on family planning was confiscated by the Customs, something which had not happened before. In family planning terms we are still a primitive backwater, and while the Supreme Court decision has important implementations for the future, it brings little or no immediate respite for those in most urgent need.[77]

Early in 1974 the national coalition government introduced an extremely restrictive bill entitled, revealingly, 'The Control of Importation, Sale and Manufacture of Contraceptives Bill, 1974'. The bill still retained jurisdiction in the Minister for Justice. Any importation or sale would require a ministerial licence and any unmarried person convicted of purchasing a contraceptive was liable to a fine of up to £100! Paddy Cooney was roundly attacked from the left and the right about the bill, the left maintaining that it was far too restrictive and the right finding it far too liberal. Throughout this debate, the *Irish*

Catholic newspaper played a strident role in attacking those deputies who dared to support this minimalist bill. In an editorial it posed the question: 'How can any deputy have on his conscience the responsibility of supporting a Bill that smoothes the way towards the spread of venereal disease in this country on a scale similar to that being experienced in countries that have already legalised contraceptives?'[78]

The Dáil debate was revealing. Paddy Cooney stressed that any person who manufactured, sold, offered for sale or advertised an abortifacient was liable to a fine of £1,000 or two years in jail. Many opponents had alleged that the pill was an abortifacient. Michael Kitt of Fianna Fáil demanded a referendum. Oliver Flanagan, Fine Gael, said 'You do not quench a fire by sprinkling it with petrol' and warned that contraceptives would add to the existing hazards to public morality represented by 'chaotic drinking, singing bars, lounge bars, side shows and all night shows'. Sean Moore, Fianna Fáil, declared that he was one of those who would 'stand up and be counted against the bill'. Dr Hugh Gibbons, a family doctor, asserted that the increased use of contraceptives must lead to an increase in venereal disease and the incidence of cancer of the womb. David Andrews, who had something of a reputation as a Fianna Fáil liberal, opposed the bill because contraceptives would become available to single persons. I strongly supported the bill as 'an essential part of social preventive medicine'. My namesake, Eileen Desmond, was as courageous as ever and supported the bill.

Then came the shock defeat in the Dáil. I was totally taken aback when the Taoiseach, Liam Cosgrave, voted against. John Kelly, the government's chief whip, and I had reassured government backbenchers that 'the boss', as they called Cosgrave, and all the cabinet would enter the 'Tá' lobby. I had personally checked with his private secretary, Frank Murray, who assured me that he had received no negative intimations from Liam Cosgrave. Neither had he received any positive indications. We were convinced that, notwithstanding a free vote, at least all members of the government would support the bill. Oliver J. Flanagan had claimed before the vote that he had in fact been responsible for forcing through the free vote on the bill at a meeting of the Fine Gael parliamentary party. I suspected, too late and well after the event, that Liam Cosgrave had been a willing, but silent, supporter of this ploy.

Paddy Cooney did not contemplate resignation that evening because to do so would only have made matters worse. Immediately after the vote Oliver Flanagan boasted[79] that he had sent a circular to the clergy and members of the Knights of Columbanus in his Laois–Offaly constituency, pointing out that of the five local deputies, four had voted against, including Tom Enright, Fine Gael, and that Charlie McDonald, his other Fine Gael colleague, had voted for in the Dáil. As Frank Cluskey ruefully remarked, 'There is real party loyalty for ye!' As a duped assistant government whip I was in despair. Brian Lenihan, then Fianna Fáil leader in the Senate, had indicated that his party's approach would be positive, constructive, generous and compassionate. It turned out to be nothing of the sort. The actions of Liam Cosgrave and his fellow minister, Dick Burke, who also voted against the bill, were all the more deplorable in that there was, in my view, a very clear imperative on the government of the day to introduce amending legislation in the light of the Supreme Court judgement.

Stella and I respected Liam Cosgrave for his defence of democracy at a critical period of political turmoil in the Dáil. However, on this issue we, and a number of backbench Fine Gael deputies, felt conned up to our teeth. The government was never to recover its internal trust. The impact of the vote was corrosive and it was the beginning of the debacle that was to be the general election of 1977.

While the political behaviour of Liam Cosgrave on this issue was deplorable all was not lost. In 1974 Mary Robinson again tabled a private members' bill. It differed from the Cooney bill in that it removed the prohibition on unmarried persons purchasing contraceptives. Mary was still determined not to throw in the towel. However, it was not until 1976 and the spring of 1977 that her bill received an extended debate in the Senate. In a forlorn attempt to be helpful and to avoid further defeat, Brendan Corish, Tanaiste and Minister for Health, intervened in the debate and proposed an all-party committee which could come forward with agreed principles to change the law. This was not acceptable, especially to Fianna Fáil, and once again the bill was defeated by 23 votes to 20.

*

During 1978 there were an elaborate series of consultations between the new Fianna Fáil Minister for Health, Charles Haughey, and a number of representative bodies prior to the publication of the Health (Family Planning) Bill, 1978. These included the Irish Congress of Trade Unions, NAOMI (National Association Ovulation Method, Ireland), representatives of the Health Boards, the various churches, the Catholic Marriage Advisory Council, the Irish Association of Social Workers and the National Health Council. This was the first formal series of consultations between the Minister for Health and the churches on the issue of contraceptive legislation. The closely typed minutes of these meetings run to one hundred pages. They range from the absolutist theology of Bishop Kevin McNamara to the fire and damnation denunciations of the Irish Family League, to the obsequious reaction of the Irish Medical Association and the constructive contributions of ICTU and the Irish Family Planning Association.

Dr McNamara, who was later to be appointed Archbishop of Dublin, was a member of the Catholic hierarchy's delegation led by Dr Cathal Daly, Bishop Lennon and Bishop Dermot O'Mahony. The minister was accompanied by the departmental secretary, Dr Brendan Hensey, whom I knew, not too well, from the period when Brendan Corish was Minister for Health from 1973 to 1977. I found him to be a most conscientious and very conservative departmental secretary. This was possibly the reason why Charles Haughey, at the outset of his meeting with the Catholic hierarchy, stated that no officer of the department was to be required to deal with matters relating to family planning if he should not wish to do so. The minister said that he was referring to the issue of conscience. My understanding, when I read this minute, was that the reference was to Brendan Hensey. Mr Haughey confirmed this when he interjected in the Dáil debate on my bill in 1985.[80]

Charles Haughey assured the bishops that there was no question of providing for abortion; that further research might be needed as regards abortifacients; that he had a keen interest in 'natural methods of family planning' and that he was considering whether the State should encourage promotion of research into this field since it had certain advantages over 'artificial methods'. Dr Daly said that the views they were now putting forward would not relate to the Church's teaching on the morality of contraception. Instead their stand would be on the social consequences on the moral environment. Regarding IUDs, Dr Daly said the problems relating to the use of IUDs stemmed from the various definitions of abortion. 'In the Church's view a person comes into being immediately fertilisation takes place. From a moral point of view the IUD was an abortifacient. A pregnancy — sometimes ectopic — may occur when a device is fitted.' Dr McNamara added that the appliance operated after conception by either preventing nidation or dislodging the fertilised ovum. From enquiries he had made there was no indication that it had effect before fertilisation. 'Officially, the Church taught that any destruction of a fertilised ovum is destruction of human life. This teaching is not entirely related to the presence of the soul. Geneticists say that from the moment of fertilisation the whole programme of a person's life is present. The Church's teaching is based on this scientific view and the probable existence of the soul from fertilisation.'

Haughey then raised the question of married versus singles and asked if it would not be better that those women who decided to pursue a certain lifestyle should have access to contraceptives rather than seek abortions if they became pregnant. Dr Daly said they would be totally against availability to single people: 'Paradoxically both unplanned pregnancies and abortions increased with availability of contraceptives. In England in 1976 the incidence of one abortion to 4 or 5 births refutes the credibility of the argument in favour of protecting single persons. The efficient use of contraception appears to require a degree of maturity in both parties which is available only in the stability of marriage.' Dr McNamara added: 'The use of contraceptives in marriage can have serious social consequences, not the least of which is the questioning of the institution of marriage. Even restriction to married couples, however, could not be enforced.'

Asked their views on an age limit only, the bishops indicated that this would be unacceptable. Dr O'Mahony remarked that, 'in particular, parents would be concerned at contraceptives being available to their children.' Dr Daly expressed concern at some activities of the family planning clinics particularly the possible referral of people to abortion clinics in England. He asserted that the international body, IPPF, promoted abortion. The secretary remarked that this was one of the reasons put forward for the involvement of health boards in family planning. Dr Lennon considered that the philosophy of the IFPA was wrongly based even if some of the people involved in the organisation were genuinely concerned. Dr McNamara wondered if the IFPA could be curtailed.

The minister's meeting with the Irish Family Planning Association provided him with a clear-cut exposition of the association's policy. The delegation was led by Dr George Henry, chairman of the IFPA and included David Nowlan, medical correspondent of *The Irish Times*. David and his wife Nora, who was a prominent member of the Labour Party, had a profound influence on my attitudes to health policy. George Henry informed Charles Haughey that a contraceptive service should be readily available throughout the country and that there should be no restriction to married couples only. In 1977 his association saw over 700 new patients. Almost 20,000 people came to the clinic for devices. These came from many areas because doctors and nurses generally, throughout the country, had little knowledge of contraceptive techniques and appliances. Questioned about IUDs, Dr Henry said he would not accept that they were abortifacient. They prevented the imbedding of a fertilised ovum but did not dislodge one already imbedded. In the normal course about 40 per cent of fertilised ova did not imbed. In his view there was even less justification for describing the mini-pill as abortifacient. The IUD was second best to the pill, and better then the pill for older women or for women who found the pill unsatisfactory.

There were occasional problems with the IUD but the major danger was in insertion by untrained people.

If Charles Haughey thought that the delegations would be plain sailing, he was soon disabused. The Irish Family League, which claimed to have a registered membership of 2,000 and had a petition of support signed by 40,000 people prior to the 1977 general election, was represented by Miss Mary Kennedy, Miss Maire Breathnach, Mr McDermott and Dr Quill. Mr McDermott bluntly informed the minister that 'Ireland was at the crossroads and that the destiny of the country depended on whether the minister's party decided that the objective moral order should give way to political expediency.' Dr Quill submitted a number of publications collected from news-stands which included nudity as evidence of growing promiscuity in Ireland, documents which, he said, 'were not meant for female eyes'. He went on to say that 'there was a group of some 4,000 perverts, law breakers, Marxists and Trinity imports appearing in all the recent radical movements and supporting homosexuality, freedom of the language etc.'

When Haughey met the delegation from ICTU he was on firmer ground. The delegation was led by Fintan Kennedy, president, Ruaidhri Roberts, May O'Brien, Brid Horan and Carmel Dunne. Congress stated that contraceptives should be made available on medical advice regardless of marital status, age or circumstances, and that holders of medical cards should have a right to the free supply of contraceptives on prescription as should women who suffered from specific chronic diseases which made the use of such drugs or devices medically necessary.

Following these consultations Charles Haughey decided to introduce a Health (Family Planning) Bill. The title was quite ingenious. As far as I know there is no such title in the statutes of any other nation. It avoided the dirty word 'contraception'. Haughey cynically described his bill as 'an Irish solution to an Irish problem'. The requirement of a general practitioner's 'authorisation' for the purchase of non-medical contraceptives was a calculated massage of the Catholic hierarchy and the conservative Fianna Fáil majority. He had no difficulty in pushing the bill through the Houses of the Oireachtas. After all,

Fianna Fáil had won the greatest overall majority ever of 84 seats out of 148 in the 1977 general election. Anyhow, he had the more pressing and very profitable prospect during this period of organising the anti-Jack Lynch forces.

*

In December 1982 when I was appointed Minister for Health, the government decided that the requirement that a prescription was needed to purchase non-medical contraceptives should be removed and that contraceptives should be made available through pharmaceutical chemists, licensed family planning clinics, health centres of Health Boards, surgeries of medical practitioners, and specified hospitals. I had asked the secretary of the department, Dermot Condon, and the assistant secretary, Joe O'Rourke, to put in hand a review of existing legislation. To their credit the internal review was completed by February 1983.

The salient point of the review was that there were no official figures available of the number of chemists who sold contraceptives in accordance with the terms of the Haughey Act. It was known that there was a strong group within the chemists' organisation that encouraged chemists not to sell contraceptives. The towns in which contraceptives were sold to chemists, by those licensed to import them, were set out on a map. There were outlets in 118 towns throughout the country. Since these licences were first issued at the end of 1980, the number of condoms authorised for importation was slightly in excess of 73 million by 1983! Contraceptives were supposed to be available only through chemists' shops owned by individuals and not by companies. It was clear, however, from advertisements in papers, that a number of other places were in fact selling contraceptives, for example, the Well Woman Clinic and Family Planning Services Ltd. It was known that contraceptives were freely available through the students' unions of the two Dublin universities.

The major objection to the existing legislation was the requirement that a prescription or authorisation of a medical practitioner had to be obtained before a person could purchase contraceptives. This was insulting to the ordinary citizen and offensive to all doctors. While in the case of some contraceptives, like the pill, diaphragms or coils, it was of course both necessary and appropriate to consult a registered medical practitioner.

I was most concerned to have the Attorney General on my side so I sent an advance copy of my proposals to Peter Sutherland. He replied the following day:

> The issues raised in the preliminary memorandum are essentially issues of policy rather than law. The 1979 Act, whilst not saying so directly, limits the sale of contraceptives to persons who, in the opinion of the medical practitioner, are going to use them in a matrimonial relationship. Of course, under present law, any person may import contraceptives into the State in personal luggage for his own use (whether he is married or not). However if the matrimonial status were to be rendered irrelevant, the government might feel it necessary to consider the question of the age of purchasers. Perhaps concern over this age factor provides the explanation for the proposal now made. The proposals made would not appear to infringe the Constitution.

I had some hopes of co-operation from Fianna Fáil considering the assurances which Haughey had given in an RTÉ radio interview when he said: 'I fully accept and acknowledge that the time has come for a major review of that particular piece of legislation, and we in Fianna Fáil will play a full part in that review, and I would hope that we will be able to come and agree perhaps with the Government when they put forward their proposals, as to what is the best thing to be done.'[81] The parties in government proceeded to consult with their parliamentary parties.

I found myself coming up against two brick walls in Labour, Sean Tracey and Frank Prendergast. Garret received a stormy reaction from Alice Glenn, Brendan Griffin, Brendan McGahon, Tom O'Donnell and Oliver J. Flanagan. It seemed at that stage that the adoption of even the most minimalist reform was going to go right down to the wire. In July, the Taoiseach wrote to me expressing concern to get the contraception legislation through the Dáil as speedily and smoothly as possible. I replied with draft heads of a bill. But I was truly taken aback when 17 medical consultants decided to go public in a major exercise against my proposals in October 1984. They wrote that if these proposals became law, the inevitable consequences would be increased promiscuity, with an upsurge in venereal diseases (syphilis, gonorrhoea, herpes and chlamydia) and carcinoma of the cervix as experienced in this and other countries.[82] They went on to state that 'legalising something which is productive of so much proven pathological and sociological sequelae is to us both reprehensible and horrific'. I was shocked that such eminent members of the medical profession as John Bonner, Professor of Obstetrics and Gynaecology TCD; Paul McQuaid, consultant psychiatrist; Arthur Barry, Past Master, Holles Street Hospital; Eamonn de Valera, consultant gynaecologist, signed that letter.

But they did not have it all their own way. Five of their distinguished colleagues, Dermot O'B. Hourihane, Professor of Histopathology; James McCormick, Professor of Community Health; J.S. Prichard, Associate Professor of Medicine; Petr Skrabanek, Lecturer in Community Health; and D.G. Weir, Regius Professor of Physics, Trinity College, Dublin, took them to task in no uncertain manner. They replied that there was no proof of such allegations.[83] They pointed out that these potential but very small risks should be set against benefits of contraception, such as the protective effect of oral contraception against ovarian and endometrial cancer, or the protective effect of condoms against venereal diseases and cervical cancer.

An acrimonious debate then occurred between Deputy Alice Glenn and Dr Paddy Leahy of the Irish Family Planning Association. Alice Glenn asserted: 'If we are not re-defining the family and we are saying we are going to make these available to all and sundry, what we are doing is advocating adultery and fornication.'[84] Dr Paddy Leahy replied: 'Our young people, Alice, are no more permissive or less permissive than the English or the Dutch or the French ... This is the old myth that the Irish are different...' By then the media was in full flight. Jack Jones of Irish Marketing Surveys assessed the issue quite clearly and showed that there had been a significant move towards the concept of having contraceptives available for all over the previous decade.[85] In May 1974, 16 per cent were in favour of their availability for all: by 1984 the percentage had increased to 41 per cent.

I became conscious that there was one singularly obnoxious contributor to the debate. Ever since the pope's historic visit to Ireland, Father Michael Cleary, a Dublin clerical populist whose hero was Charlie Haughey, had been on the bandwagon of simplistic moral truisms. He said about his bishop, whose hostility to contraception was a by-word:

> His opposition is on the basis of it being, you know, a social evil. His fears now, are the same as my fears. You see, put it this way. If you let your children have a party, and you say... leaving them to themselves... you say, there is a box of contraceptives on the shelf there. What you are saying to them is... look, I no longer trust you to behave yourselves, I am not too worried about you misbehaving, just don't get pregnant! Now, that is what the government is saying today. They are saying, kids of Ireland, we no longer trust you to behave yourselves! We don't particularly care whether you do or not, but we don't want you to get pregnant![86]

Father Cleary was a man of considerable talent, a charismatic public speaker with a wholly authentic Dublin intonation who appealed greatly to the 'ordinary' people of Dublin. But Stella and I never had any time for his base populism. Nor did we know at the time that he had a hidden family himself.

One of the most infuriating aspects of the whole debate was the silken ability of spokespersons on behalf of the Catholic hierarchy to face in apparently contradictory directions on the question. They were adamant that it was for the legislators to decide if the law would be changed while preaching that if the law was changed, great evil would be visited on the people. Their most prominent spokesperson, Bishop Joseph Cassidy of Clonfert, put forward this rationale on RTÉ radio shortly before the vote: 'First of all, it extends to unmarried people. What we will be doing then, is creating a climate, creating an environment, a moral environment for our people, for our young people especially which will make it very very difficult for them to live a decent life, to do the better thing. They will be assimilated into a kind of a culture, into a kind of a contraceptive culture if you like, in which it will be very difficult to live a decent life.' Thus, the scene was set for the deputies and senators to freely exercise their consciences on the Bill![87]

*

The debate among deputies and senators was intense, frequently emotional and invariably party partisan. Minister of State, Nuala Fennell, an outspoken feminist from South Dublin, nailed her colours to the mast. She said that she had examined the age profile of TDs and found that 66.6 per cent, or 109 members, were 43 years of age or over. She went on to confide to the House: 'Speaking for myself, I recall that sex was never discussed openly, but was always alluded to as related to vice and badness. The manner in which anything remotely connected with sexuality or female biology was dealt with in my adolescent years altogether denied girls an understanding of their basic bodily functions, left unanswered the many questions about sexuality and prepared us not at all for the roles of wife and mother.'[88]

John Kelly, also of Fine Gael, had no doubt where he stood on this issue: 'Nose poking is what this law is all about. It is the intrusion by the State into private lives. It has nothing to do with morality. There are several areas of what I might call sexual irregularity which are not crimes at all and some never were crimes here. For example, ordinary fornication is not a crime; adultery is not a crime; the act of prostitution is not a crime; it is not a crime to take money for sexual services.'[89]

Proinsias de Rossa of the then Workers Party said: 'Deputy Haughey's 1979 Act created a distinction between 'natural' and other methods of contraception purely on sectarian grounds, purely on the grounds that the rhythm method was the one acceptable to the Roman Catholic Hierarchy and that other methods were not acceptable to them. As a married man with a family I can think of no more unnatural method of family planning than the Billings or rhythm method.'[90]

Alan Shatter was a strangely unpopular deputy in the Dáil who successfully harvested the Fine Gael liberal vote in South Dublin. I served with him on Dublin County Council from 1974 to 1981 where he was somewhat unloved. He had an abrasive legal approach to most issues. Unfortunately he was devoid of political humour. He deserved, but never achieved, a senior portfolio in government. He questioned: 'Where are the women members of Fianna Fáil? Where is Deputy Máire Geoghegan-Quinn, the chairperson of the Committee on Women's Rights? Where are Deputy Mary Harney and the other members of the Fianna Fáil party who were able to do the two steps forward, one step backwards operation at the meeting of the parliamentary party last Wednesday?'[91]

But the daddy of them all was Fianna Fáil's Deputy Jim Tunney, the son of a former Labour senator, as I often reminded him to his annoyance. He had a unique pomposity and assured the Dáil: 'I have no special illusions about myself. I was a normal teenager and I took life at its various stages as it came to me. Without apology to anyone, I can say that I was happy to live along the lines that my parents and my pastors set for me. Indeed, I am indebted to them for the fact that at certain times in my life — and there were not too many of those — I was able to overcome the desires that Deputy De Rossa says we should all satisfy. These were times when I left aside what might be regarded as the ephemeral pleasures for what I know now in retrospect to have been long term happiness.'[92] Referring to the fact that in 1984 the cost to the British health scheme of the provision of contraceptives was £67 million, he said: 'Not too many in Finglas are in a position to contribute to that, so that young men can satisfy their desires on the young women of Ireland.'

Oliver J. Flanagan concluded: 'This is the first Bill to be passed in this House with the Red Flag and the clenched fist being waved outside Leinster House.'

Alice Glenn, still the formidable Fine Gael deputy, was the only woman to oppose the Bill. She was incessant in her denunciations. She said that:

> I have been given a choice which is: accept the code of immorality, of international socialism and reject the teaching of your Church or get out of the Fine Gael Parliamentary Party. The party rule concerning expulsion becomes like a clause in a Faustian contract and the full import of it will unfold very slowly. No matter what age limit is provided it will mark a break with the ethos of almost the entire known history of this country. It will have the doubtful distinction of being the first legislation since the penal days to be enacted in this land that is contrary to the law of God.[93]

Referring to the Irish Family Planning Association, Deputy Glenn added: 'They are anti-life, anti-love and anti-family. They have no tolerance of purity, chastity or honesty. They consider those virtues to be old hat and not to be bothered with. We all know that both the Minister, the Chairman of the Family Planning Organisation, Dr Rynne and Dr Leahy, also a member of that organisation, have abided by that diktat.'

It may come as a surprise to some people in Europe today to note that the former EU Commissioner for Social Affairs, Padraig Flynn, then a Fianna Fáil Deputy, held some strange views on this very question. He pontificated: 'The fashionable length of a lady's skirt or width of a gent's trousers might change but the right for young unmarried teenagers to fornicate is still unnatural and wrong.'[94] It was a great irony therefore, to note that in 1996 Padraig Flynn, as EU Commissioner for Social Affairs, launched a campaign in Brussels to distribute more than 300,000 condoms in Saint Valentine's Day cards as part of the 'Play Safe Europe Against AIDS' Programme! To his credit, Padraig allocated some 50 million ECUs for the AIDS awareness programme in 1996. I have never ceased to wonder at the capacity of former Fianna Fáil ministers to adapt to the changing social perceptions of the times.

I was profoundly grateful at that time for the support of my fellow Labour deputy, Mervyn Taylor. In 1985 Mervyn was a staunch anti-coalitionist but he faced this issue head on when he said that bald and pontifical statements have been made inside and outside the Dáil: 'As statements they are entitled to no more credence than the writings of the Emperor Justinian, a very learned man and the author of a fine legal treatise which was no doubt widely accepted at the time that homosexuality was the cause of earthquakes.'[95] This statement, coming from one of the three deputies who were of the Jewish faith, was one of great comfort to a very disturbed Catholic minister.

The support of my fellow Labour deputy, Frank Prendergast, of East Limerick was pivotal. At the final hour he found a formula. He said that he was in 'an awful dilemma' but having discussed the matter very fully over a long period with his colleagues and advisers in the Labour Party and the trade union movement in Limerick, he was guided by their advice that the only realistic and very unpalatable option he had was to abstain on this issue.[96]

Much later, Máire Geoghegan-Quinn informed me that as soon as my bill was published Charles Haughey, at the next meeting of their parliamentary party, without any consultation, bluntly informed all those present that the party would vote against. She spoke at length against this announcement pointing out that in relation to women in the west of Ireland, the provisions of the bill were quite inadequate. Mary Harney, David Andrews, Charlie McCreevy and Desmond O'Malley were clearly opposed to the Haughey line but he brushed aside their objections. In the end only O'Malley took a public stand on the issue. He paid the full price. It was a measure of the absolute control over the party by Haughey that the Fianna Fáil National Executive expelled O'Malley by 73 votes to 9. At the meeting Haughey personally recommend expulsion. Deputy leader Brian Lenihan announced the result as 'democracy in action'!

Throughout his long career Brian Lenihan persistently sold himself short. He did so within Fianna Fail, in the Dail and particularly at Fianna Faill Ard Feiseanna. He allowed himself to be cast in the role of party cheer leader. He did not use his considerable intellectual ability to stand up for himself. He did not face Haughey down when his party's interest and the national interest clearly demanded his intervention. We all held Brian in great regard. He was such a wasted talent.

In the two weeks prior to the vote in the Dáil, the pressures on the rural deputies in government in particular were intense. John Boland, Minister for the Public Service, was moved to protest during an RTÉ radio interview that it upset him deeply that he could discover in his country people who would address a member of a small minority religion in terms that were reminiscent of pre-war Nazi Germany. 'I can't see that lobbying is ever, or could ever be regarded as reasonable, nor is it reasonable to threaten the wives of deputies, that their children will be kidnapped, their house burned, nor is it reasonable to lobby deputies through their children at school.'[97]

In my response to the debate in the House, I emphasised that the bill did not in any way impose contraception on anybody, young, middle-aged or old. I pointed out that great difficulties were being experienced by a significant proportion of the adult population in gaining access to their desired means of limiting their families and engaging in contraception. I was adamant that

> there has been a demand from the medical profession to be relieved of the hypocritical requirement that I, as a married man, must go down the road to a general practitioner whom I know personally and ask him for an authorisation and a prescription, in personal humiliation, and then go along to a local pharmacist whom I also know personally and ask him for a packet of condoms across the counter. Not one woman from the opposition has spoken in this debate.[98]

However, I reserved a final criticism for Dr John O'Connell, who had taken the Fianna Fáil whip on this issue:

> For 20 years in Dáil Éireann from 1965, from his joint sponsorship of reform in this area with Noel Browne to his most recent editorials in the *Irish Medical Times*, Deputy O'Connell espoused this fundamental

reform. Now to win the award of the month for
hypocrisy, he goes with Deputy Haughey on this. I
find that embarrassing.[99]

The government won the first critical vote on second stage
by 83 to 80 votes. Three Fine Gael deputies, Alice Glenn, Oliver
J. Flanagan and Tom O'Donnell, and Labour's Sean Treacy
voted against as did Neil Blaney, the Independent Fianna Fáil
deputy. Proinsias de Rossa and Thomas MacGiolla voted for, as
did Tony Gregory, the Independent deputy. Frank Prendergast
and Desmond O'Malley, Fianna Fáil, abstained. It was a close
enough call. Had the bill been defeated the government would
have been terminally damaged. I would have been a dead duck
minister!

*

During the committee and final stages of the bill in the Dáil,
Deputy Alan Shatter shredded the preoccupation of the Fianna
Fáil spokesperson, Dr Rory O'Hanlon, who was still adamant
that the purchase of contraceptives should be confined to
'couples'. Alan Shatter said: 'What is the position, for example,
of a couple whose marriage has broken down and one of whom
has obtained a church annulment, who has been remarried
invalidly in Church and the person who obtains the Church
annulment and remarries comes to a doctor to acquire
contraceptives? Which couple are the contraceptives prescribed
for?'[100]

During this stage of the bill, I had another opportunity to
put on record my other concerns and my efforts to deal with the
broader related reforms. I stressed: 'Young people need a sense
of personal responsibility on issues relating to violence —
violence against the person, respect for the elderly and respect
for women in our society where there is rampant disrespect at
present. They need a sense of personal responsibility in relation
to respect for women and the capacity of a male to create a
pregnancy casually and experimentally and disappear into the
night leaving her alone, be she 15, 16 or 17 years of age. That is
the kind of issue this House should be discussing and trying to
ameliorate.'[101]

Monica Barnes, who had a long and passionate advocacy of women's rights in Irish society, made a trenchant intervention: 'We are talking about bleak, guilt-ridden, repressed times when a woman did not have any say, no income, no right to work away from the home and no choice as to how many children she would or would not have. I am talking about the period when if she did not get married and did not have children her value was even less.'[102]

The committee and final stages of the bill were carried by 82 votes to 79. Mary Harney, Mary O'Rourke, Eileen Lemass, also an MEP, and Máire Geoghegan-Quinn all voted against the Bill. Charlie Haughey really had 'the frightners' on them all: they all arose and followed Charlie!

*

In the Senate, I faced the same quota of hostility from Fianna Fáil. Senator Jack Fitzsimons denounced the bill: 'If religious morals are abandoned and human beings are regarded as simply a higher type of animal I could understand the promulgation of contraceptive practices. I see it as the acquiescence by women to the slave mentality that men can use female bodies for sensual gratification without any semblance of commitment or responsibility.'[103]

Senator Donie Cassidy was stridently emphatic in his denunciation. He claimed that he had 3,700 signatures from constituents and householders in Westmeath collected over a period of four days to display their enormous anger at the government and the minister for bringing in this bill. They felt that the bill had been foisted on them by a crowd of fanatics who wanted to undermine family life and flood the country with contraceptives and to promote abortion.

Senator Martin O'Toole had another family perspective. He advised his fellow senators: 'I come from a part of the country where we have our own natural family planning methods and they have worked reasonably well up to now. I have eight children — I know something about the subject.'[104]

Shane Ross pinpointed the Church and State confrontation. He said: 'I hope the government will take courage from their decision and their success in bringing this bill through the Dáil to introduce more measures of this sort on related matters. I refer to matters such as illegitimacy, the children's bill, adoption and divorce.'[105]

Catherine Bulbulia was equally emphatic in her support: 'This bill has as its backdrop the Kerry Tribunal, the tragic case in Granard, the Eileen Flynn case and, laterally, the discovery of the body of a tiny newborn baby girl in a plastic bag in Galway. Births outside wedlock have risen from 2.7 per cent of all births in 1971 to 6.8 per cent in 1983.'[106]

Another of the few women in the upper House was Catherine McGuinness, now a judge of the Supreme Court. Her contributions to radical reforms in Ireland over the decades have been outstanding. She said: 'Only recently we passed the Age of Majority Bill which clearly sets out that people of 18 years and upwards are full adults. We expect them to be able to die for their country, to vote for their legislature, to make full decisions with regard to financial contracts, to sue and be sued and to do all those other things that involve informed choices. Yet we say we cannot allow them to make informed choices in their sexual lives.'[107]

Another senator from Northern Ireland, Brid Rogers, said: 'Does anyone seriously think that the Catholics of Newry, Derry or Newtownbutler feel less bound by the teaching of their Church on matters of sexual morality than their counterparts in Dundalk, Buncrana or Clones?'[108]

But the most incisive and searing contribution of all came from my colleague Michael D. Higgins. He confronted the hypocrisy head on:

> It is traditionalism that has sent lonely women on the boat to England and has encouraged irresponsibility in paternity. It is traditionalism that has sent us the spectacle of a woman in the West of Ireland wondering how far she would have to travel to find some form of contraception. It is equally traditionalism that has given us such an appalling coldness in our relationships between men and women that have been inculcated in them over the years. It has filled the emigrant boats. It has provided all those battered people who are on the fringes of

society in London, Manchester and Liverpool, who carry with them the burden of this mixture of voodoo that was called traditionalism. I was reared in a culture that looked at an unwanted pregnancy as a woman who 'got into trouble', and when I was a teenager, as a woman who was regarded — I hope I do not offend anybody — as being 'up the pole'. Then the women disappeared to England and the child went into an institution. They all went on, traditionally happy ever after.[109]

*

Fifteen years later, I found it ironic that there were condom machines in the men's room in the Arts Block in Maynooth College and in the rooms of the students' union. Notices from the Department of Health about 'Safe Sex' were also on display.

Fifteen

A Taoiseach Who Never Was

'The canary at the Fianna Fáil coal face.'

Jim Kemmy, 1985

The debate in 1985 in the Dáil on the Health (Family Planning) Bill signalled the beginning of the end of Fianna Fáil as a cohesive, disciplined political party in the 1980s. Desmond O'Malley was the catalyst. He said that the most extraordinary and unprecedented extra-parliamentary pressure had been brought to bear on many members of the House. This was not merely ordinary lobbying, he said, but far more significant. 'I regret to have to say that it borders at times almost on the sinister.' He went on to assert:

> In many respects the debate can be regarded as a sort of watershed in Irish politics. It will have a very considerable influence on the whole political, institutional, democratic future, not just of these twenty-six counties but of the whole island. The politics of this would be very easy. The politics would be, to be one of the lads, the safest way in Ireland. But I do not believe that the interests of this State, or our Constitution and of this Republic, would be served by putting politics before conscience in regard to this. There is a choice of a kind that can only be answered by saying that I stand by the Republic and accordingly I will not oppose this Bill.[110]

I said at the time that this was the most courageous speech I had heard in my 16 years in the Dáil. I have had no occasion to change my view since then on Des O'Malley's intervention in that debate.

Following his expulsion from Fianna Fáil because of his abstention on the bill, Desmond O'Malley decided to set up the Progressive Democrats in 1986. He was rapidly supported by a group of talented, individualistic and very ambitious politicians such as Pat Cox, Michael McDowell and Michael Keating of Fine Gael, Mary Harney, Martin Cullen and Bobby Molloy of Fianna Fáil and Senators Helena McAuliffe and Timmy Conway of Labour. Helena often regretted her decision. She was 'the fall guy' in the Longford–Westmeath constituency when the PDs decided to run two candidates. She did not forgive Mary Harney.

Des O'Malley, Pat Cox and Michael McDowell dominated the party's ideological ethos. There was no shortage of wealthy supporters and media sympathisers who welcomed the 1986 version of the 'pay back time now' posturing of the PDs. Charles Haughey was a reverse magnet of support towards the PDs. O'Malley had enormous appeal among the professional and middle-income electorate. I experienced this backlash in Dun Laoghaire with the election in 1987 of Geraldine Kennedy, a talented journalist. She rapidly learned that constituency politics is a cruel trade. Upper-middle income support is very fragile. Geraldine's base was highly dependent on their measurement of their wellbeing. Her local party showed little loyalty to her in subsequent elections. That was the nature of the PDs. She survived one term and suffered a traumatic experience of electoral rejection.

The PDs' central thesis was that reductions in public expenditure could finance major cuts in personal and corporate income tax. They advanced the view that they knew where to cut, when to cut, and how to cut. By the end of 1986, O'Malley had formulated fairly detailed budget proposals for the 1987 budget. It would provide for a standard rate of income tax of 25 per cent on taxable incomes up to £15,000 for single people, £30,000 for married, all to be achieved over a five-year period. The PDs also proposed a general VAT rate of 15 per cent. The PDs' *Blueprint for jobs, fair taxation and social justice* was welcomed by the same gullible segments of public opinion and by the same gurus of the media which had hailed the 1977 Fianna Fáil manifesto. 'Happy days are here again', as in 1977, nearly became the theme song at the hugely attended PD rallies throughout the country.

Disillusioned anti-Haugheyites, some opportunistic Fine Gaelers and disgruntled Labourites transferred to the PDs. The government, although in our last few months of office, was most perturbed by the reactionary nature of the PD proposals and their serious long-term impact on the public finances. Meanwhile, the PDs in 1986 had received £277,000 in party political fundraising and donations. They received £444,000 in the 1987 general election alone, according to their published accounts: not far off one million in 2000 money terms.

What was the precise corporate and individual breakdown of these totals? We do know that O'Malley had a tempestuous roller-coaster relationship with Larry Goodman. In 1986 he wrote to Goodman soliciting money for the PDs. In January 1987 they had a very amicable meeting following which Larry sent Dessie a personal cheque for £20,000 for the party.[111] Dessie profusely thanked Larry and invited him to dinner after the general election. But it all turned very sour within the year when, according to Michael McDowell in the Dáil, Goodman brought undue pressure to bear on O'Malley over Harney's criticisms. Dessie became a major national critic of Goodman.

At a government meeting in late 1986, John Bruton, Minister for Finance, undertook an urgent costing of the PD proposals. His confidential paper gave an assessment of the PD expenditure reduction proposals; by basing their costings on the 1986 budget figures, the PDs did not take account of the £551m increase in the underlying 'no policy change' of current expenditure between the 1986 budget and 1987; the exchequer pay bill was due to rise by about £200m due to the effects of the public service pay agreement (including special increases), increments etc; and social welfare costs were due to rise by about £100m, due to the carryover effects of the 1986 increases and provision to cover cost-of-living increases in 1987.

The cuts proposed by the PDs were a quite extraordinary collection: ministers of state were to be reduced to seven; the senate was to be abolished; ministerial pensions were to be reduced; the Oireachtas restaurant subsidy was to be abolished; the budget of the Economic and Social Research Institute was to be reduced by 20 per cent; the grant-in-aid to the Dublin Institute of Advanced Studies was to be abolished; state forests were to be sold off to pension funds; the farm modernisation scheme was to be cut by 20 per cent; doctors were no longer to be paid for social welfare medical certificates; and the IDA advance factory constructions were to be reduced. The gullible supporters of the PDs, who above all else wanted their tax cuts, swallowed them, hook, line and sinker.

Fine Gael was scared to death by these exotic 'cuts' which were supposed to yield savings of some £340 million. On such flimsy postulations a new political party was spawned. In response to these proposals, the PDs polled 12 per cent of the national first preference votes and won 14 Dáil seats in the 1987 general election. On the basis of O'Malley's personal integrity and a promise of expenditure and tax cuts, it became the third largest party in the Dáil. Ironically, it posed at that time a greater threat to Fine Gael rather than to its Fianna Fáil roots. As a political party, it was yet to learn the robust realities of the real options which would face its ministers around the cabinet table. A decade later, the extraordinary incompetence of Mary Harney's general election campaign in 1997 destroyed Michael McDowell in Dublin South East, Helen Keogh in Dun Laoghaire and Mairin Quill in Cork city.

McDowell was a strange blend of orthodox economic theory, possessed of a great legal ability, and massive arrogance. It was clear from early on that he was spiked by unrequited Fine Gael ambitions. He became a toxic political cocktail which the Dublin electorate was reluctant to drink. With his demands for cuts in public expenditure, he scared the living daylights out of pensioners, the unemployed and public servants. They believed that Michael McDowell would destroy their standard of living. His turn of phrase was devastating. In 1989 during the course of the Finance Bill, he described Albert Reynolds, Minister for Finance, as having 'a neck as hard as certain portions of the anatomy of an equestrian gentleman'. Of Mary Harney, one can hardly fail to recall her fatuous claim that Ireland should emulate the economies of Hong Kong, Korea and New Zealand!

The Progressive Democrats were not so much a political party as a state of mind of the Irish electorate in 1987. They wanted to be liberal but only on Irish economic questions, as they quickly reinstated the Good Lord in their redrafted Constitution of the Republic. They wanted political power but not, initially at any rate, with Fianna Fáil and certainly not with Labour. They wanted public services but did not see why they should have to pay for them. They had mostly been in Fianna Fáil but did not want to be any longer. They wanted to be in Europe but not with the Christian Democrats and certainly not with the Social Democrats. Ultimately they wanted all their political cake but refused to eat any of it for fear of self-righteous indigestion! The fulminations of Michael McDowell often reminded me of the saying about General Patten: 'In your heart you know he's right; in your guts you know he's nuts!' They were like the Cork Militia, useless in times of war and dangerous in times of peace!

And for all this moral self-righteousness, Desmond O'Malley was quite prepared to share government again with Charles Haughey. And later Mary Harney was quite prepared to share the cabinet table with the remnants of the Haughey era despite the taunt of Prionsias De Rossa: 'Can the PDs live with Fianna Fáil's cosy relationship with Sinn Féin?' They were quite prepared to do so. As the saying goes: 'When a wasp loses its sting, it dies, but not before doing a mad dying dance.' But fair dues to Michael McDowell. He achieved a life-long ambition by being appointed Attorney General in 1999.

*

Some ministers rapidly adopt unwritten rules in relation to delegations to their offices. They quite rightly demand a written submission prior to receiving any delegation so that a brief can be prepared. Desmond O'Malley had a ceiling of five persons on all delegations to facilitate discussion. On one occasion, Pearse Wyse arrived from Cork with a delegation of 25 to see O'Malley. The minister stopped in his tracks at the meeting room door and nasally told Pearse, 'You know, now, perfectly well, the position Pearse! Now you go back in there and pick the five yourself and then you come to me.' Wyse had to pick the five Corkonians and then they saw the minister.

One did not cross O'Malley. When choleric, the hair would rise on the back of his neck. He was once being driven in the garda car to Waterford. He was late and sarcastically twanged to his driver, 'Now, sir, I want to get down there before the end of the day!' The garda duly obliged, 'Certainly, Minister!' As they came to a hump-backed bridge outside Carlow he put the boot down and took off over it. O'Malley's papers went flying. When he recovered he twanged again in very expletive terms: 'Now, sir, I forgot to tell you that I also want to get down there alive!' Dessie could be a difficult minister!

*

The appointment of Máire Geoghegan-Quinn as my successor in the European Court of Auditors was a surprise, most of all to Desmond O'Malley. Máire Geoghegan-Quinn and Des O'Malley told me that they understood that a deal had been done between the Taoiseach, Bertie Ahern, and Tanaiste, Mary Harney. Máire was to go to the Commission and Des O'Malley to the Court. But the Progressive Democrats suddenly began to focus on the prospect of drafting Michael McDowell into the cabinet as Attorney General. The upshot of all the manoeuvring was that David Byrne became commissioner, Geoghegan-Quinn went to the Court and O'Malley was not appointed

The media were assured, and some senior political correspondents foolishly fell for it, that O'Malley was too old for the job at the Court. I was furious when it was inferred by a government spokesperson that 'soundings' had been made at the Court about O'Malley's age qualification and that our response had been somewhat negative. I immediately phoned Des O'Malley and his wife to assure them that this was not so. The European Parliament has had a long-standing aspirational resolution about the qualifications of nominee members of the Court, one part of which is that candidates should not exceed 65 years of age at the end of their first term of office. But this provision is not in any way mandatory. O'Malley would have been just 66 years in 2006.

It is extremely unlikely that a candidate of Desmond O'Malley's outstanding qualifications would have been rejected by the European Parliament. In any event, the parliament does not have any veto over such appointments. I ensured through my media contacts that this spin about O'Malley was refuted. I pointed out that the Court had no function whatsoever under the Treaty in relation to these appointments. So much for loyalty to the main founder and inspirational leader of the Progressive Democrats.

As I told him the position about the age rule, Des O'Malley, in his strange half-nasal voice, snorted 'you don't say!' as if he had suddenly smelled something quite unpleasant.

Sixteen

The Politics of 'The Unborn'

'The state acknowledges the right to life of the unborn and, with due regard to the equal right to the life of the mother, guarantees in its laws to respect, and, as far as practicable by its laws to defend and vindicate that right.'

Article 40.3.3. Constitution of Ireland

Between 1958 and 1992, there were sixteen amendments to the Irish Constitution and a quarter of them were about abortion! Shortly before the June 1981 general election Frank Cluskey, leader of the Labour Party, and myself as party whip, met a delegation from the Pro-Life Amendment Campaign. They were seeking our party's support for their 'pro-life amendment' to the Constitution. After some discussion it became quite obvious that Frank had no intention of going down their road. He spoke warmly about his own adopted children and how he loathed abortion. But he was quite perturbed about the sweeping context of the amendment. I shared his concerns.

In March 1981, Garret FitzGerald, leader of Fine Gael, gave an assurance to PLAC, as it became known, that his party would, if in government, hold a referendum for the inclusion in the Constitution of an amendment prohibiting abortion. This commitment was included in the Fine Gael manifesto in that election. Frank Cluskey never received the credit he deserved for his decision and Garret's misjudgement will never be forgotten. On 10 July 1981, Julia Vaughan, MB, MRCOG, chairman of PLAC, wrote to the new Taoiseach, Garret FitzGerald, as follows:

> You will recall that at our meeting on 30 April last you indicated the full support of the Fine Gael Party for our proposal that the Constitution be amended in order to guarantee the right to life of the unborn child. We were appreciative of the manner in which our case was considered and responded to, and of the commitment to a constitutional amendment subsequently contained in the Fine Gael programme for the general election. As you are aware, this commitment is not referred to in the joint document 'Programme for Government 1981-86', and in consequence some apprehensions have been voiced within our constituent and supporting organisations. It would be extremely helpful, therefore, if we could have a brief note from you with which we could reassure our members in regard to Government intentions in the matter.

The Taoiseach replied that 'There is no significance whatsoever in the fact that the commitment is not referred to in the document "Programme for Government 1981-1986". The Government is unalterably opposed to the legalisation of abortion and is committed to taking whatever steps are necessary to ensure that an appropriate Constitutional amendment is brought forward. The Attorney General is now examining the form such an amendment might take.'

It was the beginning of a most controversial, often bitter and ultimately very sorry chapter in Irish social policy. It began when the 1981 coalition government fell over the coalition budget in January 1982. During the following election campaign, Garret FitzGerald and Charles Haughey agreed to a request from PLAC to hold a referendum on a constitutional amendment to prohibit abortion. But the outcome of the February 1982 election was a hung Dáil with the Workers' Party deputies and Tony Gregory supporting Charles Haughey as Taoiseach. In August 1983, Mother Teresa of Calcutta addressed a pro-life rally organised by the 'Society for the

Protection of Unborn Children' at the National Stadium, Dublin.

The pro-life campaigners were in a state of complete frustration about their referendum. To their chagrin, there were three general elections in the eighteen months up to November 1982. But in that election Haughey deliberately and cynically upped the abortion stakes. Three days before the election was announced, Fianna Fáil produced its wording for the proposed amendment to the Constitution, and this is cited at the top of this chapter. The Attorney General was John Murray SC. I was acutely aware of the particular 'pro-life' role of my predecessor as Minister for Health, Michael Woods, on this issue. Garret FitzGerald fell for the bait and the pro-life protagonists were all set to win irrespective of the result of the election. To his great credit Dick Spring, despite the most intense pressure, not least from within his North Kerry constituency, refused to endorse the wording. He sought the advice of John Rogers, Dermot Gleeson SC, and his brother, Arthur, who was a local general practitioner. In November 1982 we held a press conference in Dublin at which Dick reiterated Labour's unequivocal opposition to the legislation on abortion and called on the Taoiseach, Charles Haughey, to desist from his efforts to exploit the issue in the election campaign.[112] I said at the press conference that: 'Mr Haughey is simply trying to exploit this grave issue for party political purposes. I am appalled that he should descend to this level in an election campaign. I can only say that it is an act of desperation.' Dick Walsh of *The Irish Times* went on to report: 'Mr Spring explained that his reservations about the working of the proposed amendment arose because it was open to many interpretations, including one which could clear the way to the legalisation of abortion.'

But this stroke did not win Haughey the election. The programme for government agreed between the Fine Gael and Labour parties in 1982 stated: 'Legislation will be introduced to have adopted, by 31 March 1983, the Pro Life Amendment published by the outgoing government which has the backing of the two largest parties in the Dáil. The Parliamentary Labour Party reserves the right to a free vote on this issue.' I made it crystal clear that I would not introduce this bill. The government then decided to direct the Minister for Justice, Michael Noonan, to submit, as soon as possible, a memorandum to the government on the question. Thus the poisoned chalice passed from Labour to Fine Gael in government.

I did not have access to the detailed advice of the former Attorney General, John Murray SC, subsequently a judge of the European Court of Justice and now a member of the Supreme Court. The coalition Attorney General was Peter Sutherland who was well known to Dick Spring from their rugby days. At that stage I had no idea of his views on the bill, the Fine Gael ethos on such fundamental issues being very varied. It was his first major test as Attorney General and he rose to the occasion. I was soon to share his grave concern about this referendum.

Michael Noonan was a decidedly unhappy sponsor as Minister for Justice. He agonised on the question and in February 1983 he informed the government:

> The text of the amendment speaks of the right to life of 'the unborn'. A major question is what is meant by 'the unborn'. The Attorney General has pointed out that the expression is ambiguous, as it unarguably is. The former Attorney General took the view that it would probably be interpreted by the Supreme Court as meaning from conception — but that is also tantamount to confirming that the matter is not clear. The Minister, in promoting the bill, is likely to be asked what he (or the government) intends it to mean or thinks it means. He is liable to be faced with the question: if it is intended to apply from conception, why not say so?

Michael Noonan went on to advise the government that he envisaged making contact with representatives of the pro-life campaign in order to explain that the present text gave rise to problems and could have repercussions in a direction very different from what they would wish. His misgivings were indeed prophetic. They confirmed all of the advice I had received in the Department of Health. The Taoiseach was not just discomfited: he was appalled at what he and his party had walked themselves into. Dick Spring's cryptic comment was 'I wish you well, Michael, when you convey all of that to the Bishop of Limerick!'

There was no comfort for Michael Noonan from the Attorney General either. Peter Sutherland's opinion was emphatic. He advised:

> The wording is ambiguous and unsatisfactory. It will lead inevitably to confusion and uncertainty, not merely amongst the medical profession, to whom it has of course particular relevance, but also amongst lawyers and more specifically the judges who will have to interpret it. Far from providing the protection and certainty which is sought by many of those who have advocated its adoption it will have a contrary effect. In particular it is not clear as to what life is being protected; as to whether 'the unborn' is protected from the moment of fertilisation or alternatively is left unprotected until an independently viable human being exists at 25 to 28 weeks.

He went on to advise that 'the use of the word "unborn" in the proposed Amendment is significant because it has not to my knowledge been used before in a similar context, that is as a noun standing on its own. The word is usually taken in association with "child", "person" or "human being". The word, used as a noun, is not in fact defined in any of the standard English dictionaries.' Regarding the words 'with due regard to the equal right to the life of the mother', Peter Sutherland advanced the view that 'there may be cases where a doctor will have to consider whether he can treat a prospective mother for an illness which might otherwise shorten her life expectancy if this treatment will threaten the life of the foetus'. The proposed amendment would in his view tend to confuse a doctor as to his responsibilities rather than assist him, and the consequences may well be to inhibit him in making decisions as to whether treatment should be given in a particular case.

The Attorney General then went on to advise that the amendment as proposed in the Eighth Amendment of the

Constitution Bill should not be put to the people. I warmly welcomed the opinion which the minister and the government decided to release to the public in an effort to steer some rationality into the debate. However, the government did not release to the public or to the Dáil the final conclusion of the Attorney General. The convention that such advice is exclusive to the government in its deliberations was respected.

Peter Sutherland had proposed that the best way out of the morass was an amendment giving constitutional protection for a legislative ban on abortion. That, in his opinion, was the best solution to the dilemma facing the government. Michael Noonan in a very agitated response said that such an amendment would not be a substantial compliance with the pre-election commitment or with what was implicit in the introduction of the Fianna Fáil bill. He held that there was a clear party commitment, spelled out more than once, that the amendment would be adopted. There seemed to be no doubt that acceptance of the Attorney General's recommendation would mean a discarding of the central element in the commitment. The minister recalled the accusations made of a party 'U-turn' followed by another 'U-turn'.

However, all of the valiant efforts by the Minister for Justice, the Taoiseach, the Attorney General and weary hours of government debate came to nought. The self-anointed dogmatism of the pro-life zealots, and the opportunistic opposition led by Haughey, who fully understood that the pro-life amendment could not be encompassed in the Constitution with any definitiveness, had the government backbenchers on the run. The die was cast. In March 1983, only eleven deputies voted in the Dáil against putting the proposed amendment to the people. They were Joe Bermingham, Frank Cluskey, Proinsias de Rossa, Eileen Desmond, Tony Gregory, Tomas MacGiolla, Toddy O'Sullivan, Ruairi Quinn, Dick Spring, Mervyn Taylor and myself. Mervyn remarked: 'Now you know how it feels being in a minority.' My party was split down the middle on this issue. Six Labour deputies, Liam Kavanagh, Michael Moynihan, Seamus Pattison, Frank Prendergast, John Ryan and Sean Treacy, all voted in favour of bringing the issue to the people.

The campaign then began in earnest. Some of those Fine
Gael and Labour deputies who were strongly in favour were
absorbed into the PLAC campaign at constituency level. The
Fianna Fáil local machine was put at PLAC's disposal in many
areas. The Catholic Church led the way in many pulpits. The
'Yes' result was a foregone conclusion.

But the Fine Gael and Labour Party leaders were resolute.
Dick Spring and myself took the brunt of the pro-life campaign.
Dick made a passionate plea at a meeting of party workers in
Dublin. He said: 'During the general election campaign last
November, I stated that I had reservations about the then
wording of the proposed amendment to the Constitution. Since
that time events have taken place which have justified those
reservations. The Attorney General has offered his opinion
indicating the uncertain consequences of enactment of the
original wording into the Constitution, and that it is possible, if
most unlikely, that it could in fact open the door to legalised
abortion.'[113] But it was all in vain. Haughey had the pro-life bit
between his teeth and he was determined to cause maximum
damage to the government.

Garret FitzGerald made a courageous recantation of his
original error. He addressed Fine Gael's St Kevin's Branch,
Dublin South East thus:

> This wording was widely held at the time to be
> satisfactory, and both the Fine Gael Party and myself,
> in good faith, accepted that draft Amendment. In
> government, the advice given to us by the Attorney
> General, in accordance with his duties, made it clear
> to us that this Fianna Fáil amendment had several
> fatal defects and that we could not allow it to go
> ahead without risking the defeat of the very purpose
> for which the original amendment was sought. This
> Fianna Fáil Amendment left uncertain the question of
> the life to be protected — a deliberate ambiguity, Dr
> Michael Woods later informed the Dáil — thus
> making it possible that abortion could be legalised by
> a decision of the Courts. It would have been grossly
> irresponsible for us to have persisted with this Fianna
> Fáil approach.[114]

In the Dáil debate I did my best to advance coherent arguments against the bill. I had consulted widely within my Department and the overwhelming advice I had received was of reservation about the proposed text. I argued that the highest law officers of our country had confirmed for the government what seemed quite likely to the layman: that the original form of words proposed by Fianna Fáil would result in most serious uncertainty.[115] The only means of resolving that uncertainty, arising from the clash of two proposed equal rights of the mother and child, was to test it in the courts. As a result, the final decision on whether and in what circumstances the procedures amounting to abortion would be permitted would rest with the judiciary. Yet this was precisely the result which the campaigners sought originally to avoid. I pointed out to the Dáil that every year, between 300 and 500 ectopic pregnancies occurred in Ireland. Surgical intervention which can result in the death of the foetus is necessary in such cases, as it is for treatment of cancer of the womb.

I stated: 'The Dean of the School of Medicine in Trinity College holds that it is a universal feature of medical care that the mother is accorded priority where necessary treatment may harm the foetus. He instanced, for example, the use of antibiotics or treatment for acute leukaemia which might have an adverse effect on the foetus. The risk to the foetus is accepted and treatment is instituted. Similarly, the Master of the Rotunda Hospital has stated that if doctors had to give equal rights to the mother and infant, Caesarean sections to save the life of mothers suffering from high blood pressure and kidney disease could be fatally delayed.'

But the bill passed all stages by 87 votes to 13. Only Deputies Alan Shatter and Monica Barnes of Fine Gael joined us in the 'Nil' lobby that day.

*

The referendum campaign was as divisive and vicious as predicted. It was intensely denominational. The amendment was emphatically supported by the Catholic Church and strongly opposed by the Protestant churches. Three days before polling day, Dr Dermot Ryan, Archbishop of Dublin, had a letter read at all masses in his archdiocese, advising all Catholics to vote 'Yes' to block 'any attempt to legalise abortion in this country'. I had the security of my office in the Custom House but Stella at home and our family had a barrage of abusive phone calls. In the event the turnout was quite low, 54 per cent, and the amendment was passed by 67 per cent for to 33 per cent against.

However, it was not long before our innate reservations about the amendment came home to roost with a vengeance. All of the forebodings, which Dick Spring, Peter Sutherland, Garret FitzGerald, Michael Noonan and myself had expressed, were to unfold in a quite dramatic manner. It occurred in the Supreme Court in 1992. I was then an MEP and had the unenviable task of briefing the large socialist group of the parliament about the issues involved. They were quite horrified that the Attorney General in the X case would have brought an injunction preventing a fourteen-year-old alleged rape victim from going to the UK for an abortion. The basis of the injunction being sought was the 1983 Article in the Constitution. The High Court upheld the application but the Supreme Court overturned that ruling on appeal. The Supreme Court held, in general, that there was a threat to the life of the individual involved in the context of a demonstrable intent on suicide. This judgement immediately gave rise to the related issues of the right to travel to, and avail of services legally available in, the UK and to the right to information about these services.

It was a major blow to the pro-life lobby by the Supreme Court. To their consternation, it seemed to open, for the first time in the history of the State, the possibility of some form of legalised abortion. There was, however, general political agreement that the two issues of travel and information required to be clarified by way of a further Constitutional amendment. In November 1992 the freedom to travel amendment was adopted by a 62 per cent 'Yes' to 38 per cent 'No' majority. The right to information amendment was also adopted by a 60 to 40 majority. The turn-out in this referendum was quite high, 68 per cent. However, the Fianna Fáil government's attempt to amend the current Article 44.3 and, by implication, the judgement of the Supreme Court, by way of recognising a threat to the mother's life as distinct from her health as grounds for abortion, was rejected by a decisive 65 per cent.

The pro-life zealots got their comeuppance. But they have not gone away. In 1999 more than 6,000 Irish women had abortions in Britain. One could probably add another 10 per cent for those who provided an address other than one in the Republic and those who had abortions in other jurisdictions. It is not unreasonable to hold the view that by now the annual total is some 7,000. Over 280,000 abortions have been performed on Irish women in England and Wales since 1970. For these three decades, the country has had a major problem of unwanted pregnancies. And yet the Catholic Archbishop of Dublin, Desmond Connell,[116] some independent deputies, PLAC and the MEP Dana Rosemary Scallon keep demanding yet another referendum to amend the Constitution. And all for what? To have 'an absolute prohibition' on abortion? It seems that PLAC will shy away from proposing that the right to travel and to information about abortion be abolished. What unbridled hypocrisy!

The thousands of women of Ireland who have opted for abortions in the past and who will do so in the future did not and will not give the slightest heed to the sterile words of any Constitutional amendment. The public health and public education dimensions of this question are far wider than these rigid strictures. And they still need to be addressed with great urgency. And those who now demand another referendum should consider the wisdom of the distinguished Professor Thomas Flanagan when he said: 'I am in favour of a referendum about a Constitutional Amendment on abortion but the referendum I propose is one in which the electoral list will be restricted to a particular category: pregnant, unmarried women.'[117]

And what of the future of this debate? I hold that the Houses of the Oireachtas should legislate for the termination of pregnancies in certain circumstances such as rape or incest and defined clinical conditions. No doubt the constitutionality of such legislation will be challenged. So be it. Do the deputies have the bottle to do what is necessary?

I will never forget being told when I was minister that a mother with cancer of the cervix was denied treatment in a public voluntary hospital because it would harm the foetus. I had no power to intervene. The mother died in agony. That was what we were up against. I resolved to advocate abortion in those circumstances. Stella agreed with me. She, too, was a mother.

Seventeen

The Tip of the Iceberg

'Suffer the little children to come unto Me …
For theirs is the Kingdom of Heaven.'

St Mark, Ch. 10, V. 14

Liam Flanagan, secretary of the Department of Health, was a large, avuncular and blunt-speaking public servant. He took no prisoners, particularly if they came from the bruising battles with the departments of Finance and Public Service. In March 1986 he rolled into my gloomy office in the Custom House and plonked a buff-coloured file on my desk. The Department of Health had absorbed various functions from the Justice and Education departments relating to childcare.

'As an adoptive parent myself,' he said, 'I am ashamed to hand you this submission. But since we have known one another for over four years, I am sure you will see the urgent need for the proposed rationalisation programme for the mother and infant homes and the infant nursing homes.'

As he departed he added, 'And Minister, for Jasus sake, don't say a word to Finance or we will never get it through!'

His cover note on the file read: 'I do not think that we should at this time take any action in the case of the infant nursing home facility at Fahan, Co Donegal. It provides a facility which spares our national blushes in the area of the adoption of 'legitimate but unwanted children'. The resource involved at £13,600 is trivial. I will elaborate when you have had an opportunity to read the submissions.'

The proposal which Liam Flanagan brought forward was for an outline programme devised in the childcare division of the Department of Health for the rationalisation of certain facilities catering mainly for the pregnant single girl and her child. The facilities in question were the 'Mother and Baby Homes and Infant Nursing Homes'. The purpose of the programme was to bring these facilities into line with the development of support services for these families in their own communities. The suggested programme involved the gradual run-down of one of the remaining two large mother and baby homes, the Sacred Heart Home, Bessboro, Cork and three infant nursing homes, namely, St Patrick's Infant Hospital, Temple Hill, Blackrock, Co Dublin; St Clare's, Stamullen, Co Meath and St Mura's, Fahan, Co Donegal. The provision of alternative services and a strengthening of existing family and children services to deal with their increasing workloads and to enable health boards to begin to implement the provisions of the impending children's legislation was envisaged.

In their confidential submission to me, the department's staff painted a stark and chilling picture. They pulled no punches when they wrote:

> In earlier days little tolerance was shown by Irish society to the unmarried pregnant girl or to the unmarried mother and her baby. Families were unable to cope with the stigma of illegitimacy. It was in order to keep and support girls who found themselves in this predicament that a number of 'Mother and Baby Homes' were developed by religious orders and concerned lay bodies. The biggest of these homes were very large institutional-type-buildings, and were situated at St Patrick's, Navan Road, Dublin; Castlepollard, Co Westmeath; Sean Ross Abbey, Roscrea; and the Sacred Heart Home, Bessboro in Cork. Referrals to these homes were mostly by the local clergy or the public assistance authority. In those days there were usually only two choices for the unmarried pregnant girl — banishment as a social pariah to a mother and baby home or the boat to England. The unmarried mother

usually left her baby in the home, some to be placed privately in foster care, or, in later years, for adoption, by the homes' authorities. It is not known how the girls managed in the homes before and after pregnancy but there is a conventional wisdom that they had to perform 'penitential work', e.g., laundering and other domestic work. Presumably this was, in part at least, an act of atonement for the grave wrong they had perpetrated against the pristine society of saints and scholars.

I had a particular interest in the Sacred Heart Home, Bessboro, Cork, which had a capacity for approximately 200 girls a year, and was vividly aware of its role in the city. My home was then at 8 Old Blackrock Road, Cork and Bessboro was about a mile away on the Blackrock Road. As teenagers we knew that 'the fallen women of Cork' were in there. Since then I have often wondered if that famous lady 'The Mad Woman from Cork' had been in Bessboro in her youth! That was the dark side of my Cork of the 1940s and 1950s. I often wondered, when I cycled as a youth past that institution on my way down to Blackrock to play for Nemo Rangers, what went on behind these walls. I knew that the mothers of Cork used to admonish their daughters, 'If you don't watch out you will finish up in Bessboro'!

The report put on my desk in 1986 was a searing indictment of our social policy. I have no doubt that in earlier days, the department's staff would have not dared to put such words on paper. For a long time the internal culture of the department was as repressed and conventional as the climate outside. The outside political culture was that these mothers and their children hardly 'deserved' even to have the vote. But there was some courage and hope in the department. And the staff put their further views on the record:

> Over the years a greater tolerance and compassion has emerged towards the single pregnant girl. Individual cases of intolerance and prejudice can still, no doubt, be cited. However, in general it can be said that present day attitudes are more child-centred than

adult-centred and there is an increasing tendency for these girls to remain at home during most of their pregnancy. Consequently, demand for places in the mother and baby homes decreased and the homes at Castlepollard and Roscrea were closed and are now used as residential centres for the mentally handicapped. St Patrick's, Navan Road is at present being relocated to a much smaller premise at Eglington Road, Donnybrook while the Sacred Heard home, Bessboro, Cork is still operating as are some smaller homes, mainly in the Dublin area. Another reason for the reduction in places was the appearance and development in recent years of a number of voluntary organisations such as CURA, and adoption societies who provide counselling services for the single pregnant girl; ALLY, which provides a family placement scheme and has centres in Dublin, Cork, Limerick and Kilkenny; the health board social work services; and also the Voluntary Agency CHERISH which provides support, advice and information for single mothers, with a particular emphasis on those single mothers who wish to keep their children.

In 1985 there were 24 residential homes, formerly industrial schools, and 17 'approved homes'. They provided accommodation for about 1,100 children. In 1960 the number of children in such homes had been 4,000; in 1970, 2,000; in 1980, 1,258 and in 1983 and 1985, 1,086. In 1972 there were 3,880 children in full-time care in institutions in receipt of public funds from the Department of Health through the health boards and 1,730 children were in full-time care in institutions under the aegis of the Department of Education. In 1985 about 3,700 children were placed in the care of health boards to be looked after in foster care or residential care. Most were reunited with their families after a few months or weeks. But some, unfortunately, remained in care for years.

According to the statistics in 1985, about 40 per cent of these children were placed in care because they were being looked after by one parent, for example, an unmarried mother, deserted wife, widow or widower who was unable to cope. About 14 per cent of the remainder had been neglected; another

13 per cent were in care because of a short-term family crisis, 9 per cent had been abused either physically, sexually or emotionally and a further 9 per cent were in care due to marital disharmony.

I was still perturbed about the exact dimensions of the 'official situation' as perceived by the department. It placed before me a very sharp tabular reminder of the dimensions of the problem at that time.

	1976	1979	1982	1985
Illegitimacy	2,545	3,337	4,351	
Applicants for Adoption	1,277	1,234	1,254	880
Adoption orders	1,104	988	1,191	881
Unmarried mothers' allowance	3,334	4,574	7,592	11,300
Irish abortions in UK	1,821	2,504	3,653	

The submission to me also pointed out: 'Other factors which undoubtedly helped to accelerate the drop in demand or places included: The introduction in 1974 of the unmarried mothers' allowance, maximum rate of payment for an unmarried mother and one child was £54.40 per week. This rose to £56.15 from July 1986; The fall-off in the number of children being placed for adoption; and the rise in the number of Irish women going to the UK for abortions.'

The department's submission went on to point out that some of the homes had responded to the drop in demand by scaling down their operations and had developed into a welfare-counselling oriented service, i.e. Denny House and Miss Carr's. Newer facilities, such as Belmont and Newtowncunningham, had developed along similar lines. However, there were still a few homes which continued along traditional lines, staffed primarily by nursing staff, often with midwifery qualifications and providing nursing services for children who, more often than not, simply required care. The childcare staff of the department proposed that funding for these homes be scaled down and the services phased out gradually and replaced by a scheme providing supervised flatlets; a strengthened community social work service in all health board areas; and an expanded fostering programme.

The submission then came to the proposed policy reforms. The department advanced the view that accommodation and after-care should be provided for those pregnant single girls who required it. The question was, should it be shared accommodation; supervised flatlets accommodation; or a type of institutional building catering for a large number? In 1986 the new policy of the department was in favour of the smaller, and more intimate unit — preferably of the flatlet variety with supervision geared towards counselling the girls and preparing them for life following the delivery of their babies. The person responsible for the day-to-day running of a mother and baby facility should have experience in this kind of work and would preferably have nursing qualifications. However, midwifery or nursing qualifications should not be a requirement for the remainder of staff as these facilities would in future have links with the local maternity hospital; there would be regular visits by the local public health nurse and ante and post-natal care would be provided by the local maternity hospital doing the deliveries. The development of fostering schemes effectively wiped out the need for infant nursing homes.

I was determined to take urgent action on this submission. Four days after receiving the document from Liam Flanagan, I gave my approval to release our meagre financial resources and directed that they should be used for the new child and family support services. We simply went ahead, there and then, and started to implement the change. We never told the Department of Finance. We did not produce a convoluted White Paper. We did not submit a government memorandum.

Today I wonder what exactly has become of the Sacred Heart Home, Bessboro, Cork; Ard Mhuire, Dunhoyne, Co Meath; St Patrick's Navan Road, Dublin; Denny House, Eglington Road, Dublin; Belmont, Belmont Ave, Donnybrook, Dublin; St Patrick's Infant Hospital, Blackrock; Newtowncunningham, Co Donegal; St Clare's, Stamullen, Co Meath and St Mura's, Fahan, Co Donegal. Where are the records of these 'homes'? Who were the mothers? Where are these children today? And what of those Irish women, religious and lay, who staffed these institutions?

*

The necessity for reform of the childcare services had been apparent to me since the 1970s when I clashed with the Minister for Education, Dick Burke, over the issue. In 1972 I became a member of CARE, a voluntary body founded to promote actively the welfare of deprived children in Ireland and which campaigned for radical improvements in children's services. Seamus O'Cinneide and Peter Coyle were the inspired chairman and secretary of the organisation. The late Peter Shanley was the first treasurer. A memorandum entitled 'One Minister for Deprived Children' had been sent to the Taoiseach, Jack Lynch, in December 1972. It was signed by twelve leaders of the churches and the concerned professions. In 1974 I referred to 'the present public scandal of the law and the State's administrative procedures and care services relating to children'.

Dick Burke responded immediately:

> There will not be a Maria Colwell case [a child who was battered to death in Britain by a member of her family] in Ireland if I can help it. The unjust and vindictive criticism in recent issues of a Sunday newspaper of the religious orders who conduct residential homes for children should be a matter of serious concern to the public. It is poor recompense that they should be pilloried by propagandists who manipulate the forces of the media for their own ends and who are answerable to no one. On the question of centralising children's services under a single minister, there is some danger of this being regarded as a panacea.[118]

The members of the council of CARE which included the late distinguished Ian Hart, Augusta McCabe, Ercus Stewart and Michael Sweetman, SJ, flatly contradicted the minister, pointing out that chapter five of the Kennedy Report in 1970 had been explicit in its recommendation that 'administrative responsibility for all aspects of childcare should be transferred to the Department of Health'. Dick Burke flatly refused to implement this basic recommendation. It was a full ten years later, when I was Minister for Health, that we managed to bring about this change of policy.

In 1974 I wrote to my party leader, Brendan Corish, then Tanaiste and Minister for Health:

> I have had the most appalling public reaction both direct to myself and to the Labour Party concerning the views of Dick Burke and presumably of his department on this matter. Already considerable damage has been done to the standing of the government on the question. I would strongly urge you to expedite a progressive decision on this major issue of Government policy and I do not feel that any kind of so-called co-ordinating inter-departmental liaison structure is the answer. While I appreciate that the Department of Justice and Education will still be required to make substantial inputs to childcare services, nevertheless one Department and one Minister or Parliamentary Secretary should have direct personal responsibility for coordinating these services and ensuring that amending legislation is introduced.[119]

Brendan Corish replied: 'I am aware of the considerable public feeling which exists at present for the reform of our children's services and I note the point which you make in your letter concerning the need for administrative reform. As you are aware the government is considering the whole question of children's services at present and until it is finished its consideration of the question, it isn't possible for me to indicate the changes which might be agreed by the government.'

Corish had considerable difficulty in these government discussions: the most he achieved in 1974 was the setting up of a task force on childcare services. His heart was in the right place on this issue but he lacked the determination to use his position to insist on immediate change. The final report of the Task Force on Childcare Services was delayed until 1980. One of the unfortunate realities of 1974 was that there was little social work expertise and few professional childcare personnel in public administration. And the old guard in the Departments of Education and Justice dominated policy.

The Task Force on Childcare Services did not present its final report until 1980, after a protracted six years' deliberation. When I introduced the Children's (Care and Protection) Bill 1985, no less than 15 years had lapsed since the recommendation of the Committee on Reformatory and Industrial School Systems (the Kennedy Report) of 1970. From February 1983 to April 1985 I had worked unceasingly within the Department of Health in consultation with the departments of Finance, Justice, Education and Labour to have a comprehensive bill drafted. The observations of Justice alone ran to 35 pages. Between September and December 1984 we had innumerable consultations with Matt Russell of the Attorney General's office. It was an uphill battle every week. Matt used to admonish me: 'Minister, your bill is like a ball of wool. Pull a thread and it keeps on coming!' Without the intense efforts of Liam Flanagan, Dr Joe Robins, assistant secretary and Donal Devitt, principal officer, I doubt if the bill would have seen the light of day in 1985. The work of Augusta McCabe, the social work adviser to the childcare division of the department, was of enormous assistance.

Alan Shatter TD of Fine Gael was a tower of legislative experience and ability in the enactment of this bill between 1985 and 1988. When I introduced the bill in the Dáil in May 1985 he said:

> Different governments, including those of Fianna
> Fáil, did absolutely nothing in this area over decades.
> It is an indictment of all parties that this is the first
> time since 1908 that we have tried to tackle the
> legislative framework in relation to children's law
> and childcare services. It is the shame of politicians in
> all parties that it has taken so long to produce this
> legislation. It is not as if they did not know about it
> and, to that extent, some of Deputy O'Hanlon's
> comments are difficult to stomach. In the three years I
> have been in the House, I have persecuted successive
> Ministers for Health, including Deputy Woods when

he was Minister for Health, to introduce legislation on children's law. I raised it by way of Dáil Questions, adjournment debates and on the order of business. I welcome the fact that the government have at least produced this legislation and it appears that the Fianna Fáil government in office in 1982 were no nearer producing it than I was of flying to the moon because it took the department another two years to do the necessary background work to put this bill together.

At that time some 3,700 children spent time in care, either in foster care or residential homes. In the light of recent revelations, court proceedings and criminal convictions for child abuse, I have no doubt that a great deal of the incredible abuse and suffering would not have occurred had this legislation been enacted much earlier and had the governments of the day made the staffing resources available. While we, the Ministers for Health of those times, must hang our heads in shame, successive governments must accept collective responsibility for refusing to provide resources to their colleagues in the health portfolio.

It would be difficult to imagine two deputies in the Fine Gael party more opposite to one another than Alice Glenn and Alan Shatter. Alice was again in her irrepressible conspiracy mood as soon as the bill reached the Dáil. She advanced the view that the bill had 'its origins in pressure groups such as the Council of Civil Liberties, Children First, Cherish and social workers' groups, very many of whom were opposed to the pro-life amendment, support contraceptives, divorce, sex education and multi-denominational schools'.[120] Kadar Asmal, now Minister for Education in the government of South Africa, was not spared. She asserted: 'In the *Irish Independent* of Wednesday 26 January 1977 there was an article calling for the end of inalienable rights for parents written by Kadar Asmal. It is stretching credibility to think that Irish parents should be expected to accept the recommendations of these kind of groups who cast a slur on them.' Alice Glenn found me to be beyond redemption.

I was most concerned to have this bill enacted during my term of office. But the resignations of my fellow Labour ministers and I from the government overtook the substantial number of amendments I had tabled for committee stage. Brendan Howlin became the new Labour spokesperson for health in opposition. In June 1987 we tabled a major revised Private Members' Children's (Care and Protection) Bill from the Labour Party. Dr Rory O'Hanlon, the Fianna Fáil Minister for Health, responded in May 1988 with his text. At long last the impetus for reforming childcare legislation was bearing fruit. However, the Fianna Fáil bill was a watered-down version of the 1985 bill and took little account of the large number of submissions and the protracted debate which the earlier bill had provoked. The Labour Party bill of some 132 sections was reduced to 64.

Of all the reactions to the bill I introduced, the one which gave me greatest satisfaction was the statement issued by Kieran McGrath, the then public relations officer for the child-care sub-committee of the Irish Association of Social Workers. The association in particular welcomed the raising of the upper age for the receipt of children into care from 16 to 18 years; the making explicit of the role of health boards in acting as the child protection agency in this country; the updating of the grounds under which children could be taken into care to include sexual abuse, and the provision of childcare advisory committees in each health board region.

*

In 1983 guidelines were circulated for the first time by the Department of Health covering all forms of child abuse. Revised guidelines were issued in 1987. They were prepared by a working group of 22 experts in this area under the chairmanship of that dedicated public servant, Donal Devitt. The total number of confirmed cases of child sexual abuse reported to the health boards in 1985 was 133. By 1986 the number of cases had doubled to 274. We were beginning to see the tip of the iceberg.

There were many other more persistent pioneers in the struggle to respond to the needs of children in Irish society.

Senators Mary Robinson, John Horgan and Michael D. Higgins tabled a bill in the Senate, 'The Illegitimate Children (Maintenance and Succession) Bill, 1974'. This bill was to enforce the obligation on the father of an 'illegitimate' child to contribute to the support of such a child and to reform the law relating to the succession to property rights of deceased persons in such a relationship. Their pressure was also to prove successful in the long run.

*

When I took over responsibility in 1983 for the Adoption Board and the Adoption Acts of 1952-1976, I was determined to initiate a thorough review of the situation affecting children who were not eligible for adoption under these acts. Under these statutes an adoption order could be made only in respect of a child who was an orphan; or was illegitimate; or had been legitimated by the marriage of his parents after his birth but whose birth had not been re-registered. Since the Adoption Act, 1952 came into operation, a total of 33,817 adoption orders had been made up to December 1985; 882 adoption orders were made during 1985. There had been a decline in the number of adoptions in these years despite the increase in the number of illegitimate births. More and more single mothers were opting to keep their children. Society was moving away from the attitude which viewed single mothers and their babies as outcasts.

There had been many calls over the years for changes in the adoption laws to enable the adoption of children born within marriage who, for varying reasons, had been separated from or abandoned by parents. Most of these children were in the care of health boards and were either with foster parents or in residential children's homes. Some of the children were placed previously with friends or relatives and were unlikely to have come to the attention of the public childcare system. The case for amending legislation had been highlighted by the review committee on adoption services which I established and which reported to me in 1984. Its members unanimously recommended a change in the law which would enable all children deprived of normal family life to be eligible for adoption irrespective of the marital circumstances of their parents. The members of the committee consisted of a cross-section of persons involved with children in care, particularly the adoption services, and included health administrators, social workers, an adoptive parent, legal experts and a child psychiatrist.

The bill I envisaged was not intended in any way to deter families in genuine difficulty seeking to have their children cared for temporarily either in a residential setting or with a foster family. The proposed legislation was only to be appropriate in a small number of cases where all hopes of reconciliation between a child and his or her parents had been lost. The great majority of children placed in care were re-united with their parents. This was the aim of the health boards and of those caring for the children. However, where a child had no prospect of returning to his natural parents, his foster parents now had an opportunity of offering the child integration within their own family by way of adoption. After a great deal of consultation with the Attorney General John Rogers, and with considerable assistance from Declan Quigley's office, a limited Adoption Bill was initiated in November 1986.

Again time ran out on our best endeavours. A minister who fails to appreciate the extensive consultations with the Attorney General on the heads of his bill, the protracted debate in government, the five stages of debate in the Dáil and Seanad and the ultimate joy of the president's signature on his or her 'child', is foolish in the extreme. Two to three years are often the norm. Following the change of government in 1987 Alan Shatter produced a similar private member's bill. The government responded with alacrity and the legislative reforms which had taken some three or four years to bring forward were enacted.

Throughout this period, one public servant stood head and shoulders above all others. Dr Joe Robins was assistant secretary in the Department of Health. In the drift towards cynicism about the public service, Joe cared deeply for the deprived and the handicapped. He translated that concern into the quality of his official work. His books *The Lost Children* and *Fools and Mad* should be obligatory reading for all politicians.

A great deal remains to be done for the children of the nation. A truly effective child benefit scheme, included in the tax system, which I first proposed in government in 1985, remains to be implemented. One in six children lives in poverty. In 1998 there were 4,407 reported cases of alleged neglect and 2,833 cases of alleged sexual abuse. I await a government minister who will take these issues by the scruff of the neck.

Eighteen

Till Death Us Do Part

'Any Catholic who gets divorced and who then remarries may not receive the sacraments while living as husband and wife.'

Bishop Thomas Flynn, 1995

When the Irish Constitution of 1937 was narrowly approved by the people by 51 per cent, the article prohibiting divorce was included. Although W.T. Cosgrave, Leader of Cumann na nGaedheal and President of the Executive Council, was of the view in the mid-1920s that such a prohibition negated the rights of minorities, he was quickly brought to heel by Archbishop Byrne of Dublin. The archbishop not only held that divorce for Catholics was unlawful but that the Church also had the right to pronounce marriage laws for Protestants in the State.[121] And W.T. had an even more powerful conservative ally in Éamon de Valera on this issue.

Thirty years after the 1937 referendum there was a glimmer of hope when Seán Lemass set up the All-Party Committee on the Constitution. George Colley was chairman. The committee concluded that divorce should be available in extremely limited circumstances, namely, to those who were married in a religion that permitted it.[122] Seán Lemass, following his resignation as Taoiseach in November 1966, was a member of the committee. Its recommendation was unanimous. But the opposition of my constituent, Archbishop John Charles McQuaid, was implacable and the recommendation was not advanced any further.

After my election to the Dáil in 1969, I had a regular stream of deserted wives, individuals seeking advice about barring orders and separation agreements, battered wives in family chaos, and wives desperately seeking home assistance after their husbands had skipped off on the boat from Dun Laoghaire, sometimes with another woman. The Social Welfare Bill in 1970 introduced the deserted wife's allowance and I recall completing these new forms for many women in South Dublin and Dun Laoghaire. My constituency was a relatively wealthy area but marital breakdowns know no barriers of income or status. The first voluntary free legal advice centres were being set up by public spirited law students in 1969 and these made a valiant contribution.

By the early 1980s it was evident that the problem was growing each year and that the total number of people, including children, who were affected by marital breakdown was in excess of 70,000. As the years slipped by I became more and more angry about the constitutional logjam on divorce. In the 1973-1977 national coalition the subject was still taboo and Liam Cosgrave, Brendan Corish, Mark Clinton, Jim Tully, Tom O'Donnell, Richie Ryan and Paddy Cooney refused to consider the issue. As my three clinics in Dun Laoghaire dealt with more and more cases, I often felt that I should go up to the archbishop's residence in Killiney, march him down to meet these mutilated families, confront him with the real desperation of his flock and ask him to go on his knees and seek their forgiveness.

Apart from my constituency 'clinics' in which I had regular contact with persons facing marital problems, another major influence on my attitude to divorce was the publication in 1979 by William Duncan, Senior Lecturer in Law at Trinity College, Dublin, of *The Case for Divorce*.[123] He was an acknowledged authority on family law in Ireland. I invited him to address the Dun Laoghaire Constituency Council of the Labour Party on the issue. The case he put for divorce had a profound impact on us all.

*

Any politician who professes to support the liberal agenda in Ireland on property and taxation reform and on major social questions will ignore at his peril the ingrained conservative ethos of the Irish electorate. Garret Fitzgerald, Dick Spring and those of us in government in the mid-1980s underestimated the desire in Ireland to keep things as they were, or as they were perceived to be at that time. There was an immense determination by conservative forces in Irish society, notably in the convergence of Fianna Fáil and the Catholic hierarchy, to defend 'traditional values'. Thus, the government faced into the 1986 divorce referendum with Padraig Flynn declaiming that divorce was 'like a Frankenstein stalking the land'.

As early as April 1986 it was quite evident that the Catholic Bishops' Conference was lining itself up to confront the government on the fundamental issue of civil remarriage. The delegation which met the Taoiseach and the Minister for Justice was formidable: Cardinal Tomas O Fiaich, Archbishop of Armagh and Primate of All Ireland, Dr Kevin McNamara, Archbishop of Dublin, Dr Cahal B. Daly, Bishop of Down & Connor, Dr Donal Murray, Auxiliary Bishop of Dublin, Dr Laurence Ryan, Coadjutor Bishop of Kildare & Leighlin, Mrs Margaret Watchorn, Catholic Marriage Advisory Council, Mr Tom Gillen, Irish Commission for the Laity.[124] The presentation by the bishops was quite brutal.

They reiterated the message of their pastoral letter *Love is for Life* which was a comprehensively argued exposition of the policy of the Catholic Church on divorce. It estimated that some 1.6 million children in Great Britain would have divorced parents by the end of the century. It asserted: 'The figures vividly illustrate the built-in "escalator effect" of divorce. It is all too sadly true that today's remedy becomes tomorrow's disease. It was with good reason that the Vatican Council spoke of divorce as a plague (*Gaudium et Spes*, No. 47 (204)'. It also laid down their moral law in no uncertain terms:

> For those, therefore, who accept the teaching of the Catholic Church, divorce with the right to remarry is not merely not permitted, it is impossible. The bond uniting married couples is a sacramental bond, coming from God alone. No man or woman, no

> human authority, no State or civil court, can put this
> bond asunder. No legislative enactment can dissolve
> a valid marriage and leave the partners free to marry
> again.

I do not recall a copy of the minutes of the meeting between the Taoiseach and Alan Dukes and the delegation being circulated to ministers. Garret Fitzgerald's autobiography includes the sharp exchange of letters in 1990 between himself and Cardinal O Fiaich about the joint discussion on the question of bigamous marriages.[125] The cardinal's letter refers to 'The draft report of the meeting, which was never agreed'. I did not receive this draft report. Insofar as my Department of Health had responsibility for the Office of Registrar of Deaths, Births and Marriages, we had a particular interest in these deliberations. In one instance, for example, I recall our consternation when we learned that an elderly parish priest had tippexed out from his register, in all good faith, the names of those who had been granted nullity decrees! Perhaps the draft report of that meeting will see the light of day before 2016. It seems that at least there was agreement between State and the various churches that a minimum age of 18 for marriage should be introduced and that there should be a new requirement of a minimum of three months' notice for marriage.

*

It fell to Alan Dukes, as Minister for Justice, to introduce the Tenth Amendment of the Constitution Bill, 1986, in the Dáil. He pointed out that the report of the joint committee, which had been laid before the Dáil in 1985, had been extensively debated in both Houses of the Oireachtas over a protracted period. He attempted to reassure the deputies that 'very stringent conditions will have to be met which will ensure that, before a divorce is granted, the marriage has clearly failed beyond redemption and that the dependants have been properly provided for'.

When I spoke, I was determined to adopt a strong political line to ensure that there would be full Labour Party support. I said that building a consensus that something must be done to reform marriage law in Ireland had been a long and difficult process. The Labour Party had been in the forefront of the struggle. In the lifetime of that Dáil alone, there had been four attempts to initiate action to deal with the problem of marital breakdown. The Labour Party was responsible for three of the four bills tabled. Although the bills did not succeed, they served the purpose of concentrating the mind of the Dáil on the problem and of educating public opinion about the need for change. I went on to state: 'Just as banning funerals will not abolish death, a "no" vote in the referendum will not abolish marriage breakdown, and the formation of families outside marriage. The present prohibition on divorce in the Constitution conflicts with what a significant minority of people on this island consider to be a civil right.'[126]

Garret FitzGerald made one of the finest speeches ever by a Taoiseach: it was a resounding assertion of his 'constitutional crusade'. He said:

> All of us, not just in the cities but throughout the countryside, are aware of very many unrecognised unions involving people whose marriages have failed. In such cases under existing law any children born to the couple are illegitimate, and the dependent spouse has no legal rights. I believe that the existence of this restrictive form of divorce will reduce the number of unrecognised unions that now exist, in which a dependent partner has no rights, and the children are not marital children, and that by so doing we will diminish perceptibly the instability that has crept into our society with the rapid growth in the number of such unions.

*

In the referendum campaign, the battle lines were drawn between two voluntary and vehement but opposing groups. The records show that the anti-divorce campaign was particularly well organised. It was headed by William Binchy, a most persuasive barrister advocate who was never at a loss for the legal counterpoint in debate, no matter how dreadful the marital case put to him. Joe McCarroll, John O'Reilly, Senator Des Hanafin, a former seasoned Fianna Fáil campaigner and fund raiser, Michael and Mary Lucy and Bernadette Bonar, sister of Deputy Tom O'Donnell of Fine Gael (and a constituent of mine in Leopardstown) were lynch-pins. Bernadette made no secret of her desire to see me out of the Dáil. They were all seasoned veterans of the 1983 'pro-life' amendment campaign. They had very considerable resources and influence on public opinion and they put pamphlets and leaflets into every home.

By contrast the Divorce Action Group, led by the charismatic Jean Tansey as chairperson and by well known activists such as Mags O'Brien in particular, was starved of resources. They were constantly on the back pedal from such Anti-Divorce Campaign posters as 'God Says Vote No!' 'Divorce Kills Love' and 'We Want Jobs, Not Divorce'. As Minister for Health and Social Welfare, I had occasions to travel throughout the country to official functions during that period. The countryside, the school polling stations, some voluntary hospital corridors and church porches were festooned with these posters. We did not, on our side, so to speak, have a prayer.

The intervention of the Executive Council of the Irish Congress of Trade Unions in the 1986 debate was a significant development. In 1982 the annual conference of congress had adopted a motion 'that divorce should be recognised as a civil right'. That motion called on congress to campaign for the removal of the constitutional ban. Donal Nevin had just become general secretary of congress following the retirement of Ruaidhri Roberts at the end of 1981. In its 1986 statement, congress pointed out that the conditions for divorce proposed by the government in the amendment 'must be considered extremely conservative and in no way provide for quick and easy divorce. The rights of spouses and children are fully protected'. In 1985 there were 436,000 trade unionists affiliated to ICTU. On the basis of the opinion polls at the time, it is reasonable to hold that of those who voted (the national turnout was 60.5 per cent) not more than 50 per cent would have voted 'Yes'. It is clear from the actual 36.5 per cent 'Yes' vote that the plea of congress fell on many deaf trade union ears.

*

A national referendum committee was established by the Labour Party to run the campaign. Ray Kavanagh was chairman and among the members were Michael D. Higgins, Mervyn Taylor, Anne Byrne, Fergus Finlay, Dick Spring and myself. The campaign theme was 'Put Compassion in the Constitution'. It was most effective and had wide coverage. A very high Labour profile was achieved during the campaign and the Labour Women's National Council produced a very popular women's leaflet. The Labour lawyers group issued daily press releases and achieved much media coverage. But the forces ranged against the party's proposal were formidable and overpowering.

Father Denis Faul's partisan view was evident from the letters page of *The Irish Times* when he wrote on why people should vote 'no': 'It would deeply disturb [the Irish] resolution to lead the good Catholic family lives that their forefathers have lead ... despite the oppression of sectarianism from people who believe in and practise the dissolution of the marriage bond.' The role of the leader of the opposition, Charles Haughey, was substantial in ensuring the defeat of the referendum proposal. He published a speech which he had prepared for the Dáil's Committee Stage of the Tenth Amendment on 20 May. It was a carefully crafted laudation of the role of the family and, decoded, it gave little comfort to those who favoured the 'Yes' vote. He wrote:

> For my own part, I approach this issue from the point of view of the family. I have an unshakeable belief in the importance of having the family as a basic unit of our society. I fully acknowledge that in many parts of our modern world the situation has radically changed and that the family is no longer the universally accepted unit, but I do not think that it is a change for the better or that it ultimately contributes to the welfare or the happiness of people. Of course, it has an appeal for some individuals, the attraction of superficial freedom. But, in my view, the family is a great buttress for the individual. The

*The Coalition Government at Áras an Uachtaráin, 1982, with President
Patrick Hillery (front centre)*

*Receiving the Health and Social Welfare Seals of Office at Áras an Uachtaráin
from President Hillery, 1982*

Members of the Houses of the Oireachtas with President Ronald Reagan,
Leinster House, 1984

Members of the Council of State with President Hillery,
Áras an Uachtaráin, 1985

At the Pro Cathedral with Archbishop Kevin McNamara shortly before the enactment of the Health (Family Planning) Bill, 1985

As Minister for Health with the people who really matter

With Cardinal Tomás Ó Fiaich, Liam Flanagan, Secretary, Department of Health and Brother Kilian O'Leary, OH, at St John of God Centre, Drumcar

With Stella and Tony Bass after the General Election, 1987

As Minister for Health with Jack Lynch, at Croke Park

At the Berlin Wall with Stella, 1990

Martyn Turner captures the tribunal of inquiry into the beef processing industry, 1992

Fellow Minister Ruairí Quinn teases Cabinet colleagues during period of health cuts, 1986

Jim Kemmy in full flight at the Labour Party Conference, 1986

Planning tactics – Barry Desmond, Dick Spring, Sinéaid Bruton and Fergus Finlay during the November 1992 General Election

Leaving national politics, 1994

family is a support system. All I ask is that people recognise that while they favour the introduction of divorce to deal with a particular problem, divorce itself will create many problems of its own for us. [127]

In the light of the later revelations by Terry Keane about Charles Haughey, his intervention must rank as the most brazen piece of hypocrisy by any leader of the opposition in the history of the State.[128]

*

The opponents of this measure, designed to afford a basic civil right to an unfortunate minority, used every stratagem in modern propaganda methods. Misrepresentation, the generation of fear and the manipulation of captive audiences each Sunday was commonplace. Combined with this was the blatant political opportunism of Fianna Fáil. These forces represented an armoury against which the Labour Party, the trade unions, a divided Fine Gael and other groups were helpless. The success of the counter campaign can be gauged by the magnitude of the defeat suffered. This must also be judged against the background of an almost totally sympathetic national media towards the 'Yes' campaign.

These were many inquests on how and why a 20 per cent majority in the first opinion poll was turned into an almost two-to-one defeat in a matter of weeks. The turnaround was perhaps best illustrated by a leaflet issued to every household in the parish next door to where we live, in Dundrum in South Dublin, by the Sandyford-Balally Anti-Divorce Campaign which said that the introduction of divorce would allow the following: 'The first wife could be divorced against her will. It needs only one spouse to end a marriage. This could be you; The first wife would lose her inheritance rights. She would receive nothing on the death of her spouse. This could be you; The first wife would have the family home in which she lives sold without her consent. This could be you; The first wife would almost certainly receive no maintenance. Remember in Britain 60 per cent of all divorced women go straight on social welfare. This could be you.'

*

At the final Labour press conference on 25 June, we knew that we were going to lose by a wide margin. The final poll showed a 10 per cent majority against. The overall authority of the Taoiseach, Tanaiste and ministers had been seriously eroded in the preceding three and half years of unpopular budget decisions. Although the national media was supportive of our campaign, their cynicism towards the government on many issues, particularly those of employment and taxation, had a very negative impact on overall public opinion. One lesson is that if one must have a referendum on a controversial issue, one should hold it very early in the mandate of the government. However, even if that referendum had been held early in 1983 it would most likely have been lost. The dissent of our ministerial colleague, Paddy Cooney, and the denunciations of Alice Glenn were also a severe blow. Paddy reflected a strong traditional Catholic Fine Gael ethos. He signalled early on in cabinet that he would speak out against the proposal.

We knew the game was up when we gathered for the final media briefing. But Ruairi Quinn, Minister for Labour and the Public Service, was in a defiant mood. He put on the record that: 'What is now at issue is whether we on this part of the island are prepared as genuine republicans to accommodate the minority whose personal convictions do not preclude them from seeking divorce as a last resort where marriage fails — whether they be Protestant, Jewish or of no religion, or are sincere or practising Christians whose private conscience tells them this is right for them despite the orthodox teaching of their church.'

The decisive intervention of the Catholic Church in the referendum was summed up by Maurice Manning who wrote:

> From a political point of view, the most significant intervention in the entire campaign came from the Cardinal Primate, Dr O Fiaich. What was most significant about his weighty condemnation of the divorce proposal was that he made no attempt whatsoever to address the question of the rights of the minority churches within the Republic. This is

especially stark in view of the fact that all of the minority churches had spoken out in favour of the proposal.[129]

On the same day and again in the *Irish Independent*, Conor Cruise O'Brien was in a vitriolic mood: 'Hurting Fine Gael, and splitting it, and beating it on the referendum, and weakening its leader, were all fully comprehensible and acceptable as tactical steps towards the supreme end of reinstating Fianna Fáil as the party of government.'[130]

In the Tanaiste's Kerry North constituency, the vote against the amendment was a record 72.5 per cent. The most emphatic 'No' vote of 78.5 per cent was in Cork North-West. It took great courage on the part of Dick Spring to campaign in Kerry in favour of the amendment. His deputy leader had the comfort of the liberal Dun Laoghaire constituency. In the adjournment debate in the Dáil following the outcome of the referendum, Dick Spring was as forceful as ever on this issue. He said that 37 people out of every hundred voted in favour of change. Those 37 voted also for tolerance, for respect for the rights of minorities, for a greater measure of freedom. He went on to state:

> I should record my appreciation of the work of the Attorney General, John Rogers, in this area. Since his appointment he has brought an awareness and a sensitivity to his office — an awareness of the many wrongs and injustices in our society, and a sensitivity of the need for change. Perhaps the most outrageous element in Mr Haughey's behaviour in this whole affair is to be seen in the comments he made last Sunday, when he admitted that he was prepared to acquiesce in a situation where, into perpetuity, he could envisage different laws and different social systems on both parts of this island. These comments by Mr Haughey were the most succinct statement of a partitionist mentality that I have heard. His famous statement that 'the Unionists would be surprised at how generous he could be' means very little.

There was no love lost between Garret FitzGerald and Cardinal O Fiaich and when the government's proposal was defeated in the referendum, the cardinal must have felt that it was as great a pleasure as Down or Armagh bringing the Sam Maguire cup back over the border. The night of the result Garret and Joan had a thank-you drink in their home in Palmerstown Road, Dublin. They were deeply upset. Stella and I were too depressed to attend the wake. I heard later that Michael O'Leary turned up, berated Garret for a lousy campaign and was peremptorily banished by Joan.

But Garret faced down the Dáil and almost half of his deputies when he moved the vote in the Dáil for the Department of the Taoiseach and opened the adjournment debate on 3 July, 1986. He said

> Courage, resolution, patient resolve, conviction in the justice of your cause; these must be your passwords and your guiding lights out of the dark disappointment of these days. There will be better, brighter days in the future. The very large numbers who abstained, almost 40 per cent, have, no doubt, their own justifications and rationalisations. To them I would say that democracy in the modern world is a privilege, something relatively rare, to be treasured, defended and nurtured. It is better to express an opinion than to sit on the fence; to be in favour of, or against, a proposition, then to try to be in both camps at the same time.

*

Slowly but surely the momentum for reform gathered again. Most of us realised that the fatal flaw in 1986 was the lack of enacted statutes signed into the law of the land by the president and dealing effectively with particular family law issues. The expertise within the Dáil on such issues was very limited and where it did exist, very conservative. It fell to Deputy Alan Shatter, Fine Gael, in 1987 to introduce a private member's bill permitting judicial permanent orders of separation and providing for custody and the settlement of property in the procèss. Despite considerable reluctance from the Fianna Fáil government, the amended bill, the second private member's bill from the Dáil ever to be passed by the Houses of the Oireachtas, became, to the credit of Shatter, the Judicial Separation and Family Law Reform Act, 1989. Another reform for another divorce referendum was in place.

And Dick Spring never threw in the towel. The new rainbow government brought forward the Fifteenth Amendment to the Constitution (No.2) Bill of 1995 replacing the prohibition on the grant of a dissolution of marriage with a section allowing divorce under four conditions: that the couple have lived apart for at least four years; that there was no reasonable prospect of a reconciliation; that proper provision would be made for the children; and that legal provision would be complied with by the parties to the divorce.

The bill was brought to the Dáil by Mervyn Taylor, Minister for Equality and Law Reform, and embodied Labour Party policy of many years' standing. A referendum committee was established under the director of elections, Niamh Bhreathnach, Minister for Education. This time a training programme was held for constituency directors on all of the major questions likely to be raised. This fundamental preparatory work counteracted the flood of reaction from the anti-divorce lobbies. The work of Ray Kavanagh and his colleagues paid a rich dividend in the final result. Dick Spring had learned the lessons of the All-Ireland defeat of 1986. An extensive national campaign got under way with postering, leafleting and canvassing. Mervyn Taylor toured the country and spoke on local radio stations. The Labour Party campaigned vigorously with the right to re-marry campaign group and the Divorce Action Group.

Mervyn was a tower of common sense in the campaign which was reflected in the 64 per cent 'Yes' vote in Dublin. In the final week, John Bruton, Taoiseach, made a decisive and emphatic appeal to the wavering middle ground of the electorate. I believe that his late and impassioned intervention converted a vital percentage to the 'Yes' vote, particularly among the more conservative Fine Gael electorate in Leinster.

In November 1995 the national 'No' vote was 49.72 per cent, with a turnout of 62 per cent.

Another clear-cut intervention on the 'Yes' side was that of Bertie Ahern, leader of Fianna Fáil and the Opposition. Without his support also, the 'No' vote would probably have succeeded. As the campaign unfolded, many Fianna Fáil deputies and senators were opposed but, to his credit, Bertie Ahern stood his ground. The Catholic bishops were as obdurate as ever. For example, Bishop Michael Smith of Meath said 'it was Christ who said any man who divorces his wife and marries another commits adultery'[131] and in his pastoral letter, Archbishop Dermot Clifford of Cashel and Emily warned that divorced people who remarried were likely to divorce again.

To my absolute regret, I was precluded as a member of the European Court of Auditors from participating in the campaign. However Stella did so and there were eight votes in our extended family. As far as I know we all voted 'Yes'. This particular clock will never be turned back. The final confrontation between Church and State in the Republic was won by the social democrats. Stella and I have been very happily married since 1960. As a very disturbed Catholic I thank God for that privilege. But we both voted 'Yes' to put compassion in our constitution.

*

As Minister for Health in the early 1980s, I was thoroughly ashamed of the draconian laws on our statute books relating to homosexuality. Section 61 of the Offences Against the Person Act 1861, provided: 'Whosoever shall be convicted of the abominable crime of buggery, committed either with mankind or with any animal, shall be liable... to be kept in penal servitude for life.' Actually, the 1861 Act was, when introduced, a liberalising statute reducing the maximum penalty from death by hanging! Senator David Norris outlined the background: 'It was only when Henry VIII in the 1530s grabbed the monasteries and sequestered their lands that he coincidentally acquired jurisdiction over the ecclesiastical courts and homosexuality made the transition from sin to crime.'

In 1977, David Norris initiated proceedings in the High Court seeking a declaration that the laws in question were invalid having regard to a constitutional right to privacy. In 1980 the High Court dismissed his claim. Norris recalled: 'Donal Barrington prepared a detailed brief for us in the matter. He indicated that while he felt we had a good case on moral and intellectual grounds, we would meet a barrier in terms of popular and political prejudice, and this would have to be overcome.' In 1982 Norris appealed the decision of the High Court to the Supreme Court. Delivering judgement for the 3/2 majority of the court, the Chief Justice, Tom O'Higgins, said:

> On the grounds of the Christian nature of our State, and on the grounds that the deliberate practice of homosexuality is morally wrong, that it is damaging to the health both of individuals and the public and, finally, that it is potentially harmful to the institution of marriage, I can find no inconsistency with the Constitution in the laws which make such conduct criminal.

David Norris then initiated a case under the European Convention on Human Rights claiming those Irish laws prohibiting and punishing homosexual acts between consenting adults in private violated his right to privacy. I was at the cabinet table when Peter Barry, as the minister responsible, asked the government to note that a finding against the government seemed unavoidable. At that time there was no majority in the government and certainly not in the main political parties in favour of the repeal of the draconian legislation. The advice available to the government from counsel was that the AIDS argument should be used if it was a factor in the government's thinking on the desirability of retaining present laws.

My department's views in relation to health risks associated with homosexual behaviour were conveyed by me to the Attorney General, John Rogers, in May 1985. I pointed out to him that: 'I would find difficulty in identifying a reputable expert at international level who would see our present laws on homosexuality as working in the interest of public health.

Indeed any attempt to make a case for our present laws based on this premise could have a rebound affect.' The Attorney General gave his opinion to Peter Barry and the government that AIDS should not be pleaded as a defence because 'a commitment to this line of defence leads logically to a commitment to fully enforce the existing law and it is unlikely this will be acceptable in our community as it would be seen as an attack on homosexuals and there is a good chance the State would lose the Norris case before the European Court of Justice'.

In 1988 the European Court of Human Rights found the Irish statutes to be in contravention of the European Convention on Human Rights. It was a signal vindication of David Norris. The court ruling was close, eight in favour and six against. The Irish judge, Brian Walsh, was once again against. When, in December 1990, the Fianna Fáil Minister for Justice, Ray Burke, announced the government's intention to reform the law, a sea change had occurred in all of the political parties.

John Bruton said: 'I would look at this from the point of view that the European Court has made a decision that this country is acting in direct contravention of their ruling.' Des O'Malley said: 'I'm very happy that it has now been announced.' Dick Spring said that Fianna Fáil was now moving towards updating legislation on difficult issues 'in keeping with the more open attitudes of the 1990s'. Shane Ross described the government's reaction as 'a direct response to the wave of liberalism generated by the election of Mary Robinson'. But the Catholic Church in Ireland had no intention of changing its policy. Dr Michael Smith, Auxiliary Bishop of Meath said: 'The teaching of the Catholic Church on homosexuality will not change no matter what the Minister for Justice proposes in his new bill.' Archbishop Cathal Daly said he did not believe the laws in relation to homosexual acts should be changed.

In 1992, David Norris, supported by fellow senators John A. Murphy and Brendan Ryan, became quite agitated about the delay by the government in bringing forward the amending legislation. The Taoiseach, Albert Reynolds, questioned in the Dáil by the Democratic Left leader, Proinsias de Rossa, indicated that the Fianna Fáil–PD government did not propose to bring forward the bill by the end of 1992.[132] De Rossa pointed out that it was four years since the European Court had made its ruling. The chairman of the Progressive Democrats, Michael McDowell, said it was misleading to suggest that tackling economic issues was an alternative to tackling social issues: 'Human rights are human rights; and there is no room for "a la carte" commitment to respect for human rights and international law. Minorities entitled to the benefit of the rule of law, and minority status does not relegate people to the end of a list of priorities.'[133] In his 1993 Seanad election address, David Norris wrote, 'It is an issue that I will not let die.'

The Fianna Fáil-Labour coalition was committed to the reform. In particular, Dick Spring and John Rogers were adamant about the inclusion of the reform in the programme for government. Albert Reynolds was unenthusiastic but being Taoiseach was more important. As Minister for Justice, Máire Geoghegan-Quinn was straightforward and courageous in bringing the issue directly before government in May 1993. Almost five years had elapsed since David Norris had won his case.

Nineteen

The Tobacco Ring

'Cigarette smoking ... is the chief, single, avoidable cause of death in our society and the most important public health issue of our time.'

Dr C. Everett Koop, US Surgeon-General, 1982

When I was appointed Minister for Health in 1982, I was advised by senior departmental staff that they had been actively developing and implementing programmes designed to reduce both the supply of, and the demand for, tobacco products. About 16,000 people died each year from smoking-related illnesses in Ireland and it was estimated that as many as 5,000 of these were directly due to smoking. Contrary to popular belief, those who died or were disabled as a result of smoking were not elderly. Deaths from smoking-related illnesses accounted for 52 per cent of all deaths of those aged 35-64 years in 1982 and smoking was the single most significant cause of death in middle age.

Tobacco smoking in Ireland and its resultant illnesses imposed an enormous strain on the health services. Each year, about 480,000 days were spent in hospital as a result of smoking-related illnesses. The hospital costs associated with these illnesses alone were estimated in 1982 to be in excess of £50 million. The costs of outpatient services, general medical services, disability payments and days lost at work posed equally high costs to the Exchequer. The revenue receipts to government from tobacco products in 1982 were about £400 million and policy decisions to increase excise duties had been taken not only in the interests of the government's financial strategies but also from a public health viewpoint. It was estimated that for each 1 per cent increase in the price of cigarettes, demand dropped by about ½ per cent. Insofar as the implications for the tobacco industry were concerned, the industry was not then a significant provider of jobs. By and large, the tobacco industry in Ireland was becoming increasingly automated and the labour force within the industry was ageing. The gradual reduction in tobacco consumption would, therefore, be coped with through natural wastage.

The early programmes of the Department of Health centred on the educational approach through the mass media, together with voluntary agreements with the industry relating to the advertising of tobacco products. Throughout the years these programmes were developed and consolidated but, by and large, their impact was limited.

*

Charles J. Haughey and I had two good attributes in common. We were both reformed smokers and as Ministers for Health we introduced anti-smoking legislation. And we did so in the teeth of opposition from the powerful tobacco lobbies. In January 1984, following consultations with all government departments, I brought a comprehensive memorandum to government proposing the amendment of the 1978 Tobacco Products (Control of Advertising, Sponsorship and Sales Promotion) Act and the regulations made under it. It aimed to provide stronger controls in relation to health warnings on tobacco packages and advertisements; the introduction of legislation to provide for the banning of smoking in certain designated areas and facilities used by the public; the introduction of legislation to provide for the payment by tobacco companies of a fixed percentage of their advertising budgets to the Health Education Bureau to be used on public education programmes in the area of health and smoking; and the sanctioning of a sizeable increase in excise duty on cigarettes.

In the memorandum I pointed out that cigarette smoking was currently recognised as the largest single preventable cause of premature death and disability in our society. In the previous 25 years, a mass of medical and scientific research had demolished the initial and continuing claims of cigarette manufacturers and others that the scientific evidence which identified smoking as a cause of lung cancer was sketchy and that no link between smoking and cancer was 'proven'. Over two decades of continuous research overwhelmingly ratified the scientific indictment of smoking as a contribution to disease and premature death. Smoking was now known to be associated with over 20 different medical conditions including six different cancers. I further pointed out that the Department of Health had attempted to quantify the number of deaths, incidences of morbidity and other losses due to smoking in Ireland through an analysis of the international findings on the association of smoking with a broad range of medical conditions.

The results showed that smoking directly caused about 2,500 premature adult deaths per year of which close on one-half occurred before the age of 65; about 37,000 life-years were lost each year as a result of premature deaths from smoking; about 7,350 people were admitted to hospital each year as a result of smoking and these patients accounted for over 119,000 hospital bed days; the Department of Social Welfare probably received as many as 12,000 claims for disability benefit each year from people as a direct result of smoking and about 1.1 million work days could have been lost each year as a result of smoking. The analysis also indicated that smoking was the direct cause of about 900 to 1,000 serious fires each year.

I further advised the government that despite the overall decrease in numbers of smokers since 1977-1978, there had been a significant increase in smoking among the 25-34 and 45-54 age groups and this was giving cause for much concern. The increase in smoking among these age groups was primarily due to a recent but rapid increase in the incidence of smoking among women. Contrary to popular belief, I also pointed out that in 1979 the Irish were the heaviest smokers in the EU with the average Irish smoker smoking 26.5 cigarettes per day (19.8

in the UK and 16.5 in France). The number of regular smokers amongst boys changed little in the 1970s but there had been a remarkable increase in the proportion of girls smoking, particularly under the age of 15. These findings were worrying in that they indicated the failure of health education campaigns to reduce the incidence of smoking among schoolchildren.

I pointed out to the government that: 'Health warnings are required on cigarette packets under the existing legislation. The present system, which essentially uses only one warning — SMOKING SERIOUSLY DAMAGES YOUR HEALTH — Government Warning — has become ineffective. It is over-exposed and time-worn; it is no longer novel and presents no new information; and it is not likely to be perceived as personally relevant. Research by the World Health Organisation has shown that systems of "rotational" warnings can successfully overcome all of the above shortcomings.' I also proposed to increase the area of the health warning in advertisements from 8 to 15 per cent as had then been recently introduced in the UK

Another major reform I brought forward was the proposal to ban smoking in public places. A nationwide survey by the Health Education Bureau indicated that there was considerable support for the proposed ban. As a first step, I proposed a complete ban on smoking on public transport, a complete ban in cinemas and theatres, and a complete ban on smoking by visitors and staff in health institutions, in schools (including staff rooms) and in all state and semi-state offices used by the public. I also proposed to the government that there should be a major increase in the excise duty — of the order of 50 pence per packet — on cigarettes. I pointed out to my colleagues that:

> Price increases could be particularly effective in reducing the incidence of smoking among young people and in stopping people taking up the habit. The Minister would argue that any losses to the Exchequer due to decreased demand for tobacco products would be compensated for by reduced expenditure on health and social welfare services. Furthermore the Minister could suggest that a substantial increase in cigarette prices, if declared to

be in the interests of the nation's health, would be
much more acceptable to the public than if it were
merely a tax-gathering exercise.'

However, it was my proposal that the tobacco companies
should be required to pay an amount equivalent to a fixed
percentage of their advertising and sponsorship budget to the
Health Education Bureau that raised the greatest controversy.
In support of my far-reaching proposal, I pointed out that the
bureau would be required to spend this money on public
education in the area of smoking and health. The effect of this
proposal would be to ensure that the tobacco industry paid an
increased fraction of the undoubted public costs of their
activities.

These various proposals swiftly raised the hackles of my
ministerial colleagues. Alan Dukes, Minister for Finance; Dick
Spring, Minister for Industry and Energy; Ruairi Quinn,
Minister for Labour, and John Bruton, Minister for Trade,
Commerce and Tourism all opposed the major increase in
excise duty on the grounds of its impact on employment in the
tobacco industry. I argued in response to their objections that:
'The Minister for Health is aware that employment in the
industry has already declined by about 19 per cent over the past
four years — from 2,400 jobs in 1979 to about 1,800 today — but
would argue that this is largely as a result of improved
technology rather than a fall-off in sales and that these losses
will continue to occur irrespective of the level of excise duty.'
Alan Dukes also put forward the extraordinary argument that
'there may be reductions in hospital costs and disability
benefits but contends that these could be offset by increases in
other areas such as old age pensions'.

John Bruton pointed out that a 50p increase in excise duty
would raise the Consumer Price Index by 1.4 per cent and,
therefore, the rate of inflation. I replied quite sharply to this
assertion by stating that: 'The Minister would also argue that
the validity of including tobacco products on the CPI is now
questionable in view of the serious health hazards associated
with smoking.' Alan Dukes advanced the further argument that
all smokers should be required to pay a greater share of the
medical cost of treating smoking related illnesses. I contended

that while I agreed in principal with this approach, the only practical way of doing this was a significant increase in taxation. The Minister for Education, Gemma Hussey, was not satisfied that it would be practicable to introduce a ban on smoking in school staff rooms. Alan Dukes and Michael Noonan, Minister for Justice, were also of the view that Gardaí should not be involved in enforcing restrictions in public areas.

Regarding the proposed levy related to tobacco companies' advertising budgets, Alan Dukes could not agree that the proceeds should be used in aid of the Health Education Bureau activities. He requested the government to assign the levy proceeds to health expenditure generally with an option to use part of the levy for the HEB. I strongly disagreed, pointing out that 'The proposed levy is specifically designed to link the resources of the Health Education Bureau in the area of "Smoking and Health" to the activity level of the tobacco industry. Failure to use the proceeds of this levy for health education will make it impossible for the HEB to counter the constant and persuasive stream of advertising, sponsorship and promotion funded by the tobacco industry.'

Within the echelons of the departmental secretaries there was an equal lack of enthusiasm for my proposals. Four departments made submissions: Social Welfare, Justice, Industry and Energy, and Labour. The latter considered that it might be difficult to implement a smoking ban in public offices and in workplaces. I was thus faced with a marked lack of enthusiasm from most of my government colleagues for these reforms. The fear of offending the smoking electorate and the industry was very powerful.

Thus, the battle lines were drawn. The Taoiseach, Garret FitzGerald, was entirely sympathetic but we were faced with an unenthusiastic government. The smoking habit was so ingrained at government meetings that early on we had to bring a mobile filter machine into our meeting room. Only Garret FitzGerald, John Bruton, Austin Deasy, Michael Noonan and Jim Mitchell did not smoke. Paddy Cooney smoked a pipe, others cigars and cheroots. Some colleagues such as the late Frank Cluskey, Alan Dukes, Liam Kavanagh and John Boland were very heavy smokers. I smoked, but only four or five per day. I simply could not smoke in public as Minister for Health. There was great hilarity when, in the heat of debate, I regularly borrowed cigarettes from Alan Dukes at government meetings. Alan was a chain smoker. The air at these meetings was simply poisonous. Every government meeting was an exercise in prolonged passive smoking, the dangers of which were not fully appreciated. The Taoiseach had a weeping eye condition but that did not deter the smokers. Dermot Nally and Frank Murray, secretary and assistant secretary to the government, regularly emerged from those long meetings red eyed and leaving a blue fog behind. I stopped smoking in 1987 and Stella also kicked this dangerous habit a few years later.

However, I was deeply impressed by the wealth of expert evidence on the smoking epidemic presented to me by the medical officers of the Department of Health and I was determined to press forward with my proposals. After considerable debate at several government meetings, during which most of my 'smoking colleagues' were appreciative of my health concerns, I won over their support in the end. The government in March 1984 finally approved stronger controls in relation to health warnings on tobacco products, provided for the banning of smoking in certain designated areas and the introduction of the advertising levy. The latter two decisions required the drafting of a Tobacco (Health Protection) Bill.

*

There then began a protracted and heated period of consultation with the Irish tobacco industry, the advertising industry and the trade unions in the industry about the proposed reforms. These contacts continued over a period of eighteen months while regulations and the new bill were being drafted. The Tobacco (Health Protection) Bill did not appear until 1986 despite my best efforts to harass the Attorney General, the parliamentary draftsmen and the cabinet to approve the bill for circulation to the Houses of the Oireachtas. Meanwhile, there had been sustained opposition to the proposal for a levy from the Association of Advertisers and the Institute of Advertising Practitioners in Ireland. They lobbied all deputies and senators and members of the government. The

Federated Union of Employers joined in, as did the Confederation of Irish Industry. Michael Noonan, as the new Minister for Industry and Commerce, was intensively lobbied by all of the tobacco manufacturers and reopened the whole question of the levy. Dr A.J. O'Reilly of Independent Newspapers joined in the campaign and wielded a major influence.

But I did have some important support. Dr Risteard Mulcahy, Director, Cardiac Department and Professor of Preventive Cardiology, St Vincent's Hospital, Dublin and University College, Dublin wrote in the *Irish Medical Journal*:

> There is no doubt that his new legislation will be bitterly resented by certain vested interests and particularly by the tobacco companies, the advertising industry, and some of the media. Influences still exist which frustrate the abolition of tobacco advertising and sponsorship, but government should be aware that there is not a single reason why tobacco smoking is essential for the economic wellbeing of this country, and the savings in medical expenditure and human suffering from such measures would be immense.[134]

Dr Luke Clancy, Medical Director, Peamount Hospital, wrote to me in December 1986:

> I had the honour of representing Ireland as a Constituent Member of the International Union Against Tuberculosis at the 26th World Conference recently in Singapore. It was therefore a great pleasure and source of pride for me to hear the Chairman of the conference, Sir John Crofton, pay singular tribute to yourself as Minister for Health. This praise concerned your exemplary action in banning the sale of 'Skoal Bandits'. He pointed out how important this was and stressed how his adopted country, i.e. Britain, because as you will know he was born and reared in Ireland, had failed to take early action.

I was also very pleased when, in January 1986, a statement of support was made by leading academic and scientific medical organisations. I had met representatives from the Royal College of Surgeons in Ireland, the Royal College of Physicians of Ireland, the Irish College of General Practitioners, the Royal College of General Practitioners, the Irish Cancer Society, the Irish Thoracic Society, the Irish Cardiac Society and the Irish Heart Foundation. For once the medical profession and the minister of the day were in total harmony!

However, politics still prevailed and, by mid-1986, I had received further strenuous representations on the levy from three of my Labour ministerial colleagues, nine of my Fine Gael ministerial colleagues, 16 government backbenchers and ten opposition deputies and senators. The controls on smoking in public places were the most vital part of the bill. I deliberately delayed until December 1986 before conceding the deletion of the levy. The government approved all other sections of the bill and agreed that it should be introduced in the Seanad. Meanwhile I had introduced, with effect from July 1986, comprehensive Tobacco Products (Control of Advertising, Sponsorship and Sales Promotion) Regulations 1986.

During the course of these negotiations I received outstanding cooperation and advice from Liam Flanagan, secretary of the Department of Health, and Dermot Smyth, principal officer. The exceptional personality on the side of the tobacco manufacturers was the late John Lepere, managing director of PJ Carroll Ltd. His sheer ability and charm around the conference table was a lesson to all involved. His knowledge of domestic and European Union legislation relating to tobacco was most impressive. At a time when the Gallagher (Dublin) Ltd spokesperson was accusing the government, not just the Department of Health, of being 'prepared to mutilate, and thus destroy, international brands', John Lepere held his nerve and negotiated the best possible deal for his industry.

And the chairman of Carroll Industries PLC, Don Carroll, did not pull his punches on the issues. His reaction to my initial draft of the regulations was that they were 'a flagrant and violent destruction of commercial property, trade marks and labels built by many millions of pounds of investment over many years, of a kind without precedent in a Western democracy'. He had led a strenuous delegation from Player and Wills Ltd and Gallagher (Dublin) Ltd to the Taoiseach and Tanaiste in February 1986. I found Don Carroll gracious enough in my meetings with himself and John Lepere. I gathered that one of my predecessors, Charles Haughey, had treated him with scant regard when he met him in the Custom House prior to the introduction of the 1979 regulations. I could sense that Carrolls were under considerable pressure from Rothmans International who had licensed them to manufacture and sell Rothmans King Size. I was quite impressed by the efforts of Carroll Industries PLC to diversify their commercial enterprises in non-tobacco areas particularly in projects in the west of Ireland.

However, one particular episode in this campaign left me with a very sour taste. At the time the Independent Newspapers Group, as pointed out by *The Irish Times* in a feature in May 1986, earned about £1 million per annum from cigarette advertising. The *Sunday Independent* in a pre-Christmas supplement in 1984 had used a particular Santa Claus cigarette advertisement which was clearly in breach of the existing 1979 regulations. The newspaper was warned by the Department of Health not to repeat the advertisement. The Independent Group management was outraged. When they proceeded to make an issue of it we had to stand our ground or be, in effect,, party to a statutory offence. The industry was closely watching the outcome of this confrontation. Government ministers were appraoched but I refused to agree to a repeat infringement. The Independent backed down.

In the aftermath of the government reshuffle in early 1986, I suspected that the advertising, newspaper and tobacco lobbies had pressurised Fine Gael for my replacement by a more cooperative minister. I compared my fate to that of Sir George Young MP, the junior minister in Mrs Thatcher's Conservative government in 1979 who, after a valiant campaign to implement a total ban on all cigarette advertising and sponsorship, was moved to the Department of the Environment in her reshuffle of September 1981. Peter Taylor in his outstanding book *The 'Smoke Ring', The Politics of Tobacco*[135] clearly documented this episode and the ring of defences which ensured that the power of the tobacco industry was kept intact. The industry in Ireland and indeed some of my union colleagues in the industry would have been very relieved to see the same fate befall myself during those years.

*

One of the most important actions I took during my tenure in the Custom House was my decision, in January 1986, to ban the importation and sale in the Republic of a particular tobacco product known as 'Skoal Bandits'. At a press conference in the department, I displayed the product, a circular tin containing about twenty small sachets similar to tea bags. The sachets were placed in the mouth between the cheek and the gum and sucked, a practice known in the USA as 'snuff dipping'. The product was being manufactured in Scotland by an American company for distribution in Europe and was available in Northern Ireland. At about £1 per tin it was particularly attractive to teenagers and less obvious to parents. It was a potent source of cancers of the mouth and throat and caused serious dental disorders. The sachets were pure tobacco and highly addictive. A Dublin firm, Tobacco Distributors, intended importing the product.

I decided to ban them under a little known section 66 of the 1947 Health Act which gave the minister power to ban a substance which he deemed injurious to public health. It seems that, amazingly, at an Easter meeting of the Catholic Hierarchy in 1944, the use of a new sanitary tampon called 'Tampax' was discussed. Following a discussion the bishops disapproved: I wonder if the minutes of this meeting exist. However, we do know that Dr John Charles McQuaid, the Catholic Archbishop of Dublin, did contact Dr F.C. Ward, Parliamentary Secretary to the Minister for Local Government and Public Health, to convey their concerns and explain that, in their opinion, such tampons could harmfully 'stimulate girls at an impressionable age'. Dr Ward was asked if he could prohibit their sale and, amazingly, acceded to their request with Section 66 in the 1947 Act.[136] Presumably to avoid public ridicule and protest, the section was rather vaguely drafted, hence my opportunity to encompass 'Skoal Bandits'.

This course of action had been recommended to me by the ever resourceful officers of the department. At first I thought that they were 'having me on'. When I told some of my fellow ministers of my action, they concluded that at last I had gone completely round the bend. United States Tobacco International Inc. was not amused: they issued a summons and statement of claim against myself, Ireland and the Attorney General in February 1986. The case was heard in the High Court in July 1987 after the Labour Party had left government. Not for the first time did Justice Liam Hamilton, then President of the High Court, face a strange piece of ministerial ordering.

The High Court found the order to be invalid but I had bought valuable space and had exposed this pernicious prospect. To his credit Dr Rory O'Hanlon, the new Fianna Fáil Minister for Health, promptly ensured that the Tobacco (Health Promotion and Protection) Bill 1988 provided for the prohibition of the supply of oral snuff. Not surprisingly, the Irish Tobacco Manufacturers' Advisory Committee opposed the provision but to no avail.

It was not until May 1990 that the regulation under the 1988 act finally came into force. It was against the law to smoke in public offices, schools and third level colleges, food preparation areas, bus and railway stations, sports centres, cinemas, libraries, trains, DART and buses, health premises including all hospitals, centres for the mentally handicapped and for the physically handicapped, restaurants and canteens, and airports and ferry ports. We had come a long way, indeed, from Charles Haughey's first regulations in 1979 and my government memorandum of 1984.

In the 1850s, John Snow ended an epidemic of cholera in London by removing the handle of the Broad Street pump. In the 1980s in Ireland, the tobacco regulations were the handle towards coping with the smoking epidemic. One of the regressive decisions of Fianna Fáil in the 1980s was to abolish the Health Education Bureau. The bureau had done tremendous work in public health education, particularly in relation to smoking. The Fianna Fáil cuts in the 1987 budget transferred the functions of the bureau back to the Department of Health. And with all the constraints of the department and its limited budget, the profile of health education has not exactly blossomed.

In 1985 the bureau organised the World Conference on Health Education in Dublin and I had addressed the inaugural session thus:

> You must oppose the tobacco companies as strenuously as you oppose the drug pushers. Companies who peddle drugs unrelated to real health care must be exposed and excluded from the market. Advertising must be controlled in the common good. This is of course draconian. But health means money and profit and there is no soft option in dealing with such influences. I am under no illusion that such market forces have enormous influence to oppose public health needs. They unceasingly manipulate politicians, the health professions, public opinion and those who are most vulnerable — young persons and in particular young women. As such they must be opposed.

I was particularly pleased when Charlie McCreevy, Minister for Finance, put an extra 50p on a packet of 20 cigarettes in the 1999 budget. Furthermore, this revenue was allocated directly to the Department of Health. And the decision of the Minister for Health, Micheál Martin, to ban all advertising of tobacco products from June 2000 must be warmly welcomed. It took 15 years to bring about these policy changes during which 97,500 Irish people died from tobacco related cancer. The Society of Actuaries in Ireland has shown that male smokers aged 40 or more are twice as likely to die in a given year as non-smokers. Their report said that both sexes could expect to reduce their life span by seven years if they are smokers.

It is a measure of progress that the government in 2000 is setting up the Office of Tobacco Control to co-ordinate government policy and help enforce existing anti-smoking legislation. When I still see so many young people in the throes of this addiction, I know that we have a long, long way to go.

Twenty

Reshuffling the Pack

'You are always dangerous with a chip on your shoulder.'

Nickey English, 2000

From time to time it has been alleged that various ministers in government have resigned or threatened to resign unless they got their way on certain key issues of policy. Noel Browne is the celebrated case although he was more fired than resigned. John Bruton was wont to threaten to do so. Kevin Boland did so after Taoiseach Jack Lynch fired two other ministers during the Arms Crisis. Paddy Smith, Minister for Agriculture, resigned because Taoiseach Seán Lemass confirmed an increase in the basic wage of agricultural workers which he considered excessive. And for a more mundane reason, Bobby Molloy allegedly threatened to resign if the West Galway Dáil constituency was revised by Jack Lynch's government.

I faced a somewhat similar situation during the Taoiseach's changes in the portfolios of ministers in February 1986. I was apologetically but bluntly informed by Dick Spring that I was being moved from the Health and Social Welfare portfolios to Justice as and from the following day. He informed me that he had discussed the matter with the Taoiseach. Up to that point there was no indication whatsoever that I was to get the bump. I was a very disturbed minister when informed. I enquired from Dick about the other ministers. Apparently, John Bruton, then Minister for Industry, Trade, Commerce and Tourism, was about to take over Finance from Alan Dukes who was to transfer to Education. Gemma Hussey, then Minister for Education, was to become Minister for European Affairs, and Peter Barry was to retain the Foreign Affairs portfolio. Michael Noonan was to transfer from Justice to Industry and Commerce. It was intended to move John Boland from the Public Service portfolio to Health and Social Welfare. Paddy Cooney and possibly Paddy O'Toole were, in my opinion, destined for the drop. Sean Barret, chief whip and fellow constituency deputy was, it seemed to me, one of those on the up and up to a full cabinet post.

Dick Spring made a most persuasive case to me for my reshuffle. I was under enormous political pressure after three years plus of grinding endeavours to control health and social welfare expenditures and to initiate long overdue reforms. I had faced down the cynical Fianna Fáil dominated health boards whose accounts were often submitted to the department years out of date. I had challenged the proliferation of private beds in publicly funded hospitals which were a licence to print money for some very well paid consultants under the extremely generous common contract given to them by Charles Haughey when he was Minister for Health. And I had attempted to turn around the conservative ethos of the psychiatric hospitals, some of which fully merited closure. Others were in dire need of fully integrated nursing care. On the public health policy side, my legislative reforms in relation to the nursing profession, contraception, clinical trials, childcare and tobacco advertising had met virulently hostile reaction from entrenched vested interests.

In short, Dick and Garret knew, and I certainly knew, that I was most unpopular. The newspaper industry deeply resented my reforms in relation to tobacco advertising. The hierarchy was hostile in relation to contraception and divorce. The health boards and the health trade unions were screaming for more money but opposed vital reorganisation. Some voluntary hospital matrons and boards adamantly opposed a common trainee nurse recruitment system under An Bord Altranais and wanted to see the back of me. To add to the pressure, I was denounced as an abortionist from the pulpit at a novena in my Dun Laoghaire constituency in Dalkey parish Catholic church:

to his credit the parish priest repudiated his visiting preacher at the masses the following Sunday. Many of these interests were determined to remove the incumbent minister from the Department of Health as a matter of urgency.

The backbench Fine Gael and Labour deputies had a severe dose of the health runs when I announced, in the Dáil, following a government decision on my 1986 health estimate, that I intended to close two psychiatric hospitals in Carlow and Castlerea and four other outdated local hospitals from the end of 1986. One of these facilities, St Patrick's, Blackrock, was in my constituency. These decisions caused local uproar. I knew as I watched the shocked reaction of government backbenchers that confrontation was inevitable. Such was the reaction that Garret and Dick resolved that I had to be removed to Justice where, presumably, I could provide some tough medicine to the Provos which would be more appreciated by the electorate.

When my immediate opposition to the move became apparent to Dick, I went and discussed the situation with the Taoiseach, the Tanaiste, the Attorney General, John Rogers, and separately with Alan Dukes. Alan said, 'Barry, it is your privilege to serve as the Taoiseach so decides!' They reproached me for not having had extensive prior consultations on the closures with the backbenchers. I pointed out that the government had decided that my health estimate clearly foreshadowed these closures and that I had conveyed the decision, in the first instance, directly to the Dáil itself. I had no intention of being the fall guy. I knew that 'prior consultation' would have meant that no decision could be implemented.

Late that bleak winter evening, I met Jim Downey, secretary of the Department of Social Welfare, and Liam Flanagan, secretary of the Department of Health, in my sparse room in the Dáil. I was again under considerable pressure, particularly from Alan Dukes in the privacy of his office. He and I, despite our ferocious disputations over my health and social welfare estimates from 1982 to 1986, were by then close associates. He was a social liberal with an elongated Finance mandarin mentality. Jim Downey, an outstanding secretary of the Department of Social Welfare, had little time for the Taoiseach. He had deeply offended Jim by his personal criticisms in 1981 of the computer capacity of the Department of Social Welfare, which were starved by Finance's sparse allocation of resources. When I informed Jim of my proposed demise, he stressed that a government reshuffle was entirely outside his remit. But I had no doubt that he wished me to continue in Social Welfare.

Jim Downey had been plucked by Charles Haughey from the principal officer ranks of the department for elevation to the secretaryship. He was a vastly experienced and shrewd public servant from Macroom and had an encyclopaedic knowledge of social welfare administration and its consolidated statutes. He brooked no special pleadings from the annual estimate-cutting campaigners of the public expenditure division of the Department of Finance. And he had a tenacious and highly progressive social conscience as he protected his succession of ministers and their estimates. He invariably routed the Department of Finance. 'Yerra, Garret and Dukes have nothing on us at all, boss!' he would say when we regularly adjourned to the Kingsland Chinese restaurant in Dame Street after out-manoeuvring Finance once again.

Liam Flanagan, by contrast, was a much more flamboyant civil servant, and very articulate about health issues. There was an extraordinary group of professional administrators with him in the department which he dominated. He was very knowledgeable and energetic with a hint of paranoia about the politics of the health boards. He was a Glasnevin resident, a St. Vincent's GAA admirer and a no-holds-barred Clontarf Golf Club activist. He had a healthy contempt for most Dublin 4 politicians. He had succeeded Dermot Condon, a Corkman from Blarney and the 'North Mon', a shrewd contemporary of Jack Lynch who was the last secretary in that department to be appointed by government solely on a minister's recommendation prior to the introduction of the top level appointments scheme.

I also informed Liam of the proposed reshuffle. He advised me, on a very personal basis, to sit tight. Duly fortified, I returned to the Taoiseach and the Tanaiste. I informed them at 4 a.m. that I would 'consider my position' and would inform them of my 'decision' at 8 a.m. My short journey home in the state Mercedes to Stella was very subdued indeed. I recalled

Michael O'Leary's famous saying: 'By their tyre marks shall ye know them!' He had heard that when he had the misfortune to visit the Dunlop tyre plant in Cork in his state car which had Semperit tyres. To make it worse, he had a Dublin registered Mercedes to boot, not even a decent Ford from Cork. 'Mickie Léari' from the Court House Bar, off Washington Street in Cork, was never allowed to forget his gaffe.

As dawn came up, I awakened Stella and told her the full story. She was very angry and I was exhausted. We knew that my refusal to budge could precipitate a general election. Dick Spring could not force through the reshuffle and I would bring the fury of government supporters in both Houses of the Oireachtas around my head. In the Dun Laoghaire constituency, my prospects were even grimmer. We had no money and a young school-going family. My ministerial salary was paying off the personal election overdrafts from the three elections in 1981 and 1982. We did not ask for or receive any special treatment from our Bank of Ireland manager in College Green. In short, our situation was rather desperate. There loomed the prospect of a redundant politician at 51 years of age.

However, Stella never faltered. She adamantly supported my view that to throw in the towel in the health portfolio would be an abject surrender to the hard core of reactionary backbenchers on the government and opposition benches. The former Minister for Health and Opposition leader, Charles Haughey, would glory at my forced exit from the Custom House. The multiple vested interests in the health services would be vindicated in their incessant representations to vulnerable deputies and senators. Stella knew that I still had many reforms to develop our health services for *all* our people. Like a captain of a doomed battleship in war, I was determined to go down with all guns blazing. And I would ensure that some enemy crews would not see the dawn either!

*

I have been asked: why was I so adamant? Was it a stubborn personality streak or the outcome of deeply held beliefs about the future direction of our health services and particularly for those who were in psychiatric care? Dick Walsh, the political correspondent of *The Irish Times*, who himself has had more than his share of ill health, summed up the core issues when he wrote:

> If there is a policy — as there is — of moving towards community care for people who need psychiatric treatment, how can the retention of hospitals which have outlived their usefulness be justified? In some small towns, hospitals had come to be viewed merely as sources of employment and revenue for those who provided ancillary services: agents of an industrial policy which had as much to do with provision of jobs as with the provision of an efficient and humane hospital service. Local politicians are fully aware of this and their objections to the changes that Mr Desmond announced have more than a hint of hypocrisy.[137]

Central to my approach was my report *The Psychiatric Services — Planning for the Future* which was published in 1985. It represented the collective wisdom of senior departmental staff, psychiatric nurses, doctors and hospital administrators. They were unanimous in their recommendations for a community-based rather than a hospital-based psychiatric care system. The emphasis was on prevention, health and social education, early and accurate assessment and treatment in new short-stay units in the general hospitals. Nursing staff would be integrated. Long-stay psychiatric hospital residence would be a treatment of last resort. Mentally handicapped persons would be removed from psychiatric hospitals to community homes under professional supervision.

The psychiatric services I inherited in 1982 were largely hospital based, with in-patient treatment provided in 22 health board psychiatric hospitals and at a few acute units attached to some general hospitals. There was also a small number of private psychiatric hospitals. I was determined to reform this structure with a comprehensive, community-oriented psychiatric service and to integrate the treatment of mental illness with general health care as much as possible. The main components of the community services would be day hospital units, halfway houses, group homes, out-patient clinics, hostels, sheltered workshops and day care facilities. I had been so taken aback by the poor conditions of most of our psychiatric hospitals in 1983 after I took over the portfolio that I authorised £9.5 million in minor capital schemes to improve living accommodation for long-stay patients.

It was in this policy setting that I decided to recommend to the government that St Dympna's Hospital in Carlow and St Patrick's in Castlerea, Co Roscommon, should be closed. Carlow was one of five district psychiatric hospitals in the South Eastern Health Board and Castlerea was the third and the smallest of the psychiatric hospitals in the Western Health Board area. The closure of these hospitals would require detailed planning to ensure that the needs of the patients were properly met and the staff effectively redeployed. However, the decision on closure had to be taken first and the government fully accepted my proposal. All of the interested parties were fully aware of the general closure guidelines as stated in the *Planning for the Future* report. However, the decision was immediately transformed into a political football, epitomised by the cynical analysis of the late journalist, John Healy, who dismissed the exercise: 'Pitching a couple of hundred mental patients on the charity of ill equipped villages is not a reformation.'[138]

*

As the reshuffle crisis developed, I was acutely aware that Dick Spring was now in an impossible situation. I had agreed to contact him at 8 a.m. by phone on the morning of the proposed announcement to convey my decision. I restated my determination not to move and said that I would do all possible not to damage his position in government and in the party. Dick was not surprised and knew that he had little option but to inform the Taoiseach that I could not be ditched. Despite our differences in temperament, age and political experience, Dick had been a tower of support in government when Alan Dukes and John Bruton had repeatedly cut loose with proposed cuts in social welfare and health.

I had resolved, but did not inform him, to bring the whole debacle down to the wire and then, as a final and only compromise, to vacate Social Welfare but, most emphatically, to remain on in the Custom House in Health. I kept this strategy entirely to myself, for once. I did not wish to raise false hopes to Stella as I left for Leinster House. The Labour Party officers met at noon with Dick Spring: general secretary Colm O'Broin; Minister of State, Joe Bermingham and Ministers Liam Kavanagh and Ruairi Quinn present, as were Fergus Finlay and John Rogers, the Attorney General. I again restated to this larger audience my opposition to the proposed reshuffle. I well recall Liam Kavanagh's offer to serve in any portfolio to resolve the impasse.

Dick Spring had, by this time, begun to draft his speech for the resumption of the Dáil at 2.30 that afternoon in which he proposed to explain why Labour was withdrawing from government that evening. We were now facing into an inevitable motion of no confidence. I then asked Dick if I could see the Taoiseach alone in his office in a final effort to resolve the crisis. At this stage his patience was razor thin but, wearily, he contacted the Taoiseach. I had played my last card.

*

When I entered the Taoiseach's office, Garret was alone, pale and slumped against the marble fireplace. He looked shattered. I told him that I had a proposal to resolve the situation. I would move from Social Welfare because of the excessive work load of two major departments, and remain in Health. I further suggested that with all the problems we were then having in government with equal treatment disputes in Social Welfare and the need to devote particular care to the recommendations of the recent Report of the Commission on Social Welfare, which I had established, that Gemma Hussey should move from Education to this portfolio. On the grapevine I had learned that by now it was quite clear that the other deputy leader in government, Peter Barry, Minister for Foreign Affairs, had furiously rejected the Taoiseach's proposal to split his department. Garret had seriously underestimated another Corkman and failed to appreciate the extent of the statutory changes required to meet his aspirations for Gemma. Needless to note, the senior officers of the Department of Foreign Affairs were aghast that their erstwhile ministerial hero of the 1970s would surrender *their* department on a plate of political convenience.

Garret agreed to consider my proposal and said he would inform Dick Spring of his decision. I disappeared while Garret sent for Gemma. I returned to the Labour gathering and explained how the crisis could be averted. Dick went off to see Garret and when he returned, it was clear that the crisis was over. We were barely on speaking terms. It was a real head to head. And it was a real mess. A half an hour later I met Gemma in the corridor where we shared offices. She was in tears. I phoned Stella, gave the bad news to the Secretary of Social Welfare, Jim Downey, locked my office door and had a large Paddy and water, all alone, as I braced myself to go to the Dáil Chamber for the Taoiseach's statement. I knew going into the Dáil that I was in the same position as was de Valera at his own funeral! Half of those who attended came to confirm that he was dead. The other half came to ensure that he was buried.

*

I was acutely aware that my refusal to be moved from both portfolios had seriously diminished the government's credibility. A major reshuffle had turned into a complete shambles. The Taoiseach could not exercise his most fundamental constitutional entitlement — the right to hire and fire his own government ministers. He could have, and some to this day still say should have, fired me on the spot but, as in almost all coalitions, he would have brought down the entire government in the process. But his panic about the future of Fine Gael and his initial support from the Tanaiste for the reshuffle was understandable. The Progressive Democrats had arrived on the doorsteps with populist political banalities and soft tax options. Fine Gael, on the Monday prior to the reshuffle had, as a consequence, plummeted to a 23 per cent first preference vote in an opinion poll. The alarm bells were ringing in Mount Street and Joan FitzGerald was on the phone 'goodo'. Joan was a truly formidable analyst and she did not spare

Garret her trenchant views on most issues. And the January 1986 Alan Dukes budget had been deemed to be pretty lousy for the country by 56 per cent of the electorate.

Dukes did not deserve the drop either. There was no precedent for the removal of a Minister for Finance between the introduction of a budget and its adoption by the Dáil. He was head and shoulders above the government, both literally and in ability, on most budgetary issues. However, in government and even to the electorate, he could not resist portraying himself as the brightest boy in the class. Well after he had won many a budget argument at bilateral meetings with other ministers and their senior staff, he invariably persisted in proving how clever he really was. This was his undoing in the short term and later as leader of Fine Gael.

Gemma was, in many ways, also unfortunate. She was clearly out of her depth in the pay negotiations with the teachers' unions, and the die-hard operators of Carysfort College gave her an unmerciful partisan drubbing on the overdue closure of the college.

Gemma should have decided to remain a Fine Gael senator after she joined that parliamentary party in 1979. She was already 41 years old and would probably have been re-elected to the Seanad in 1981 and 1982. Had she moved to a middle-class Dublin constituency instead of Wicklow she would have hardly retired from active politics in 1989 when she was 51. The Seanad role was her real forté and her record there was excellent. She and her husband, Derry, a successful businessman and an influential backroom adviser to Fine Gael, were the embodiment of Dublin 4 and Dublin 6; well off, well connected, the elite middle-class of Fine Gael activists. And they knew that too.

When she was appointed to cabinet, Garret FitzGerald completely misplaced her abilities. She had a real interest in European affairs and would have made a successful minister of state in that area. She would also have been fireproofed from domestic political trauma. Joan and Garret FitzGerald and Gemma and Derry Hussey were close friends and they must have been aware that Gemma was, by her own statement a 'non practising, lapsed Catholic'.[139] This was known to the Catholic

Church authorities who were the dominant influence in education. And yet Garret conceded to Gemma's approaches that she should become the first Fine Gael woman Minister for Education in 1982 and only the second woman minister in the history of the State to have four successive years of office in an Irish government.

I had expected a serious analysis of the fundamental issues we faced in government in Gemma's diaries on the 1982-1987 government, *At the Cutting Edge*. Instead she sounded like a Mount Anville prefect ensuring that the reverend mother Taoiseach was aware of the problem pupils in the class. We both experienced the crisis of public debt and expenditure which shocked us to the core in December 1982. We shared a resolve not to visit another four years of Charlie Haughey and Sean Doherty on our country. This vital background was indeed worthy of serious analysis in any diary. Unfortunately, Gemma failed to record in any coherent way the social perspectives of our government decisions on divorce, the 'pro life' amendment, family planning, legislation affecting children, the National Social Services Board, the Commission on Social Welfare and the Combat Poverty Agency. These issues concerned real people, not just the social preoccupations and ambitions of a narrow Dublin political circle. As far as I know she was the only minister, in my time, to write up a daily diary. Most ministers I knew were too exhausted at day's end to do so.

And what of Gemma's relationship with Garret FitzGerald? He was a real leader of public opinion who was, on many issues, courageously ahead of his time. It is not to Gemma's credit that she failed to so acknowledge in her diaries. She did not understand Dick Spring; he came from a constituency which was much more conservative than Delgany or Greystones. Their great integrity in government was, for the most part, ignored in her diaries. Gemma's comments about Garret were also grossly unfair. As leader of Fine Gael, he promoted her and several other Fine Gael women such as Nuala Fennell, Mary Flaherty, Avril Doyle, Nora Owen, Monica Barnes and Mary Banotti in the teeth of conservative reluctance within her party.

Gemma was in a unique position coming into government. She had palavered Garret into giving her the Education portfolio weeks before he and Dick Spring formed the government despite the fact that John Boland had been shaping up to be the best Minister for Education ever. Within months of office, Gemma had the nerve to start blaming the Labour Party, the civil service, Fianna Fáil and Workers Party union officials for the pressures of office. The only real sympathy I had for her was her ordeal in facing cynical opposition from Mary O'Rourke, the Fianna Fáil opposition spokesperson, the Cilla Black of the Fianna Fáil front bench.

The Labour Party has a substantial number of trade union teacher activists in its ranks. Dick Spring was aghast at her approach to negotiations with the leaders of the teachers' unions. He later wrote:

> Gemma made some disastrous mistakes in office. Few who were involved will forget the furore that erupted when she chose to lecture the teachers about the morality of their pay dispute. That was a personal mistake — not one which was forced on her by collective Cabinet responsibility. It was a gratuitous thing to do. But you will spend a long time searching her diaries for any acknowledgement, or even recognition, of the fact that it was a mistake.[140]

His general assessment of Gemma Hussey's role in government was equally critical:

> But that's part of the schizophrenia she suffered from, as a Fine Gael Minister with liberal views on many issues, but right-wing convictions about public spending. 'If only we didn't have to put up with the Labour Party,' she moans throughout the first half of the book. But by page 250 she's very glad that Labour is there to insist on full indexation of social welfare rates.

However, it would be unfair to regard Gemma's contribution in government as entirely non-reforming and unconstructive. In 1985 I wrote to her pointing out that I had received a report from the Health Education Bureau on the development of a clear-cut policy for post-primary schools in regard to personal relationships and sex education. I knew that some schools already had excellent programmes in operation and that her department and the Health Education Bureau had been co-operating on specific projects. But there was no national policy for health education in the schools. I knew that she was as concerned as I was about some of the misfortunes involving young persons which had their origins in sexual ignorance and social prejudice. I sought her personal support for early action. Gemma promptly replied that same month assuring me that her programme for action in education, for 1984-1987, included encouragement for health education in the school curriculum at both primary and post-primary levels.

Early on in government, I had detected that Gemma was somewhat disillusioned by her mundane political work. The life of a woman deputy in a multi-seat semi-rural constituency under proportional representation is dog rough. She also soon found out that life in government, surrounded by all male colleagues, all equally ambitious and ruthless in their own self-interests and policy objectives, was a bed of thorns, particularly in a period of budget stringency.

Nevertheless, she put up a brave and courageous front to the world following the reshuffle. She said that she did not regret her handling of the teachers' pay dispute. From my own trade union background and knowing the work of my late sister Noreen as a teacher in a special school in Waterford, I had a good deal of sympathy for the Minister for Education. The teachers' unions were of course ruthlessly selective and determined in their own self-interest. With the exception of those employed in the European schools of the European Union, which is the most expensive system of education on earth, the conditions of service of Irish teachers at all levels are exceptionally favourable today. Gemma did not possess the particular flair of negotiating skill to respond to their demands.

I have had great difficulty in writing in a critical vein about Gemma not least because being a woman minister in an Irish government is a daunting and hostile experience. The Irish civil service and the Irish political structure are interlocked in their male camaraderie. I had, in 1969, met Gemma's sister, Ann, who is married to Neville Keery, the Fianna Fáil candidate whom I narrowly defeated for the last seat in the Dun Laoghaire constituency in that general election. Neville and I have been close friends ever since, our mutual interests being the future of Northern Ireland and Ireland's future in Europe.

Perhaps the most objective assessment of Gemma Hussey came from Christina Murphy, the outstanding education correspondent of her generation, when she wrote in *The Irish Times*[141] after the reshuffle that Gemma Hussey was only 10 days in the ministerial chair in December 1982, when she announced the introduction of charges for school buses which had been free up to then. It caused a political furore, but it was nothing compared to the row that erupted two weeks later when she announced cutbacks in teacher allocations to schools. The teachers' unions mounted a massive campaign to force her to back down on the cuts, but she stuck to her guns. Christina stressed:

> She organised elections to set up a national parents council; she set up an independent Curriculum and Examination Board which quickly set about a wide ranging programme of reform of the intermediate certificate examination. She extended vocational preparation and training courses to secondary as well as vocational and community/comprehensive schools and waged an extremely successful battle to get millions of EEC Social Fund money allocated to port-primary and third level education. This resulted in pupils being paid £30 a month to stay and do vocational preparation courses at school and also in over 80 per cent of regional technical college students getting social funds grants and fees remission.

Christine Murphy concluded: 'She should be remembered for her work on curriculum and examinations, but she'll probably be remembered for the "morality" speech that caused a strike.'

Gemma was undoubtedly the biggest loser in the government reshuffle. In effect, the debacle terminated her political career. She had little conception of the political and administrative unlikelihood of the Department of Foreign Affairs being split in two. To this day I cannot fathom why Garret FitzGerald embarked on that particular proposition. If it was to ensure the transfer of his Minister for Education to a more congenial political portfolio, it went horribly wrong.

*

A further major consequence of Gemma's role in the reshuffle was the enmity it subsequently provoked from John Boland who had been Minister for Education in the 1981-1982 government. John was perhaps the shrewdest political brain around the cabinet table from 1981 to 1987. He had an ability to see around political corners which were blind to many of his colleagues. His long apprenticeship in the Seanad, on Dublin County Council and County Dublin Vocational Education Committee was an invaluable preparation for government. To his great credit, he abolished corporal punishment in our system of education, and he introduced the radical reform in the appointments' system of senior civil servants, TLAC.

He despaired of trying to impress on Garret FitzGerald the political sensitivities of major economic and social issues. Garret did not appreciate his insight into the thought processes of Fianna Fáil and particularly of Charles Haughey. He suspected that John Boland had been far too 'political'. However, he could not do without John Boland's experience in government. John was later to write: 'Most issues which reach that table are complex and have delicate nuances in whatever decision may be taken. The stuff of cabinet decisions is compromise — the accommodation of varying ministerial views, policy and national considerations and departmental demands. The cabinet which does not bring a degree of political consideration into the flavour of its discussion does so at its peril.'[142]

He was of the view that Gemma had personally handbagged him out of the Education portfolio when the new government was being formed in late 1982. He was scathing about his fellow party and ministerial colleague in his review of her diaries. He wrote:

> Whilst acknowledging that Gemma found her move to Social Welfare traumatising it is, nonetheless, quite a shock to read that, when she learned Pat Cooney was to become her successor in Education, she rang Garret FitzGerald and asked that Pat NOT be appointed! Pat Cooney, it will be recalled, is a senior figure in Fine Gael, having been first elected to the Dáil in 1970, after previous local authority experience, and had served as Minister for Justice in the 1973-77 government, and Minister for Transport in Garret's first government and Minister for Defence up to that time. The diaries do not record whether Gemma made any other such phone calls.[143]

*

Paddy Cooney was the most fortunate minister of all. Paddy was cool, calm and collected at government meetings, pragmatic on all issues unrelated to 'morality'. We differed on the issues of contraception and divorce. But Paddy and I had long shared a mutual detestation of the Provos. We had walked behind too many coffins of the Gardaí and army they had murdered. Garret was never to forgive him for being forced into a 'parties in government' as distinct from 'the government' advocacy of conditional divorce in the June 1986 referendum. At that point in the Dáil the second stage vote on the Tenth Amendment of the Constitution (No. 2) Bill loomed large. Paddy had made it clear that he would resign if there were to be an announcement before the poll that 'the government' as such agreed to the proposition.

Paddy Cooney had survived in government largely because Peter Barry, John Boland and, strange as it may seem, myself had strongly advised him during that confrontation with the Taoiseach in the run in to the Divorce Bill, not to put himself out on a complete limb on the issue. However, Garret had much earlier resolved to dump him at the first available opportunity. The other reshuffle ructions offset Paddy's intended demise. The outcome was that he had an elevation to Education from Defence, a portfolio he had thoroughly enjoyed with his background as the son of an army medical officer.

Shortly after Paddy's appointment, he displayed his customary common sense and, together with Ruairi Quinn as Minister for Labour and Public Service, resolved the teachers' pay dispute. They did so by largely having minimal debate on the issue in government. This was a clever ruse given Garret's determination to have a finger in every pie. Finally, John Bruton could thank the PDs for his reinstatement in Finance as Garret desperately tried to prevent the drift of the so-called 'enterprise community' to Desmond O'Malley.

*

Throughout this episode, the role of Dick Spring as leader of the Labour Party in government was facing extinction on all fronts. Frank Cluskey was lodged in the backbenches in sullen self-imposed exile having failed to get his way for a major State subsidy for Dublin Gas, arising from pressure from his union. Frank could not abide John Bruton and John, in turn, had no appreciation at all of Frank's conspiracy theories. Mervyn Taylor had turned down Dick's invitation to fill the ministerial vacancy following Frank's resignation. Mervyn was deeply hostile to Fine Gael perhaps because he felt he had suffered so much at the hands of the Fine Gael councillors on Dublin County Council on many planning issues. A *Cork Examiner* editorial summed up the situation quite accurately at that time: 'Mr Spring's dilemma is that his chances of regaining electoral support in government now look slim indeed. But the prospect of precipitating an election when the party's rating may be as low as 4 per cent is a daunting alternative. An interesting statistic for Mr Spring is that 44 per cent of the Progressive Democrats' support comes from working class voters.'[144]

Dick Spring's back was truly to the wall. The chairman of the Parliamentary Labour Party, Joe Bermingham, also a Minister of State, had offered to resign his position as part of the reshuffle package and indicated that he did not propose to contest the following general election. That reshuffle package too was ill-devised. Both Joe Bermingham and his fellow Fine

Gael Minister of State, Donal Creed, were deeply respected figures in both parliamentary parties. They greatly resented having to stand aside. I was perplexed by the Taoiseach's decision to drop Donal Creed as Minister of State for Education. Garret had a very bad habit of treating his Ministers of State in a cavalier fashion. Donal's redundancy came weeks before celebrating his 21 years of service as a Fine Gael deputy: his three-seater Cork North West constituency had returned two Fine Gael deputies. Donal Creed had been most effective in his advocacy in government of the setting up of the National Lottery for sport. This decision by Garret alienated a large Fine Gael tranche of supporters in North Cork and it is resented to this day.

*

Following the Taoiseach's announcement about the reshuffle to the Dáil, Charles Haughey immediately tabled a motion of no confidence. He said that no Taoiseach should attempt to continue in office who allowed his capacity to rearrange his cabinet to be disrupted by one single minister who flouts his authority with impunity. He said:

> The Minister for Health over the last three years had set about demolishing the health services of this country, as we have known them, with perverted zeal. In making these closures, Deputy Barry Desmond as Minister for Health was acting with the approval of the Government and the Taoiseach. It is therefore particularly reprehensible for the Taoiseach, when the public anger burst forth, as he should have known it would, that he should try to throw his minister to the wolves in an effort to keep them away from his own door.

Deputy Haughey went on to make the interesting observation that he had seen references in some newspapers to the possibility that one of the principal reasons for the anxiety to get me out of the Department of Health was because of my insistence on pursuing the campaign to curtail the advertisement of tobacco products. He went on to say: 'From my own personal experience I know the sort of pressure that can be mounted by the tobacco lobby and I would not be prepared to dismiss these suggestions. Can we have the truth about this aspect?'

Dick Spring had the unenviable task of leading off on behalf of the government and did extremely well in the circumstances, concentrating on Fianna Fáil's record in the previous government: 'When we came into office, a number of things became apparent. First, a whole series of shady and sinister events had undermined public confidence, particularly in the Garda Síochána. Many of these events, which were, to say the least of it, suggestive of a willingness to manipulate the gardaí for personal and political purposes, were suspicious in the extreme. I shudder to think what the consequences for democracy might have been had this process been allowed to continue.' He wisely decided to omit any reference to the detail of the reshuffle other than to pay a particular tribute to Joe Bermingham.

When I spoke during this debate I received an uninterrupted hearing. I had decided not to elaborate in any way on the circumstances of my confrontation with the Taoiseach and the Tanaiste. The wounds were still too raw to be touched upon and, in any event, the Taoiseach was due to reply to the debate. I pointed out that I had strongly recommended to my party that we should join in coalition with Fine Gael. I bluntly told the House that Deputy FitzGerald, as leader of his party, stood head and shoulders over any other aspirant for the office of Taoiseach with his wide experience, his personal abilities and his national commitment. In terms of national commitment, what had influenced me most were his views on Northern Ireland. He was most clearly fitted to undertake the introduction and implementation of economic and social policies which were so badly needed.

And Garret did not concede the battle despite such a self-inflicted gunshot. He put up a sterling performance in the Dáil debate, particularly about my ministerial role at a time when I half expected to be shredded in public. He said:

> Even by the standards of what must be the hardest working Government since the early days of the

State, the Minister for Health is an extraordinarily energetic and committed Minister who works in his Department sometimes seven days a week, and has a complete mastery of the very complex issues involved. Pursuing the task of bringing health expenditure under control, the Minister for Health incurred considerable unpopularity even before he had to undertake the closure of several hospitals decided on by the Government as part of its decisions in the preparation of the Budget. On the night of Wednesday week we both pressed on Deputy Desmond the desirability from his own point of view of a change to a different post, and I make no secret of the fact that we pressed him quite hard on the point.[145]

The motion of no confidence was defeated by 82 votes to 77. The government was to survive another year. But that vital spark, necessary in both parties for the re-election of the government, had been quenched by stupid mistakes in the budgetary and reshuffle strategies.

*

After the reshuffle there was a public avalanche of political abuse, local special pleadings, and gross exaggerations of the effects of the decision to phase out the redundant hospitals. In the midst of these attacks there was the occasional glimpse of truth. At a quarterly meeting of the association of health boards of Ireland in Cork, Joe Arkins, a psychiatric nurses' representative on the Mid-Western Health Board, pointed out that 'Most of these places are not hospitals, they are asylums with saints' names in front of them — but, even so, they must be closed in a structured way.'[146] Councilor Camillus Glynn from the Midland Health Board, however, was having none of this constructive analysis: 'He (Desmond) is a one-man demolition squad!'[147] The Cork Council of Trade Unions decided to revisit the issue of funds for cancer treatment at the Cork Regional Hospital. Bart O'Mahoney, ITGWU delegate, said, 'There were some glaring inconsistencies in what the Minister was doing. On the one hand, he is saying there is plenty of money available for family planning services, and on the other that there is no money available for life-saving equipment.'[148]

Deputy Kieran Crotty, the senior Fine Gael figure in Carlow–Kilkenny, demanded in the Dáil that there be no time limit on the closures. My Labour colleague from South Kerry, Minister of State, Michael Moynihan, who was a retired senior psychiatric nurse, appealed for 'something else to be pruned other than Killarney Isolation Hospital'. Deputy M.J. Nolan, Fianna Fáil, Carlow–Kilkenny, said that my decision 'smacked of dictatorship'. Ireland's future EU Commissioner, Deputy Padraig Flynn, predicted 'the abolition of the health boards next'. Tom Dolan, a psychiatric nurse at Castlerea and a member of the Western Health Board, said that 'Castlerea will be a ghost town if the hospital is closed'. Deputy Terry Leyden went further: 'Mr Desmond is a cold, callous and uncaring man who cared little about Roscommon because Labour had no support there.'

This was the level of public debate about a long overdue proposal to reform the psychiatric hospital services. Ironically, the most severe reaction I received from the government parties was from the Fine Gael organisation. Finbarr Fitzpatrick, general secretary of Fine Gael and National Director of Organisation, wrote to me in February 1986 pointing out that he was 'facing uproar in the constituencies concerned, that public representatives from the Fine Gael Organisation were not briefed or prepared for the announcements. Great emphasis has been put in the past on the proper handling of good news being announced on behalf of the government and in my opinion, even greater thought has to go into the method by which bad news will be announced'.

Finbarr had a perfectly valid point to make. The only problem was that any such briefing would be immediately leaked and opposition whipped up overnight. I would also be accused of not first informing the Dáil. I replied to Finbarr, pointing out: 'You and I are hardly so naive to think that consultation would have made the slightest difference to the difficulty which our backbenchers have had in accepting that in government we most govern and be seen to do so at all times.

Your party has been most vocal about the need to control and redirect public expenditure. Now your colleagues know that the process cannot be brought about with fine words and no shock or reaction.' In his analysis of the situation, Joe O'Malley, political correspondent of the *Sunday Independent*, wrote that 'Anybody who knew Barry Desmond could not have mistook his passion for the reforming aspects of health — both on the administrative (changing the health boards, reforming the general hospital services) and social side (adoption reform, the new children's bill and development of family planning services).'[149]

*

In his reply to the Dáil debate on the reshuffle, the Taoiseach was much more circumspect on his very serious, and potentially much more damaging, clash with his deputy leader, Peter Barry. Peter had had a very severe confrontation with Garret about the proposed emasculation of 'his department'. He was a formidable, always immaculately dressed, traditional Fine Gael heavyweight. My parents had known his father, Tony Barry, quite well in Cork politics. His political pedigree was impeccable. Both of our fathers had been elected Lord Mayors of Cork which for most Cork people is an honour which is only exceeded by winning an All-Ireland hurling medal. Peter was not a particularly articulate politician which detracted from his shrewd ability. We felt that he had little time for the Labour Party in government, particularly in relation to our taxation policies. This was reciprocated by Dick Spring, the prickly son of a Tralee trade union official, who would not suffer being patronised, however innocently, by the son of a Cork merchant prince. I was more tolerant, being from Cork!

A remarkable aspect of that government reshuffle was the failure of the media and the opposition to dwell on the acute tension at that time between Peter Barry and Garret FitzGerald. Peter always regarded Garret as being somewhat impractical. He was, however, a totally loyal deputy leader who was very circumspect about his criticisms of Garret in private and never in public. Peter regarded politics as a dour responsibility in the best interests of the country, Fine Gael and Cork, in that order. I was more determined to enjoy my politics and relished stirring up the establishment of the day. Peter Barry's wife, Margaret, reminded me of Stella. Both longed for the day when they would have more time with their husbands and less of the sheer constituency grind.

In that reshuffle, Garret learned that however difficult one Desmond was, the other Barry was most certainly not for turning. He put a gloss on the internal Fine Gael situation in the Dáil debate when he said: 'I have been considering the question of how it might be possible for the next eighteen months to lighten the load of the Minister of Foreign Affairs, whose responsibilities in respect of Northern Ireland have now become so heavy following the signing of the Anglo-Irish Agreement. I came to the conclusion however on Thursday morning that given the technical obstacles to dividing the work of the Department of Foreign Affairs between two Cabinet Ministers without dividing the Department itself — a course of action which I considered would be very undesirable: it was not appropriate to proceed along these lines ...'

While the reshuffle was most damaging to the government, it was of profound importance for the future of Garret FitzGerald. It would sow the seeds of his abrupt resignation as leader of Fine Gael after the 1987 general election. That weekend was far worse for Garret than his 'out-out-out' dismissal by Prime Minister Margaret Thatcher. As Gerry Barry pointed out in *The Sunday Tribune*, I had been 'personally more loyal to Garret FitzGerald than almost any cabinet minister'.[150] Bruce Arnold, the political columnist of the *Irish Independent*, critically summed up the role of the Taoiseach: 'The reshuffle has revealed a number of Garret FitzGerald's weaknesses. First, he has a susceptibility to the findings of opinion polls, and to their subtleties and intricacies. Second, he has an almost total disregard for the human factor in politics, a direct result of reading percentages as if they were the stars. Third, he has raised serious doubts about his ultimate political judgement, perhaps the most important aspect of which, in any politician, is knowing when to do nothing. He was found wanting in this.'[151]

*

When the furore died down, I immediately implemented the government decision. In June 1986, with no hysteria abroad, the Fianna Fáil spokesperson on Health, Deputy Rory O'Hanlon, who himself was to be Minister for Health some months later, asked for a progress report on the closures. I informed the Dáil that: 'Longford Surgical Hospital: this hospital is now closed. Roscrea District Hospital: the closure will be completed with the placing of five residents in more appropriate accommodation. Carlow and Castlerea Mental Hospitals: the main outstanding issue is the location of acute admission facilities in Carlow and in Roscommon. St Patrick's Infants Hospital, Blackrock: agreement has been reached on its closure in June 1986. St. Patrick Duns Hospital: this hospital will close in August 1986. Cork Eye and Throat Hospital: ENT services will transfer from this hospital to the South Infirmary/Victory Hospital complex by the end of August. Ophthalmology services will transfer to the Cork Regional Hospital. Killarney Isolation Hospital: this hospital has now closed as an isolation hospital.'

Most of the staffs concerned were assured of continued employment in other services. It was notable that a special meeting of the Midland Health Board voted by 14 votes to 11 in favour of closure after I announced my decision about Longford Surgical Hospital. Contrary to the popular political prejudice that my relations with all of the health boards were disastrous, I had excellent working relationships, particularly with Denis Doherty, Chief Executive Officer of the Midland Health Board; Donal O'Shea, Chief Executive Officer of the North Western Health Board, and the late Pat Clarke, Chief Executive Officer, North Eastern Health Board. They were outstanding professional administrators. Relative to the multi-million pound budgets they administered, and the complex political, policy and personnel issues they faced on a daily basis, they and their programme managers were poorly paid. I frequently berated the government and the Department of Finance on this issue but, such was the climate of retrenchment, I got nowhere. However, there was very little media comment on my Dáil reply about these hospitals. Their preoccupations can be very fickle indeed.

Twenty-One

Anti Bloody Well Everything!

'I think that if the questions that were asked in the Dáil were answered in the way they are answered here, there would be no necessity for this inquiry and an awful lot of money and time would have been saved.'

Justice Liam Hamilton at the Beef Tribunal

Dick Spring was looking for me. I knocked at the party leader's door in the 1932 annex in Leinster House. One did not take Dick Spring for granted. He was alone on the phone and beckoned me to come in and sit down. He said to the person on the phone, 'Can I say to you again, Desmond does not want anything! He is not looking for anything in raising these questions. He is not that kind of guy!'

The person at the other end seemed perplexed. Dick then told him that I had arrived and that he would discuss the matter with me. As he put down the phone, Fergus Finlay came in. Dick announced, 'Well, Desmond, you have really fucked up the beef industry this time. That was a rugby pal giving out holy shit about your allegations. Larry Goodman is going ballistic. He has denied everything. Unless the pol corrs see the body, Charlie and O'Kennedy will tear you to shreds!'

I knew that I was in dire difficulty. I had been challenged to repeat my assertions outside the Dáil that Anglo Irish Beef Processors (International) Ltd had a penalty of £1.084 million imposed on it by the Department of Agriculture for irregularities at Waterford and Ballymun. Our sources were impeccable but were absolutely terrified about forwarding the evidence. I had, however, sufficient detail to 'take a flyer' in the Dáil debate on 15 March 1989 and specified the situation at the plants at Waterford and Ballymun. The Dáil was about to go into the Easter recess. I knew that writs would fly if I were forced to broach these issues outside the Dáil.

However, Larry Goodman, Charlie Haughey and Michael O'Kennedy were about to fall for the bait. They denounced me from on high. In doing so they so incensed the prospective sources of Dick, Fergus and myself that a copy of the letter of 16 January 1989 from the Department of Agriculture to AIBP's chief executive was faxed to our office. The game was up. As Brian O'Shea, minister of state at the Department of Agriculture, Food and Forestry, put it in the Dáil debate on the Beef Tribunal Report some five years later: 'Material became available to my party that something wrong was happening within the beef industry.'[152]

*

I could never fathom why Justice Liam Hamilton's report was such a sloppy piece of work. One had to search for the definitive conclusions. The punches did not seem to land. There was no indexed executive summary. When I was doyen of the Agriculture Guarantee sector in the European Court of Auditors, which included the beef industry, had our auditors presented me with such voluminous incomprehension I would have immediately sent it for review to our quality assurance unit. The drafting of this report took place over a period of no less than three years. But there were some inescapable findings in the report.

Justice Hamilton found that in relation to Goodman International, allegations about under-the-counter payments to employees were fully substantiated;[153] that the Goodman Group evaded payments of income tax; that fictitious payments were made to hauliers and farmers; that the Revenue authorities were deceived; that fictitious invoices were produced; and that according to the Revenue Investigation Branch, this concealment was 'professionally put together'. Justice Hamilton also found that bogus stamps were used at the

AIBP plant in Waterford thus giving the appearance that the carcasses were eligible for intervention.[154] This was a most serious finding by the tribunal and the judge rejected the attempt by the senior management of the Goodman Group to disassociate itself from this 'improper practice'.[155]

When the report was debated in the Dáil in September 1994, Deputy Michael McDowell of the PDs was scathing. He said:

> The proof of the pudding will be in the eating. Will any of the top brass of the Goodman organisation, who engaged in a massive criminal conspiracy to defraud the Exchequer and taxpayers and who, because of that, are open to be tried, convicted and sentenced to any term of imprisonment up to life imprisonment, darken the District Court door? Will any of them spend a night in jail and hang their Armani suit on the back of the cell door in Mountjoy? They will not. Not a single person will be brought to account for the most substantial and highly organised tax evasion in this country.[156]

*

One of the most infuriating aspects of political disputation in this island is the level of personalisation of issues raised by individual deputies. Displaying monumental arrogance, Charles Haughey and Larry Goodman went down this track as soon as questions were raised. I never had any contact whatsoever with Larry Goodman; I bore him, his family and his business no personal animus. It was not a matter of concern to me if Larry Goodman was or was not a member or supporter of any political party. I had no plot or hidden agenda about the beef industry or about Goodman International and I never set out to be an anti-farmer or anti-private sector agitator.

I simply had a series of very disturbing observations and anecdotal stories brought to my attention by persons associated with the industry. Then I began to hear that some public servants, particularly in the public storage and beef exports areas, were decidedly unhappy about certain practices. I knew, of course, that Goodman International was a major player in the industry. The identity and private ownership of this company was not my preoccupation. My main motivation was that I had over many years an abiding disaffection about any waste of hard-earned taxpapers' resources irrespective of the budget area. It is a prime function of every deputy to discharge this obligation whether in government or opposition. It was a great irony of this whole episode that had Larry Goodman, Michael O'Kennedy and Charles Haughey confirmed, in a straight-forward manner, the amount of the penalty notified by the department to AIBP International and stated that all measures were being implemented to ensure full compliance with EU regulations, the episode would probably not have resulted in such a considerable fall-out. Mary Harney put it succinctly in the Dáil debate on the Tribunal Report: 'Fianna Fáil's only problem is being caught out and if one is caught one is a fool.'[157]

But the culture of the time was that these happenings were no business whatsoever of any deputy and hardly that of the minister of the day. And the minister's ploy was to disclose the minimum of information to any enquiring deputy. It was as if the department existed solely for the industry. And if the deputies in the Committee of Public Accounts in due course did not ask the right questions, that was their tough luck. There was no Freedom of Information Act. But Joe Meade of the Comptroller and Auditor General's Office did ask pertinent questions. So did Paddy Cooney. Then the storm broke. In the event this hidden culture was hoisted by its own side of beef and the noose began to slowly tighten around the career of the chief defender, Charles Haughey.

Had these issues been treated by the government of the day in a transparent manner, a conflict of evidence at the tribunal would never have arisen between Taoiseach Albert Reynolds and Minister Desmond O'Malley, leading eventually to the collapse of that government and the November 1992 general election.

During the course of my intervention in the Dáil in March 1989, I gave the extent of the sanctions notified by the Department of Agriculture and Food to AIBP International. Charles Haughey's response was immediate: 'I, in turn, accuse

Deputy Desmond, with a full sense of responsibility, of trying to sabotage the entire beef industry in this county.' My allegation was true and accurate. Haughey, however, not only accused me of attempting to sabotage the industry, but also repeated the allegation in his evidence to the beef tribunal: 'Of course he was. He made reckless allegations and accusations continuously in the Dáil around that time'; and 'The other constant harassing attacks on the beef industry and on the Goodman organisation in particular were in my view irresponsible.'[158]

Larry Goodman, Dick Spring and myself were certainly involved in a number of common events. Our confrontation between May 1989 when the tribunal was set up and August 1994 when Justice Liam Hamilton finally reported, was a prime cause of an historic general election. There were three important Supreme Court cases, disciplinary hearings by the Bar Council and an investigation by the Public Accounts Committee of the Oireachtas. The issues thrown up were of such importance that the new Fianna Fáil–Labour coalition government which came into office in 1993 committed itself in advance to implementing the tribunal's recommendations, nearly eighteen months before those recommendations were issued. I recall Dick Spring's adamant assurance to the Labour negotiators that he would walk away if Albert did not give an emphatic commitment to implement the expected recommendations. Unfortunately, Liam Hamilton's report was poorly formulated and Albert blew himself out of the Taoiseach's office by his inept response to the report and his utter failure to appreciate the position of the Tanaiste.

*

As soon as I made allegations about AIBP International in the Dáil, I was subjected to extraordinary political hostility. My colleague from Louth, Michael Bell, wanted to know why I was 'after Larry, in my own constituency'. He was most upset. We received anonymous threatening phone calls at home warning us to mind our own business. Fianna Fáil sources put out a spin that my eldest son, Ciaran, who had worked as a clerical officer in the Department of Agriculture office in Kildare House, was the source of my information. I wondered if I had poured my eldest son's career down the drain. He was then an executive officer in the Revenue Commissioners. Later I saw a tribunal note from the secretary of the department to the minister that my son was in no way involved.

Other Fianna Fáil 'spinners' rumoured that I was in the pay of Larry's competitors. For this whole period the climate of hostility was acute. Stella asked, 'Barry, what are we letting ourselves in for?' I met Susan O'Keeffe, an intrepid journalist, with whom I had no earlier connection whatsoever. We cautiously compared notes. She rang me only from public telephones. She went on to research the ITV *World In Action* programme which proved to be the final trigger for the setting up of the tribunal. Susan told me that she had feared for her personal safety when doing the research. The political climate was one of extraordinary intimidation. By May 1991, Desmond O'Malley was, fortuitously, Minister for Industry and Commerce. After intense pressure from him, Taoiseach Charles Haughey and the Minister for Agriculture and Food, with great reluctance, set up the tribunal of inquiry.

I have no doubt now, from the evidence to the tribunal and from my audit contacts with the Department of Agriculture and Food over the past six years in the European Court of Auditors, that had the department then ensured that effective controls were in place and had rigorously enforced such controls, the need for this tribunal would not have arisen. Many media and political commentators worked themselves into a frenzy about the costs of the tribunal. A total cost of £30 million to £35 million was the common assessment. In fact the final cost to the taxpayer was about £16 million gross or £12 million net. I have no doubt that the beef tribunal succeeded in bringing about major improvements in the public accountability of this industry. As such it was money well spent. And until the great fall-out between Larry Goodman, Desmond O'Malley and Mary Harney, it was pointed out by Minister Joe Walsh that in January 1987, Deputy Desmond O'Malley wrote to Larry Goodman as follows: 'I was delighted to meet you the other evening but I'm sorry that through nobody's fault, things were rather rushed. I hope that you will have dinner with me in Dublin some evening after the election when we can discuss matters in more detail in a more relaxed atmosphere (perhaps over a bottle of Beaujolais or a bottle of '82).' At that time the Progressive Democrats were the toast of the business lunches in Ireland. Desmond O'Malley and Mary Harney were the most promising prospects of 'getting the State off our backs'.

*

During the Dáil debate on the tribunal report, the Tanaiste Dick Spring, a central figure in the allegations made about the industry, made a trenchant comment about one aspect of the report. Justice Hamilton had stated that he was satisfied that financial contributions made by companies engaged in the food processing industry were 'normal contributions made to political parties [which] did not in any way affect or relate to the matters being inquired into by the Tribunal'.[159] Dick Spring vehemently disagreed with Justice Hamilton:

> I believe he is wrong. I do not accept that the tens of thousands of pounds paid or offered to Fianna Fáil, Fine Gael, and the Progressive Democrats were gifts based on a philanthropic desire to further the cause of democracy in Ireland. It may stand to the credit of the recipients if that money never played any part in the decision-making process, but it would be naive to assume that it was not intended to.[160]

I agree with Dick Spring. All such contributions from public and private companies should be banned and a strict ceiling on private personal contributions should be introduced. All such personal contributions should be declared by all candidates and all parties. There can be no half-way house on this fundamental issue. Deputy Willie Penrose pointed out in the Dáil debate that in the nine-year period to 1991, Fianna Fáil received £374,700 in political contributions from the beef processing companies. Fine Gael received £138,550 from similar sources from 1987 to 1991.[161] Nobody in the Labour Party knows better than Willie Penrose about the beef industry.

Throughout this controversy, I was acutely aware that some 100,000 farmers were dependent on a full or part-time basis on the production and bringing to the market of some two million cattle each year. The beef processing industry alone employed about 4,500 permanent employees growing to about 6,000 at peak periods. Live cattle and beef exports had a value of about £1 billion Irish pounds a year. No politician in his right mind would wish to place any part of this industry in jeopardy.

One of the beneficial developments from the tribunal was the measures taken by the Department of Agriculture and Food to strengthen its audit structure and staffing. In government, Dick Spring, Fergus Finlay and William Scally kept up the pressure. In 1994 the department established, not before its time, an external audit committee to monitor and co-ordinate the audit of EAGGF beneficiaries by the department and by Revenue. From my meetings with the department from 1994 to 2000 as a member of the Court of Auditors, I am convinced that there is now a greater determination to enforce all EU and national controls.

In his outstanding book *Meanwhile Back at the Ranch* in 1995, Fintan O'Toole wrote a perceptive analysis of the focus of the controversy: 'Larry Goodman, through single-mindedness, brilliance and an eye for the main chance, made himself one of the most powerful men in the country. Yet he continued to see himself as an outsider, a loner, a marginal man beset by foes and conspirators waiting to drag him down.... Through it all, he could never understand "why have we been identified, pulled aside and torn to pieces?"'

*

Next to waiting for the returning officer to declare the result of an election count, the ordeal most feared by a politician is being on the witness stand at a tribunal of inquiry. From the date of my allegations in the Dáil, to my appearance before the tribunal, a period of some thirty months, I had maintained a Cistercian-like silence. For once I followed the advice of Brian McCracken, my senior counsel, and Donal Spring, my solicitor. Brian said very little during our consultations. But in the Dublin Castle witness box, one flick of an eyebrow from him clearly signalled that I was going off track or being far too elaborate in my replies. I was fortunate when Donal Spring made the thousands of pages of evidence and transcripts available to me, together with detailed advise on the issues likely to arise. A close friend, Aidan McNamara, did a massive job of indexing and cross-referencing. As a consequence I had instant access to most anticipated questions. His work was invaluable. To recall with precision events and data of some years past is never an easy exercise for any witness.

I was particularly fearful of a grilling from Dermot Gleeson, senior counsel for Larry Goodman. His capacity to get to the nub of each issue was formidable and his cross-examination technique left no room for any witness to obfuscate. I sighed with relief when he concluded. The rumbustious style of Seamus McKenna, also for the Goodman team, was a complete contrast. The relaxed and accommodating style of Justice Liam Hamilton was disconcerting. He seemed to adopt a style of 'let them all have their say and their day'. As a consequence the proceedings were protracted. I still retain a copy of Hammo's election address when he stood as a Labour candidate in the Pembroke Ward for Dublin Corporation in 1957. Stella canvassed for him and had many a door slammed in her face in Leeson Park when she mentioned his name and the Labour Party.

The real credit for the beef tribunal must go to those public servants who blew the whistle; to Susan O'Keeffe who showed rare courage; to my Dáil colleagues, Tomas MacGiolla, Pat Rabbitte and Desmond O'Malley who stood up and were counted; to Dick Spring who put the boot in and stood by me when I was facing the political abyss; to Brian O'Shea for his courage in the crisis; and to Fergus Finlay who gave us his unswerving support. I have promised Stella not to repeat the exercise.

By mid-1995, Larry Goodman and his associates were on the threshold of resuming 60 per cent control of his meat processing operation, Irish Food Processors Ltd. Within five years he had regained 100 per cent control. He is undoubtedly the most remarkable and successful operator in the industry. It is now a decade since his operations were put under the protection of examinership after new legislation was enacted by the Dáil. One must hope that severe lessons have been learned by him and by all those associated with the industry from these traumatic events. And I wonder if Desmond O'Malley and Larry Goodman will ever get to share that bottle of '82!

Twenty-Two

The Uneasy Peace

'A piece by piece process, little by little, line by line, easing and teasing Ulster out of the United Kingdom at the behest of Dublin and a treacherous London administration.'

Rev Willie McCrea, DUP

I met Cardinal Thomas O Fiaich on a number of occasions at Drumcar, Co Louth at the Brothers of St John of God, at state receptions and dinners at Dublin Castle and at the funerals of State and Church dignitaries. He had no time at all for Labour deputies and ministers. We were 'soft' on the national question. He was the foil to Willie McCrea when, in 1978 as Archbishop of Armagh, he stated, 'I believe the British should withdraw from Ireland. I think it is the only thing that will get this thing moving!' Willie McCrea and Tommy Fee encapsulated to me all the sectarian politics of Northern Ireland's cauldron of territorial disputation.

My first experience of it was in the 1962 Stormont elections. I was sent by John Conroy, president of the Irish Transport and General Workers' Union, to Derry to help Stephen McGonagle, the union's district secretary who was contesting the Foyle constituency as an Independent Labour candidate. Stephen was a charismatic union leader and a powerful speaker. He opposed Eddie McAteer, the outgoing Nationalist leader and MP. I campaigned with Stephen and Seamus Quinn, his colleague and secretary of the Derry Trades Council. We did a door-to-door canvass in the Bogside and had our final rally there. I experienced for the first time the raw nationalist politics of that city. McGonagle was denounced as a communist candidate by the Catholic clergy who unashamedly supported 'Big Eddie'. Nothing was further from the truth as far as McGonagle was concerned.

I attended McAteer's final rally in the Diamond. After the veteran republican, Cahir Healy MP, then 85 years of age, had addressed the gathering in front of a massive tricolour, a clergyman called on the large gathering to join with him in a decade of the rosary to pray that McGonagle be defeated. On polling day, McAteer's loudspeaker cars toured the Bogside arousing the people with the claim that 'the Protestants were all voting for McGonagle'. And then the Fianna Fáil fleet of cars and their droves of canvassers arrived from Donegal, headed by Neil Blaney and Joe Brennan. The workers from the clothing factories, mostly women, were unmercifully canvassed to vote against their own union secretary who had ably represented them year in and year out. It was my first experience of the Blaney machine. To cap it all, the Unionist headquarters in Belfast urged the Protestant voters in rural Foyle to vote McAteer. He was much less dangerous than McGonagle.

McAteer won by 8,720 votes to 5,476. It was a real baptism for me. In 1969, Eddie met his match in the young nationalist John Hume who took the seat. Steve McGonagle went on to become president of the Northern Ireland committee of the Irish Congress of Trade Unions; he was Northern Ireland ombudsman from 1974 to 1979; chairperson of the Police Complaints Board 1977 to 1983 and a Labour senator — quite a record for a dangerous Marxist from Derry.

I was not the first canvasser to go north. It was a political measure of those times that in 1950 Seán MacBride and Noel Browne intervened in the Westminster elections and spoke in support of Healy in the Fermanagh-South Tyrone constituency. But then in another Westminster election in the early 1970s, Conor Cruise O'Brien and Michael O'Leary spoke on a platform in support of Bernadette Devlin.

That foray into Northern politics was also my first experience of political parades. There is a vast gulf between people in the Republic and Northern Ireland concerning such

political and religious gatherings. Apart from the annual
Corpus Christi parades in some areas and Saint Patrick's Day
parades in the Republic, other manifestations of nationality and
religion are almost now extinct. The situation in Northern
Ireland is still in sharp and vicious contrast. In 1960 I was in
Manor Cunningham, Co Donegal at a union meeting of
members employed in an industrial alcohol-making potato
plant on a Sunday morning. I was asked to join the annual
parade of the local Ancient Order of Hibernians after the
meeting. I did not wish to offend them but I felt ridiculous as I
marched behind a fife and drum band with my union
colleagues.

There is of course a streak of national mischievousness in the
Irish psyche in relation to such events. I heard of one village in
the midlands where the local pub populace decided to hold a
unique Saint Patrick's Day parade. After viewing all the major
parades on RTÉ, they decided to hold a parade going
backwards. The locals assembled on either side of their only
street and applauded as the occupants of one pub shakily
paraded backwards into another pub, pints in hand. The
following year the village had an even more exotic parade. It
was to be invisible! All the excited citizens gathered on either
side of their one and only street and applauded the invisible
parade going by. By all accounts the parades were a great
success. No doubt Saint Patrick was not amused but some
invisible parades would solve the problems in some areas of
Northern Ireland.

*

Following the initial shock of the crisis in Northern Ireland in
1968-1972, some movement emerged in the Dáil favouring a
more liberal and pluralist society in the Republic. This
development offered the unionist people of Northern Ireland
some hope for the first time that an Ireland of peace and
reconciliation would not necessarily encompass an enlarged
version of what most of them had always feared — a Republic
dominated by Catholic teaching and influence and violent
republican anti-partitionism.

In 1971 the Dáil set up an all-party committee to review the implications of Irish unity. The Fianna Fáil Ard Feis early in 1972 rejected the hard-line strategy that any internal constitutional reform should be postponed until negotiations started towards a united Ireland. That was a significant step forward; it reflected a growing willingness by Jack Lynch to swim a little with the tide of public opinion in favour of a review of the constitutional and social aspects of life in the Republic. An all-party committee was set up in May 1972. It was composed of James Tully and Conor Cruise O'Brien of the Labour party; Frank Carter, Vivion de Valera and Michael O'Kennedy of Fianna Fáil and Patrick J. Harte, Thomas F. O'Higgins and Richie Ryan of Fine Gael. Michael O'Kennedy was elected chairman.

In November 1972 it issued invitations to all the political groups in Northern Ireland to meet it. The committee also proceeded with an examination of all of the articles of the constitution of the Republic during the second half of 1972. Some 22 Articles of the Constitution were examined and viewpoints noted and agreed on many of them. Shortly after the 1973 general election and the change of government, the committee was reconstituted as an inter-party committee on Irish relations.

The membership of the committee was Garret FitzGerald, Minister for Foreign Affairs; Declan Costello, Attorney General, Paddy Harte, Conor Cruise O'Brien, Minister for Posts and Telegraphs and myself, representing the national coalition government: Joe Brennan, Frank Carter, Michael O'Kennedy, Vivion de Valera, and Paddy Smith representing Fianna Fáil. Paddy Harte was elected chairman. The committee requested the government departments dealing with legal, economic, social and cultural matters to undertake comparative studies within their departments identifying the areas of divergence between North and South. This was the first occasion that such an exercise had been commissioned by the Houses of the Oireachtas. The committee also agreed that, as an essential prerequisite of its work, it should seek submissions from, and meet the representatives of, a wide range of political, religious, trade union and other bodies.

The committee also proposed in 1974 to commence examination of each article of the constitution. However, the view was expressed by the Fianna Fáil deputies that no steps should be taken at that time to proceed with this exercise. In effect, their view was that the questions of amendment(s) to the constitution or the drafting of a new constitution should only be considered when politicians, North and South, were jointly authorised to come together to discuss the future of the Six Counties, as they called them. This Fianna Fáil viewpoint was in direct conflict with the general view of Labour and Fine Gael on the committee that we should work towards a consensus on the amendment(s) or otherwise and removal, if necessary, of those obstacles to a better climate.

The committee decided that, in view of this fundamental lack of consensus regarding constitutional change, the members should report to their parties on the situation. Conor Cruise O'Brien and I did so in July 1974. The Parliamentary Labour Party endorsed our work on the committee but its role petered out. There was virtually no shift in the traditional policy of Fianna Fáil until it inherited the Anglo–Irish Agreement in 1987 which obliged it to adhere to this international treaty registered at the United Nations and supported by successive American presidents.

*

I was in the Vimar restaurant in Place Jordan in Brussels in 1995 when Dick Spring as Tanaiste and Minister for Foreign Affairs met Jim Nicholson, MEP, chairman of the Ulster Unionist Council. The occasion was unplanned and quite informal. After some discussion on the situation in Northern Ireland, Dick turned to Jim and said 'Look, you and I know that the best prospect of a solution lies between yourselves and Fianna Fáil. No matter how much you and I may agree, unless Fianna Fáil are central to the exercise they will sabotage any progress we might make.' Jim got the message. Dick was a realist from Kerry.

Notwithstanding Fianna Fáil's imprimatur, Dick and I were very proud that our party had been a member of coalition governments which had produced three substantive contributions to the amelioration of Northern Ireland strife. The first, in 1973, was the Sunningdale Agreement which carried great promise for positive and peaceful development in the North, although it was later destroyed by loyalist intransigence and because of the inclusion of a 'Council of Ireland' at the insistence of the Irish government negotiators. This was singularly ill-advised. Unfortunately the SDLP and some national coalition ministers pushed Brian Faulkner over the brink in these negotiations.

The second was the New Ireland Forum which reported in 1984 and whose discussions were of great value in clarifying the precise views of all the constitutional parties outside of unionism, including, of course, the 13 members of Fianna Fáil who all agreed with the conclusions of that forum. As Garret FitzGerald stated at Hillsborough, the agreement was in full accord with the principles agreed by all the forum participants as the 'necessary elements of a framework within which a new Ireland could emerge'.[162] As a result, the coalition parties would at least have expected the support of all the constitutional parties who fully endorsed the forum report in their third substantial initiative towards a solution of Northern Ireland's problems — the 1985 Anglo-Irish Agreement.

*

At the time of the Sunningdale Agreement in 1973, I was only four years out of my job with the Irish Congress of Trade Unions and I contacted some former colleagues in the Northern Ireland Committee of ICTU for their opinions. They all held the view that Brian Faulkner had seriously misjudged the situation. The SDLP saw the whole exercise as an imminent step towards a united Ireland with an interim government buttressed by a Council of Ireland. Liam Cosgrave and Brendan Corish, in government a mere eight months after 16 years of opposition, had completely misjudged the mood of the unionist electorate. To cap it all, Ted Heath treated Brian Faulkner as a truculent hireling from an outer colony. He thought that his government could treat Northern Ireland like Rhodesia. In 1974 the Ulster Unionist Council rejected the Council of Ireland by 427 votes to

374 — shades of the UUC votes in 2000. Faulkner was forced to resign.

But the real gain from Sunningdale was the long-term effect of the parallel declarations of both governments that there could be no change in the status of Northern Ireland until the majority of the people of Northern Ireland desired a change in that status. The joint declaration was to cut the ground from under the Fianna Fáil hardliners, the IRA and Sinn Féin, and from under some old-style nationalists in Fine Gael. The Keating socialist republican wing of the Labour party with their simplistic hope for a united Ireland were also put in their place. In May 1974 the UWC general strike put the tin hat on the situation.

At long last the Dáil deputies and senators were getting the message. A sense of reality about Northern Ireland began to pervade the Houses of the Oireachtas. A great irony of course was that Conor Cruise O'Brien was involved up to his eyeballs in the Sunningdale negotiations. He has been one of the great educational forces on this island on the real politics of Northern Ireland. I have been one of his often infuriated admirers. More than any politician in the Republic in the 1970s, he demolished the popular myths about extreme republicanism and paramilitary unionism. He exposed the naked sectarianism of Northern Ireland and the clever ambiguities of Fianna Fáil. In the early 1970s, he ensured that the Labour Party in the Dáil advanced the precondition of the consent of the majority of all of the people of Northern Ireland on future structures of government. For all that, the peoples of these islands will be forever in his debt. However, in his challenges to armed Irish republicanism and its sectarian nationalist ideology, he seriously diminished his arguments by his association with the UK Unionist Party from 1996 onwards. These aberrations detracted greatly from his central contribution.

*

While Sinn Féin–IRA were engaged in their nefarious bombing and murdering campaign in the 1980s, I fully supported Section 31 of the Broadcasting Authority Acts which directed the RTÉ authority not to broadcast propaganda from that organisation.

Furthermore, I refused to receive any delegation or representations that included members of Sinn Féin. This included Phil Flynn who was elected vice president of Sinn Féin in 1983. He was elected general secretary of the Irish Local Government and Public Services Union in 1984. By 1985 he no longer held a leading position in Sinn Féin.

Section 31 was a very controversial issue. In the State (Lynch) -v-Cooney (1982), the constitutionality of the Minister's Order and of Section 31 was challenged by a Sinn Féin candidate for the Dáil. The then minister, Paddy Cooney, set out in an affidavit to the Supreme Court the evidence of facts which he had before him relevant to the aims, methods and aspirations of Sinn Féin. These facts, which were not denied by the plaintiff, included an *Irish Times* report of the statement of Ruari O'Bradaigh, president of Sinn Féin, that: 'The fight in the North was in grave danger of leaving the 26 counties far behind. We must show them that we want to disestablish both States, North and South.'[163] The minister also informed the court of an article by Sinn Féin, headed 'By Ballot and Bullet': 'As it was aptly put at the Sinn Féin Ard Fheis, "who here really believes we can win the war through the ballot box?" But will anyone here object if, with a ballot paper in this hand and an Armalite in this hand, we take power in Ireland.'[164]

Paddy Cooney also submitted an IRA staff report, produced at the trial of Seamus Twomey in the Special Criminal Court in 1977, which said: 'Sinn Féin should come under army organisers at all levels. Sinn Féin should employ full-time organisers in big republican areas. Sinn Féin should be radicalised (under army direction) and should agitate around social and economic issues, which attack the welfare of the people. Sinn Féin should be directed to infiltrate other organisations to win support for and sympathy to the movement ...' Of the eight candidates nominated by Sinn Féin for the February 1982 general election in the Republic, three had been convicted of being members of the IRA, one had been convicted of the unlawful possession of firearms, and another was awaiting trial for the possession of firearms. At that period, of the eight-man officer board of the party, two had been convicted of membership of the IRA, one had been convicted of attempting to import arms and one had been convicted of causing explosions.

The Supreme Court unanimously held that the minister had cogent grounds for believing that Sinn Féin aimed at undermining the authority of the State, that he was justified in forming the opinion which he did form, and that he could not have formed any other. Therefore, any broadcasts which sought support for such an organisation could properly be regarded by him as being likely to promote crime or incite to crime or to tend to undermine the authority of the State. The Supreme Court found: 'A democratic State has a clear and bounden duty to protect its citizens and its institutions from those who seek to replace law and order by force and anarchy, and the democratic process by the dictates of the few.'

These were the considerations which strongly influenced me in the governments of the 1980s. We faced down Sinn Féin–IRA just as every other previous government had to do on occasions. Had we shown any weakness they would have walked all over us.

My antipathy for Gerry Adams began with the IRA bomb in Brighton during the 1984 Conservative Party conference. The IRA came close to murdering many of the British cabinet and killed five people, including Roberta, the wife of John Wakeham, the government chief whip. They paralysed Margaret Tebbit. This attempted mass assassination was a huge setback to Anglo-Irish relations. For months afterwards, Thatcher simply disengaged from any Irish dialogue. I was infuriated by Adams' callous comment: 'The Brighton bombing was an inevitable result of the British presence in this country. Far from being a blow against democracy, it was a blow for democracy.'[165]

I was shocked when Patrick Magee, who was convicted of this murderous act and who was released after 14 years, under the terms of the Belfast Agreement, was a given a soft RTÉ 50-minute interview, during which he sought to speak away his act of war. There can be no justification for these murders. I agree with Muiris MacConghail when he wrote: 'What will happen in the future when, for example, the killers of Detective Garda Jerry McCabe are released?'[166]

*

My 11 years' working in the institutions of the European Union provided me with first-hand experience of communities consisting of two or more groups with significant social, cultural, religious, national or racial differences. Such communities can live in reasonable peace and stability in countries like Belgium, Switzerland, Canada or Holland. It took time to achieve. It required complex administrative structures, much support from neighbouring countries, and especially the will to make a new start and to try to move out of embattled ghetto mentalities.

Apart from more than three thousand deaths and the inhuman suffering inflicted on many people in the North and in Britain and the Republic as a result of the Northern conflict, we were also only too well aware of the monetary costs of the violence. The extra exchequer security costs to the Republic on the border alone rose every year from 1970 onwards and had cost more than £150 million per annum in 1985 when I was in government.

As a minister responsible for Health and Social Welfare at that time, I was acutely aware of the great uses to which such money could have been spent. I was, therefore, furious at the cynical opposition of Charles Haughey to the Anglo-Irish Agreement. It was deplorable to find that our common resolve to seek unity by consent was broken by the hostile attitude of Haughey towards the agreement. It was not too difficult to work out why his views had changed so drastically since 1980-1981. The only major change was that Haughey was in opposition. And worse still, he prevailed on his deputy leader Brian Lenihan to travel to the US in opposition. Ted Kennedy and the US State Department had more sense and they sent Brian home with a flea in his ear. But so dominant was Haughey that in November 1985 he marched, among others, deputies Bertie Ahern, David Andrews, Seamus Brennan, Raphie Burke, Gerard Collins, Brian Cowan, Padraig Flynn, Máire Geoghegan-Quinn, Charlie McCreevy, Ray MacSharry, Robert Molloy, Rory O'Hanlon, Mary O'Rourke and Albert Reynolds into the 'Níl' lobby in the Dáil against the agreement.

To their credit Mary Harney and Desmond O'Malley voted 'Tá'. The Dáil endorsed the agreement by 88 votes to 75.

One must contrast Haughey's approach with that of Garret FitzGerald in opposition; of Jack Lynch and of the major opposition parties in the United Kingdom where the bipartisan approach gave added strength to the British government's position on Northern Ireland. Neil Kinnock, in opposition, adopted a principled bi-partisan approach to Northern Ireland's crisis. We knew that Fianna Fáil was deeply divided on the issue with at least one-third of their deputies supporting the agreement. But they dared not oppose Charlie. He has a lot to answer for to our future generations.

Gerry Adams, Martin McGuinness and Gerry Kelly have a lot more to answer for. I walked behind the coffins of the gardaí and army public servants who were murdered in cold blood by the Provos. As I tried to convey my sympathy on those awful occasions, I never forgave these IRA apologists for the pain and suffering I witnessed on the faces of the widows and children they maimed for life. They may cynically tease the body politic with promises to decommission their arms but they will never decommission their consciences.

*

John Hume arrived on the political scene in 1969 with all the equipment necessary to become a statesman with an enduring impact. He had a sound theological training, he had a personal charisma, a devoted wife, oratorical skills, a loyal Catholic constituency, supportive business friends in the Republic, legions of US and European friends and understanding Irish governments. But after the abolition of Stormont, after Sunningdale and after the collapse of the Northern Ireland Executive in the mid-1970s, John Hume decided to abandon the fundamental principle of power sharing. As the single most influential nationalist leader in Northern Ireland since 1969, he decided to try the short route home. He kept hankering after a joint role for the Irish government towards one objective — a united Ireland 'settlement'. He badgered successive Taoisigh and Prime Ministers along these lines but to no avail. He and

Charles Haughey were soul-mates in this carefully cloaked ambition.

For a short time while I was in government in the 1980s, I thought John might face down the Provos. He said: 'They bomb factories and shout about unemployment; they shout at a teacher in the classroom; kill school bus drivers; kill people on campuses and then lecture us about education ... They rob post offices leaving people without benefit payments, then they preach to us about defending the poor ... One of these days Sinn Féin will disappear up their own contradictions.'[167] And yet because John had himself taken the narrow 'final solution' negotiating stance with successive governments, he and Gerry Adams lived off one another throughout the 1990s in a riverdance of Hume-speak and Adams ambiguities. It was all too clever by half. In 1993 they issued a joint statement that 'an internal settlement is not a solution because it obviously does not deal with all the relationships at the heart of the problem'.[168]

And why was John Hume ensnared into talks by Gerry Adams? Because at all events he had to be centre-stage. John was wholly expendable in the Provo strategy. The Provos knew well of his self preoccupation and astutely played up to it. From 1988 onwards Adams, Kelly and McGuiness were under tremendous pressure as the counter-terrorist capabilities of the Gardaí, the RUC and army intelligences, North and South, and throughout the UK, perfected their responses. Joint co-operation with the US anti-terrorist forces also began to produce results. The network of informers was expanding North and South. The bitter experiences and painstaking co-ordination of the security forces, North and South, were slowly closing the net. The Provo leaders knew that they themselves were facing incrimination or assassination by the loyalist paramilitaries. Tit for tat was the order of the day. They badly needed a cease-fire. They did so not because of John Hume's pleas but because they had run out of options. The SDLP allowed themselves to be used.

John Hume did not believe in power sharing or in an elected assembly in Northern Ireland. In 1992 he stated, 'experience has shown that if an assembly controls the government of Northern Ireland, whether it is power sharing or not, it won't work because any one party, by walking out, can wreck the whole thing'.[169]

In October 1993, an IRA bomb exploded in a Shankill fish shop. One of the bombers, Thomas Begley, was killed and Adams helped carry his coffin. Nine others were murdered and 57 injured. Dick Spring decided to propose in the Dáil six major principles in a major attempt to unhinge the paramilitaries from violence. He advanced that the Northern Ireland situation should not be changed by the use or threat of violence; any political settlement must depend on freely given consent; there could be no talks between governments and those who use, threatened or supported violence; there could be no secret agreements and those claiming to advocate peace should renounce the use or support of violence for good.[170] In effect, Spring put it up to the paramilitaries. They knew what to do if they wanted doors to open. At that stage, the IRA was going nowhere.

*

Perhaps in this millennium, the Sinn Féin–IRA leaders have some residue of compassion in their bones to reflect on the murders of 3-year-old Jonathan Ball and 12-year-old Timothy Parry by an IRA bomb in Warrington in 1993. Timothy would now be a fine young man of 20 celebrating a new millennium as do my own sons. Since then, many of these Sinn Féin–IRA leaders have become grandparents. Do they have any regrets about the butchery of this young teenager? Their historic claim is that they are the real defenders of the Catholic community in Northern Ireland. Yet between 1969 and 1999, they killed some 400 Catholics. Many of those so-called community leaders never did a day's work in their lives. They lived off their local communities; they blackmailed businesses for 'protection'; they murdered those who did not pay up; they abused clerics like Father Denis Faul and they robbed banks and post offices. They now expect us to bend the knee in retrospective admiration for the 'armed struggle'.

Adams, McGuinness and Kelly 'understood' the slaughter at the Abercorn Bar, Enniskillen, Warrington, Birmingham and Guildford. We now pat them on the arm and appreciate that they are 'moving the peace process forward'. The IRA condescends not to blow more innocent people to pieces. In their arrogance they merely wish to keep their powder dry. Now and again, Adams did suffer a teeny weenie twinge of concern. At the 1989 Sinn Féin Ard Feis he urged the IRA 'to show more circumspection than ever before' about killing or injuring civilians. However, he quickly went on to stress that 'the IRA's armed struggle sets the political agenda'.

Perhaps Gerry Adams is heading down the same road that Cathal Goulding and the Official IRA travelled in 1972; that the Sinn Féin–IRA leaders have at long last broken with the cult of the blood sacrifice; that they have abandoned plans to assassinate loyalists, the RUC and the army in Northern Ireland and that they no longer propose to recruit, fund and arm their private army. I am strongly of the view that we all need much clearer evidence that this is so. The people of Ireland need to know that their current parliamentary entryism is not merely a tactical phase in 'the struggle'. As Dick Walsh of *The Irish Times* pointed out, 'Republicans are still deadly at the theology.' My allegiance is to the army of the Republic of Ireland, not to the army council of the so-called IRA. My father was a Volunteer in 1917-1921. He believed and I believe that there can be no place in any government in our republic for those who wish to subvert our army, our president, our government and our constitution. Otherwise our democracy is not, in the words of Fergus Finlay, 'worth a penny candle'. Time will tell.

John Hume's Catholic nationalist agenda of a united Ireland has been cleverly cloaked by him over the decades. In 1973 he saw the Sunningdale Council of Ireland as a lever in that ambition. He was to avail of the Anglo–Irish Agreement 12 years later as 'an implicit declaration by the British that they have no interest of their own in staying in Ireland'.[171] John Hume and Gerry Adams were *ad idem* on this issue. They seriously differ on the means to the end. So far neither have prevailed. Hume has provided an alibi for peace to the IRA. They both now live with a devolved Northern Ireland Assembly and an Executive. In giving the cloak of resepctability to Sinn Fein–IRA, John has sacrificed the SDLP. The IRA still have their weapons. And there has been no British declaration of withdrawal. Ulster unionists are no petty people!

But by 2000 they were both deeply involved in the administration of an internal settlement. Martin McGuinness had transmuted himself from IRA propagandist to Minister of the Crown. And Gerry Adams accepted the Queen's cheques for his services to his people. There is nothing to beat cash from Westminster! They still have the IRA card close to their chests. Their ultimate clear objective of a united Ireland on their terms remains unchanged. Their non-decommissioned weapons are the collateral security for their final solution. John and Gerry know this.

And I am not without hope. The political landscape of Northern Ireland is substantially different from that when I was first elected in 1969. Northern Ireland is now part of a Europe of the regions. We in the Republic have left our irredentist claims for the four green fields behind. Our prosperous economy is opening up to the North. The present cease-fire is three years old. Ian Paisley is 74 and a declining demagogue. Catholic participation in the administration of Northern Ireland has increased greatly. Civil rights are more protected. The Assembly and the Executive are slowly learning all about compromise. The Troubles are not without a long-term federal solution. Paddy Devlin's and Gerry Fitt's ambition of a Social Democratic and Labour Party might yet unfold in the decades ahead.

Meanwhile, when I hear some of the spokespersons of Sinn Féin–IRA and the DUP, I am reminded of the comment of Henry Kissinger during the Iran–Iraq war: 'It's a pity they both can't lose!'

Twenty-Three

Over in Europe

'The Gregory deal was a precursor to destructive localism in politics.'

Garret Fitzgerald, August 2000, *The Irish Times*

Stella and I and our four sons faced into the 1987 general election confidant that I was going to lose my seat. All of the omens, most of the political pundits, the opinion polls, public and private, concluded that I was going to be dumped. Fianna Fáil had demonised me with the slogan 'Health cuts hurt the old, the sick and the handicapped'. After the first week of canvassing my son Mark, then 25, came home and said, 'Mom, Dad, the seat is gone, there will be no tears, we will go out holding our heads up high.' Liam Cosgrove Jnr, in his usual racing parlance, said that young Eamon Gilmore of the Workers' Party was 'coming up fast on the inside'. Kevin Fitzpatrick, the local Sinn Féin hard man, had capitalised on the local drugs situation.

A consolation was that the outgoing Taoiseach, Garret FitzGerald, expressed the view that it would be most unfortunate if I were to lose my seat. For that endorsement I was most grateful. We fought on, doorstep by doorstep. Some slammed doors and gates in my face. And slowly the tide began to turn in the second and third week of canvass. Stella was a key canvasser, morning, afternoon and evening. She felt the sympathetic vibes. I had issued an unapologetic 'I Stand By My Record' letter to every household. The hostility began to decline as our 40 Labour canvassers patiently put rational explanations to the electorate about my policies in Health and Social Welfare. There was perceptible support from Fine Gael voters. Canvass reports from the shopping centres on the final Saturday were more and more understanding. Some of Sean Barrett's key Fine Gael supporters switched, to his consternation. In the end I won the fourth seat in the five seat constituency with 6,484 first preference votes or 11.6 per cent of the first preference vote, well ahead of Eamon Gilmore.

One of the most upsetting episodes for Stella and our family, in the whole of my political career, was the circulation in my constituency by John P. Clerkin, secretary of the 'Children's Protection Society' during that campaign of a document entitled 'Mr Barry Desmond and Sexual Exploitation'. He wrote that I was 'perhaps the only member of the outgoing Dáil to have called for child contraception as such'. He added, 'in such a society, too, incest would be more difficult to oppose'. He also alleged that those I associated with called for explicit repeal of the major child molesting law in other countries. Irate constituents began to ring me.

I had no option but to go immediately to the High Court and seek an injunction. I obtained an interlocutory injunction and claimed damages in libel. I was granted the injunction. Clerkin undertook not to publish or circulate such defamatory documents in future. John Rogers had suggested that I brief Dermot Gleeson SC for the case. He handled the proceedings with great aplomb and he wrote that there was no question of fees. That was the only occasion in 30 years in public life that I had to have recourse to the courts to clear my name. I have always cautioned my colleagues to steer well clear of the protection of the law on political issues. I did not proceed for damages because nobody can put a price on his or her good name. In any event I was more than pleased to be returned to the Dáil.

*

During all these 20 years in the Dáil, including those years in government, I attended my constituency clinics at Blackrock, Dun Laoghaire, Sallynoggin and Deansgrange every Saturday morning and afternoon and every Sunday morning except for the month of August. I had unstinting and loyal assistance from Mary and Tom Byrne, Councillor Eric Doyle and Eileen Doyle, the late Councillor Joe Durning, John Mulcahy and his late wife Marjorie, Councillor Frank Smyth, Councillor Archie Dixon, the late Martin Hughes, Pat and Aileen Shanley, the late Hugh Nevin, Aidan McNamara, Matt McQuirk, Frank Greene, William Scally, Betty Clifford, Nora Nowlan, Carmel Treacy, Gerry Wrigley and Niamh Bhreathnach. Shortly after the 1987 election, I decided that by the next contest in Dun Laoghaire I would have enough. Opposition politics are very sterile. Incessant weekend clinic work began to take its toll. Stella and I had little time to ourselves. I yearned to spend more time with my sons.

At the end of the following year I found Christmas to be a time of joy but also of reflection. My feeling was that, except for a small number of deputies, the hidden Ireland was off the agenda of the Dáil. The emigrants, the long-term unemployed, the public hospital patients with no beds and waiting for hours in outpatients; the public psychiatric patients, the elderly with no money for the nursing home — they were the hidden Ireland whose fears and needs that Christmas were, I felt, no longer on the Clár of the House. And why was this so? Because we had the dominant consensus of the comfortable. Public servants were given £98 million in 1988-1989, £18 million more than expected, to retire early with topped-up pensions, tax-free lump sums and severance payments. They were unlikely to disturb the consensus. That hundred million did not go to the poor, the old and the handicapped of the Fianna Fáil poster in the 1987 general election.

I felt that it was the negation of the fundamental philosophy that 'I am my brothers' and sisters' keeper'. That bond had been broken by health cuts, by cleverly hidden social welfare cuts in eligibility, and by the virtual abolition of the local authority house construction programme. And to cap my concern, we had the first tax amnesty for those with ready money who had never paid their due taxes. That was a political disgrace. There was no amnesty for those in 1989 who faced another £8 million in public hospital in-patient and out-patient charges. In 1989 despite £500 million more in the budget from the tax amnesty,

£40 million more in the lottery, £120 million more in income tax and £100 million more in VAT, the cuts in health, education, social welfare and environment services continued because the consensus ordained that there was no other option.

When I pointed out that one senior tax adviser assured me that only one in six of his clients who had tax arrears liability actually paid up, the consensus still said that there was no option to cuts in public expenditure. And when I pointed out that the waste refuse fleet of Co Dublin was then 14 years old, with no money for replacements and escalating maintenance costs, I knew that the shoulders of the comfortable would shrug and say that there was no other option. Meanwhile those who lectured the left perfected their DIRT and offshore deposit scams and Ministers for Finance scarcely pressurised the Revenue Commissioners on tax compliance. Their senior officers in Finance saw all solutions emanating from public expenditure cuts and little else. At that stage I had had enough of the Dáil.

I decided to aim for the European Parliament elections in 1989, work there for five years and then, at 59 years, Stella and I would have a hard-earned break from elective politics. I had a particular interest in European affairs since the early 1970s when I became active with Mary Robinson, Garret FitzGerald, Louis Smith, Tony Browne, the late Michael Sweetman, Miriam Hederman O'Brien, the late Charlie McCarthy, to whom I am related, Denis Corboy, Brendan Halligan and the late Michael Kileen, in the Irish Council of the European Movement. I was a vice president of the ICEM for many years from 1974 onwards. I had also served as an Irish delegate to the Council of Europe from 1973 to 1981. I decided to seek a party nomination for the European Parliament elections in 1989. I assured the party that I would make a major effort to win back a Labour seat in Dublin and the convention agreed that I should run alone.

*

In the 1989 European Parliament election I was faced with a formidable array of candidates. Although I had never lost a parliamentary or local government election over 20 years, I was a very poor populist campaigner. The larger the street crowd, the more I wanted to hide. Stella, Ita McAuliffe, Aidan McNamara and my sons pushed me in front of the curious electors as they gave out the literature. They were only curious because they saw 'the elder lemon' at last. Women said to me 'You look much bigger on TV'. While I had no reticence in addressing political meetings, in the crowded streets I shrivelled away from small talk and eye contact with votes. I had to compete with the frenetic *bonhomie* of Mary Banotti; the stately campaign of the vague Niall Andrews; the charismatic and elegant coat over the shoulder of Proinnsias De Rossa and the magic Dublin name of Eileen Lemass. The PDs still held a populist attraction in the youthful Mary Harney and the Greens also had an articulate candidate in Trevor Sargent. Raymond Crotty had cornered the anti-EU protest vote. He was supported by Kevin Boland, Desmond Fennell, Noreen Kearney, Sister Stanislaus Kennedy, Matt Merrigan, Tony Coughlan and Senator John Robb.

My campaign suddenly became secondary with the general election on the same day. To make matters worse, my party decided that, because of that election, I would have to personally bear half the cost of the Euro billboards in Dublin, about £17,000. But I had one advantage which I stressed on every occasion in the campaign. De Rossa and Mary Harney were 'dual mandators' whereas I had vacated my seat in Dun Laoghaire to run for Europe. The electorate, and particularly those public service trade unionists who had always strongly supported me in South Dublin, appreciated the point of principle. But when I saw the expensive 'battle buses' of De Rossa and Harney and the custom-painted jeeps of Andrews and Lemass, I knew that we had a major electoral battle ahead.

I had no wealthy party or commercial sponsors. Candidates then did not have to file any accounts. Stella and I had to borrow another £10,000 from our bank manager for another gamble with the electorate. And I had to sign a monthly debit to repay with interest similar to any other customer. De Rossa ran a brilliant campaign with the help of Eoghan Harris. He and Niall Andrews headed the poll with 71,000 and 72,000 first preference votes respectively. Eileen Lemass and I came next with 58,000 and 57,000 first preferences. But Mary Banotti and

Chris O'Malley, the grandson of Kevin O'Higgins, polled 77,000 between them and were well on their way to a Banotti quota of 89,681 votes. In the event I won the final fourth seat from Eileen Lemass. I then had to opt to take the lump sum portion of my Dáil pension to pay off our election debts. In this regard I was no different from the vast majority of deputies I knew in my two decades in the Dáil. They came into the House in debt and most left in debt. In my experience the great majority were not beholden to any trade union, employer or business tycoon. We had no offshore accounts or business contacts to tap for our lifestyle or election campaigns. Our constituency treasurers, Stella and I paid all our election invoices and we and our sons 'did without' in order to do so.

Some politicians regard the European Parliament as a comfortable, pensioned parachute from national politics. For some who have had long tenure in the Dáil, it can be a second career. However, it is of vital importance that the European Parliament should not be regarded as an elephant graveyard for retiring politicians. In 1989, the parliament was a growing political institution of the Union with increasing democratic powers in its relationship with the European Commission, the European Council, the European Court of Justice and the European Court of Auditors. As an Irish delegate to the Council of Europe from 1973 to 1981, I knew that there was no joyride. I decided to stress major policy issues and in the election I laid out my stall:

> We will work for a social community in which individual ability to pay for health services, educational opportunity and income security in later life will not be a dominant yardstick of a good society. We will work for a co-operative society in which we will reach out across the twelve member states to the rapidly changing east and outside Europe to the poverty-stricken peoples in the South of our World and join with them in the development of their economies and societies. This is the policy vision of the Labour Party in Europe.

I went on to warn the selection conference that there was another vision in Europe — the dangerous, infectious appeal to the greed of individualism. This was the purpose of the political right. It was all-pervasive. For them, the future of Europe was full deregulation in a free market economy with marginal social obligations. For them, a crude, personal wealth accumulating market was paramount. For them, economic development was a dog-eat-dog society where the powerful dominated with no commitment to the common needs of the young, the unemployed, the disabled and the elderly. For them, there was no common sense of justice, no common sharing of opportunities for growth. These principles were to them social democratic impediments to the individual pursuit of swelling bank accounts. I rejected these economic and social criteria of the right.

*

In 1994 I was nominated a member of the European Court of Auditors by the Irish government. The court is the external auditor of the European Union and bodies set up by it. The treaty stipulates that the court assists the parliament and the council in exercising their control over the implementation of the budget.

The court carries out its control and consultative functions independently. It is responsible for the audit of all EU expenditure and revenue in much the same way as the Comptroller and Auditor General audits government departments and certain State bodies in Ireland. In 2000, the EU general budget amounted to some IR£70 billion. The court audits and reports on the reliability of the Union's accounts and the legality and regularity of the underlying transactions. It also checks, on a systematic basis, that the financial management of these resources is sound. The court conducts its audits not only at the commission but also in the member states where some 85 per cent of EU expenditure, notably under the Common Agricultural Policy and the Structural Funds, is administered by government departments, regional authorities and other agencies.

Despite its title, the court has no judicial powers or functions. It is organised in accordance with the principle of collective cabinet responsibility similar to that of the Irish government. Each member takes an oath of office to act in a completely independent manner. In the performance of their duties, members may neither seek nor take instructions from any government or other body and they may not engage in any other occupation. The members of the court can only be removed from office by a decision of the European Court of Justice. I was the third Irish appointee since 1977. A fellow Corkman, Michael Murphy, former secretary of the Department of Finance, served at the court until 1986 and was president of the court from 1977 to 1981. His successor from 1986 to 1994 was Richie Ryan, the former national coalition Minister for Finance and the Public Service and a former Fine Gael TD and MEP.

To me, our involvement in European affairs is vital because all of our political parties have strong residues of an anti-European intellectualism and cultural isolationism. For decades we related obsessively to the English-speaking British Isles and the United States. Our post-war foreign policy forays by Frank Aiken were mostly to New York. Fianna Fáil contained in its early years some rare backwoodsmen, as when deputy Martin Corry from the East Cork constituency said in 1928, 'Irish diplomats posture abroad so that they might squat like the nigger when he put on the black silk and the swallow tail coat and went out and said he was an English gentleman.'[172] Such sentiments ensured that Corry, a Volunteer from 1914, was re-elected in every subsequent Dáil election until 1969. He lived to see his fellow Corkman, Jack Lynch, lead his party into the European Communities.

During my six years in the court in Luxembourg, I frequently injected doses of bluntness into our deliberations. I always believe in robustly 'telling it as it is' rather than dancing to the delicate slow waltz of polite officialese. But such inclinations can lead one into trouble. One evening at dinner in the Irish Embassy in Luxembourg, Ambassador Geraldine Skinner sat me next to the wife of the British ambassador. She broke the ice remarking that she knew the president of our court. She asked me how I enjoyed working with André Middlehoek. I was polite but ventured that with André's 14 years as a member I found his strictures somewhat overpowering. She asked why he was that intimidating. I jokingly responded, 'Well you know the Dutch! They can be very dogmatic at times! You know they are not very subtle!' 'Oh,' she exclaimed, 'that's very interesting, I am Dutch myself.' There was no recovery! We slowly ate fish and beef and dessert. When the mouth comes before the brain ...

*

The Union's budget is now one of immense complexity. Throughout the community there are 90 national and regional paying agencies with, for example, 23 in Germany and 17 in Spain where they have considerable autonomy in making payments to producers. In the commission's budget alone there are some 600,000 commitment and payment transactions each year and millions in member states. The commission's financial control is only able to examine about 60,000 of these each year. In Ireland alone in 1997 there were 543,000 claims to the Department of Agriculture and Food for premium payments. Total payments by the department amounted to one billion euros and encompassed 1.7 million payments to 135,000 applicants.

During my time in the court, examples of irregularities in the area of agriculture found by our auditors were over-declarations of arable area for a given crop; over-declarations of area set-aside, such as land which had never been used for agricultural production; and supplementary milk levies not being paid by the producers who exceeded their quotas, but being borne by the member state administrations concerned. In my opinion, the three billion euros paid each year as subsidies to olive oil and tobacco producers are open to serious abuses.

Contrary to some mythology in Ireland about my views on the reform of the Common Agriculture Policy, I am acutely aware that EU direct payments of some 1.6 billion euros per annum to Irish farmers constitutes half of their income. These payments are of vital importance to farm families and the entire rural economy. However, from my 11 years' experience in the

European Parliament and in the Court of Auditors, I am only too well aware that many agricultural products are extremely difficult to monitor and audit in terms of production, marketing and the payment of subsidies on such as oranges, lemons, tomatoes, apples, peaches, citrus processing, cereals, olive oil, skim milk powder and tobacco. The major problems relating to payments for cattle and sheep are also well documented. The blatant deficiencies of the common market organisation of the above products are riddled with expediencies inserted largely at the behest of member states and powerful vested interests. This is where the real reforms must start. In my opinion, more far-reaching measures need to be considered to reduce the share of the aid received by the largest farmers. The impact of enlargement and the WTO negotiations will be acute for Irish farmers. The net contributors to the EU budget will strenuously oppose any new increases on their part.

It is often overlooked by many commentators that the Council of Ministers is a Union institution with far-reaching treaty responsibilities, legal obligations, a permanent staff of 2,500 and a budget of 360 million euros. Peter Sutherland, former Commissioner and Director General of the WTO, rightly observed that: 'In regard to the "democratic deficit" in the Union, much has yet to be accomplished in achieving democratic accountability over the Council.'[173]

There is no doubt that the proceedings of the council could be made more transparent. The opposition parties in the member states are virtually excluded from the deliberations of the council. The various European affairs committees of the national parliaments exert little influence over the permanent representatives and the ministerial councils. The co-decision procedures between the council and the European Parliament are far removed from the elector in the street. There is an urgent need to review these aspects of the public accountability of the council without introducing another layer of competence in the decision-making processes of the Union. However, it is vital that such reforms should not create further inertia and scope for blockages in the decision-making processes.

Part of the explanation for the alienation of citizens from Union affairs relates to the embezzlement of Union funds and

cases of incompetent management of these funds. Unfortunately, these frauds set off an avalanche of media and Euro-sceptic reaction and can destroy citizens' faith in community legislation and in the staffs of the institutions. Public acceptance of the single currency, the future work of the European Central Bank and adherence to economic policy guidelines by every member state demands that the resources of the Union are fully accounted for.

Frauds are frequently of a complex transnational nature. For example, criminal charges were brought against 119 people for a conspiracy of fraud against the community budget, involving smuggling, tax evasion, forgery and corruption concerning a 'meat carousel'. This concerned imports of live cattle from Eastern Europe to Italy, which were re-exported as low-quality cuts and offal to Malta, re-exported from Malta to Italy, and further re-exported to non-member countries, mostly Gabon, with refunds. It involved 18.5 million ecu in evaded levies and 24 million ecu in wrongly paid export refunds; 42 persons were convicted. The investigative difficulties in this work are, of course, immense because some 18 million transit documents are issued annually in the Union.

Fundamental reforms are absolutely necessary in the personnel administration of the Union's institutions. There are some 35,000 civil servants working in these institutions and there are more than 8,000 retired staff. They work in an extremely complex and demanding multi-lingual and multi-national environment. For the most part they serve the institutions very well. However, the staff regulations within which they work are in need of considerable reform, having first been framed some 30 years ago. No less than 76 staff regulations have now been consolidated into a complex text of 229 pages in 11 languages. These range from the special conditions of employment for officials serving in third countries to the weighting of the purchasing power of community staff allowances in member states.

EU staffs are recruited in outmoded public service categories of A, B, C and D. Category A, for example, ranges over eight steps from Director-General to Administrative Assistant at A8. These are the outmoded staff structures of the 1970s. A

fundamental reform is that the posts of Director General and Director in all of the EU institutions and agencies should be made by an absolutely independent appointments board. For example, 350 senior management staff are directly appointed by the commission within a system which is seriously lacking in transparency. How many of these appointments are based on real merit? How many are made on national considerations alone? Directors General should be appointed for a non-renewable fixed term of seven years. These appointments are subject to the constraints of the staff regulations and an appeal system to the European Court of Justice. But these are not enough to inspire real confidence.

Effectively, the European institutions have a top-level appointments system which we in Ireland abolished in the mid-1980s. Basic reforms in the European civil service structure are long overdue. These structures are rigidly hierarchical. Those in the middle grades have a major disincentive to question the actions of their superiors because promotions and notations may be dramatically affected.

One of the fundamental reforms which should be introduced in relation to the appointment of members of the European Court of Justice, the Court of First Instance and the Court of Auditors is that of a single maximum mandate of six years with no renewal. All members of such institutions take an oath of office, in a solemn ceremony before the assembled Court of Justice of the European Communities, to act at all times with absolute independence and integrity and not to take instructions from any member state in the discharge of their functions. The treaty requires the members to act independently yet they depend on the governments of their member state for re-nomination. There is an innate contradiction here. Is there not a temptation to cultivate one's home administration to ensure that one is well thought of when the next request for a nomination is sent by the council to their member state government?

One way or another, these appointments should have a very clear-cut limited term. I am also of the view that all members should not exceed 65 years of age on completion of their six-year term. The regular infusion of new blood in the institutions at the highest level would also be of major benefit. I am very strongly of the view that before government nominations are sent to the Council of Ministers, they should appear before the appropriate committee of the Houses of the Oireachtas, to assess and report on their suitability. This would apply to the EU Commissionership, the European Court of Justice, the European Court of Auditors, the European Investments Bank and the European Bank for Reconstruction and Development.

I am also convinced that there is a very urgent need for the fundamental reform of the financial regulations relating to the agricultural payments. These are initiated by the commission, decided by the Council of Ministers, acting unanimously, following consultation with the European Parliament and having received the opinion of the Court of Auditors. In my opinion, the regulations urgently need reform to ensure that there is full transparency of all transactions at institution and member state level. These regulations are drafted with deliberate flexibility and ambiguity to enable member states and their paying agencies to appeal at three or four levels, to the commission, the Conciliation Committee and the European Court of Justice in the event of corrections or penalties being imposed by the commission. If irregularities and fraud are to be rooted out, this basic change must be implemented.

Secondly, the regulations relating to the tendering procedures and controls over outside contractors engaged by the commission and its agencies are also in clear need of urgent reform. There are many large-scale technical assistance programmes where financial control, value for money audits, and reporting systems are entirely unsatisfactory. The Court of Auditors has pinpointed many of these defects. Does real political will exist at council, commission and member state level to tackle this serious problem?

During my in Brussels and Luxembourg, I have seen the constant improvisations and emergency measures introduced by the commission, often at the behest of political expediency at council summits. These are a ready-made prospect for the waste of resources and irregularities. Attempts to carry out ex-post evaluations of Structural Fund expenditures in certain member states are almost pointless. In the CAP expenditures the integrated administrative control system, IACS, is still not fully operational. Advances paid to member states under the Structural Funds are often treated as definitive expenditure and their ultimate utilisation is very poorly controlled.

Above all else, I am convinced that the basic structure of the European Union's budget is in dire need of fundamental reform. The differentiated system of multi-annual programming of commitments and payments is fatally conducive to maladministration. For example, has one ever tried examining a cancelled expenditure commitment which is carried over, revived in the following year, partly paid in that year, with the balance being refused in year three? This is an audit nightmare. The lack of annuality in the budget is a constant source of criticism, a recipe for malmanagement, an incentive for misappropriation and conducive to ever-mounting layers in the financial regulations. This budget structure of deliberate complexity is suited to many member states, particularly those who are net beneficiaries. I am also strongly of the opinion that it would be an enormous sea change if the EU budget were to be transformed into a real cash-based annual budget. We urgently need compulsory year-end closures with absolutely transparent carry-overs and mandatory reversions to the general budget.

Many governments are so beholden politically to their agricultural lobbies that they are most reluctant to propose a root and branch reform of the Common Agricultural Policy and its regulations. The CAP reforms to date have failed in a major way to deal with serious pollution from agriculture. Today we pay the polluter not to pollute: we must implement the principle 'the polluter shall pay' as a matter of utmost urgency. Meanwhile, the agri-food conglomerates and the major farmers cream off the incomes of Europe's industrial labour force.

I believe that in relation to Common Agricultural Policy reform, there is a real imperative to create a healthy, highly efficient and competitive farming industry which guarantees the future of high quality food production, rewards food producers fairly, controls the agri monopolies, maintains the rural environment, meets consumer entitlements to high quality and safe food at a reasonable cost, and enables the new Eastern

European states to enter the markets on a fair, competitive non-excessively subsidised basis. David Byrne, the Irish Commissioner, is well-equipped to contribute in this area.

And what of the future? The European Union is still maintaining its momentum. The historic goal of economic and monetary union is within reach; common strategies towards the fullest possible employment of all EU citizens need to be developed; there is consolidation and completion of the single market; the largest enlargement in the Union's history is being planned; and slowly but surely elements of a common foreign and security policy are being forged. I brought many Irish visitors to Luxembourg to see the graves of the 16,000 American and German soldiers in two cemeteries outside the city killed in the bitter World War II battles of 1944–1945. It is our duty to ensure that 'no longer will old men make war and young men die'.

Twenty-Four

Finally and In Conclusion

'That diary will be the death of me.'

George Redmond, 2 June 2000, Flood Tribunal,
regarding his 1988 IPA diary

When I was an Irish MEP in Brussels between 1989 and 1994, I quickly learned that the wheels of Belgian politics were well oiled by *diensthetoom*, a system of reciprocal political favours between the different factions. It put to bed awkward problems. The spoils of office were shared.

When I moved to Luxembourg in 1994 for six years in the European Court of Auditors, I had a further learning experience. I discovered at first-hand the extent of irregularities in the disbursement of EU funds in member countries, including Ireland. The world of transnational fraud came sharply into focus.

I realised that, contrary to the perceived wisdom at home, Ireland had no exemption when it came to corruption. The light began, almost accidentally, to shine on Ireland's golden business and political circles. All members of the court were circulated with summaries of the press stories from each member state. The litany of scandals and tribunals in Ireland appeared with regularity. How does one stand up for one's country in that situation?

Memories of my time on Dublin County Council flooded back. I was elected to the council, for the first and only time at the top of the poll, in the 1974 local elections and thus entered the strange world of Section 4 planning motions and draft development plans. After seven years on the council, I was elected chairman in 1981.

I was shocked at the preoccupation of some councillors with Section 4 motions on planning issues directing the county manager to vary county development plans or to give planning permissions. These motions were often tabled in the teeth of opposition from the planning and roads engineering staffs of the council. There was an unholy alliance between a group of the Fianna Fáil and Fine Gael councillors. I recall the developers in the public gallery smiling broadly as the motions were ruthlessly voted through. They would gather in delight in Conway's lounge after the meetings. My cynicism knew no bounds and my protests as chairman about orderly planning and development in the county were treated as socialist nonsense. The values of the lands and properties concerned soared overnight. And most of these councillors were also re-elected.

For most of these meetings, George Redmond, Dublin Assistant City and County Manager, sat next to me at the top table and dispensed advice. Little did I know!

In late 1981, the process of drafting the County Dublin Development Plan got under way. By the time the draft plan went on public exhibition in late 1982, some 3,500 acres had been rezoned by the councillors. Dublin was about to become a concrete urban sprawl as developers realised that they were in possession of goldmine lands. I publicly estimated at that time that only about 500 acres for new or revised designations were justified on planning criteria. The Minister for the Environment, Ray Burke, was constrained to put on record that he regarded the councillors' rezoning proposals as 'highly objectionable'.[174] I was sceptical!

The leader of Fine Gael, Garret FitzGerald, instructed his councillors to vote in accordance with the recommendations of the council's planning staffs. They were not amused: to them Garret was an innocent abroad. Time and again, I and a minority of councillors, including Eithne Fitzgerald, Frank Smyth and Mervyn Taylor, strenuously objected to these rezoning motions being pushed through. Frank McDonald and Frank Kilfeather of *The Irish Times* were foremost in exposing the insistent demands of landowners, speculators and the various vested interests. Is it any wonder that the social and economic infrastructure of County Dublin is today in such a mess?

Thanks to the work of the various tribunals, we now know a lot more of the truth of what lay behind events in those days, not just in relation to planning but also in relation to the corruption of political life presided over by Charles Haughey.

However, no politician can claim credit for the setting up of the Flood Tribunal into the planning affairs of County Dublin. It was the chairman of An Taisce, Michael Smith, by his instigation of a reward of £10,000 in conjunction with Colm McEochaidh, for information in respect of planning corruption. James Gogarty and others came forward which, in effect, obliged the Dáil to set up the Flood Tribunal.

I never thought I would see the day when Ray Burke resigned from government and the Dáil. I never thought I would see the unmasking of George Redmond as a corrupt local government officer. And I certainly never thought I would hear the startling revelations of Frank Dunlop. My colleagues in the Court of Auditors in Luxembourg asked me if I knew those characters. I assured them that I did indeed, to my shame. Any lingering illusions I had about Ireland being a country of higher ethical standards were shattered.

We urgently need in the Houses of the Oireachtas an absolute determination to ensure full public accountability at all levels of Irish society. We need political parties which will keep the monied lobbies and the vested interests firmly at arm's length. We need an absolute protocol in the public service which will insist on a clear moratorium between a public servant's retirement and his taking up analogous appointments or consultancy in the private sector. The golden circle must be squared.

But when I returned to Dublin in March 2000, I was in for a bigger shock. I met universal cynicism about our politicians. In my local pub I was jocosely offered brown paper bags by my friends. The issue is far from funny. Ireland has now dropped from being the fifteenth to the nineteenth least corrupt country. We are now ranked just behind Chile according to the

Transperancy International Corruption Index. It is imperative that the good name of our country be restored.

When will the Houses of the Oireachtas enact major reforms in the sources of finance and expenditure of the political parties? When will we see the end of the 'hospitality tent' at Galway races and the ubiquitous golf classics, with individual contributions of £450 to avoid publication. These events tell a great deal about the interaction of politics and business in Ireland. And perhaps we need the sanction of a loss of pension and other perks for any politicians who are convicted in court of corruption.

We need in Ireland a society proud of its public servants. I have been a public servant in its broadest sense since 1969. Those of the political right will never understand those who gain great personal fulfilment from their public employment. The right will never understand that for many, the concept of personal success does not necessarily revolve around making a personal fortune.

As a former member of the Dáil's Committee on Public Accounts I was proud of the work done at the committee's hearings into the Deposit Interest Retention Tax. This proves conclusively that tax evasion and avoidance are not the preserve of a minority in public office. The infection permeates a wide cross-section of our society. Deputy Jim Mitchell has proved to be an outstanding chairman in bringing this scandal into the public domain.

Finally, we need an Ireland of social consensus and national cohesion opposed to sectional demands. I vigorously dispute the view of Mary Harney 'that liberalism, not leftism, is what has transformed this country over the last ten years'.[175] This is a bit rich coming from a party which disdained the successive social partnership agreements which were supported by the left and which underpinned a great deal of our social and economic development.

And, in conclusion, I was one of the very fortunate deputies who never lost his seat. Some 60 out-going deputies lost their seats in the last two general elections in 1992 and 1997. In fact, 1,064 deputies have been elected since 1918 and, on average, each deputy has won 3.8 elections. I was double the average. I was extremely fortunate. I lost many a political argument and some fair-weather supporters but never the seat. Stella and I saw defeated deputies and their families leave the counting centres all alone late at night. As the returning officer slowly read out the result, count by count to elimination, we saw the humiliation of public rejection etched on their faces.

The defeated deputy dredged up his last reserves of pride, thanked his weary wife, family and supporters and publicly vowed to be back in the Dáil. But they knew his prospects were grim.

They knew that his replacement would also have a honeymoon with the constituency. He would enjoy the salary, expenses and secretarial assistance. He would now have the inside track in the party. Meanwhile, the phone and the fax of the defeated would grow silent. There are few offers of employment for a rejected former TD. Recriminations begin within the family and the local party.

His only hope is to run for the Senate. Stella and I greeted many such dejected candidates on our doorsteps over seven such elections. They travelled thousands of miles seeking votes from that most mendacious electorate of all — fellow deputies, outgoing senators, city and county councillors. My father was a senator so we knew the score.

After being witness to all this over 20 years, Stella and I resolved not to encourage our sons to consider elective politics. This was probably unfair but we are opposed to dynastic politics. Our family has no regrets. We stand by our record. And we thank the people of Dun Laoghaire for the generosity of their support.

Appendix I

Barry Desmond has served in public office in Ireland and in the European institutions for over thirty years:

Dáil Éireann	1969–89
Dublin County Council	1974-82
Council of State	1973-91
Council of Europe	1973-81
Minister of State, Finance	1981-82
Minister for Health & Social Welfare	1982-87
European Parliament	1989-94
European Court of Auditors	1994-2000

Presidents of Ireland 1973–Present

Erskine Childers	1973–74
Cearbhall Ó Dálaigh	1974–76
Patrick Hillery	1976–90
Mary Robinson	1990–97
Mary McAleese	1997–

Fianna Fáil leaders 1966–Present

Jack Lynch	1966–79
Charles J. Haughey	1979–92
Albert Reynolds	1992–94
Bertie Ahern	1994–

Fine Gael leaders 1965–Present

Liam Cosgrove	1965–77
Garret FitzGerald	1977–87
Alan Dukes	1987–90
John Bruton	1990–

Labour Party leaders 1932–Present

William Norton	1932–60
Brendan Corish	1906–77
Frank Cluskey	1977–81
Michael O'Leary	1981–82
Dick Spring	1982–97
Ruairi Quinn	1997–

1 Jim Cronin, Cork GAA historian, has this episode recorded in his outstanding compendium, *An Chéad Chéad 'A Rebel Hundred'*
2 The O'Kief Volumes, Millstreet Public Library
3 *James Larkin: Lion of the Fold*, Ed. Donal Nevin, Dublin, Gill & Macmillan, 1998
4 'Cosgrave's Kingdom', *Hibernia*, 07.01.1977
5 *Magill*, August, 1999
6 Basil Chubb, *The Government and Politics of Ireland*, London, OUP, 1970
7 *Irish Independent*, 12.08.1999
8 Labour News Bulletin, January, 1971
9 *Irish Independent* 23.10.1982
10 *Irish Independent*, 21.10.1999
11 Dáil Debate, 11.12.1979
12 1977 Fianna Fáil Manifesto pp 5-9
13 *Irish Times* 19.07.1978
14 *Irish Times* 19.07.1978
15 RTÉ broadcast, January 1980.
16 ESRI Quarterly Bulletin, November 1980; NESC Report No 53, 1980 and Central Bank Autumn 1980 Quarterly Bulletin
17 03.02.1983. Extract from memorandum circulated by Paul Mackay FCA to Fianna Fail TDs, 23.03.2983, quoting Charles Haughey
18 Dublin, Blackwater Press, 1996
19 *Sunday Independent* review by John A. Murphy of *Against the Tide*, Noel Browne, Gill & Macmillan, 30 November1986
20 Dáil Debates, April 1951
21 David Thornley, *Sunday Press*, 04.10.1970
22 *Health Medicine & Politics in Ireland 1900-1970*, Ruth Barrington, IPA, 1987
23 Review of *Against the Tide* by Dr James Deeny, *Irish Medical Journal*, August 1986 Vol. 80
24 *Health Medicine & Politics in Ireland 1900-1970*, Ruth Barrington, IPA, 1987
25 Maurice Manning, *Irish Independent*, 18.11.1986
26 David Hanly, *Colour Tribune*, 11.01.1987
27 Brian Trench, *Sunday Tribune*, 16.11.1986
28 David Hanly, *Colour Tribune*, 11.01.1987

29 Vol I, 1997, Obituary by Joe Deasy, President, ILH Society
30 The Journal of the Medical Association of Eire, 1946
31 Professor Ronan Fanning, UCD, *Sunday Independent*,
     12.06.1998
32 Professor Ronan Fanning, UCD, *Sunday Independent*,
     12.06.1998
33 Notes from Dr McQuaid's Archives, opened to the public
     April 1998
34 *Irish Historical Studies* No. 98, 1986, Church State Relations,
     Eamon McKee
35 David Thornley TD, *Sunday Press*, 04.10.1970
36 Memorandum to the Party Officers, Flor O'Mahony,
     25.10.1977
37 Eamon McCann, *Sunday World*, 08.01.1978
38 *Irish Times* 16.05.1978
39 *Irish Times* 16.05.1978
40 *Irish Independent* Report 30.01.1978
41 *Thanks for the Tea, Mrs Browne* by Phyllis Browne, New Island
     Books, 1998
42 *The Sunday Tribune*, 25.10.1998
43 Dáil Debates 9.07.1943
44 Interview with Sean Cryan, *Sunday Press*, 05.10.1975
45 *Evening Herald*, 21.03. 1985
46 *Sunday Independent*, 05.10.1975
47 RTÉ. TV1. Transcript, 14.02.1985
48 *Irish Times*, 08.05.1976
49 *Irish Times*, 08.05.1976
50 *Irish Times*, 31.07.1972
51 *Irish Times* 30.06.1975
52 *Evening Herald* Report 18.02.1976
53 *Business and Finance*, 27.08.1981
54 *Irish Independent*, 22.05.1976
55 *Irish Times*, 21.02.1985
56 *Irish Times*, 21.02.1985
57 *Irish Times*, 11.08.1992
58 *Doctor John* by John O'Connell, Poolbeg, 1988
59 *Sunday Tribune*, 06.04.1995
60 *Magill* Interview, 21.03.1985
61 Stephen Collins, *Sunday Tribune,* 28.09.1997

62 *Irish Times*, 08.07.1981
63 *Sunday Business Post*, 28.09.1997
64 *Irish Times*, 09.1997
65 *Sunday Independent*, 06.04.1986
66 *Irish Press* Editorial, 29.08.1984
67 *Sunday Independent*, 02.07.1977
68 *The Government and Politics of Ireland*, by Basil Chubb, Longman, London, 1982
69 *The Sunday Tribune*, 18 August, 1991
70 *Irish Times*, 10 February, 1996
71 Page 112, *Mary Robinson*, by John Horgan, Dublin, The O'Brien Press, 1997
72 Interview with Henry Kelly, *Irish Times*, 02.11.1974
73 Review of *Fine Gael 1923-1987* by Brian Maye, Dublin, Blackwater Press, 1993
74 *Irish Medical News*, 12.1986
75 *The Irish Times*, 22.02.1974
76 Mary Magee v The Attorney General and The Revenue Commissioners, The Supreme Court (148-1972)
77 *Hibernia* 18.01.1974
78 *Irish Catholic*. 04.07.1974
79 *Irish Press*, 25.07.1974
80 Dáil Debate Col. 448, 20.02.1985
81 RTÉ GIS Transcript, 17.02.1985
82 Letter to Deputies, 23.10.1984
83 *Irish Times*, 06.11.1984
84 *Day by Day* Programme, RTÉ Radio, 08.11.1984
85 RTÉ Radio, 12.02.1985
86 RTÉ Radio, 12.02.1985
87 RTÉ Radio Transcript, 13.02.1985
88 Dáil Debate, 19.02.1985, Volume 356 No.1
89 Dáil Debate, 19.02.1985, Volume 356 No.1
90 Dáil Debate, 19.02.1985, Volume 356 No.1
91 Dáil Debate, 19.02.1985, Volume 356 No.1
92 Dáil Debate, 19.02.1985, Volume 356 No.1
93 Dáil Debate, 19.02.1985, Volume 356 No.1
94 Dáil Debate, 19.02.1985, Volume 356 No.2
95 Dáil Debate, 20.02.1985, Volume 356 No.2
96 Dáil Debate, 20.02.1985, Volume 356 No.2

97 RTÉ GIS Transcript, 17.02.1985
98 Dáil Debate, 20.02.1985, Volume 356 No.2
99 Dáil Debate, 20.02.1985, Volume 356 No.2
100 Dáil Debate, 21.02.1985, Col. 500
101 Dáil Debate, 21.02.1985, Cols. 514, 519 and 520
102 Dáil Debate, 21.02.1985, Col 617
103 Seanad Debate, 27.02.1985, Col 520, 521 and 522
104 Seanad Debates, Volume 107 Number 7, 28 February 1985
105 Seanad Debate, 27.02.1985, Col 504 and 505
106 Seanad Debate, 27.02.1985, Col 509, 513 and 517
107 Seanad Debate, Volume 107 Number 8, 06.03.1985
108 Seanad Debate, Volume 107 Number 8, 06.03.1985
109 Seanad Debate, Volume 107 Number 8, 06.03.1985
110 Dáil Debate, 20.02.1985, Volume 356 No.2
111 Letter of 20.01.1987 Beef Tribunal
112 *Irish Times*, 10.11.1982
113 Address to Labour Party workers, 19.04.1983
114 Address to Fine Gael Branch, 12.04.1983
115 Dáil Debate Col. 2029 and 2030, 27.04.1983
116 *Irish Independent*, 14.06.1999
117 Professor Thomas Flanagan, *Irish Times*, 06.07.1982
118 Department of Education statement, 06.09.1974
119 Letter to Tanaiste, 18.09.1974, Department of Health
120 Col. 282, Dáil Debate, 22.01.1986
121 SPO. S4127, E.J. Duggan to W.T. Cosgrave 1923
122 Report of The Committee on the Constitution, PR 9817, 1967
123 Commissioned and published by The Irish Council for Civil Liberties, Dublin, 1979
124 Press Release, Catholic Press and Information Office, 07.04.1986
125 *All in a Life*, Garret FitzGerald, pages 628-9, Dublin, Gill & Macmillan, 1991
126 Dáil Debate, 15.05.1986
127 *Irish Times*, 21.05.1986
128 *Sunday Times*, May-June 1999
129 *Irish Independent*, 28.06.1986
130 *Irish Independent*, 28.06.1986
131 *Sunday Tribune*, 04.04.1999
132 Dáil Debate, September 1992

133 *Irish Times*, 12.09.1992
134 May 1986
135 *Smoke Ring — The Politics of Tobacco*, Peter Taylor, The Bodley Head, 1984
136 Notes of interview between John Whyte and Dr F.C. Ward, 18 June 1966, *Health, Medicine & Politics, in Ireland, 1900-1970*, Ruth Barrington, IPA, 1987
137 *Irish Times*, 06.02.1986
138 *Irish Times*, 08.02.1986
139 *Irish Times* Interview, 04.02.1999
140 *Evening Press*, 19.04.1990
141 *Irish Times*, 14.02.1986
142 *Sunday Business Post*, 22.04.1990
143 *Sunday Business Post*, 22.04.1990
144 *Cork Examiner*, 24.02.1986
145 Dáil Debate, 21.02.1986
146 *Cork Examiner*, 13.02.1986
147 *Cork Examiner*, 13.02.1986
148 *Cork Examiner*, 14.02.1986
149 *Sunday Independent*, 16.02.1986
150 *Sunday Tribune*, 16.02.1986
151 *Irish Independent*, 15.02.1986
152 Col. 477, 01.09.1994
153 Pages 335–6, Tribunal Report 1994
154 Page 50 Tribunal Report 1994
155 Page 553 Tribunal Report 1994
156 Dáil Debate, 02.09.1994 Col 534
157 Dáil Debate, col 860, 03.09.1994
158 Page 9, Day 127 Evidence, Beef Tribunal
159 Page 12 of The Report of The Tribunal 1994
160 Dáil Debate, 01.09.94 Col. 271
161 Dáil Debate, 02.09.1994 Col. 742
162 Forum Report, s.5.2
163 *Irish Times*, 14.12.1971
164 *An Phoblacht*, 05.11.1981
165 *Irish Times*, 5.11.1984
166 *Irish Times*, 6.09.2000
167 John Hume 09.11.1985
168 Joint Statement 26.04.1993, *Irish Times*

169 BBC 26.09.1992

170 Dáil Debate, vol 435 col 257 1993

171 *The Uncivil War: Ireland Today*, Padriag O'Malley, p. 423, Beacon Press, 1997

172 Dáil Debate, 21.11.1928 cols 430-500

173 Jean Monnet Lecture, European University Institute, 10.02.1995

174 *Irish Times*, 28.10.1982

175 Mary Harney, *Irish Times*, July 1999

W

Wakeham, Roberta, 353
Walsh, Brian, 296
Walsh, Dick, 142–3, 154, 167,
    177, 259, 316, 358
Walsh, Edmund, 20
Ward, F.C., 308
Watchorn, Mrs Margaret, 284
Weir, Professor D.G., 239
Well Woman Clinic, 237
West, Trevor, 229
Whitaker, T.K., 88, 93–4, 95, 96
Whyte, Professor J.H., 115, 117
Wilson, Harold, 79–80, 96
    IRA meeting, 150–1
Wilson, Joan, 226
Wilson, John, 148
Woods, Dr Michael, 259, 263,
    276–7
Woods, Paddy, 186, 187
Workers' Party, 72, 166, 241–2,
    258, 322, 360
Workers' Union of Ireland
    (WUI), 24, 25, 28, 30, 35
    rivalry with ITGWU, 31
Wrigley, Gerry, 362
Wyse, Pearse, 254–5

Y

Yeates, Padraig, 155
Young, Arthur, 307
Young, Dr Jim, 82